A CULTURAL HISTORY OF TRAGEDY

VOLUME 6

A Cultural History of Tragedy
General Editor: Rebecca Bushnell

Volume 1
A Cultural History of Tragedy in Antiquity
Edited by Emily Wilson

Volume 2
A Cultural History of Tragedy in the Middle Ages
Edited by Jody Enders, Theresa Coletti, John T. Sebastian, and Carol Symes

Volume 3
A Cultural History of Tragedy in the Early Modern Age
Edited by Naomi Liebler

Volume 4
A Cultural History of Tragedy in the Age of Enlightenment
Edited by Mitchell Greenberg

Volume 5
A Cultural History of Tragedy in the Age of Empire
Edited by Michael Gamer and Diego Saglia

Volume 6
A Cultural History of Tragedy in the Modern Age
Edited by Jennifer Wallace

A CULTURAL HISTORY OF TRAGEDY

IN THE MODERN AGE

VOLUME 6

Edited by Jennifer Wallace

BLOOMSBURY ACADEMIC
LONDON • NEW YORK • OXFORD • NEW DELHI • SYDNEY

BLOOMSBURY ACADEMIC
Bloomsbury Publishing Plc
50 Bedford Square, London, WC1B 3DP, UK
1385 Broadway, New York, NY 10018, USA
29 Earlsfort Terrace, Dublin 2, Ireland

BLOOMSBURY, BLOOMSBURY ACADEMIC and the Diana logo are trademarks of
Bloomsbury Publishing Plc

First published in hardback in Great Britain 2020
This paperback edition 2023

Copyright © Jennifer Wallace and contributors, 2020

Jennifer Wallace and contributors have asserted their right under the Copyright,
Designs and Patents Act, 1988, to be identified as the Authors of this work.

For legal purposes the Acknowledgments on p. xii constitute an extension of this copyright page.

Series design by Raven Design

Cover image: Mourners console the mother of 15-year-old Palestinian teenager Azzam Oweida during
his funeral in Khan Yunis © MAHMUD HAMS/AFP/Getty Images

All rights reserved. No part of this publication may be reproduced or transmitted
in any form or by any means, electronic or mechanical, including photocopying,
recording, or any information storage or retrieval system, without prior permission
in writing from the publishers.

Bloomsbury Publishing Plc does not have any control over, or responsibility for, any
third-party websites referred to or in this book. All internet addresses given in this
book were correct at the time of going to press. The author and publisher regret
any inconvenience caused if addresses have changed or sites have ceased to
exist, but can accept no responsibility for any such changes.

A catalogue record for this book is available from the British Library.

A catalog record for this book is available from the Library of Congress.

ISBN: HB: 978-1-4742-8809-5
HB set: 978-1-4742-8814-9
PB: 978-1-3504-1681-9
PB set: 978-1-3504-1692-5

Series: The Cultural Histories Series

Typeset by RefineCatch Limited, Bungay, Suffolk
Printed and bound in Great Britain

To find out more about our authors and books visit www.bloomsbury.com
and sign up for our newsletters.

CONTENTS

List of Illustrations	vi
Notes on Contributors	ix
Series Preface	x
Editor's Acknowledgments	xii
Introduction: Tragedy Since 1920 *Jennifer Wallace*	1
1 Forms and Media: Fragmented, Torn, Multiplied *Ramona Mosse*	23
2 Sites of Performance and Circulation: The Ecology of Modern Tragedy *Drew Milne*	41
3 Communities of Production and Consumption: Modernism and the Rebirth of Tragedy *Olga Taxidou*	57
4 Philosophy and Social Theory *David Kornhaber*	75
5 Religion, Ritual and Myth *Ben Quash*	93
6 Politics of City and Nation: Tragic Politics and the Incommunicable Experience *Tony Fisher*	109
7 Society and Family: Vibrant Affiliations *Kélina Gotman*	127
8 Gender and Sexuality: Watching as Praxis *P.A. Skantze*	145
Notes	161
Bibliography	187
Index	207

ILLUSTRATIONS

INTRODUCTION

0.1	Paul Nash. *We Are Making a New World*. 1918.	2
0.2	Alberto Giacometti. "Walking Man II."	10
0.3	Khmer Rouge prisoners of the S21 Tuoi Sleng security prison under Pol Pot's regime, Phnom Penh, Cambodia, about to be killed.	11
0.4	An unidentified Tutsi man who survived the Civil War in Rwanda, June 1994.	11
0.5	Residents from the nearby city of Weimar walking with eyes averted past a pile of corpses in the courtyard of Buchenwald concentration camp following its liberation, April 1945.	12
0.6	The assassination of Martin Luther King Jr., April 1968.	14
0.7	Atomic Shadow. The "shadow" of a ladder and a Japanese soldier after the Atomic bombing of Nagasaki by the U.S. in August 1945.	16
0.8	A child laborer carrying coal he has scavenged from the edge of an open-pit coal mine on former agricultural land in Jharkhand State, northeast India. 2010.	19
0.9	Firefighters stand in the smoldering wreckage of the World Trade Center, New York City, September 13, 2001.	21

CHAPTER 1

1.1	*Mount Olympus*, created and directed by Jan Fabre. Foreign Affairs 2015, Berliner Festspielhaus.	24
1.2	Heine Müller's *Hamletmaschine*. Deutsches Theater, Berlin, 1990.	28
1.3	Paul Klee. *Angelus Novus*. 1920.	29
1.4	The Wooster Group's *Hamlet* at The Performing Garage, New York City, 2007.	35
1.5	Richard Mosse. Moria in Snow, Lesbos, Greece, 2017.	38–9

CHAPTER 2

2.1	The Thiepval Memorial to the Missing of the Somme.	44
2.2	A shadow of a man is cast upon one of the 72,000 names of soldiers killed in the Battle of the Somme. Thiepval Memorial.	45
2.3	A fresco along the memorial "Slave Route" depicting slaves compelled to circle the "Tree of Forgetfulness" before being forcibly shipped off to the New World. Ouidah, Benin.	45
2.4	Former U.S. president Barack Obama and King Filipe VI of Spain view Picasso's *Guernica* in the Reina Sofia Museum, Madrid. July 2017.	47
2.5	The Judenplatz Holocaust Memorial, Vienna, created by Rachel Whiteread.	47

ILLUSTRATIONS

CHAPTER 3

3.1	Isadora Duncan dancing.	63
3.2	Edward Gordon Craig. *Hecuba*. 1908.	65
3.3	Brecht. *Antigonemodel*. Photographed by Ruth Berlau. 1948.	72

CHAPTER 4

4.1	Jean-Paul Sartre's *The Flies*, directed by Juergen Fehling, at the Hebbel Theater, Berlin, 1955.	81
4.2	Simone de Beauvoir's *The Useless Mouths*. Theatre of Carrefours, Paris. October 1945.	82

CHAPTER 5

5.1	Larry Burrows' photograph of a grieving widow crying over the remains of her husband killed by the Viet Cong during the Tet offensive the previous year. Vietnam, 1969.	96
5.2	Oren Goldenberg. *Requiem for Douglass*. 2015.	104
5.3	Teresa Margolles. *Plancha*. 2010.	106
5.4	Doris Salcedo. *Shibboleth*. Turbine Hall, Tate Modern. 2007.	106

CHAPTER 6

6.1	Dustin Hoffman (as Willy Loman) and John Malkovich (as Biff Loman) in a staged-for-television version of *Death of a Salesman*, 1985.	116
6.2	Japanese salarymen. Tokyo, 1980s.	121
6.3	Beckett's *Happy Days*, directed by Deborah Warner at Bam Harvey Theater, New York City. January 2008.	124

CHAPTER 7

7.1	An American family in a backyard bomb shelter. Garden City, New York. 1955.	129
7.2	A group of women, under a Women's Liberation banner, march in support of the Black Panther Party. New Haven, Connecticut, November 1969.	132
7.3	Romeo Castellucci's *On the Concept of the Face, regarding the Son of God*, for Socìetas Raffaello Sanzio. Barbican Theatre, London. April 2011.	134
7.4	A young couple dance with joy in Athens' Syntagma Square during a political demonstration to celebrate the "No" result in a popular referendum. May 2015.	138

CHAPTER 8

8.1	Billie Piper in Lorca's *Yerma*: Young Vic, London, August 2016.	149

8.2	Sondheim's *Pacific Overtures*, directed by John Doyle. Classic Stage Company, New York, May 2017.	152
8.3	*A Midsummer Night's Dream*, directed by Joe Hill-Gibbins. Young Vic, London, February 2017.	154
8.4	Caryl Churchill's *Escaped Alone*, directed by James Macdonald. Royal Court Theatre, London. January 2016.	157

NOTES ON CONTRIBUTORS

Tony Fisher is Professor of Theatre, Politics and Aesthetics at the Royal Central School of Speech and Drama, University of London. He is the author of *Theatre and Governance in Britain, 1500–1900: Democracy, Disorder and the State* (2017) and *The Aesthetic Expression: Essays on Art, Politics and Theatre* (forthcoming).

Kélina Gotman is Professor of Performance and the Humanities at King's College London. She is the author, among other books, of *Choreomania: Dance and Disorder* (2018), and editor of the 4-volume *Theories of Performance: Critical and Primary Sources* (2022).

David Kornhaber is Associate Professor of English and Comparative Literature at the University of Texas at Austin. He is the author of *Theatre & Knowledge* (2019) and *The Birth of Theatre from the Spirit of Philosophy: Nietzsche and the Modern Drama* (2016) and the co-editor, with James Loehlin, of *Tom Stoppard in Context* (2021).

Drew Milne is Judith E Wilson Reader in Poetics in the Faculty of English, University of Cambridge. His academic interests span comparative drama, poetry and critical theory, with a particular recent focus on ecological poetics and politics. His collected poems, *In Darkest Capital*, were published in 2017.

Ramona Mosse is the head of Theatre at the Zurich University of the Arts, Switzerland, and formerly Fellow of the International Research Center for Interweaving Performance Cultures at the Free University, Berlin. She is the co-editor, with Anna Street, of *Genre Transgressions: Dialogues on Tragedy and Comedy* (forthcoming).

Ben Quash is Professor of Christianity and the Arts at King's College London, and Director of the Centre for Arts and the Sacred at King's. He is editor of the Visual Commentary on Scripture (TheVCS.org) and author of *Theology and the Drama of History* (2005).

P.A. Skantze is currently Visiting Professor in Performance Studies at NYU's Tisch School of the Arts and was formerly professor at Roehampton University. A theatre writer, director and composer making work in Italy, Croatia, London and New York, her academic publications include *Stillness in Motion in the Seventeenth-Century Theatre* (2003) and *Itinerant Spectator/Itinerant Spectacle* (2013).

Olga Taxidou is Professor Emerita of Drama and Performance Studies at the University of Edinburgh, and Visiting Professor in Hellenic Studies at New York University. Her recent books include *The Edinburgh Dictionary of Modernism*, co-edited with V. Kolocotroni (2018), and *Greek Tragedy and Modernist Performance* (2021). She also works on adaptations of Greek tragedy for performance.

Jennifer Wallace is Harris Fellow and Director of Studies in English Literature and Comparative Drama at Peterhouse, University of Cambridge. Her published books include *The Cambridge Introduction to Tragedy* (2007) and *Tragedy since 9/11: Reading a World Out of Joint* (2019).

SERIES PREFACE

A cultural history of tragedy faces a daunting task: how to address tragedy's influence on Western culture while describing how complex and changing historical conditions have shaped it over two and a half millennia. This is the first study with such an extensive scope, investigating tragedy's long-lived cultural impact and accounting for its material, social, political, and philosophical dimensions.

Since antiquity, tragedy has appeared in a myriad of forms, reinvented in every age. It has been performed as opera, dance, film, and television as well as live theater. From the beginning, concepts of tragedy have also surfaced in other literary genres such as narrative poetry and novels, as well as in non-literary forms, including journalism, visual art, and photography. Tragedy never appears in a vacuum: the conditions of performance and production and its communal functions always affect its form and meaning. Tragedy has never belonged solely to elite culture, and who creates and consumes these forms of tragedy also makes a difference. Not only has the status of tragedy's producers—the writers, actors, artists, and performers—evolved over time, but so has the nature of the audiences, viewers, and readers as well, all significantly affecting tragedy's aesthetic and social impact.

Tragedy also does more than simply represent or perform human catastrophe or suffering; it is a mode of thought, a way of figuring the human condition as a whole. Philosophers and social and cultural theorists from Plato to Lacan have long pondered the idea of the tragic, while in turn literary models have influenced philosophy, social thought, and psychoanalysis. Tragedy has always had a complex relationship with religion and ritual practices, both complementing and conflicting with religious orthodoxies concerning fate, the power of the gods, and the meaning of suffering. At the same time, since its earliest staging in fifth-century Athens as a civic as well as religious event, tragedy has both echoed and challenged relationships of power and political events in societies experiencing conflict or change.

While tragedy in all its versions has thus profoundly tapped into broad social, intellectual, and political movements, it has often represented those themes through individual experiences, ranging from the titanic sufferings of princes to the sorrows of ordinary men and women. While tragedy's themes of ambition, authority, transgression, and rebellion are grounded in religion and politics, its plots often play out through family relationships that both mirror and conflict with social and political norms. When tragedy thus engages familial and personal themes, it often involves tensions of gender and sexuality. Sexuality is a powerful driver of tragic catastrophe, when desire is granted its own kind of fatal power.

As with other *Cultural History* series, here the story of tragedy writ large is divided into volumes covering six historical periods from antiquity to modernity. Although the boundaries between those time are necessarily fluid, the volumes are divided as follows: 1. Antiquity (500 BCE–1000 CE); 2. Middle Ages (1000–1400); 3. Early Modern Age (1400–1650); 4. Age of Enlightenment (1650–1800); 5. Age of Empire (1800–1920), and 6. Modern Age (1920–present). While such a history naturally focuses on Western culture and history, at the end it also touches on tragedy's later post-colonial adaptations, which put its fundamentally Western concerns in a global context. Each volume has its own introduction by an editor or co-editors presenting an original and provocative vision of tragedy's manifestations in one historical era. Each volume also covers the same eight topics as the others in the *Cultural History*: forms and media; sites of performance and circulation; communities of production and consumption; philosophy and social theory; religion, ritual, and myth; politics of city and nation; society and family; and gender and sexuality. Readers may thus follow one topic over a wide historical span, or they may focus on all dimensions of tragedy in one period. Either way they read, they will be able to appreciate the power of tragedy to shape our understanding of human experience, and in turn, how tragedy has changed over time, both reflecting and challenging historical conditions.

Rebecca Bushnell, University of Pennsylvania, General Editor

EDITOR'S ACKNOWLEDGMENTS

The editor is hugely grateful to Sunita Sharma-Gibson for her photo research and advice on illustrations and to the following photographers and artists who generously gave their images for nothing or for reduced permission fees: Robert Wallis, Richard Mosse, Oren Goldenberg, P.D. Rearick, Teresa Margolles, and Joan Marcus. Ramona Mosse and Kélina Gotman read an earlier draft of the Introduction and offered helpful comments and advice. Rebecca Bushnell has been a wise and encouraging counselor throughout the process and generally a force for good.

Introduction

Tragedy Since 1920

JENNIFER WALLACE

1920. The starting date for this volume. Europe has been torn apart by the Great War. In total, about 15–18 million people throughout the continent and its colonies across the globe have been killed, in combat and from malnutrition and disease caused by war. About 20 million more men have returned wounded, limbs missing, breathing difficulties from gas attacks, terrible burns. And there is a new kind of injury, shellshock, a new word coined to describe a novel condition, the physical and emotional breakdown of a man with no visible injury, enough to make Sigmund Freud in Vienna radically rethink his psychoanalytical beliefs. Machines and technology have transformed war as well as peace, from the automatic machine guns that killed nearly 20,000 British soldiers on the first day of the Battle of the Somme in 1916 to the arrival of the tank that continues in the 1920s to haunt the cultural imagination.[1] In the 1920s, the German Weimar republic is burdened by the demand for reparations so punitive that debt, hyperinflation, extreme poverty, and political violence are a factor of daily life. The Bolshevik revolution in Russia has provoked a civil war between the communist Red army and the White counter-revolutionary forces that stretches over many fronts across the empire from Ukraine to Siberia. Meanwhile the fall of the Ottoman empire has led to instability in the Middle East, with the British betrayal of their wartime promise of land and independence made to Arab leaders and their ruthless crushing of the Iraqi revolt.[2]

But there are, in 1920, signs of hope too, a determination not to revert back to the old ways before the Great War but to engage in international cooperation. With this aspiration, The League of Nations is founded in January 1920 to prevent conflict in the future. Its remit also stretches to a range of social welfare responsibilities, including improving employment conditions, health provision, and the protection of minorities; forty-four states sign the agreement in the first instance. Meanwhile women are given the (limited) right to vote for the first time in the UK in 1918 and in the United States in 1920; French women would have to wait until 1944. Modernity ushers in the widening of the franchise, dramatic drops in rates of illiteracy, the widening of universal education and the growth of popular culture. Indeed, the pace of change is bewildering for some. "Culture is at a crisis," observes F.R. Leavis in *Mass Civilisation and Minority Culture* in 1930. Radio, cinema, and newspapers have brought about "an overthrow of standards."[3] Photography opens up the opportunity for recording everyday events or "mechanical reproduction" for the masses.[4] Millions more people have access to the news and learn about the hopes, fears, and suffering of others.

The postwar optimism shared by many people was tempered by anxiety, the intellectuals fearing the deadening effect of technology and the frightening democratization of culture.[5]

And lurking behind that anxiety was the shadow of the past war (Figure 0.1) and the ominous signs of the next war soon to come, signs that many were urgently trying to ignore in their flight into escapism. "It's the war that makes you lead such a fantastic life," declares the earnest twenty-year-old Helen Banner to the jaded, alcoholic, inveterate party-goer David Scott-Fowler, thirty-eight, in Terence Rattigan's 1938 play *After the Dance*.[6] Dancing, drinking, and deceiving themselves and others are the Bright Young Things' method of coping in the postwar era, a forced pretense at happiness and an abrogation of responsibility which the younger generation, deaf to the underlying anguish of their elders, castigate. Rattigan's play might be considered paradigmatic of the tragic anti-tragedy of the modern age. The Scott-Fowlers pretend they don't love each other, turning even the heartbreak of betrayal and infidelity into a flippant joke. Comedy and tragedy are intertwined in their lighthearted, flapper dialogue. The emotional implications of actions taken or not taken are understated, evaded, or only indirectly implied. In its generic blurring, the play is both a response to and escape from contemporary events, symptomatic of the doggedly unserious atmosphere and static inertia of the interwar years.

To cover so vast a subject as tragedy, in all its myriad forms and meanings across the globe, in the hundred years since 1920, is immensely challenging. And to pick one text, not even categorized by its author as tragic, as paradigmatically my starting point might seem counter-intuitive. But, taking my cue from *After the Dance*, I want, in this introductory

FIGURE 0.1: Paul Nash. *We Are Making a New World*. 1918. © Imperial War Museums (Art. IWM ART 1146).

chapter, to consider first the difficulty of defining what tragedy means in the modern age. As the distinctions between tragedy and comedy collapse and the social conditions traditionally considered essential for the genre—heroism and social hierarchy, the presence of gods or God, a small, close community—decline, is it possible to speak meaningfully of tragedy in the twentieth century at all? Secondly, if we accept that the definition of tragedy changes during this period and that categories widen and become more fluid, then the forms in which we might encounter the tragic mode must diversify in unexpected directions beyond the traditional focus upon drama. I want to consider what a twentieth- and twenty-first-century canon of tragedy might look like. What is the range of material that could legitimately be included in a volume of cultural history like this? As *After the Dance* demonstrates, the relationship between literature and history is complex. The irony is that, while the modern age has supposedly witnessed the much-heralded "death of tragedy" in the literary/aesthetic sense, it has been marked by a century of tragic events on a vast scale. So my third priority in this introductory chapter is to consider the historical events, long-term developments and experiences of suffering as tragedies too, drawing upon traditional hermeneutic tools used to analyze literary tragedy to consider how history and our lived experience have altered or strengthened our understanding of the tragic mode. And finally, in an era punctured by two world wars and nuclear weapons, I must consider the global dimensions of twentieth-century tragedy. The modern age brings into sharp focus the comparative nature of tragedy and its very different forms and functions in cultures across the world. To what extent, then, can we think about global tragedy as a cross-cultural encounter? Of course, throughout the modern age there lurks that alternative meaning of tragedy as a total catastrophe on a planetary scale, an apocalyptic vision that was already latently there after the First World War.

DEFINING TRAGEDY IN THE MODERN AGE

As many of the contributors to this volume point out, the twentieth century is often considered to have witnessed the "death of tragedy." Of course, tragedy has been deemed to have died many times before over the centuries, as other volumes in this *Cultural History of Tragedy* series will testify. But the emphasis upon equality, progress, and secular government, which characterized modernity, was particularly felt to be unsuitable for the traditional concerns of classical tragedy. George Steiner famously mourned the disappearance of the theatrical genre, on the grounds that "there is nothing democratic in the vision of tragedy" and it was therefore no longer relevant or adequate to the age.[7] While Steiner regretted the alleged demise of traditional tragedy, other playwrights and thinkers have celebrated the emergence of new generic forms that they consider more suitable to the non-hierarchical and rational twentieth century. Berthold Brecht replaced traditional tragedy with what he called Epic theater, in which the dialectical progress of history supplanted the conventional shape of dramatic plot.[8] Aristotle's theory of tragedy is "coercive," according to Brazilian theater director Augusto Boal, since it advocates plots in which the central character is punished for his hubris and transgression and it schools the audience into an acceptance of the status quo through the process of catharsis.[9] Instead, Boal promoted participatory theater and role-play, which would encourage positive thinking and empowerment, amongst the oppressed in the slums of Rio. Immersive theater, drama that democratically breaks down the divide between actor and spectator and which explores an inclusive, demotic world, might be considered the most relevant form for the modern age.

Yet other writers would claim that the twentieth century has been particularly haunted by and responsive to tragedy. The declaration by "The Madman," in Friedrich Nietzsche's *The Joyous Science* (1882), that "God is dead! God remains dead! And we have killed him!", has overshadowed the century, prompting both guilt-ridden epistemological crises and also opportunities for thinking about what could replace him.[10] In the case of Nietzsche, the metaphysical void once occupied by God was filled by art. The spirit of Dionysus, or tragic theater, offered the transcendent, transfiguring power that gave meaning to mortal existence. Inevitable destruction could therefore be celebrated joyfully, rather than received as a rupture that shatters all belief and certainty, negating everything. The French existentialist thinkers like Jean-Paul Sartre and Albert Camus, heavily influenced by Nietzsche's legacy, replaced God not with art, as such, but with human consciousness. The mind need only realize the absurdity of everyday, purposeless existence, they believed, and that humdrum meaninglessness could be superseded and transfigured by the human imagination.[11] Tragedy as conquest and submission is also inherent in psychoanalytic approaches to the subject. Freud's ego and id operated rather like Nietzsche's Apollonian and Dionysiac forces, attempting to regulate and give expression to various acceptable or unacceptable desires. Is the pleasure of tragedy, according to Freud's theories, derived from the "formal control" it exerts, like the repression of the unconscious?[12] Or is it based upon our perverse attraction to destruction and violence, the pull of the death drive identified in Freud's later work? It is in this respect that Oedipus becomes the paradigmatic figure for Freud, since he both solves the riddle of the sphinx *and* commits incest, using his philosophical reason, in Miriam Leonard's words, to "shine a redemptive light onto the hell of the unconscious."[13] Following Martin Heidegger, Christopher Hamilton has recently argued that the loss of belief in God, together with the horror of Auschwitz, has left the twentieth century particularly tragic in its nature and philosophical condition. "Human beings are not at home in the world; we are like wanderers on the face of an earth wholly indifferent to us," he notes, claiming that this disenchanted and futile stance constitutes fundamentally a "tragic view of life."[14]

In light of these very different attitudes to a post-Nietzschean world, what does it mean to talk about tragedy in the twentieth century? As many commentators have pointed out, there are three recognized meanings for the term tragedy: the literary and theatrical, the philosophical, and the vernacular. But even within and between these categories there are areas of confusion and overlap. When we speak of the theatrical notion of tragedy, are we referring to the traditional Greek understanding of tragedy, practised by the ancient Athenians and analyzed by Aristotle, which may or may not be relevant to our age? The thirty-two plays, by Aeschylus, Sophocles, and Euripides, which have survived from antiquity were created to serve very different historical and cultural needs but continue to be adapted and performed in new contexts for different audiences around the world. The plays take on new meanings in each century as different theatrical productions are influenced by the particular concerns and interpretations of their age. Indeed, as Edith Hall observes, the "mythical, dysfunctional, conflicted world portrayed in the archetypal plays of Aeschylus, Sophocles and Euripides has become one of the most important cultural and aesthetic prisms through which the real, dysfunctional, conflicted world of the late twentieth- and early twenty-first centuries has refracted its own image."[15] Or by theatrical tragedy do we speak, rather, of a whole evolving history of tragic drama—Shakespeare, Racine, Goethe—to which new dramas for the modern age have been added?

There is also, now, a long history of philosophers, political thinkers, and theologians who discuss the aesthetic or political idea of tragedy, beyond its dramatic embodiment upon the stage. Certainly, some of these writers formulate their ideas by thinking about the tragic as it is instantiated in drama. As David Kornhaber describes in this volume, twentieth-century philosophy has been shaped by two plays, *Oedipus the King* and *Antigone*. On the other hand, other philosophers think about the tragic as inherent in the human condition itself. Or, in the case of theologians like Donald Mackinnon or Rowan Williams, one could locate the tragic within the religious ideas of sacrifice, atonement, incarnation, and kenosis (literally "emptying out" or Jesus' self-renunciation). In many ways, our approach to the literary form of tragedy is inevitably impacted by the philosophical tradition, going back to the German Idealist interpretation of tragedy in the late eighteenth and early nineteenth centuries.[16] Hegel and Nietzsche have continued to inform thinkers, such as Freud, Arendt, and Heidegger, who in turn influence both the theoretical and the dramatic conceptualization of tragedy.

And then there are the devastating public events that ruptured the century: wars, revolutions, economic depressions, famines, genocide. In our common everyday parlance, in which we describe our response to daily crises, tragedy is a term used to refer to a terrible event without identifiable cause or explanation: the death of a child, the massive loss of life in an accident. The popular use of the term appears to deny the possible political implications of a disaster by emphasizing its origins in chance or fate. In this case, we might consider it "a powerful term that can serve as a veil concealing difficult truths," as noted by Helene Foley and Jean Howard.[17] But other interpretations of the effect of calibrating historical events with the philosophical or literary notions of the term are motivated by completely different concerns, by the desire not to demarcate the elite literary or aesthetic notion of tragedy from the ordinary experience of devastating loss or suffering. In this case, an attention to tragedy can deliver a radical political purpose, for "only by grasping our constraints can we act constructively."[18]

One of the most helpful definitions of tragedy is the one prompted by the cryptic observation of Raymond Williams in his book *Modern Tragedy*: that tragedy is born out of the connections between "event and experience and idea."[19] The event produces a feeling or range of feelings, experienced by the participants and witnesses in diverse and varying ways. These feelings might be prompted by the disparity between hope and despair, between expectation and reality, between question and answer, provoked by the event which tests deeply our resources for confronting these things and shatters the security of easy theories or explanations. The thoughts and emotions are usually—but not always—communicable, since they emerge from what Williams calls the "structures of feeling" shared by the wider community, whether that be grief or anger, despair or loss, or even the empty guffaw of bleak futility. But these feelings in turn are shaped by the idea that this is how one *should* feel or respond or represent one's experience. So the idea of the tragic shapes the feeling and the feeling shapes the idea, and both become filtered by layers of tradition and cultural practice. Thus the process of recognition is often a vital component of tragedy. Setting an event and experience in context, as part of a pattern of human activity and in conformity with a history of tragic representation, forms the process of recognition which helps to shape a tragedy and, often, to make it bearable—and sharable. The peculiar self-consciousness of tragedy is perhaps one reason, I believe, why the modern age, with its ironic self-knowingness and capacity for parody and citation, might be considered particularly receptive to tragedy.

But as indicated by my attempt just now to delineate what Williams might have meant by his brief definition of tragedy ("event and experience and idea"), classifying these terms and distinguishing one from another is fraught with difficulty. What is an event, an experience, an idea? Raymond Williams himself acknowledged that it is not possible to separate an event from the response to an event.[20] Where should we locate the tragic feeling? In the consciousness of the tragic here or in the audience? Is it felt by those who are directly implicated in a disaster or is it registered in the act of witnessing? These distinctions between experience and witness, between event and representation, between history and narrative, start to break down under detailed scrutiny. And indeed, such distinctions become particularly ambiguous in the context of postmodernity when temporalities and epistemological registers are newly interrogated.

TRAGIC CANONS

The difficulty of defining exactly what tragedy is in the modern age leads to an uncertainty about the twentieth-century tragic canon. This is partly because it is still too early for the twentieth-century tradition to be sharply defined. Canons require some historical distance in order to be firmly established in common critical consensus. But the uncertainty is also partly owing to the fragmentation of the genre and its boundaries, the re-assemblage so well described by Ramona Mosse in her chapter in this volume. We could, for example, describe a modern tragic canon based upon new, influential, and important plays written in the twentieth century and shaped by traditional generic expectations established by tragic dramatists and theorists. Such a canon might begin with George Bernard Shaw's *St Joan* (1923), which, while dealing with a Christian subject, is structured along Aristotelian principles of hubris and hamartia. Key plays of the 1930s, influenced by Nietzsche's ideas of Dionysiac irrational impulses and surrealistic experimentation, would follow: W.B. Yeats' *Purgatory* (1938), Federico Garcia Lorca's rural trilogy *Blood Wedding* (1932), *Yerma* (1934), and *The House of Bernarda Alba* (1936), and T.S. Eliot's Christian and classical plays: *Murder in the Cathedral* (1935) and *The Family Reunion* (1939). Terence Rattigan's *After the Dance* (1938) and *The Deep Blue Sea* (1952) and Noël Coward's *Private Lives* (1930) might be there, the work of closet gay writers, masking their identities with polished well-made plays. Their tragi-comedies depend upon understatement and the brittleness of wit, powerfully dependent—like Anton Chekhov—upon what is not said. After the war, there was a golden age of new American tragedy. Eugene O'Neill's *The Iceman Cometh* (1940) and *Long Day's Journey Into Night* (1941) drew on dramatic techniques, utilized by Henrik Ibsen and August Strindberg, to represent the New World experience. O'Neill was to go on to influence the work of Tennessee Williams (*The Glass Menagerie* [1944], *Streetcar Named Desire* [1947], *Cat on a Hot Tin Roof* [1955]), Arthur Miller (*All My Sons* [1947], *Death of a Salesman* [1949], *A View from the Bridge* [1955]), and Edward Albee (*Who's Afraid of Virginia Woolf* [1962]). Along with the tensions of immigration, these dramatists explored the fantasies and delusions of postwar America and the tragic intensity of commitment shown by their protagonists to what Eagleton described as a "spurious goal."[21]

Meanwhile postwar and politically-divided Europe was dominated by ideologically or philosophically conceived theater: Berthold Brecht and Heine Müller in the GDR, examining the flaws in political structures and revolutions; Albert Camus, Jean-Paul Sartre, Eugène Ionesco, Jean Genet, and Samuel Beckett in Paris, dramatizing the tragic alienation at the core of the Theatre of the Absurd. In postwar Britain, influential plays which must be counted in the tragic canon include John Osborne's shatteringly squalid *Look Back in Anger* (1956) and the equally angry, absurdist, and class-conscious work of Harold Pinter: *The Birthday Party* (1958), *The Caretaker* (1960), and *The Homecoming* (1964). While these early plays of Pinter were described as "comedies of menace," their debt to Beckett and evocation of terrifying and violent alienation place them within the tragic tradition.[22] Across in the United States, African American dramatists, like Lorraine Hansberry and August Wilson, wrote plays that utilized similar plot structures and middle-class aspirations as their white counterparts but with a black perspective. Both *A Raisin in the Sun* (1959) and *The Pittsburgh Cycle* including *Fences* (1985) offer politically empowering depictions of black experience, but their underlying evocations of social aspiration and frustration, delusion and betrayal echo similar tragic concerns to those of O'Neill, Williams, and Miller. Nigerian tragic drama, spearheaded by Wole Soyinka, Ola Rotimi, and—later—Femi Osofisan, flourished in the 1960s and 1970s, despite, or maybe because of, the political situation in the country and the forced exile of its writers. In the last two decades of the twentieth century, surreal and shockingly violent plays by Edward Bond, Caryl Churchill, Sarah Kane, and Mark Ravenhill, among others, responded to modernity's rampant consumerism, political apathy, and sexual exploitation with explosive results.

This brief sketch, which inevitably omits many important and relevant dramas and is far from definitive, is just one way to classify the tragic canon of the twentieth century. But one could equally point to a canon that included ground-breaking productions of classical tragedy, which became new plays in this transformation. This would have to take account of Gilbert Murray's pro-peace *Trojan Women* (1905), which toured the U.S. during the First World War; Jean Anouilh's *Antigone* (1944), which drew contemporary parallels with the Nazi occupation and the French resistance; Brecht's *Antigone* (1948), which in its first version began with two sisters and their brother a deserter from the Second World War; the Michael Cacoyannis film trilogy *Electra* (1962), *Trojan Women* (1971), and *Iphigenia* (1977), set against the changing backdrop of turbulent Greek politics; Athol Fugard's *The Island* (1972), set on Robben Island in apartheid South Africa; Wole Soyinka's *The Bacchae of Euripides* (1973); Seamus Heaney's Irish version of *Philoctetes* entitled *The Cure at Troy* (1991); Ariane Mnouchkine's ten-hour-long *Les Atrides* (1992); Caryl Churchill's *Thyestes* (1994); Yael Farber's *Molora* (2008), the *Oresteia* reset in the context of South Africa's Truth and Reconciliation Commission. Or it could be a canon of fresh approaches to Shakespeare, including the stimulating partnership of director Peter Brook and critic Jan Kott in the 1960s which resulted in the Beckettian production of *King Lear* (1962) and an important re-evaluation of the play.[23] The canon should also comprise the Noh and Kabuki-influenced productions by Yukio Ninagawa since the late 1970s and the renewed appreciation of the late "problem plays" as well as the revival of interest in Shakespeare's *Titus Andronicus*, following Jonathan Bate's Arden edition; and most recently the new fashion for epic-length productions that merge history plays with tragedy: Ivo van Hove's *Roman Tragedies* or the BBC's *The Hollow Crown*.[24] Meanwhile the canon of plays indebted to Chekhov, for example, grows continually from Richard Nelson's Apple Family plays like *Sorry*, set during the 2012 Presidential election, through the ironically titled *Three Sisters on Hope Street* (2008), by Diane Samuels, a bleak hopeless drama set in wartime Liverpool, to Bonnie Greer's African American version of *The Cherry Orchard*, entitled *Hotel Cerise* (2016). These playwrights have found in Chekhov's ensemble dramas which look forward to an uncertain future a means of addressing the contemporary moment and of thinking through the relation between history, tragedy, and comedy.

Every century has performed and re-performed canonical tragedies, going right back to antiquity when fifth-century BCE Athenian tragedy enjoyed a theatrical afterlife around the Greek diaspora, from Sicily to the Black Sea littoral. To pinpoint exactly what is the tragedy of each particular age therefore brings its own challenges in any era. But the problem is most acute in the twentieth century, with its increased capacity to record material and its self-conscious use of allusion. The distinction between text and scholarship, between tragedy and meta-tragedy, breaks down. And the postmodernist collapse of those distinctions is itself a source of tragic aporia as well as playful absurdity. Anne Carson's *Antigonick*, for example, which has been performed in deconstructive, experimental ways on both sides of the Atlantic, explores Sophocles' play, its many versions and interpretations over the centuries, and the act of translation itself in a complex, hand-lettered, and illustrated art book.

> [ENTER ANTIGONE AND ISMENE]. **ANTIGONE:** WE BEGIN IN THE DARK AND BIRTH IS THE DEATH OF US **ISMENE:** WHO SAID THAT **ANTIGONE:** HEGEL **ISMENE:** SOUNDS MORE LIKE BECKETT **ANTIGONE:** HE WAS PARAPHRASING HEGEL **ISMENE:** I DON'T THINK SO **ANTIGONE:** WHOEVER IT WAS WHOEVER WE ARE DEAR SISTER EVER SINCE WE WERE BORN FROM THE EVILS OF OIDIPOUS WHAT BITTERNESS PAIN DISGUST DISGRACE OR MORAL SHOCK HAVE WE BEEN SPARED . . .[25]

Although some of the chapters in this volume (Olga Taxidou, P.A. Skantze) locate the tragic sense exclusively in the theater, thus legitimately reflecting one line of interpretation of the genre in a hotly contested debate amongst critics, it is indeed the case that tragedy has rarely been limited to the theater in any age.[26] Aristotle included Homer in his account of tragic mimesis in *The Poetics*, and Nietzsche's *Birth of Tragedy* was subtitled "out of the spirit of music" and intended as a contribution to the appreciation of Wagner. Since, in the twentieth century, theater is no longer the pre-eminent cultural form, other media such as novels, films, photography, and popular music have also played a role in shaping the public imagination and constituting a response to the critical concerns of our times. As Rita Felski argued in *Rethinking Tragedy*, in the twentieth century tragedy should perhaps be thought of as a "mode" rather than a "genre," allowing for the hybrid, mixed nature of contemporary artistic expression and the broadening of its scope beyond the narrow conceptions of classical drama.[27]

Various nineteenth-century novels, such as Leo Tolstoy's *Anna Karenina*, George Eliot's *Middlemarch*, and several of Thomas Hardy's works, have been identified by critics as tragic.[28] But there are many twentieth-century examples too. F. Scott Fitzgerald's *Great Gatsby* (1925) and Richard Yates' *Revolutionary Road* (1961) explore the dark side beneath the glittering exterior of aspirational American domestic life; Camus' *The Outsider* (1942) and Franz Kafka's *The Trial* (1925) dramatize the ramifications of existential nihilism and absurdity, coupled with an attention to the political anxieties and tensions at Europe's borders. Meanwhile the injustice and violent repression of African American history are given expression in Ralph Ellison's *The Invisible Man* (1952) and Toni Morrison's *Beloved* (1987). Short stories, such as those by Raymond Carver, can match the linear shapeliness and concision of traditional dramatic tragedy. And then there are tragic memoirs, which cross between art and history: *The Diary of Anne Frank* (1952), Primo Levi's *If This is a Man* (1959; first published in Italian in 1947), and Anne Michaels' *Fugitive Pieces* (1996). The "Canto of Ulysses" chapter in Levi's Auschwitz memoir, which combines poetry and literary allusion, autobiography, and a degree of fiction, is arguably the most powerful example of the tragic mode in twentieth-century prose. Levi recalls trying to teach Jean, the "Pikolo," Italian by reciting Dante as they walk to collect the day's food rations. He stumbles to remember the lines describing Ulysses' assertion of the human spirit beyond the pillars of Hercules, the rhythm of the *terza rima* matching the movement of their walking, and he declares himself prepared to sacrifice that day's soup rations to recall Dante's words.[29] It is a testimony to the importance of memory and the grief of forgetfulness, to the whole European classical tradition which is threatened with extinction in Auschwitz but nurtured with such fervor. This central moment of the book makes the case for the value of humanity beyond the fact of its brute survival.

Film critics have written relatively little on the subject of tragic cinema, as Rita Felski noted.[30] Yet as films develop particular generic expectations and then consciously interrogate and depart from them, and as cinema explores the boundaries between the private gaze and various forms of tacit collective understanding or its limits, we can see various tragic tropes coming into play. Postwar film noir developed conventions of style and plot which are still alluded to in more recent films such as *Taxi Driver* (1976), *Mulholland Drive* (2001), or indeed *Drive* (2011), and which evoked existential despair, urban loneliness, and a certain feeling of fatalism and entrapment. The western, with its traditional ethics of colonial expansion and conquest, has been interrogated by Sergio Leone and Clint Eastwood to tragic effect.[31] As Rita Felski noted, film raises the question of the distinction between tragedy and melodrama. The work of David Lean, for example (*Dr Zhivago*, *Bridge over the River Kwai*, *Lawrence of Arabia*), explored this generic faultline, with the paradoxically melodramatic understatement of his *Brief Encounter* echoed in the Korean film *In The Mood for Love*. At the opposite end of the spectrum, European art cinema has created work deeply informed by philosophical or theological theory and the work of past film makers, producing films which self-consciously reflect on their own medium and its history in ways that might seem to conform with traditional dramatic tragedy. We could include in this category Krzysztof Kieslowski, Michael Haneke, Lars Von Trier and the Danish Dogma group, Iranian directors Abbas Kiarostami and Asghar Farhadi, and the Turkish filmmaker Nuri Bilge Ceylan, himself influenced by Andrei Tarkovsky, Michelangelo Antonioni, Robert Bresson, Ingmar Bergman, and Yasujiro Ozu.

Just as music played a vital function in classical Greek tragedy—the song of lament, the choral song of memorialization—so the events of the twentieth century have been registered in the memory by sonic, melodic intervention. "The Last Post," played on the trumpet at the Menin Gate First World War memorial in Belgium nightly since 1928, has set the pattern for memorial services around the world and was incorporated into Karl Jenkins' *The Armed Man* (1999). There are many classical musical works which could be deemed tragic: the tragic operas of Benjamin Britten, Alban Berg, and Francis Poulenc.[32] But the foremost musical response to the experience of pain and suffering in the twentieth century is jazz, which grew out of the blues, along with other forms of popular music such as soul and—later—rap. With a tight chord structure like an Aristotelian plot, the jazz chorus finds form to shape the sad experiences of romantic loss, forced migration for work, poverty, and racism. The tension between aesthetic form and mournful content is inherent in the music of Lonnie Johnson and Bessie Smith; Billie Holiday and Nina Simone; Miles Davis' *Kind of Blue*; Amy Winehouse's *Back to Black*. In many cases, the tough or tortured lives experienced by these singers and musicians, heard in the timbre of the voice, also determines the reception of these songs as tragic. But the music also transfigures those experiences, pointing to the poignant contrast between lyrical beauty and suffering, or what Paul Gordon has described as "the relation between rapturous blues music and its supposedly pessimistic lyrics."[33]

Artists are limited in their tragic expression, Lessing believed, because of the lack of narrative in their work and their focus rather upon a single moment.[34] Yet, as Ben Quash explores in his chapter in this volume, many twentieth-century artists have conveyed a tragic sense of narrative and grief, by indicating the passage of time and the accretions and losses of history. The German artists Anselm Kiefer and Gerhard Richter, for example, reflect on the Holocaust, history, guilt, and memory by layering their canvases with paint and other materials, covering and uncovering unplumbed trauma. Responding, arguably, to a similar sense of mid-century traumatic history, Giacometti pared down the human figure to "very little . . . almost nothing," comparable in its minimalism—and simultaneous evocation of a lost plenitude—with Beckett's just-surviving narrators (Figure 0.2).[35] In contrast, the power of photographs is often derived from their ability to capture a single moment. When one looks at a photo from the Jewish ghettos of Eastern Europe by Roman Vishniac, for example, or a portrait of a victim of the Stalinist Gulag or Cambodian Khmer Rouge (Figure 0.3), one is caught between acknowledging the ordinary humanity of the photo's subject and possessing knowledge of their subsequent fate.[36] Tragedy is inherent in the gap between innocence and knowledge, between areas of recognition and non-recognition. The Vishniac or the Khmer Rouge portraits hold the viewer's gaze. But other photographs draw attention to the refusal to look or to the limits of our witness and understanding. Since, as Susan Sontag pointed out, photographs risk transforming suffering into spectacle, often the most powerful images are ones in which the subject turns away from our gaze and experiences something we cannot see (for example Figure 0.4).[37] Margaret Bourke-White's picture of German woman averting their eyes from the sight of the dead in the Nazi concentration camp, for example, draws attention to what is at stake in looking or not looking at—and within—photographs (Figure 0.5).

FIGURE 0.2: Alberto Giacometti. "Walking Man II" in the Kröller-Müller Museum, Otterlo, Netherlands. © Maurice Savage/Alamy Stock Photo.

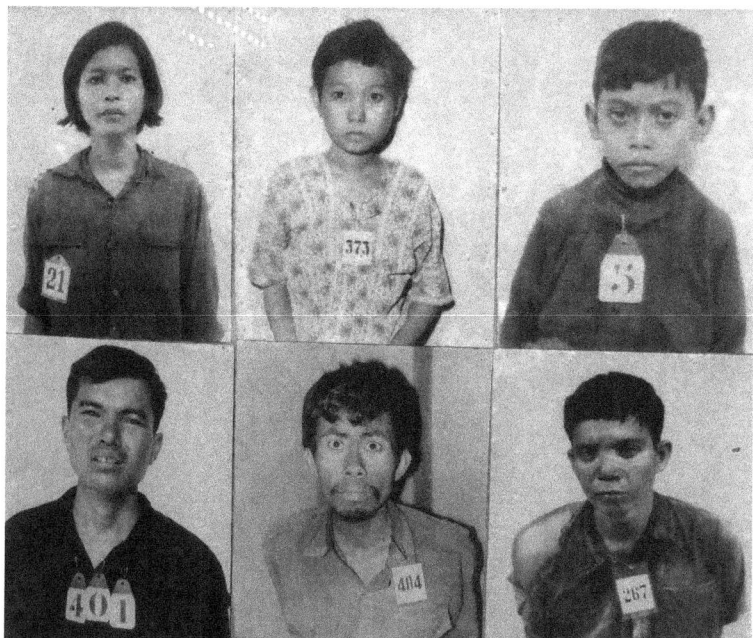

FIGURE 0.3: Khmer Rouge prisoners of the S21 Tuoi Sleng security prison under Pol Pot's regime, Phnom Penh, Cambodia, about to be killed. Credit: Clay Gilliland/Wikimedia Commons.

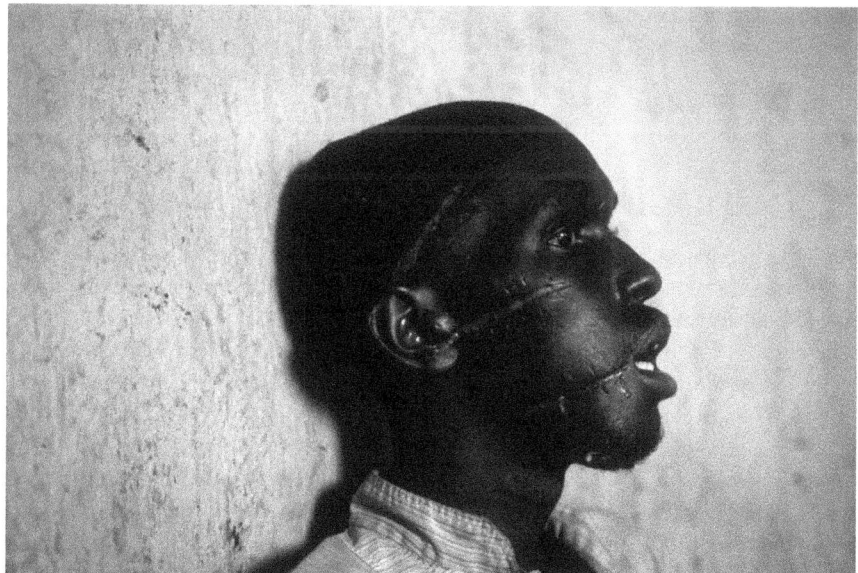

FIGURE 0.4: An unidentified Tutsi man who survived the Civil War in Rwanda, June 1994. © Scott Peterson/Liaison via Getty Images.

FIGURE 0.5: Residents from the nearby city of Weimar walking with eyes averted past a pile of corpses in the courtyard of Buchenwald concentration camp following its liberation, April 1945. © Margaret Bourke-White/The LIFE Picture Collection/Getty Images.

TRAGIC EVENTS, TRAGIC RESPONSES

I've sketched here some tentative canons of tragic art: drama, fiction, films, music, visual culture. But even these draw our attention to some of the fault-lines in speaking or writing definitely about tragedy: namely the question of the relation between historical event and aesthetic response. On the one hand, any analysis of the tragic import of a work of art must necessarily take account of its referential relation to historical experience and factual knowledge. The knowledge of Amy Winehouse's death at age twenty-seven, for example, influences one's reaction to her songs "Back to Black" or "Valerie." Picasso's painting *Guernica* acquires extra significance from its title and our awareness of this event in 1936 as the first aerial bombardment of civilians in history.[38] On the other hand, it is hard to conceive of an event which would be unmediated by our response to it. History is turned into narrative almost as soon as it is experienced.[39] That metamorphosis is the process by which the cultural imagination tries to make sense of what has happened or is still occurring. And the twentieth century, with the development of news and documentary reporting, through newspaper, radio, film footage, and television, gave the population access to events around the world more extensively and immediately than in any previous age. The distinction between historical events and their mediation—and arguably between historical and aesthetic tragedy—became even more blurred than in previous centuries. The language of tragic theater "bleeds out" of the theater into public space, and vice versa, as Kélina Gotman notes in this volume. It is possible to focus with as much serious critical attention upon historical tragedies that have been witnessed in our world since 1920 as it is upon fictional tragedies on the stage or the page.

Any account of twentieth-century tragedy, for example, cannot fail to consider the experience and impact of the two world wars. The first "Great" war, which begins the period covered by this volume, "the biggest collective blunder in the history of international relations," strikingly illustrated the futility of war, exemplified not only by the way the leaders "sleepwalked" into military battle but also by the static nature of the four years of trench conflict in which 400,000 British men's lives might be lost in the Battle of the Somme to gain six miles of land.[40] In this case, the war can be characterized as tragic, due both to its apparent pointlessness, encapsulated in Wilfred Owen's poem "Futility," and to its frequent tropes of sacrifice for one's fellow man and for an inept and heartless older generation.[41] In contrast, the Second World War was much more geographically diffuse, clearer in its political purpose and eclectic in its cost to military and civilians alike. There is no single tragic narrative of the Second World War, in the way that the trenches of the first war took on such existential, metaphorical significance. Instead there are many stories and theaters of war, reflecting its refracted nature, from the London Blitz and the siege of Stalingrad, to the firebombing of Tokyo and the Japanese kamikaze pilots, the beaches of Dunkirk and Normandy, the French Resistance, and the Burma railroad. This was truly a global war, and its consequences did not end in 1945 but arguably continued with the Cold War, first experienced in the bitter civil unrest in Greece in 1944, and continuing until the fall of the Berlin Wall in 1989. Totalitarianism and ideological division, with global, imperial reach, dogged the century. From the Soviet Gulag, as described by Aleksandr Solzhenitsyn, to McCarthyite America, alluded to in Arthur Miller's *The Crucible*, through Korea, the horror of Vietnam, and the heartbreaks across the divide in Berlin, the Cold War persisted for nearly five decades.[42]

But besides the wars and ideological conflicts that undergirded the century, the period covered by this volume was characterized by a series of revolutions related to human rights. Race, gender, sexual orientation: the personal was political in the twentieth century and it was frequently the locus for tragedy too. The Civil Rights struggle in America in the 1950s and 1960s drew attention to long-term systemic abuses and injustice—segregation, voter suppression, lynching—which underpinned individual tragic events, such as the murder of Emmett Till, the Birmingham church bombing, and the assassination of Martin Luther King Jr. Indeed, King's murder (Figure 0.6) echoed other dramatic assassinations in the period: John F. Kennedy, Robert Kennedy, Malcolm X, and—a little later—Harvey Milk. It seemed, in the 1960s, as if any individual who tried to campaign for justice and equality (heroic virtues) would be targeted by darker forces.[43] The fate of these individuals could be read in Schlegelian terms, poised between external oppression and individual "transcendent" courage.[44]

The historical divisions and tensions of race in America have produced many complicated tragic narratives but none more widely publicized than the rise and fall of O.J. Simpson in the 1990s. O.J had been one of the most successful football players of the 1970s, who crossed into advertising and Hollywood, a shining example for white

FIGURE 0.6: The assassination of Martin Luther King Jr., Memphis, April 1968.
© Joseph Louw/The LIFE Images Collection/Getty Images.

Americans supposedly of a post-racial United States. But arrested, after a televised car chase down the Los Angeles freeway, on the charge of killing his (white) wife Nicole Brown and her friend Ron Goldman, Simpson's trial lasted for eleven months and was a media sensation; 150 million Americans tuned in to watch the verdict in October 1995. As revealed in the well-researched ten-hour-long documentary, *OJ: Made in America*, itself arguably a work of tragedy too, the trial, in which O.J. was controversially acquitted, threw a spotlight on key concerns in late twentieth-century America: the obsession with celebrity, the mistrust of law enforcement, the continuing deep divisions of race.[45] On the one hand, O.J.'s was a classic tale of hubris and hamartia, a latter-day Icarus whose years in the sun of success were followed by a downward spiral of drink, violence, and destruction. On the other hand, it was a complex story of manipulation, opportunism, and omission. O.J., who had always ignored Civil Rights protests and been studiously silent when African Americans were brutalized by the police in his own city, blatantly exploited race during his trial, opening the lid publicly on racial mistrust and persuading the majority black jury to find him innocent, despite the overwhelming evidence against him. His acquittal shone a light, therefore, on a third, overlooked injustice in America: the violent domestic abuse and murder of women. The further tragedy of the O.J. Simpson case is that the story of the rise and fall of O.J. often eclipses the fate of Nicole Brown in the popular imagination.[46]

The trial of O.J. Simpson can be read as tragedy because it dramatizes, on an individual level, much larger currents of American social and political life, making history particular rather as traditional theatrical tragedies do. It also became a televised event. It is impossible to understand O.J. Simpson without taking into account the role of the media in recording and shaping his life, and therefore his was a natural tragic narrative in the making. At the opposite end of the scale, there are two tragic events or episodes in the twentieth century that are so catastrophic in their physical range and ethical implications that they interrogate the very possibility of representation and interpretation. I am referring to the Holocaust and to the detonation of nuclear bombs over Hiroshima and Nagasaki. The attempted genocide of an entire race, six million Jews killed by the Nazis, has overshadowed the century, testing the boundaries of what we consider is humanly possible or thinkable. "Writing poetry after Auschwitz is barbaric," Theodor Adorno famously observed.[47] It was not that artistic creation after the Holocaust was impossible, although that strangely seemed to be implied by Adorno when he returned some years later to retract his earlier statement: "Perennial suffering has as much right to expression as a tortured man has to scream; hence it may have been wrong to say that after Auschwitz you could no longer write poems."[48] But it was rather that aesthetic appreciation had been centrally part of the culture that had also produced the Nazis, that to put faith in the old artistic values of beauty, poetic expression, or tragedy itself was to evade or even be complicit in the horrors of the genocide. After Auschwitz, we are "tainted and can never again be made clean."[49] For some writers and philosophers, this meant that it was impossible to believe in God, in humanity, in the possibility of adequate comprehension or representation.[50] Yet for some theologians, like Donald Mackinnon or Juergen Moltmann, the Holocaust was a pivotal event in shaping their beliefs about an incarnate God who suffers with us, the crucified God, plumbing the depths of what is thinkable.[51] Auschwitz calls up the tragic turn in theology, which is still powerfully felt today.

The Second World War ended with the other cataclysmic event of the twentieth century, the atomic bombs dropped over Hiroshima and Nagasaki. Around 129,000 civilians were killed immediately by the two bombs and another 100,000 from burns and radiation in the months afterwards. Casualty statistics are hard to establish because the bombs continued to claim their victims for years after their detonation. Sadako Sasaki, arguably the Anne Frank of Hiroshima, died from leukemia ten years after she survived the bomb when aged two. Before she died, she folded many origami paper cranes, because she had heard the legend that anyone who folds a thousand cranes will be granted a wish. Allegedly she died before she could reach her target number. But paper cranes made by children from all over the world hang from her memorial statue in Hiroshima, a symbol of their longing for peace. Since 1945, no nuclear bombs have been used in war. But the world has been living all this time under the possibility that these weapons could be detonated at any time, that, in other words, we now have the capacity to blow ourselves up several times over. Is this to live with the permanent possibility of absolute tragedy, a possibility that became more acute, for example, during the thirteen days of the Cuban missile crisis in 1962? According to Hannah Arendt, nuclear weapons radically altered the limits of thought itself.[52] Perhaps we could say the same about tragedy, that the nuclear age ushered in the necessity for new modes of tragic thinking.

As Drew Milne describes in this volume, one tragic form that has taken on a new resonance and importance in the twentieth century, as a focus for public feeling around these events, is the memorial. Sometimes these are commissioned artistic monuments, designed to convey the collective, contradictory response to a traumatic episode in a nation's history as well as a site of reflection and mourning for individuals involved. One example is the Vietnam War Memorial in Washington, D.C., conceived by Maya Lin in 1982, which consists of two adjoining walls of names—American soldiers killed in the conflict—sunk into the ground. Families can walk down the path to the wall and touch the name of their dead relative, mourning his individual death with that tactile encounter. Visitors looking at the black, shiny gabbro walls can see themselves reflected simultaneously with the names and ponder the relation between past and present. And overall, from a distance, the memorial looks like a dark wound in the ground, symbolizing an unpopular war which was lost and a tragic episode in U.S. history. More recently, the Holocaust Memorial inaugurated in Berlin in 2005 succeeds in registering a powerful sense simultaneously of lament, guilt, and bewilderment. Indicating the serious enormity of the atrocity by the centrality of the monument's location (it is beside the Brandenburg Gate, almost underneath the Reichstag), the five-acre site is covered with dark, concrete, tomb-like slabs, laid out in a grid pattern and some as tall as fifteen feet. To walk between them

FIGURE 0.7: "Atomic Shadow. The 'shadow' of a ladder and a Japanese soldier after the Atomic bombing of Nagasaki by the USA in August, 1945." © Authenticated News/Archive Photos/Getty Images.

is to feel both regimented and lost in an oppressive labyrinth, disturbingly both victim of, and participant in, "the rigid discipline and bureaucratic order that kept the killing machine grinding along."[53]

But other memorials are created from ruins and relics of the past, which derive their power from the contrast between the physical retrieved object viewed and the lives that have been lost. To return to Hiroshima and Nagasaki, the bombs obliterated the centers of the cities (five and one square miles respectively) and killed many thousands of people instantly. The scale of destruction was hard to fathom. Yet the tragic significance of what happened is measured by small traces on an individual, human scale. For example, the photographs of human "shadows" (Figure 0.7)—the traces of people created when the heat from the explosion burned off the surface of a building except where it was shaded by a victim's body—testify to the unimaginable power of the bomb (which instantly incinerated the body to nothing, beyond its shadow) but also to the specificity and humanity of the individual.[54] Meanwhile the museums at Hiroshima and Nagasaki contain objects discovered after the bomb: torn and burned children's clothes, a watch face with the hands stuck at the exact minute of the explosion. These memorials also can be considered tragic on account of their simultaneous testament to destruction and survival. The body of the Japanese man has been entirely incinerated but the shadow lingers on. The watch hands have stopped but the watch remains.[55] This is, again, the "almost nothing" of tragedy, the double sense of nihilism and hope, or the "inability to speak and the inability to be silent" that animates Beckett. "I can't go on. I'll go on," as the narrator says in the final line of *The Unnameable*.[56]

GLOBALIZING TRAGEDY

In the past, tragedy was confined to the nation-state. Greek tragedy emerged in the particular political context of fifth-century imperial Athens. Shakespearean tragedy was founded upon the anxieties of late-Elizabethan, early-Jacobean England, its portrayal of foreign kingdoms shaped by the conflicts and turbulent politics of the pre-Tudor age as explored in the history plays. Even the postwar golden age of American tragedy was focused upon the new country with its recent immigration from the old world and its aspiration towards prosperity and safety in the future. August Wilson's *Fences* has its main character building a boundary around his backyard for most of the play as a visible symbol of his sphere of concern, the private home a metaphor for the family and his patriotic feelings towards his country.

But tragedy in the twentieth century has generally been much more international in subject matter and reach. Two world wars, the Cold War, and de-colonization have opened up the sphere of tragic concern as has the development of mass communication: television, film, and now the Internet. We are now more informed about the suffering of others around the world than ever before and more aware of cultural responses to disasters across many different societies. Critics have often argued that tragedy is a Western art form, that other civilizations have never been able to "achieve tragic knowledge."[57] But it is clear that every society experiences pain, loss, and disaster, even if they choose to respond to these episodes in different ways. Tragedy, we might then argue, is the form in which a culture attempts to explain and express unbearable, inexplicable experience, shaped by its particular religious beliefs, history, and traditions.

The Chinese, for example, have no specific word for tragedy, preferring to speak of "sad plays" ("bei-ju"), and indeed some Chinese critics would deny that there is a tradition of Chinese dramatic tragedy.[58] Yet comparisons can be made between classical Chinese plays and stories and Western tragic drama, while still being attentive to the different approaches and beliefs.[59] In particular, Chinese tragic stories often focus upon the suffering and stoic resilience of the ordinary citizen whose own life might be lost but, watched over by ancestors, will be commemorated and ultimately vindicated by a cosmos which is basically just. It is possibly to place the filmmaker Zhang Yimou in this tradition, his films such as *Red Sorghum* or *Not One Less* closing with some glimpse of hope despite individual death or hardship. But other writers and artists are much more questioning of traditions. Early twentieth-century short story writer Lu Xun, well read in Chinese, Japanese, and Western literature, exposed cynically the "moral cheapness of catharsis" by ironizing the attitudes of the rural peasants to the disasters and suffering of others.[60] Meanwhile, working in the wake of the Cultural Revolution and Tiananmen Square, the artist Ai Weiwei has produced installations and videos that point to the repression of the individual in the name of the national collective interest and the public omission of care for ordinary citizens. In particular, his series of works relating to the 2008 Sichuan earthquake, which resulted in the deaths of an estimated 70,000 people, including many schoolchildren, drew attention to the government neglect of proper building construction and attempted censorship of the news while it also participated in a material form of tragic lament.

Japanese ideas of tragedy, as evidenced in Noh drama and Kabuki, attracted the interest of Western writers like Yeats and Pound at the beginning of the twentieth century. But its Buddhist Zen traditions were reinterpreted and given renewed life by Mishima Yukio following the humiliation of defeat in the Second World War. His novel *The Temple of the Golden Pavilion* (1959) explored the "tragic beauty" which is revealed at the moment of destruction, the exquisite building burned by a Zen monk. Echoing this tragic paradox, Mishima turned his own death into a work of art by committing *seppuku*, or ritual suicide, in 1970 according to traditional Samurai custom.[61] In both these examples, it is arguable that Buddhist ideas were actually subverted by Mishima to support what was ultimately a very personal, violent, and nihilistic philosophy, troubled by the loss of empire. More recently, the 2011 earthquake, tsunami, and meltdown at the Fukishima nuclear plant resulted in new reflection upon the way in which the Japanese respond to these natural disasters.[62] The precariousness and preciousness of life, lived in the shadow of the colossal destructive power on land (volcanoes, earthquakes) and sea (as typified by Hokusai's "The Wave"), have been celebrated by poets and artists both in Japan and abroad.[63]

Tragedy in the twentieth and twenty-first centuries has frequently become hybrid in form: neither exclusively Western or non-Western, leaking beyond the boundaries of particular cultures, genres, or traditions. As Erin Mee and Helene Foley have recently demonstrated, classical plays like *Antigone* can travel to different contexts.[64] And playwrights like Wole Soyinka transferred classical Greek ideas of tragedy, such as beliefs about sacrifice, the individual, and the chorus, to Nigerian culture and what he described as "the universe of the Yoruba mind," in plays such as *Death and the King's Horseman*.[65] As well as utilizing tropes from both traditions, Soyinka's play also dramatizes the complications and tragic consequences of the cross-cultural encounter between the British colonial rulers and the indigenous African culture.[66] Beyond the hybridity of many modern tragic dramas, however, and what might be described as the "glocalism" of different traveling tragic texts, it is possible to view the tragedy of the modern age as uniquely global in character. The effects of industrial globalization have been devastating on the lives of indigenous peoples, with extraction industries listed on the London Stock Exchange displacing tribal communities from their land, polluting their waters and throwing millions into precarious, marginalized existence (Figure 0.8). Moreover—following two world wars, the Holocaust, Hiroshima and the development of even more powerful nuclear weapons, the AIDS epidemic in the 1980s—this has been the age to imagine total catastrophe.[67] How can we speak of a planetary tragedy which, by its nature, would annihilate a race, a nation, a whole world, and defy speech and thought? As Maurice Blanchot mused, "to think the disaster . . . is to have no longer any future in which to think it."[68]

The planetary tragedy we are facing now is climate change. This threat challenges traditional ethical thinking both because it is global by nature—the sins of one nation in terms of carbon emission have an impact upon the lives of other nations that might be far less polluting—and also because of the extended temporality of the crisis.[69] There is a time lag of around forty years between carbon emission and temperature rise, so the connection between cause and consequence, or *hamartia* and *peripeteia* in Aristotelian terms, is greatly attenuated and hard to confront. This is a novel type of global tragedy. Caught in an already decided fate and continuing to transgress, we are living in limbo, in a dying planet, as the walking dead.[70]

FIGURE 0.8: A child laborer carrying coal he has scavenged from the edge of an open-pit coal mine on former agricultural land in Jharkhand State, northeast India. 2010. © Robert Wallis/Panos Pictures.

TRAGEDY IN THE TWENTY-FIRST CENTURY

The final volumes of other *Cultural Histories* published by Bloomsbury close the period of their coverage in the year 2000+. But this *Cultural History of Tragedy* pointedly takes the story up to the present moment. For it is our contention that the concept of tragedy, and the cultural function of tragic drama and performance, changed dramatically on September 11, 2001. We were, in the last decade of the twentieth century, supposedly living in "the end of history," as Francis Fukuyama put it, with the Cold War over and the values of Western liberal democracy, capitalism, and secularism prevailing.[71] It was possible, back then, to put forward theories about tragedy that in fact are still being articulated by some critics, namely that the tragic condition is a response to a world without God, that Auschwitz was the event that tragically made God both unthinkable and most needed.[72]

But after two planes flew into the World Trade Center on 9/11, the West woke up to the fact that history for many people around the world was still very much ongoing and that there was a powerful sense of God for whom it was necessary to sacrifice a great deal (Figure 0.9). On the one hand, philosophers, literary critics, and theologians have seen, in 9/11 and its aftermath, an opportunity for renewed thinking about how we relate to others. Martha Nussbaum pointed out that "terror has this good thing about it; it makes us sit up and take notice" and that "Americans [made] real to themselves the sufferings of so many people whom they never would otherwise have thought about."[73] Judith Butler considered the opportunity that 9/11 offered us for realizing our "shared precarity" with others and for questioning whose life is considered "grievable."[74] And for these writers, like Martha Nussbaum, classical tragedy seemed the most useful form through which to think about the responses of pity and fear, the politics of compassion and moral cognition located in the emotions. Inter-subjectivity has become the prevailing trope through which to read tragedy in the twenty-first century, from the renewed interest in Antigone's relation with Ismene, for example, to new approaches to Shakespeare.[75]

But on the other hand, 9/11 ushered in a two-decade war, first on the "axis of evil" and then more widely on "terror." And the religious extremism on one side prompted a retaliatory fundamentalism, similarly employing a religious rhetoric of crusade, heroes, and sacrifice, on the other. What Rowan Williams foresaw, back in January 2002, as a dangerous choice he urged his readers to avoid—"Violence is a communication, after all, of hatred, fear or contempt, and I have a choice about the language I am going to use to respond"—has come to pass.[76] Conflict seems unending, terror and terrorism is spreading, and refugees forced to migrate pose an ongoing challenge. With a sense of tragic events escalating in scale, interdependency, and frequency across the world, there is concomitantly an increasing appetite for tragic representation in our theaters, amongst our artists. The number of productions of Greek tragedy in Britain and America, for example, has spiked in the last two decades. And there are new plays written as responses to the world we find ourselves in, as well as new exhibitions, art installations, and further musical, visual, aesthetic interventions.[77]

It is sobering in many ways to acknowledge that the body of material on tragedy in the modern age is expanding exponentially. This volume of Cultural History has no definitive ending, no final conclusion. If it begins with the cataclysmic, hellish vision of the Great War from which the population sought to escape, it closes with uncertainty, an endless war without geographical location or clear political focus; a nationalistic retreat into

FIGURE 0.9: Firefighters stand in the smoldering wreckage of the World Trade Center, New York City, September 13, 2001. © Mario Tama/Getty images.

isolationism in the Anglophone world; deep social and economic division and distrust; a global environmental crisis with a terrifying timescale. The future seems open-ended, unpredictable, and hugely disturbing, matched by the forms and concerns of our modern idea of tragedy.

CHAPTER ONE

Forms and Media

Fragmented, Torn, Multiplied

RAMONA MOSSE

"Fuck. Fuck. Fuck. Fuck. Fuck!" The expletive echoes through the auditorium—not once, not twice, not even four or five times but as a 40-minute incantation. Fists raised up high, the performers hurl their insult at the gods. Tragedy today: that is *Mount Olympus*: To Glorify the Cult of Tragedy, the 24-hour performance by Belgium artist and director Jan Fabre, which opened at the *In Transit*-Festival Berlin in 2015 before touring internationally. Fabre and his ensemble created a miniature festival with tents to camp out, resting areas, food stalls, a fortune teller as the Oracle of Delphi, cathartic restrooms, and an atmosphere reminiscent of Glastonbury. The performance itself, as the subtitle announces, was "to glorify the cult of tragedy" in all its conceptual shades: tragic heroes from *Oedipus, Medea*, or *The Bacchae* riled against their fate; ritualistic violence paired with illicit desire; the burden of power captured in the figure of the king; finally, the workings of blind fate. *Mount Olympus* offered a staged kaleidoscope of tragedy fragmented, a memory of tragedy in Western culture. Or, as Luk Van den Dries sums it up on the *Mount Olympus* website: "The 24-hour project cannibalizes theatre. For a whole day and night the remnants are digested and ejected through the passage where everything ends up"[1] (Figure 1.1).

The theatrical cannibalism of Fabre's performance piece is more than just a provocation. It marks a fundamental shift in the way tragedy has been perceived in the twentieth and twenty-first centuries. Tragedy no longer is limited to a serious dramatic action depicting the fall of an exceptional individual; instead, the place of tragedy in the Western tradition has itself become an object of reflection in a variety of forms and media. The hyperbole in the phrase "to glorify the cult of tragedy" offers both: a way of distancing and ironizing the cultural validation tragedy has received while highlighting the ritual origins of tragedy. In its breakdown of borders between drama, event, and experience, *Mount Olympus* offers an entry point to thinking about the formal peculiarities of modern and contemporary tragedy. To offer a variation on Van den Dries' image of cannibalism: like Pentheus in the *Bacchae*, the body of tragedy is dismembered and torn. Yet, tragedy is not buried but rather reassembled over and over: in acts of rewriting; as performance event; or as processes of adaptation across media. Part of tragedy's modernity is to present itself in fragmentation.

At the gates to tragedy in the twentieth century stand the odd couple of Friedrich Nietzsche and Richard Wagner, the philosopher and the theater maker. Philosophy had remade tragedy fundamentally over the course of the nineteenth century by creating a complex theoretical body of work on the tragic. The crucial contributions made by

FIGURE 1.1: *Mount Olympus*, created and directed by Jan Fabre. Foreign Affairs 2015, Berliner Festspielhaus. © Wonge Bergmann.

nineteenth-century German idealism—in the works of Friedrich Schlegel, Arthur Schopenhauer, or Georg Friedrich Wilhelm Hegel—served to reposition tragedy permanently on the margins of drama and literature and at the nexus between philosophy and history.[2] Yet, of all the philosophers engaged with tragedy, it was not Hegel but Friedrich Nietzsche whose reshaping of tragedy would carry the greatest impact back into the realm of the theater. Nietzsche offered a radical reimagination of tragic conflict as a purely aesthetic phenomenon in *Die Geburt der Tragödie* (Birth of Tragedy) and made a call for a new tragic art: "A storm seizes everything that is worn out, rotten, broken, and withered, wraps it in a cloud of red dust . . . Tragedy sits in the midst of this superabundance of life, suffering, and delight, a sublime ecstasy . . ."[3] The poetic force of Nietzsche's description was formative for the many attempts of twentieth-century aesthetic production to break with the cultural tradition, particularly because "it offers a theory of tragedy that can maintain itself without almost any reference to content."[4] Nietzsche's call continues to echo through the theaters. More specifically, Wagner's new conception of opera as the *Gesamtkunstwerk* that fused all the arts was one manifestation of this renewal of tragedy.

Beyond Wagner's vision for his own theater, which shape would such a renewed tragedy actually take in the twentieth century? In 1966, Raymond Williams created a canon of modern tragedy in his book of the same title, which spans a range of texts from the late nineteenth century to the 1960s and includes core modernists such as playwrights Henrik Ibsen, Anton Chekhov, August Strindberg, Eugene O'Neill, T.S. Eliot, Luigi Pirandello, Albert Camus, Jean-Paul Sartre, Arthur Miller, Samuel Beckett, and Eugène Ionesco as well as novelists Leo Tolstoy, D.H. Lawrence, and Boris Pasternak. Strikingly, the equation "tragedy = drama" does not hold here. Instead, tragedy is a broadly literary genre comprised of narrative and dramatic works. Williams' list has remained relatively stable and received minor expansions, particularly when it comes to the tragic novel, including Hermann Melville, William Faulkner, or George Eliot, Thomas Hardy, and Henry James as well as Fyodor Dostoyevsky.[5] The current definition of tragedy in the *Online Oxford Dictionary of Literary Terms*, as "a serious play, (or, by extension, a novel)"[6] equally supports this framing. However, this broader scope of modern tragedy points to a crisis in genre theory itself, evident particularly in Gerard Genette's critique of the inconsistencies of established genre divisions into dramatic, epic, and lyric, or Jacques Derrida's attack on the prescriptive qualities and naturalization of genre categories in "The Law of Genre" (1980). To draw on an alternate conception of genre: Medieval usage of the term "tragedy" was far more fluid and referenced a set of prose and poetry, containing "sad stories about commonwealths and kings."[7] Hence, Julie Orlemanski, in her exploration of genre in the Middle Ages, proposes a nominalist understanding of genre, which "functioned mainly as an empty category."[8] Lacking knowledge of the classical tradition, the Medieval artist did not have sufficient reference points of, for example, Classical Greek tragedy to draw on. I would like to borrow this notion of an "empty category" to point to the various shapes that tragedy in the twentieth century takes. Here, the sense of an "empty category" stems not from a lack of but rather an intensely heightened awareness of the rich and often paradoxical cultural tradition of tragedy. In this chapter, I would like to argue for an understanding of tragedy in the twentieth century as exploding traditional genre categories in order to move through a more fluid set of forms and media. This kind of tragedy is not so much an adding to the corpus or canon of the tragic tradition but instead a self-conscious practice of questioning and revaluating that tradition. Tragedy in the twentieth century looks backward rather than forward.

Tragedy as a genre shifts. In order to show the mechanisms of this shift, I will first consider Raymond Williams' tragic theory in the first part of *Modern Tragedy* and put it in dialogue with George Steiner's *Death of Tragedy* (1961) and Lionel Abel's *Metatheatre: A New View of Dramatic Form* (1963), all published in close proximity to one another. In combination, these contributions to the theory of tragedy mark a turning point in our cultural conception of tragedy in the twentieth century. As Susan Sontag remarked, the "death-of-tragedy"-debate was an "exercise in cultural diagnostics" and "the burial of a literary form [is] a moral act."[9] In the context of the 1960s, the question of the cultural place of tragedy is part of a wider debate about how to relate to or rebel against the cultural tradition. Culminating in the Student and Civil Rights Movements of the 1960s, the question of renewal v. conservation took to the streets and remade not just aesthetic but also social values. The crisis of values forms the basis of George Steiner's particular argument about the impossibility, or death of tragedy. It is a crisis that stems from the ethical breakdown in human relationships and the scale of destruction produced by two world wars that had dominated the first half of the century. Steiner's understanding of tragedy is built on its exceptionalism and marries ethics and aesthetics: to classify as tragedy itself implies a value judgment of extraordinary excellence.[10] Tragedy dies because the idea of such excellence, be it in the tragic hero or in the sense of a shared ethics, rings hollow in the aftermath of Hiroshima, Auschwitz, and Stalingrad. Tragedy, in Steiner's conception, is fundamentally a conservative form.

In an inversion of precisely this argument, Raymond Williams asserts the need for tragedy because of the scale of such suffering. Tragedy does not die, it can adapt, Raymond Williams asserts. Echoing Arthur Miller's "Tragedy and the Common Man," Williams calls for a democratization of tragedy and the relevance of human suffering per se.[11] In reflecting on the immediate history of the two world wars, Williams argues for the revolutionary potential inherent in tragedy: "we have identified war and revolution as the tragic dangers, when the real tragic dangers, underlying war and revolution, is a disorder which we continually re-enact."[12] Instead, the incommensurability implied in the tragic conflict justifies resistance and political change. Ultimately, Williams' focus on the revolutionary potential of tragedy echoes the cultural revolution embedded in his own historical moment of the 1960s.[13]

In contrast, Lionel Abel offers metatheatre as the next evolutionary step of drama to move beyond tragedy. Working with a very similar list of modern dramatists to Williams, such as Ibsen, Pirandello, Beckett, and Brecht, Abel asserts that "tragedy w(ill) be replaced by metatheatre"[14] because metatheatre's playfulness about the status of reality is able to address modern individual consciousness more fully. While Abel's definition of metatheatre as a celebration of the individual's powers of self-consciousness is not without its problems, he rightly points to the overwhelmingly important role self-reflexivity plays in twentieth-century drama and performance. It also speaks to a rising prevalence of generic hybrids in modern drama,[15] which echoes Polonius when announcing the arrival of the Players to Hamlet: "The best actors in the world, either for tragedy, comedy, history, pastoral, pastoral-comical, historical-pastoral, tragical-historical, tragical-comical-historical-pastoral, scene individable or poem unlimited" (2.2.368–72). The fluidity between these categories is indicative of modern and contemporary drama while the apparent redundancy of an excess of classification points to the already mentioned crisis in genre theory itself. While Steiner's evocation of death actually points to a shift in conceptualizing tragedy, Williams and Abel give accounts of tragedy in transformation. Williams' understanding of the revolutionary dimension of tragedy underscores how tragedy exists in history as much as in drama, while Abel identifies self-conscious playfulness as a fundamental feature of twentieth-century theatre.

Let's return briefly to the Wagnerian *Gesamtkunstwerk*, since it also offers another less abstract innovation to artistic production: the Bayreuth Festival House. When it opened in 1876, Wagner's theatre was a marvel in modern technology, spatial innovation, and acoustics that reshaped audience experience. Wagner's dimming of the houselights by extension marks the use of electric lighting on and off the stage in the theaters. Herein lies the other game changer for tragedy: technology. It offered not only a radically different experience of space and atmosphere in the theatrical event, but it also expanded the possibilities for aesthetic expression with the rise of broadcast media, photography, and film. Walter Benjamin's 1936 essay "Das Kunstwerk im Zeitalter Seiner Technischen Reproduzierbarkeit" (The Work of Art in the Age of Mechanical Reproducibility) famously argues that technology, particularly the medium of film, reorganizes spatial and temporal experience in the creation of its essentially visual narrative. It also undercuts the organic unity of the artwork and replaces it by processes of reproduction, which ultimately allow for a wider distribution and hence democratizing of the function of art. The broad-ranging expansion of aesthetic media, then, crucially affects the arts and their engagement with the world. Tragedy is no exception. Tragedy after 1945 absorbs these technological, philosophical, and political developments and undergoes a transformation that extends it beyond the sphere of drama, shaped by how it responds to the question of its own reproducibility. If one can speak at all of a death of tragedy, it would be a death of it as dramatic genre only. Rita Felski has powerfully argued for "emancipat[ing]" tragedy by conceiving of it as the more flexible mode in order to avoid "equating the tragic with a now virtually defunct form of poetic drama."[16] In the remainder of this chapter, I will trace the various ways, in which tragedy, modal, fragmented and multiplied across various media, self-consciously reflects on its processes of reproduction and self-aware adaptation.

I would like to start where modern tragedy tends to come to a close, with 1945 and the postwar period, looking at tragedy as metatheatre, tragedy as performance, tragedy as adaptation, and tragedy in its triangle with history and democracy.

TRAGEDY AS METATHEATRE

The story of modern tragedy often ends with Samuel Beckett, the playwright who pushes drama to its formal limits. Instead, I would like to begin with Beckett as the author who experiments with a wide range of genres including drama, prose, radio, and film. In doing so he pays particular attention to how different media impact our ability to tell stories, use language and create fictional worlds. *Breath*, the shortest of Beckett's plays, consists of a tableau of the stage littered with objects, while a rhythmic sound and light pattern marks the stage itself as a breathing spectacle. The theatrical conditions cease to be tools of storytelling; they become the story. Beckett is concerned with the notion of tragedy. His Theatre of the Absurd places its protagonists into bare spaces to explore the most basic conditions of their existence. Beckett's characters are governed by necessity, which makes them tragic, but it is also a determination that has lost any meaningful frame since they exist exclusively onstage, which makes them comic. Beckett creates self-consciously metatheatrical plays that oscillate between tragedy and comedy. His drama defines itself by keen awareness of the theatricality of the situation and it is out of that theatricality that the tragic dimension emerges. *Endgame* exemplifies such tragic metatheatricality in a variety of ways. Most immediately, *Endgame* is a rewriting of Shakespeare's *Hamlet* with Beckett's Hamm retaining only a crippled version of the Shakespearean hero's name. But Beckett does not so much retell and illuminate a new aspect of the famous tragedy. He rather halts the play at Hamlet's inability to act and makes that the raison d'être of his characters. Temporality is no longer a linear progression but rather a cycle of repetition, in which the characters are caught up. As Hamm puts it in his opening speech: "Can there be misery—(*he yawns*)—loftier than mine? No doubt. Formerly. But now?"[17] He is the tragic hero without a purpose or an action. Drama has been emptied out of anything but its theatrical condition.

Beckett becomes a major influence on GDR playwright Heiner Müller, whose own metatheatrical intervention systematically rewrites Ancient Greek and Shakespearean tragedy and explodes dramatic form entirely. Müller couples tragedy from his early verse version of *Philoctetes* in the early 1960s to *Hamletmaschine* (Hamletmachine) (1977) with his immediate historical realities. Jonathan Kalb likened Müller's strategies of rewriting old texts to "occupying the corpus like a vampire or virus in order to explode it from within."[18] Müller's texts turn into attacks on dramatic form itself. That is particularly true for his internationally most acclaimed text, *Hamletmaschine*, a complex web of quotations, intertextual and historical reference of eight pages in length, yet without a clear division into dramatic roles. The opening of the play makes *Hamletmaschine* into a running commentary on Shakespeare's tragedy: "I was Hamlet. I stood on the shore and talked with the surf BLA BLA, The ruins of Europe in back of me."[19] In Müller's theater texts that have ceased to abide by dramatic convention, the metatheatrical challenge lies in the impossibility of their staging and the immense onslaught of reference (Figure 1.2). David Barnett calls it "a dramatic confrontation between the text and history."[20] That is to say, Müller does not write a tragedy but a reflection on the status of tragedy, a drama of theoretical commentary rather than a representation of an action. Hamlet, Ophelia, and Horatio inhabit the piece as much as Charles Manson, the German

FIGURE 1.2: Heine Müller's *Hamletmaschine*. Deutsches Theater, Berlin, 1990. © DRAMA. Agentur für Theaterfotografie.

RAF terrorist group, and references to the Soviet crushing of the Hungarian uprising of 1956. The image of the ruins of Europe as a backdrop ties Müller to Walter Benjamin's Angel of History in his pivotal essay "Theses on the Philosophy of History," an angel who is caught powerless between the forces of past and future (Figure 1.3):

> Where we perceive a chain of events, he sees one single catastrophe which keeps piling wreckage upon wreckage . . . The angel would like to stay, awaken the dead, and make whole what has been smashed. But a storm is blowing from Paradise; it has caught in his wings with such violence that the angel can no longer close them . . . this storm is what we call progress.[21]

Tragedy, to both Benjamin and Müller, lies in the self-contradiction of teleological history, which smashes those it allegedly liberates; radical transformation goes hand in hand with violent destruction. Müller takes from Benjamin the sense that tragedy in the twentieth century no longer takes place in literature but rather in history. Müller's acts of rewriting tragedy are both paradoxical because they announce both at the same time: the necessity and impossibility of tragedy in the present. To Müller, the realities of the two dictatorships of the Third Reich and the GDR can only be expressed through tragedy but also can only exist shattered and in fragments, since the level of systemic political violence and ideology has also made the agency required in tragedy impossible. One can draw interesting parallels to British drama of the 1970s through 1990s, when playwrights such as Sarah Kane and

FIGURE 1.3: Paul Klee. *Angelus Novus*. 1920. © The Israel Museum, Jerusalem, Israel/Carole and Ronald Lauder, New York/Bridgeman Images.

Edward Bond foreground the exploration of a violence that comes to mark a social and political breakdown rather than reconstitution. Howard Barker sketches a modern version of tragedy in his Theatre of Catastrophe, "overwhelming the normal barriers of tolerance in its audience"[22] which goes beyond any aspect of social and ethical reconstitution that might close tragic violence. In his "Forty-nine asides for a tragic theatre," Barker states that "[t]ragedy is not about reconciliation. Consequently, it is the art form of our time."[23] Tragedy turns into a site of resistance, collective for Müller and individual for Barker.

This device of fragmentation and citation in the writing process also is at the core of the less pessimistic rewriting project of tragedy by American playwright Charles Mee and his Internet-based *(re)making project*. Mee uses Greek tragedy (among other cultural artifacts) as material for his plays and simultaneously encourages his audience and other artists to do the same: "Please feel free to take the plays from this website and use them freely as a resource for your own work: . . . pillage the plays as I have pillaged the structures and contents of the plays of Euripides and Brecht and stuff out of Soap Opera Digest and the evening news and the internet, and build your own, entirely new, piece—and then, please, put your own name to the work that results."[24] Mee's plays are radical text assemblages that borrow freely from the theatrical tradition. As open sources downloadable from the Internet, they undercut existing conceptions of the artist, intellectual property, and originality: "There is no such thing as an original play."[25] The titles of Mee's plays, such *as Iphigenia 2.0*, or *The Bacchae 2.1* create a palpable relationship between the Internet, the structure of his plays, and the history of tragedy for that matter: both can be accessed not in linear progression but as a growing network of interconnected references. On the surface, this interconnectivity makes Mee's plays comic and full of absurd surprise. Yet, as Mark Chou states: "Beneath the folly, hilarity and gratuitousness of Mee's dramatization, the audience is given a sense that the civilization we have created—refined, just and progressive as it seems—depends on repressed violence."[26] *Big Love*, Mee's version of Aeschylus' *The Suppliant Women*, follows fifty sisters being pursued by fifty unwanted grooms and eventually has forty-nine women kill their husbands on the wedding night while one finds romantic fulfillment. Comedy becomes a tool with which Mee brings home the irrational motor of a self-perpetuating violence from which there is no escape. As Constantine, one of the pursuing grooms, states:

> you can say, yes, it was the men who started this
> there is no such thing as good guys and bad guys
> only guys
> and they kill people
> but if you are a man who doesn't want to be a bad guy
> and you try not to be a bad guy
> it doesn't matter
> because even if it is possible to be good
> and you are good
> when push comes to shove
> and people need defending
> then no one wants a good guy any more
> they want a man who can fuck someone up[27]

There is no escape from role-play for Constantine, as the social role of masculinity inevitably pairs with violence in the moment of crisis. In another twist, the play ends in a sumptuous wedding ceremony with garters and bouquets thrown into the auditorium. Mee has it both ways: *Big Love* opts for two consecutive endings, one comic, one tragic.

In contrast to the citational reassembly of tragedy that re-enacts violent acts in the fragmentation of language, American playwright David Mamet explores language in the form of institutionalized discourse as a motor for tragic conflict in his 1992 play *Oleanna*. In an interview with John Lahr for the *Paris Review*, David Mamet explicitly identifies the play as a tragedy: "The most challenging dramatic form, for me, is the tragedy. I think I'm proudest of the craft in the tragedies I've written—*The Cryptogram*, *Oleanna*, *American Buffalo*, and *The Woods*. They are classically structured tragedies."[28] *Oleanna* was a scandal when it opened, specifically because it confronted inherently liberal values with each other. Set in the ivory tower of the American university, Mamet created a contentious chamber play about a meeting between John, a professor and his student Carol that turns awry when she accuses him of sexual harassment. The play starts with an apparently ordinary meeting in John's office. Carol is concerned with her grade and struggling in class:

> Carol: Nobody *tells* me anything. And *I sit* there . . . in the *corner* In the *back*. And everybody's talking about "this" all the time. And "concepts", and "precepts" and, and, and, and, and, WHAT IN THE WORLD ARE YOU TALKING ABOUT? And I read your book. [. . .] I DON'T KNOW WHAT IT MEANS AND I'M FAILING.[29]

Carol does not just fail in class. Rather, any attempt at communication is doomed to fail. John's attempts to reach out to Carol only worsen the impasse. Exasperated, when in Scene 2 the accusation of sexual harassment threatens his tenure and family life, John talks about the fundamental conventionality of language and the need to reach beyond its surface: "I don't think we can proceed until we accept that each of us is human. (*Pause*) And we still can have difficulties."[30] However, as the progression of the action shows, precisely this move from language as convention to making language an expression of one's self does not take place. Both John and Carol are caught in the structures of discourses no longer their own. John, while attempting to de-escalate what he sees as a misunderstanding, loses all and is driven to precisely the violence he had so abhorred. Fundamentally, the tragic conflict is not so much one that circles around an illicit action, such as Antigone's burial of her brother Polyneices. All action in *Oleanna* can be read in more than one way, as the method of intellectual self-inquiry is pushed to an extreme. Language becomes the obstacle. Two orders of language and reality clash in the encounter between student and professor, as the play poses the question of who has been manipulating whom and how individual speech and established discourses relate to one another. David Mason terms *Oleanna* "both metatheatre and tragedy, the play with no meaning and the play with more meanings than it can bear."[31] David Mamet's case is an example for a metatheatrical tragedy that is not based in its self-referentiality to the tragic tradition and intertextual play with existing tragic figures and plots. Instead, the self-referentiality in *Oleanna* is focused entirely on the use of language itself.

In the pairing of tragedy and metatheatre, self-conscious reflection does not move these theatre texts beyond the tragic, as Abel had envisaged. Instead, self—both in the broader historical sense that Müller and Barker employ and in the personal encounter between Mamet's characters and Mee's montage figures—is what creates the tragic conflict. Our understanding of tragedy is deeply embedded in our understanding of our place in the development of history and in the Western context. Such acknowledgment is no longer celebratory but, qua Benjamin, keenly aware of the high price of suffering there is to pay for what is called progress.

PERFORMING TRAGEDY

The arguably most radical formal shift that tragedy undergoes in the twentieth century is away from the dramatic text and towards exploring the advent of performance. While the nineteenth-century philosophical engagement—Hegelian re-readings of *Antigone*, *Hamlet* and *Oedipus* at their helm—prioritized the reading of tragic drama and the philosophical reconceptualization of tragic conflict, the mid-nineteenth century also witnesses the first attempts to put Greek tragedy back on the stage. We return to Richard Wagner's Bayreuth Opera Festival, which first opened in 1867, as "the single most important event in the pre-history of modern festivals of Greek drama."[32] Even earlier, in 1842, Ludwig Tieck and Felix Mendelssohn-Bartholdy staged the so-called Potsdam *Antigone*, which counts as the first such modern attempt at performing Greek tragedy unabridged. Its success turned the production into "a new model for staging Greek tragedy" that exported internationally and "proved highly successful for productions of *Antigone* in Paris, London, and New York."[33] Similarly, the institution of the "Greek play"—Greek tragedy performed in Ancient Greek—at Cambridge University in 1882 (that continues today) speaks to the range of burgeoning interest in the possibilities of performing Greek tragedy. While there was a distinctly historicist motivation in recreating Greek tragedy in performance, the beginning of the twentieth century shows that performance also led to radical new theater aesthetics such as Max Reinhardt's landmark productions of Greek tragedy in the early 1900s that aimed to perform with the masses for the masses.[34] Performance itself began to redefine what role tragedy might play in the modern age. In fact, it may be argued that in the twentieth century performance, not the writing of new tragic drama, is the privileged site of tragedy's formal transformations.[35]

In his 2013 book *Tragödie und Dramatisches Theater* (*Tragedy and Dramatic Theatre*), Hans-Thies Lehmann captures this new perspective on tragedy when making the crucial and somewhat counterintuitive distinction between drama and tragedy. The "and" between the two suggests a curious inequality between the two. Tragedy, rather than being the epitome of drama as George Steiner would have argued, is a theatrical event that shape-shifts throughout Western history, passes through drama when it is the dominant form of theatrical expression and then moves into the sphere of the post-dramatic. Tragedy is not a body of texts but rather an experience based in the performance in front of an audience. It is at heart the experience of a fundamental transgression of our intellectual and perceptual parameters:

> ... consciousness loses its footing, concepts falter, the certainty of judgment wavers, and the sphere of the calm (and calming) resolution of contradictions by thinking is shut out – or shut down altogether. Certainty of what "acting" [*Handeln*] even means, disappears.[36]

Lehmann's redefinition of the tragic experience of and in performance is primarily a formal one: no longer the hero stumbles and falls but rather we as audience stumble over the rigidity of our own expectations. Performance, rather than text, lies therefore at the heart of Lehmann's understanding of tragedy. Bringing tragedy into performance has been a preoccupation throughout the twentieth century, which comes to a particular culmination point in the last thirty to forty years.[37] The following examples explore tragedy's ritual foundation in performance, as well as the relationship between the individual and the choral collective.

Lower Manhattan, the Performance Garage in 1969: the newly constituted Performance Group under director and performance theorist Richard Schechner opened with their rendition of Euripides' *The Bacchae*. The production also doubled as the testing ground for Schechner's idea of an environmental theater that broke down the divide between stage and auditorium and united performers and audience members in a single space, in which the audience was repeatedly asked to join in. Loosely based on Euripides' play, the production used devised texts that allowed a gap between performer and character. *Dionysus in '69* offered a glance at an understanding of tragedy beyond textual reference but rather based in a primarily physical experience of a series of rituals relating to birth, death, and most fundamentally, the opposition between individual and community. In one of the most famous sequences of the performance, the Dionysus-performer crawls through a birth canal made up of the naked bodies of the other performers and is born by them. The performer then addressed the audience:

> Here I am. Dionysus once again. Now for those of you who believe what I just told you, that I am a god, you are going to have a terrific evening. The rest of you are in trouble. It's going to be an hour and a half of being up against the wall. Those of you who do believe can join us in what we do next. It's a celebration, a ritual, an ordeal, an ecstasy. An ordeal is something you go through. An ecstasy is what happens to you when you get there.[38]

Theater with its spatial and conceptual division of audience and actor gives way to single, shared performance environment, in which ultimately everyone turns into performer. The shared experience of the performance ritual culminates in the chase and sacrifice of Pentheus. We see *The Bacchae* primarily through the eyes of the chorus of Maenads rather than the power conflict between Dionysus and Pentheus. In some sense, the audience doubles up as the chorus. Schechner redefined tragedy primarily through this audience–performer relationship, describing the theatrical event as "a network of obligations and expectations"[39] negotiated in direct interaction in a single space. Schechner's experiment with tragedy became also foundational for the academic discipline of Performance Studies, which, in drawing on ideas from Anthropology and the Social Sciences, ushered in the performative turn in the Humanities.

More immediately, however, Schechner also drew on the work of the American avant-garde ensemble The Living Theatre, which under the artistic direction of Judith Malina and Julian Beck had worked to implement a new theater aesthetic inspired by Antonin Artaud's Theatre of Cruelty. The Living Theatre's work on *Antigone* (1967) in turn based itself on Brecht's 1947 version of *Antigone* at the Stadttheater in Chur, Switzerland with which he re-entered the European theater scene in the postwar period.[40] This genealogy is important since Brecht's project to reshape tragedy was informed by a core concern with performance: "it is not so much a new school of playwriting as a new way of performance being tried out on an old play."[41] But Brecht's journal entries at the time also suggest tragedy as a platform for investigating the anatomy of violence in the aftermath of the Second World War and the Holocaust.[42] Likewise, Schechner as much as Malina and Beck conceives of the relationship between the individual and the community as structured by a core of violence, echoed in René Girard's anthropological study *La Violence et le Sacré* (Violence and the Sacred). Girard sees the expulsion of a scapegoat as the fundamentally stabilizing moment of the community; the individual is sacrificed for the group.[43] This view of community stands in stark contrast to the more utopian visions of a performance collective as a new kind of peaceful political community, which plays a substantive role in the self-understanding of The Living Theatre but also The Performance Group. A similar tension can be traced in the *Antikenprojekt I* (Antiquity Project I) under the direction of Peter Stein at the West Berlin Schaubühne am Halleschen Ufer in 1974, which exposed the violent undercurrents of social formations while formulating principles for an egalitarian theater collective based upon the principles of co-determination for the running of their theater, perched in close proximity to the Berlin Wall.[44] Each was an experiment not only in the realm of aesthetics but also in social organization, formulating alternatives to modern institutionalized society.

If tragedy turns into a privileged site for exploring the make-up of the community, the collective or the mass, this has also given rise to a series of further performance experiments that focus specifically on the tragic chorus. In Greek tragedy, the chorus had offered a mediating function between protagonist and audience, providing a space for reflection on the action (even if not all Greek choruses have a privileged access to knowledge about the development of the action). In modern drama and performance, the chorus is a site of deep ideological contention for twentieth-century culture.[45] It apparently lies close at hand in order to express the multiple and fragmented modern experience of mass culture and our modern experience of history as an institutionalized bureaucratic apparatus, no longer dominated by individual figures but movements, parties, and factions. At the same time, the staging of de-individualization and collective unison reverberates with the threat of dictatorship, whether in the shape of National Socialism or Soviet Communism. The potential and partiality of the chorus lie side by side. Bertolt Brecht's choruses of the

1930s *Lehrstücke* inhabit a position grounded in materialist dialectics when reflecting on the stage action. Furthermore, the chorus here is something to join rather than watch, as Brecht envisaged the *Lehrstücke* as a participatory form without audiences.[46] Tyrone Guthrie's 1957 rendition of *Oedipus Rex* at the Canadian Stratford Festival returned to performing with masks, requiring a non-realist, intensely physical acting style that emphasized the rhythmic and musical nature of the chorus. Ariane Mnouchkine, in turn, makes the chorus a site of intercultural celebration, joining Ancient Greek with Asian acting traditions in *Les Atrides* (1990–2). As Helene Foley points out, "the use of mask, dance, music, ritual and poetry and other world theater traditions not only overlaps with that of Greek tragedy, but offers an opportunity to bring to life those aspects of ancient drama that are alien to the tradition of Western nineteenth-century realism."[47] Foley foregrounds the physical dimension of tragedy: in the rhythmic body, then, different cultures begin to relate to one another where language would divide them.

Contemporary theatre continues to be attracted to the politics of the choral form, as the latest adaptation of Scottish playwright and director David Greig shows. Greig adapted Aeschylus' *The Suppliant Women* in 2016 as the first production of his tenure as Artistic Director of the Edinburgh Royal Lyceum Theatre together with director Ramin Gray and composer John Brown. At its core is an amateur chorus of fifty local young women, aged 16–26, who voice the plea of the fifty daughters of Danaus for a refuge and a new home. A teaser trailer for the production shows the fifty women in a small, enclosed space surrounded by metal walls. They are on a threshold of what could be the backstage area of a theater or the container of a ship. As they move towards the camera, rhythmically stomping, it is the small step of the threshold that dominates the frame.[48] It is the threshold to the past of Aeschylus' play with its choruses of lay citizens as much as it is a threshold to the present-tense of this community theater that brings the politics of the current refugee crisis into shared space for debate. We all are or at least could be refugees, is one underlying message of Greig's Suppliant chorus.

Finally, to acknowledge tragedy in performance as its own separate form of aesthetic engagement is to accept a fundamental shift in the treatment of tragedy. As performance departs from embodying the tragic canon to reflecting on the underlying structures that make up that canon, it becomes a field to reimagine tragedy independently of any given play. The importance of performance as its own category goes hand in hand with the development of audio-visual recording devices, namely photography and video. Despite all the insufficiencies and incongruities that the concept of a performance archive implies, it remains a fact that audio-visual recording technology has entirely reshaped what is collectible and can be retained for future reference. Performance leaves behind a more diverse, sophisticated, and accessible set of traces thanks to the development of these technologies. The immense audio-visual and photographic collections of the New York Library of Performing Arts at the Lincoln Center or the National Video Archive of Performance at the Victoria and Albert Museum in London speak to this development. The same goes for the establishment of the Archive of Performances in Greek and Roman Drama by Oliver Taplin and Edith Hall at Oxford University in 1996. It is worth recognizing that academic knowledge of and interest in the conditions of Ancient Greek theatrical performance have expanded as evident in publications from Oliver Taplin's groundbreaking *Greek Tragedy in Action* (1978) to Simon Goldhill's *How to Stage Greek Tragedy Today* (2007). The performance of tragedy and performing the tragic provide a fascinating alternative to the much cited text-and-performance divide. Instead, tragedy straddles both, foundational dramatic texts and equally foundational conditions of live theater making.

FIGURE 1.4: The Wooster Group's *Hamlet* at The Performing Garage, New York City, 2007. © Paula Court.

The Wooster Group's production of *Hamlet* (Festival Grec, Barcelona, 2006) eloquently captures this transfer between liveness and archival storage, by using the legendary 1964 Richard Burton film production of *Hamlet*—in the 1960s hailed as a "new form of 'theatrofilm'"[49]—as a foil for their own live performance. That is to say, the dramatic text does not create the score for the performance but rather the visual record of a previous performance does so. As the Wooster Group performers repeat and subvert their Richard Burton double, the temporality between what is live and what is recorded is called into question (Figure 1.4). William Worthen sees theater as existing suspended between archive and repertoire: "The archive preserves writing, enabling readers to encounter and imagine the work of dramatic writing, and the work that dramatic writing might do, anew. But the repertoire is the drama's difference engine, the machine of its (dis-)appearance, and so of its transformative survival."[50] The Wooster Group explores how multifaceted such a transformation between archive and repertoire can be, using *Hamlet* as one of the most canonical tragedies. Instead of a before and after, the relationship between live body and image turns into a near endless loop. Likewise, it becomes difficult to locate this *Hamlet* as film or theater; instead the Wooster Group's production marks the intermedial mash-up that theater and, with it, tragedy in performance is exposed to in the late twentieth and twenty-first centuries. As tragedy becomes enmeshed and confronted with new media and forms, performance offers some of the most radical reimaginations of tragedy.

TRAGEDY AND ADAPTATION

The camera pans down a rainy New York street and into a French bistro, where four intellectually combative diners are discussing the prevalence of a tragic or comic view of life. This is the opening scene of Woody Allen's film *Melinda and Melinda* (2004), in which a single story turns into a tragedy or a comedy depending on the teller. The film echoes Felski's approach to tragedy as a mode that can essentially shift; tragedy and comedy are effects of a negotiation between author/director and audience. It is no longer understood to reside in the work. While Woody Allen was not necessarily able to deliver successfully on the challenge he sets himself with this film, the question of whether tragedy is rendered through form or content is one that lies at the heart of the tradition. As we have seen in the previous parts of this chapter when dealing with metatheatre and performance, adaptation lies at the core of tragedy, it is not a modern afterthought. From its origins in Athens onwards, tragedy is fundamentally implicated in a process of adaptation between religious ritual, dramatic text, and theatrical performance. In the following, I will highlight the processes of adapting tragedy to two distinctly modern narrative forms, i.e., the novel and film. Tragedy, as stated at the beginning of this chapter, may not only describe a particular piece of serious drama but also constitute a sad tale about an excess of human suffering reflected in or conditioned by the conditions and failures of public life. Both the novel and the film can both deliver on that front. One might say: while modern and contemporary drama and performance foreground the theatricality and formal dimensions of tragedy and its cultural tradition, the continuation of individual tragic plots and stories occurs in the narrative genres of the novel and film. Herein lies also the peculiar logic of discussing them jointly in a single section.

When Raymond Williams drew up his canon of modern tragedy to include the novel, he distinguished between a "social" and a "personal" tragedy in order to show how the novel shows up social conflicts by staging them as internal:

> There is social tragedy: men destroyed by power and famine; a civilization destroyed or destroying itself. And then there is personal tragedy: men and women suffering and destroyed in their closest relationships; the individual knowing his destiny in a cold universe, in which death and ultimate spiritual isolation are alternative forms of the same suffering and heroism. One version of tragedy or the other, it seems, we must choose between them.[51]

Williams' distinction between a public and a private tragedy can only apply to the modern context; Greek and Shakespearean tragedy, the Spanish Golden Age and even eighteenth-century bourgeois tragedy either operate entirely within an alternately aristocratic and divine realm or have at least an overtly public context. The democratization of tragedy to ordinary men and women like Arthur Miller's Willy Loman becomes relevant only from the drama of Henrik Ibsen, Gerhard Hauptmann, and August Strindberg onwards. It also fundamentally relates to the rise of the novel over the course of the nineteenth century to become the dominant form of literary expression. When French novelist and playwright Emile Zola exclaims that "I am waiting, finally, until the development of naturalism already achieved in the novel takes over the stage,"[52] he substantiates the notion that the novel is at the forefront of aesthetic expression. He is also very literally waiting for drama to model itself on the novel, which includes engaging with the personal and private in the ordinary day-to-day. Jeanette King emphasizes nineteenth-century closet drama as another way in which drama approached the novel and concludes: "The novel obviously presented itself as a more satisfactory vehicle for modern tragedy than drama had become. When serious drama was itself reduced to a form of private reading, the novel was a formidable rival."[53] If the modern experience is marked by its fragmentation and plurality, postwar tragedy reflects this turn through its own formal diversification. It does not only allow for exceptions to a dramatic or theatrical norm but is rather entirely multi-medial; different media reflecting different aspects of the tragic tradition.[54] Put another way, "modern tragedy is the tragedy of the modern."[55]

Swiss author Max Frisch explores this theme of "the tragedy of the modern" very explicitly in his 1957 novel *Homo Faber*. Already the title announces a defining shift in the conception of modern man as no longer a *Homo sapiens* but a *Homo faber*, i.e., a maker but no longer wise. Walter Faber is the protagonist, an engineer whose rational and pragmatic worldview is shattered by a series of events that show up the limits of human mastery over both nature and life. Technology persistently fails Walter, most dramatically in the opening of the novel where Walter survives a plane crash. At the center stands the love affair with the young girl Sabeth who turns out to be Faber's daughter from a previous lover, Hanna. She dies from a fall after being bitten by a snake, while Walter's ultimate fate remains uncertain after a cancer diagnosis. Frisch re-enacts the Greek myth of Eurydice and the tragedy of Oedipus in an industrialized and technology-driven modern environment. Faber who wanted to make his own fate ends up being destroyed by it. Or, as Hanna says in the novel: "You don't treat life as form, but as a mere sum arrived at by addition, hence you have no relationship to time because you have no relationship to death."[56] Modern technology reshapes human consciousness and that turns into a key source of tragedy in the novel.

This pairing of technology and tragedy also reappears in film, most markedly perhaps in Ridley Scott's 1982 feature film *Blade Runner*, loosely based on Philip K. Dick's novel *Do Androids Dream of Electric Sheep?* (1968), which is considered a postmodern masterpiece of fusing film noir with science fiction as well as the thriller. Again, the question of human consciousness and technology takes center stage, although here the tables have been turned. For Rick Deckard, the protagonist of Ridley Scott's movie, there is no alternative to the post-industrial urban landscape in constant darkness and perpetual rain dominated by various forms of surveillance. Deckard is a Blade Runner, that is a bounty hunter, whose task it is to kill or "retire" bio-engineered creatures originally used to colonize other planets, but which have started to turn against the humans that created them. In this case, four fugitive replicants have returned to force the humans to extend their relatively short life spans. In the process, Deckard falls in love with the replicant Rachel and ultimately tries to flee with her. Frisch's exploration of technology positivism is pushed to its ultimate conclusion with the creation of the replicants or cyborgs, a fusion of human and robot into a single being. The film self-consciously plays with genre classifications, given the wide range of its literary and filmic references critics have traced, such as Dante Alighieri, William Blake, and E.T.A. Hoffmann, and most notably Milton's *Paradise Lost* with Satan as a version of the classic tragic hero.[57] More generally, Elizabeth Bronfen has explored the tragic dimension of the film noir, which could function both as a commentary of the political instability after the Second World War but also as "fantasy scenarios . . . with its protagonists fatefully entrapped in a claustrophobic world and unable to master their destinies."[58] As a *neo-noir*, *Blade Runner* could easily belong to that category. The ominous ending of the Director's Cut version suggests that Deckard might also be a replicant, slated to die soon; hence neither Rachel nor Deckard seem able to escape their fate. Fate, however, comes no longer in the shape of a cruelly divine sphere of Delphic oracles but rather as a stringent technological determinism. Human agency becomes impossible because the status of what it is to be human is itself under threat. In addition, the Voigt-Kampff-Machine test that can distinguish between replicant and human makes its distinction based on the test person's capacity for compassion, resonating with the response of pity and fear experienced by the tragic audience. In pairing science fiction with tragedy, *Blade Runner* also exemplifies a shifting context for the realm of myth. No longer a story of origin (which here takes place in a laboratory or sterile factory setting of the Tyrell Corporation), science fiction's utopian thrust locates myth in the realm of the future. The limitless possibilities of technological advancement and particularly AI as its most burgeoning field reinstate a quasi-divine sphere.

Film's visual narration links it to photography as the other major visual medium of the twentieth century. Jennifer Wallace has convincingly argued for a consideration of visual culture in the context of tragedy, citing tragedy's focus on the act of displaying maimed or dead bodies.[59] Photography offers another way for such a display of bodies that suffer, linking it to processes of reproduction as a mass media. Reproduction challenges any representational distance to the subject of the photograph, thus raising ethical questions about what may be depicted. Susan Sontag's critique of photography in 1977 in talking of images of violence and suffering has a bearing today: "To suffer is one thing, another thing is living with the photographed images of suffering, which does not necessarily strengthen conscience and the ability to be compassionate. It can also corrupt them."[60] In other words, the purging effect of catharsis is replaced by an addiction to see more. Forty years later, this charge of sensationalism still holds, given the even more widespread distribution of still images via the Internet. Websites such as lifedaily.com or omglane.com offers viewers the opportunity to gloat over a series of photographs entitled "Final Photos Taken Before Tragedy Struck." Tragedy here is equated simply with accidental death. The effect on the

FIGURE 1.5: Moria in Snow, Lesbos, Greece, 2017. Digital C on metallic paper, 35.5" × 120". From *The Castle* by Richard Mosse, published by Mack Books, 2018. Image courtesy of the artist and Jack Shainman Gallery.

viewer is to revel in a position of smug superiority in the face of those either unaware of imminent danger or already in agony. Nevertheless, it is also true that photography has found intricate ways to play with the implicit realism of its medium and highlight the mechanics of its own production processes when depicting suffering and crisis. In his 2017 video installation "Incoming" at the Barbican Centre in London and the accompanying photography exhibition "Heat Maps" at the Jack Shainman Gallery in New York, Irish art photographer Richard Mosse repurposes a military infra-red surveillance camera able to track body heat at long range. Inverting its military status as a weapon, Mosse uses it to follow the humanitarian plight of the refugees along their most commonly traveled routes to Europe. The photographs in "Heat Maps" are large-scale shots that transform the camps and refugees en route into luminous silvery silhouettes in the midst of gray landscapes of tents and shelters. Architectural structure and bureaucratic stratification coincide. The three-screen video installation "Incoming" enhances the stunning unrealism of the visuals: the people here remain de-individualized but in their transformation through the eye of the camera powerfully alluring at the same time. Mosse's experimentation with the medium throws the viewer back on the medial processes of production. The question of scale and its limits is particularly noticeable: not just the scale of the refugee crisis but the obsession with scalability at the heart of Western culture (Figure 1.5). In the Artist Statement, a video on his website, Mosse connects the refugee crisis with the increasing pressures of climate

change that have transformed homelands into deserts.[61] The camera's mapping of heat takes on a different dimension in the environmental context and produces complex tensions between the tracking of body heat and the threat of temperature rises due to global warming. Strikingly, the camera in Incoming transforms not only our perception of the humans in the video, the environment equally shifts, so that the rocks of a Mediterranean beach appear much closer to cool slabs of ice in a pseudo-Arctic landscape, connecting the mass migration of people with environmental degradation. "Heat Maps" and "Incoming" are examples of contemporary photography's multifaceted engagement with tragedy in other media. Mosse's installation furthermore expands the possible focus of tragedy beyond the human to the complex theme of tragedy and ecology.[62]

TRAGEDY AND DEMOCRACY: BY WAY OF A CONCLUSION

Over the course of this chapter, I have traced the shifts that twentieth-century tragedy undergoes in a variety of media. Overall, a peculiar tension exists between the high level of aesthetic self-consciousness when engaging with tragedy, and the urge to locate tragedy politically, i.e., beyond aesthetics and in history. The first half of the twentieth century with its two world wars and the Holocaust are one important reference point in this context. Theater since the 1960s has born witness to the past and in doing so foreshadows a more general culture of reparation that has gained prevalence with the end of the Cold War. John Torpey has argued that the lack of a clearly defined utopian future in the aftermath of ideological collapse has implied a shift towards righting the past: "When the future collapses, the past rushes in."[63] Tragedy marks this past of human suffering. It turns into the flipside of modernity's story of progress and human advancement, politically in terms of democracy, and technologically in reshaping the idea of the human and what lies beyond the human, i.e., ecology. Twentieth-century tragedy is a highly self-conscious reflection on that tradition and how it may still bear upon modern society, albeit understanding itself as a break with that tradition. That is to say rather than merely continuing to write in the tragic tradition, playwrights, performers, artists, and philosophers made the processes of that tradition apparent, in acts of embodiment, of adaptation, and of metatheatrical playfulness. Their work becomes based in the idea of reproduction rather than production. The academic debate on tragedy and its form is also currently entering new territory. The recent Festival of International Drama (F.I.N.D.) at the Schaubühne Berlin in April 2017 ran under the banner of "Democracy and Tragedy." Yet, the festival stood out by its apparent absence of tragic forms or reworkings of the classic tragic myths onstage. Tragedy seemed not to occur within the confines of the theater but outside, in the rise of populism and the self-contradiction of democracy that undoes itself by its most fundamental tools: the electoral vote. Tragedy, then, is here to stay.

CHAPTER TWO

Sites of Performance and Circulation

The Ecology of Modern Tragedy

DREW MILNE

Will Eno's theater play *Tragedy: the Tragedy* (2001) is set within an American live television broadcast reporting a tragedy. The tragedy, it emerges, is that the sun has set for the last time. The play represents a rolling news channel reporting weather that has taken an apocalyptic turn, offering both a prophetic representation of climate breakdown and a satire on infotainment. Early on, the doubling of the play's title is made concrete: a radically unfamiliar tragic event is mediated by a familiar processing of unfolding responses.

> FRANK IN THE STUDIO The sense of tragedy must be almost palpable there.
> JOHN IN THE FIELD I'm sorry? *He checks his earphone.*
> FRANK IN THE STUDIO Is the sense of tragedy palpable?
> JOHN IN THE FIELD Absolutely, Frank. You can feel it. Something is out there, or in here, and this is what we are watching.[1]

The theater audience watches a theatrical representation of the way tragic news is packaged for a digital audience. Eno's play reads and performs less as a tragedy than as a dark satire of the way packaged news oscillates between newsroom anchor and reporter, between studio and field. Which of these is the real site of contemporary tragic performance? The play hints that the way television mediates environmental tragedy has become part of our sense of tragedy, might even be "the" tragedy, a critical part of the emerging tragedy of climate breakdown as fundamental as the prospect of the sun setting forever.

Tragedy: the tragedy is symptomatic both of a new media ecology mediating the sites of tragic performance, and of a new sense that the underlying tragedy of modern life is environmental and not the action of dramatic heroes. How might such a play be sited? Written by a New Yorker, given a rehearsed reading at the Royal National Theatre in London in 2000, and then premiered at the Gate Theatre, also in London, in 2001, the play nevertheless remains North American. Is its site of performance *transatlantic*? It received its U.S. premiere in Berkeley Repertory Theatre, California in 2008, a production for which there are trailers and clips on YouTube. The play also circulated through reviews, as printed play text, subsequently as an eBook readily available on Amazon, but also in an anthology of downtown New York theater.² Such hybrid processes of international dissemination are characteristic of twenty-first-century dramatic forms, involving performance, print and e-print, along with television and digital media.

Less than six months after *Tragedy: the Tragedy* was first performed in London, the attack on the Pentagon and the World Trade Center in New York that became known as 9/11 further intensified the sense of tragedy as media spectacle. Television generates a smokescreen of cultural vertigo, offering seemingly Olympian and yet personal and anchored perspectives on globalized scenes of destruction and suffering. This was perhaps the most widely watched live catastrophe in history, with rolling news coverage repeatedly screening footage of planes as missiles and the towers imploding. As Richard Schechner reflected, the destruction and media ecology of 9/11 challenged avant-garde aesthetics of tragedy.³ Many plays resist the cultural consumption of tragic spectacle associated with 9/11: notably Anne Nelson's *The Guys* (2001, 2002); Neil LaBute's *The Mercy Seat* (2002); Meron Langsner's documentary drama *Bystander 9/11*; Sam Shepard's dark comedy, *The God of Hell* (2004); and Ismail Khalidi's monologue, *Truth Serum Blues* (2005).⁴ But such plays, often first performed in relatively small chamber theater contexts, can appear dwarfed in their impact by global media representations. Any reckoning with the tragedy of 9/11 also has to reckon both with the intense mediatization of tragic events and with the more local environmental catastrophe and toxic debris centered on what became known as Ground Zero. As 9/11 makes clear, the sites of twenty-first-century tragedy can be found in both local environments and globalized media spectacle: the ecology of tragedy emerges as the intermediation of these different sites.

Struggling for perspective amid global conflicts, local sites of theatrical performance nevertheless remain significant for the scale, argument, and impact of plays such as Eno's *Tragedy: the Tragedy*. The history of contemporary chamber theater plays indirectly representing and confronting worldly tragedy can be traced back to Beckett's *Waiting for Godot* (1953) and the pocket theaters of postwar Paris.⁵ *Waiting for Godot*, like *Tragedy: a Tragedy*, is not formally a tragedy, but nevertheless affords tragic-comic glimpses of a tragic environment that is not named or made fully explicit. Plays such as Bertolt Brecht's revised version of *The Life of Galileo* (1945–7) more directly confronted the science of the nuclear catastrophe at the end of the Second World War. *Waiting for Godot* can nevertheless be read as the exemplary tragic drama of unspoken but palpable postwar trauma. Analogously, Beckett's *Endgame* (1957) is often taken as a meditation on some kind of post-apocalyptic, post-nuclear refuge, and yet the tragic environment of nuclear weapons is never mentioned in the play. Beckett's postwar drama emerged contemporaneously with global film, newsreel, and television news coverage, part of a deep structure of complicity that *Tragedy: the Tragedy* makes explicit as shared sites of modern tragic performance. Framed as a specifically *theatrical* performance, Eno's play implies a critique of television's role in the ecology of tragedy. As well as satirizing tragic news, the play also dramatizes deeper resistances to the recognition of environmental crisis. The tragedy of unfolding environmental disaster in the "field" is mapped on to the construction of tragic news as "human interest" entertainment. In the wake of Raymond Williams' conception of drama in a dramatized society, this is tragedy in a tragic environment.⁶

Televisual packaging of news for rapid consumption is the antithesis of the struggle to find radical new forms capable of articulating the emergent conflicts of worldly tragedies. Tragedy in the world is painfully evident, but nurturing environments in which performances can articulate the pervasive awareness of tragedy has proven difficult.

Modern tragic forms seek to deflect, revivify, and politicize the way television news has become one of the main sites of performance through which recognition of tragedy is produced, consumed, and domesticated. As such, contemporary tragedy seeks to resist becoming complicit with Guy Debord's "society of the spectacle"[7] and what Edward Hermand and Noam Chomsky call "manufactured consent."[8] Performances of modern and contemporary tragedy necessarily constitute themselves through critical resistances to more dominant media, such as news and the history of popular *drama*, from melodrama to soap opera. Whether such resistances have been primarily political or aesthetic, the sites of performance identifiable with modern and contemporary tragedy have been diffusely cosmopolitan, often developed as reflexively self-critical media hybrids. Although theater remains one critical site of performance, the place and space of tragedy has become *intermedial*, as Ramona Mosse explored in the previous chapter. Tragedy is now both site-specific and global, mediated by visual art, photography, film, television, and digital platforms including "social media." Screen media, from film and television to digital media, have reshaped global awareness of local tragedies as modes of representation, reproduction, and consumption. Screen media, however, are largely structured around entertainment and are rarely developed as sites of *critical* performance. Tragic events are continuously glimpsed but scarcely articulated with a sense that screen media might become tragic forms or sites of tragic performance. The ecology of modern tragedy remains torn between intermedial forms and the pressure of site-specific and live performance.[9]

What, then, can be learnt from the history of this intermedial globalization of tragedy? The enormity of humanly-produced suffering over the last century has transformed the substance and ecology of tragedy. The Second World War is often taken as marking a paradigmatic break in the cultural history of tragedy, but the First World War was itself so unprecedented in scale, technology, and devastation as to be experienced as the war to end all wars. The end of the First World War marked a new culture and global recognition of tragedy. One symptom of this new culture was Sigmund Freud's conception of the death drive, in part to account for the compulsion to repeat or re-enact traumas of war such as shellshock.[10] The war's many aftermaths included widespread grief and trauma, but also the worst recorded global flu pandemic, a disaster that killed more people than died in the war itself.[11] The impact of the war can be traced through forms of tragic drama, from R.C. Sherriff's *Journey's End* (1928) to Frank McGuiness' *Observe the Sons of Ulster Marching Towards the Somme* (1985), and from Sean O'Casey's *Silver Tassie* (1928) to Michael Morpurgo and Nick Stafford's *War Horse* (2007). In such plays, war and its associated *pathos*, mourning and melancholy, overshadow tragic *ethos*. It is evidently too glib to draw on world war to evoke a sense of human waste. Theatrical responses to the First World War have struggled to articulate the enormity of the global tragedy. Joan Littlewood's Theatre Workshop production *Oh What a Lovely War!* (1963), to take one example, belatedly hints at tragic waste, but its dominant mode is of dark satire through musical comedy. Harley Granville Barker's political tragedy *Waste* (1906 and 1927) has proved more enduring as a modern tragic drama, with a string of well-received revivals at the Barbican (1985), the Old Vic (1997), the Almeida (2008), and the National Theatre (2015), perhaps because the forms of waste that are dramatized are more human in scale than those of global war. Somehow theaters in London, Paris, Berlin, or New York never quite became critical sites for public mourning and tragic argument. This difficulty only intensified after the Second World War, a culture ghosted by Adorno's question as to the very possibility of poetry, and by extension, of tragedy after Auschwitz.[12]

In search of alternative sites of tragic performance, it could be argued that war memorials have become more enduring places of mourning and of tragic negotiation with the legacies of war, even amid persistent divisions, such as those in Ireland.[13] Edwin Luytens, the principal architect of British war memorials, for example, designed the Cenotaph in Whitehall, London, India Gate, New Delhi, and the Thiepval Memorial to the Missing of the Somme (Figure 2.1). Memorials have become part of the structure of feeling through which humans come to terms with the enormity of humanly-produced disasters, from the Somme and Auschwitz to the 9/11 Memorial (Figure 2.2). Daniel Libeskind's work is central to the recent critical history of memorials. He designed the Jewish Museum Berlin and many subsequent memorials, including the National Holocaust Monument in Ottawa, Canada, as well as being the architect responsible for the overall master plan of the rebuilt World Trade Center site in New York. Memorials of the Holocaust and indeed of war have created new sites of tragic performance that seek to register and bear witness to the scale of humanly-produced disasters.[14] From the Anti-Slavery Arch in Stroud (1843) to the memorial "Slave Route" in the port city of Ouidah, Benin (1993–) and London's Fen Court (2008) there are also memorials to the history of slavery (Figure 2.3). Yet, for all that disaster and oppression memorials provide sites of collective witness, grief and reflection, they are primarily sites of remembrance rather than sites of performance. Any performance that takes such sites too readily as a given context for new tragic art risks appearing crudely opportunist or deeply insensitive. The struggle to articulate tragic arguments is forced to go elsewhere to engage with the ecology of global ruins and suffering.

FIGURE 2.1: The Thiepval Memorial to the Missing of the Somme. © Popperfoto/Getty Images.

FIGURE 2.2: A shadow of a man is cast upon one of the 72,000 names of soldiers killed in the Battle of the Somme. Thiepval Memorial. © Scott Barbour/Getty images.

FIGURE 2.3: A fresco along the memorial "Slave Route" depicting slaves compelled to circle the "Tree of Forgetfulness" before being forcibly shipped off to the New World. Ouidah, Benin. © Xavier Desmier/Gamma-Rapho via Getty images.

Global institutions founded in the aftermaths of world war, such as the League of Nations and the United Nations, became new theaters for negotiating global conflict and injustice. Symptomatic of the difficulty of situating justice, the trials of German war criminals took place in Nuremberg, the ceremonial birthplace of the Nazi Party. Abby Mann's play *Judgment at Nuremberg* was originally produced for television in 1957 before becoming a well-known Hollywood film in 1961, later adapted for a Broadway production in 2001. Courtroom drama, in the theater and on film and television, continues to be a significant form for lightly fictionalized documentary tragedy. Court settings provide an ecological fit between documentary and fictional tragic action, whether as a way to stage conflicts of liberal justice, as in the film *Twelve Angry Men* (1957), or to dramatize racism and injustice, as in films such as *To Kill a Mockingbird* (1962) and *Marshall* (2017). The 1999 Tricycle Theatre London production of *The Colour of Justice*, later made into a television film (2001), offered a documentary dramatization of the Stephen Lawrence inquiry and played a small part in the recognition of "institutional racism" in Britain. The struggle to address the institutionalized histories of racism, imperialism, and colonialism is part of the modern ecology of tragedy across documentary forms, theater, and screen media.

The International Criminal Court now sits in The Hague, alongside the United Nation's International Court of Justice. The different built environments of the United Nations provide significant multi-lingual sites for negotiating tragic conflicts. As theaters of legal, cultural, and political representation, such global institutions nevertheless remain all too flawed and limited, all too institutionally racist and bound up with the legacies of imperialist wars. Such institutions are nevertheless significant as existing and potential forms of global theater against which global media and more local forms of theater and art have articulated their sites of performance. To take one example, Pablo Picasso's painting *Guernica* (1937), perhaps the most famous example of a tragic anti-war painting, was exhibited in Paris initially before traveling across the world, from the Museum of Modern Art (MoMA) in New York City to Brazil and back, before returning to be displayed initially behind bomb and bullet-proof glass screens in Madrid in 1981. A full-size tapestry copy of *Guernica*, first commissioned by Nelson Rockefeller in 1955, has hung, not without controversy, at the United Nations in New York since 1985. The painting's many politically charged sites of exhibition are nevertheless secondary: Picasso's painted memorial of Guernica's tragic destruction remains potent as a global symbol, at once local and yet addressed to an imagined court of public opinion (Figure 2.4).

The specificity of the site of tragedy, both the worldly tragedy represented and its exhibition as tragic art, specifies the political ecology of *Guernica*. It is possible to imagine more deracinated forms of art by analogy with tragedy, but without environmental specificity. This can suggest rather impressionistic and ahistorical analogies, as, for example, in Frank O'Hara's remarks on David Smith's sculptures: "The primary passion in these sculptures is to avert catastrophe, or to sink beneath it in a major way. So, as with the Greeks, it is a tragic art."[15] Cultural analogies require greater historical and environmental specificity to make sense of art's relation to tragedy. The work of Rachel Whiteread perhaps more successfully intimates a sculpture of tragic architecture and negative environment, whether in *House* (1993–4), a life-sized cast of the interior of a condemned terraced house in London's East End, or around the Judenplatz Holocaust Memorial in Vienna (2000) (Figure 2.5). Imagined global courts may always have been significant horizons for tragic art, but twentieth-century catastrophes have focused tragedy through new questions of environment and global perspective.

FIGURE 2.4: Former U.S. president Barack Obama and King Filipe VI of Spain view Picasso's *Guernica* in the Reina Sofia Museum, Madrid. July 2017. © Handout/Casa Real/Getty Images.

FIGURE 2.5: The Judenplatz Holocaust Memorial, Vienna, created by Rachel Whiteread. © Spieg/ullstein bild via Getty images.

Rescuing tragedy from its commodification as ideological entertainment remains an ongoing dynamic in the ecology of tragedy. Arguments against the continuing relevance of tragic forms have often suggested that tragedy is complicit with the suffering it represents rather than part of any solution. Brecht and Boal argued for new hybrids such as *epic theater* and *forum theater*. Along with other radical approaches to tragedy, notably those associated with Antonin Artaud, Jerzy Grotowski, Eugenio Barba, and Ariane Mnouchkine, such hybrids position tragic texts within new ecologies. These new ecologies engage with theater as a representative and artificial site, differentiated in its "liveness"[16] against "dead" media, but also as an ongoing process of repurposing the "technology" and audience dynamics of theater. More traditional theatrical institutions that revive classical and canonical tragedies, such as the Royal Shakespeare Company or the National Theatre, have also tried to resist merely reproducing or institutionalizing canonical works. Sean Carney argues, moreover, that a political poetics of tragedy is central to recent English theater, from David Hare and Howard Barker to Caryl Churchill and Jez Butterworth.[17] A recent collection of essays, *Visions of Tragedy in Modern American Drama*, traces a longer history, from Eugene O'Neill to Suzan Lori-Parks and *Hamilton* (2015).[18] Part of the ongoing work of remaking tragic theater involves recognition of the complicity of canonical tragedies with historical injustices and often unacknowledged tragedies of race, gender, and class. The weight of tradition, and the problem of tragedy as "heritage" culture sponsored by public and private funding, forces new, more critical work to emerge from more marginal sites of performance. A notable example is the work of Socìetas Raffaello Sanzio, a theater company based in Cesena, near Bologna in Italy, whose work "Tragedia Endogonidia" (2002–) was nevertheless performed across Europe in Brussels, Rome, Strasbourg, London, and Marseille.[19]

Alongside new conceptions of theater, an emerging but fundamental shift in twenty-first-century understandings of tragedy is the recognition that the environment itself has become a tragedy. Debates about the death of tragedy are now overshadowed by "the end of nature"[20] and the ethical conflicts of climate change.[21] The emerging world of climate instability and environmental disaster deepens the crisis of tragic representation already posed by the humanly created disasters of war, genocide, famine, and nuclear catastrophe. The question of what it means to produce tragic art after Auschwitz and Hiroshima, or indeed after 9/11 and Fukushima, is further burdened by global warming and the universal pollution of the Anthropocene or "Capitalocene."[22] Strains on tragedy's traditional resources for representing *homicide* and *suicide* are stretched to breaking point by *genocide*, and then undermined by the crises of environmental disaster, mass extinction, and *ecocide*.[23] The performance of contemporary tragedy necessarily engages with this new sense of tragic ecology as an underlying but unacknowledged condition of tragic performance. New understandings of the sites and settings of tragic performance have also emerged,[24] alongside new types of environmentally aware art practice.[25] Somewhat belatedly, theater institutions have attempted to come to terms with environmental politics. London's Royal Court Theatre, a significant site for new developments in the performance of tragic drama, has, since 2012, offered a symptomatic environmental policy statement on its website: "We aspire to address, through our artistic programme, the ideas and questions about environmental sustainability and to help raise the profile of these ideas through productions and related events."[26] The sites of contemporary tragic performance have been forced to reflect on their own role in environmental sustainability.

Ecological crisis turns out to have been an implicit condition of the cultural history of modern tragedy, and in ways now made newly explicit. The avalanche humanly provoked at the end of Ibsen's *Brand* (1865) prefigures both the wider sense of ecological peril but also the limits of what can be staged. The theater of the imagination can conjure humanly-produced avalanches and reflect on the disastrous consequences of human agency, but it is less evident how this can be sited within existing theater technologies. Ibsen's *Enemy of the People* (1882) and Chekhov's *The Cherry Orchard* (1903) also dramatize human agency's complicity with environmental tragedies taking place just offstage. The bombing at the end of George Bernard Shaw's *Heartbreak House* (1919) provides a comparable tragic twist to an otherwise Chekhovian comedy. Using elaborate theater technology to represent the threats of technology risks hubris. Tragic theater artifice tends to work with knowingly theatrical rather than spectacular special effects, emphasizing individual human complicities rather than environmental tragedy. In such forms, environmental tragedy remains offstage, glimpsed only in omens and portents. This is loosely analogous with the ways older tragic forms intimate that "nature" is polluted or unnatural. Intimating tragic ecology underneath comic theatrical surfaces exemplifies the way modern drama often suggests tragic depths by hinting at some more pervasive environmental doom.

In what Raymond Williams called "liberal tragedy" the theater provides a humanly-made and knowingly artificial environment in which the conflicts of inter-human action are foregrounded while environmental tragedy appears marginal.[27] Collective human agency has nevertheless shaped global forces and emerging environmental tragedies, endangering many other species and the future of the human species itself. Environmental tragedy and what has become known as "the sixth extinction" engulfs traditional conceptions of human agency.[28] As climate conditions become more dangerous, the previously unacknowledged ecology of the "sites" in which tragic art has been staged or performed become apparent.

"Liberal tragedies" prefigure an environmental turn in the performance and ecology of tragedy itself. New tragic plays, such as Steve Waters' *The Contingency Plan* (The Bush, 2009), work with the "well-made" dramatic forms pioneered by Ibsen and Chekhov. Waters' play is part of a wave of recent plays about climate change that also includes Clare Pollard's *The Weather* (2004), Mike Bartlett's *Earthquakes in London* (National Theatre, 2010), and Richard Bean's *The Heretic* (2011).[29] This environmental turn hit critical and commercial difficulties with *Greenland* (2011), a National Theatre production collectively authored by Moira Buffini, Matt Charman, Penelope Skinner, and Jack Thorne. *Greenland*'s intersecting narratives attempted to dramatize the politics and culture of climate change but the play was widely perceived as well-intentioned rather than dramatically persuasive. The most incisive of this group of plays, *The Contingency Plan*, makes sophisticated and engaging drama out of family, individual, and generational conflicts. Personal arguments are mapped on to wider social arguments about government policy and global warming, in ways that are informative and engaging. The play has its own ecological specificity in relation to London and East Anglia, marking the presence of the "sea" in the place names of London—Chel*sea*, Batter*sea*—and thus reminding London theater audiences of their proximity to potential flooding from the Thames.[30] But the play could be performed, with subtle modifications, in any metropolitan city threatened by rising sea levels, which is to say nearly every major city in the world, from New York to Mumbai, from Rio de Janeiro to Shanghai.

Globally mediated by ecocidal capitalism, the sites of tragic performance, not least those associated with the artificial space of nineteenth-century theater forms, are no longer neutral conditions of poetic possibility. While it is still possible to make intelligent liberal tragedies that address climate politics using the forms and technology of nineteenth-century theater, new forms of tragic performance often break with the conventions of "theater" as a building.[31] Part of the recurrent difficulty is the scale of humanly-produced tragedies. The enormity and tragically sublime scale of human horror overwhelms the resources of realist art. One response has been recourse to documentary forms, perhaps most powerfully in Claude Lanzmann's film *Shoah* (1985), which juxtaposes oral testimony of the Holocaust with documentary film of the sites of the Holocaust. Another part of the difficulty is the crisis in metaphorical, symbolic, or allegorical modes that might represent tragedy more indirectly or obliquely. Adorno's brief critique of Brecht's critical dramatization of fascism, for example, argues that: "The illustration of late capitalism by images from the agrarian or criminal registers does not permit the monstrosity of modern society to emerge in full clarity from the complex phenomena masking it."[32] The scale of modern society's monstrosity cannot be reduced to natural or mythic parables: the "nature" of modern humanity's genocidal and ecocidal world exceeds natural analogies.

The crises associated with the death of "nature" and what has become known as the "Anthropocene" are both global and local. This mediates the significance of site and space for any modern tragic performance. Mohammad Al Attar's Syrian play *While I Was Waiting*, for example, represents the tragedy of the Syrian civil war through the family drama, set in Damascus, of a person in a coma. The person serves as a metonym for a country in a coma. *While I Was Waiting* toured Europe, including the Avignon Theatre Festival in 2016, and the Lincoln Theatre Festival, New York, in 2017, but a performance in Damascus remains, as yet, unimaginable. Performances in exile have only minimal or mediated resonance for the contexts they would articulate. The "nature" of the conflict in Syria has also been understood as reflecting a deeper environmental crisis. Although the specific evidence is contested,[33] humanly-induced climate change helped trigger large-scale human migration. Global migration in response to climate change can be mapped on to racist perceptions of immigration, a structure of emerging global conflicts that unsettles any stable concept of the home, "oikos" or "domus." Part of the complexity is that the ecology of global tragedy demands inter-disciplinary scientific analysis, and in ways that undermine the human-centered forms of tragic drama. Recent environmental science has suggested, for example, that the seemingly "biblical" famines of sub-Saharan Africa in the 1970s were associated with global anthropogenic climate change.[34] But how could the scale of humanly-produced famine become a subject for a play or a performance?

Places such as Darfur need to be understood, then, not just as local sites of tragic climate change, but as part of an emerging global conflict involving millions of humanly-produced deaths and migrations.[35] In this sense, Damascus and Darfur are part of a long list of place names that could be understood as tragic sites: from the Somme to Abu Graib, from Moscow to Phnom Penh, from Hiroshima to Chernobyl, from Rwanda to Myanmar. Writing in 1979, Raymond Williams updated an analogous list: "In 1965. . . I argued that 'Korea, Suez, the Congo, Cuba, Vietnam, are names of our struggle.' That perspective was verified, and it came to include new names: Czechoslovakia, Chile, Zimbabwe, Iran, Kampuchea."[36] Such lists can be extended with alarming ease. Many place names have become synonymous with tragedy without it becoming clear how such places could be sites for tragic performance capable of articulating truth or reconciliation. The cordoned off "zone rouge" in northeastern France is still so polluted by weapons and chemical damage from the First World War that it remains uninhabitable. The site around Chernobyl will remain polluted for longer than humans can readily contemplate.[37] As Michael Marder construes the Chernobyl sarcophagus: "we are, at the same time, Creon and Antigone, the sovereign who disrespects ecological realities, burying alive the one who cares for them, and the suffering prisoner, deprived of the elements, of everything that makes life possible."[38] Symptomatically, it seems more natural to publish a *history* of Chernobyl as a tragedy, than to write a play dramatizing this social tragedy through tragic art.[39] The memorial to the immediate victims of the Chernobyl disaster in front of the entombed power station remains an isolation zone rather than a place for shared mourning and reflection. Nuclear catastrophe also supervenes over earlier disasters that might yet deserve memorials, such as the mass killings and deportations under Stalin's regime and the mass murder of the Jewish community during the German occupation. Some of the darkest tragedies of the twentieth century are so compounded and so catastrophic as to displace any site from which reconciliation might be imaginable.

Tragic drama can nevertheless play some part in communal conflict resolution, as it has in the north of Ireland[40] and South Africa,[41] but the intensity of local political conflicts often marginalizes global ecology. Metropolitan centers and regional cultural festivals have been the sites most likely to produce performances that reflect the ecology of tragic places. Steve Waters' theater play *World Music* (2003), for example, places the genocidal conflicts of Rwanda in the longer-term perspective of European colonialism and its legacy. Rather than claiming to document the historical Rwanda, Waters uses fiction to create some critical distance:

> Every act of fiction is an addition to the world, creating a parallel universe alongside, but not identical to, reality; this is the promise inherent in the word 'play'—the promise that the play will in itself be an act of making sense of what seems unimaginable in advance.[42]

A fictional site of performance offers some "play," some space for reflection that is freed from the burden of representing reality, but also thereby risks aestheticizing the historical suffering implicated in counter-factual fiction. *World Music* makes explicit some of the human mediations involved, not least European responsibility for creating the conditions of genocide, but the difficult scale of the mediations is also suggested by the play's title. Even if local sites of tragic violence are articulated within the artificial space of a metropolitan theater, any link between a local theater and the larger scale of human tragedy remains globally mediated. Tragedy's ecology—its setting, context, or performance environment—is no longer background, a natural backdrop against which human struggle is represented, but has become a defining condition, the unrecognized protagonist even, in the performance of tragedy.

Once recognized, the importance of the environment for performances of tragedy can be traced back into Greek tragedy. The sites of Greek tragedy's performances, notably in Athens, were already sites of ecological, cultural, and religious significance. The ancient "theater" is not merely an artificial or humanly-made context, but part of an ecology of environmental reflection performed under the eyes of watching gods, not least the sun. Questions of human miasma, pollution, and environmental violence are persistent parameters of ancient tragedy that run through European drama.[43] As Lucien Goldmann suggests, the hiddenness of the gods becomes a critical question for neoclassical tragic drama,[44] but this is also bound up with the historical move indoors to artificially lit theater. Shakespearean tragedy is a more moveable feast, performed in more evidently secular and artificial sites of performance, from the wooden "O" of Shakespeare's Globe to performances at court, in universities and inns of court.[45] This plurality of Shakespeare performance environments prefigures modern drama's secular indifference to the ecology of theater's artifice. Western theater has developed out of its ancient associations with sacred, court, and public spaces into what Peter Brook famously called "the empty space."[46] Setting aside the intricate history of Athenian tragedy's site-specific qualities,[47] Brook suggests how significant theater might now take place almost anywhere, in any place. But as David Wiles argues in his history of Western performance space, "Theatre space is not so much a given, but rather a concept produced by a specific spatial practice."[48] Any stress on theater's secular, conceptual and local site-specificity also has to reckon with the global and digital mediation of tragedy. Climate conflicts reveal how even the most conceptual forms of site-specific theater depend on a global environment that cannot be taken as a given.

Wagner's Beyreuth Festival remains perhaps the most famous modern reinvention of tragic performance within a specific performance site, though tainted by its association with Nazi Germany.[49] The early twentieth century also saw attempts to reinvent both Greek and Shakespearean tragedy for new sites. A tradition of performing Greek plays in Greek emerged in Cambridge in the 1880s and continues to the present.[50] Recreations of Greek tragedy in ancient sites has been an ongoing feature of the Athens and Epidaurus Festival since the mid-1950s. William's Poel's Elizabethan Stage Society, founded in 1895, sought to recreate Shakespearean staging conventions, and this ambition lives on in the New Globe Theatre on London's South Bank.[51] Recreations of classical and early modern tragedies have been a staple form in modern culture but what is perhaps at first surprising, and then revealing, is the new emphasis on the ecology of original conditions and sites of performance. It is as if reimagining the very sites of ancient and early modern performances might reanimate modern performance to become more than a museum culture.

Isadora Duncan's performances and the work of the Association of Teachers of the Revived Greek Dance were informed by a comparable interest in reviving aspects of Greek performance and in ways that proved significant for modern dance.[52] Vaslav Nijinsky's choreography for *L'après midi d'un faune* (1912) and *The Rite of Spring* (2013) marked a symptomatic attempt to find pre-Greek and pagan sources for the new kinds of tragic dance and performance pioneered by the Ballets Russes.[53] Reanimating Greek and ancient mythic forms continued to be an important dynamic in modern dance, notably in the work of Martha Graham's "Greek Cycle."[54] Modern dance since Graham, however, has been less explicitly concerned with tragedy as a cultural form and genre. Yvonne Rainer's influential and symptomatic "No Manifesto," for example, said "No to the heroic" and "No to the anti-heroic."[55] Tragedy has nevertheless been a continuing point of reference for intermedial forms of dance theater, such as those pioneered by Pina Bausch.[56] Her dance theater work *Café Müller* (1985), widely toured by Tanztheater Wuppertal, offers a series of profoundly suggestive images of manipulation and dependence, energy and exhaustion. These images are given further depth by recognition that Bausch choreographed the work partly out of childhood memories of her father working in his café in Germany during and immediately following the Second World War.

Overshadowed by the specter of Wagnerian ambitions, opera houses in the twentieth century have also been a persistent site for the reproduction of nineteenth-century tragic operas, preserving what were often radical or innovative in their original conceptions more as an aesthetic experience than as an attempt to grapple with modern society. In contrast, modern tragic operas, from Dmitri Shostakovich's *Lady Macbeth of Mtsenk* (1934) and Alban Berg's *Lulu* (1937/1979) to Anthony Davis' *X, the Life and Times of Malcolm X* (1986) and John Adams' *The Death of Klinghoffer* (1991) and *Doctor Atomic* (2005), have controversially confronted tragic material. Yet contemporary operas produced by talents as various as Adams, Philip Glass, Robert Wilson, Louis Andriessen,

Peter Greenaway, Peter Sellars, Steve Reich, and Beryl Korot have offered performances more engaging as studies in dramatic indeterminacy than as tragedies. Such work has not established opera as a key site for tragic performance. Indeed, while "tragedy" continues to be revived within the traditional institutions and technologies of the performing arts, such revivals tend to confirm Adorno's suggestion that "tragedy and comedy perish in modern art and preserve themselves in it as perishing."[57]

Perhaps the modern cultural form in which it is clearest that tragedy is a genre of diminishing but persistent relevance is cinema. A case can be made for performance as the modern space of tragedy, from theater, the performing arts, and post-dramatic theater to opera. And yet this is to sidestep the extent to which film and screen media are also dominant spaces and representations in the mediation of tragedy and tragic representation. Any number of films could be reclassified as tragedies or tragic films. The way such films are marketed and discussed, however, suggests that they are made, distributed, and watched as dramas, or through some associated generic category. Tragic materials are appropriated and incorporated but largely by skirting around the genre of tragedy itself. Tragedy persists in film, then, not so much as a genre, than as a ghost, a lyrical tendency or as a lamentable sense of unnatural history amid other kinds of dramatic narrative, whether as tragi-comedy or, more often, simply as drama or action. Among early classic silent films such as Fritz Lang's *Metropolis* (1927), F.W. Murnau's *Sunrise* (1928), and Carl Theodor Dreyer's *The Passion of Joan of Arc* (1928), it is possible to discern the lineaments of individual, tragic passions set in tragic environments, whether historical, urban, or dystopian. Many of the more explicitly tragic Hollywood films are adaptations of tragic novels, such as Lewis Milestone's *All Quiet on the Western Front* (1930), John Ford's *The Grapes of Wrath* (1940), Robert Mulligan's *To Kill a Mocking Bird* (1962), and Steven Spielberg's *Schindler's List* (1993). Such films risk making entertainment out of the tragic ecologies they selectively adapt. *Schindler's List*, for example, was criticized by Claude Lanzmann for making "the extermination" a "setting" for "kitschy melodrama."[58] The dramatization of individual stories such that the wider environment and tragic context remains a "setting" misrepresents historical truth, he contended. In classic westerns, too, such as Howard Hawks' *Red River* (1948), John Ford's *Searchers* (1956), and *The Man Who Shot Liberty Valance* (1962), there are often tragic, almost Hegelian ethical conflicts between culture and nature, with individuals pitted against their environments. Although the planting of "civilization" in such films offers glimpses of the tragedies of the genocide of indigenous peoples and the environmental violence of the railroad and gun law, the dominant site of imagined tragedy is the existential crisis of patriarchal Western "man" rather than the crisis of the environment damaged by this "man."

The existential turn to Western "man" away from a tragically conflicted environment used as mere setting is perhaps best exemplified by Francis Ford Coppola's *Apocalypse Now* (1979). Films as different as Charles Frend's *Scott of the Antarctic* (1948) and Yasujiro Ozu's *Tokyo Story* (1953) suggest the importance of environments as frames for tragic human drama. It is relatively rare, however, for film drama to make the environment itself the protagonist for more than ominous interludes and reflective moments. Insofar as fictional film drama continues to be dominated by human action, the dramatic action largely remains within the modes of liberal tragedy. Films with explicitly collective, political, and environmentally tragic subtexts, such as Gillo Pontecorvo's *Battle of Algiers* (1966), Roman Polanski's *Chinatown* (1974), and Mike Nichols' *Silkwood* (1983), tell their stories by foregrounding the psychological drama of individual human agents.

Environmental concerns loom large in the history of cinema, not least because film so often evokes images of the natural world in crisis as a contextual metaphor.[59] Contemporary cinema—whether as science fiction, eco-noir, psychological horror, or disaster movie—is suffused with tragic environmental material,[60] but it is the tragedy of the climate and its future that is perceived as tragic, rather than any drama or action of tragic performance that might confront the pervading sense of climate disaster.

The awkward relevance of environmental tragedy for cinematic genres and the limits of auteur cinema as a tragic artform are perhaps best exemplified by Michelangelo Antonioni's film *Zabriskie Point* (1970). Antonioni's film offers a tragic pathology of "America" in the late 1960s, from black power and student politics to unsustainable real estate development on the desert lands of indigenous people. Antonioni's film gestures towards the tragic ecology of American history but iconic sequences, such as the Open Theater's orgy in Death Valley, inscribe the artificiality of theatrical practice on the landscape to offer tragically inarticulate symbols of countercultural revolt. The film comes close to suggesting a tragic environmentalism that concludes in a spectacle of quasi-terrorist spectacular destruction: a model home is blown up in an obscurely imagined, symbolic dream protest against corporate, establishment America. *Zabriskie Point* offers an almost clinical account of the naivety of countercultural protest set against the many tragic layers of ecological violence constitutive of "America." The sense of environmental tragedy is palpable, but the film's argument descends into inconsequential dialogue and overdetermined symbolism. If *Zabriskie Point* makes Death Valley into an awkward site of performance, the film nevertheless registers landscape and context as environments that reflect the deeper ecological violence of America.

Part of the environmental sensitivity of film is the way it can blur differences between staged locations and documentation of existing landscapes. The documentation of natural landscapes can turn film into a tragic form in which the environment itself is both site and tragic agent.[61] *Blue Planet II*, the 2017 British television nature documentary series, has been widely credited with raising awareness of plastic pollution, and a case could be made for understanding nature documentary as a tragic form of film, not least in the way it juxtaposes damaged landscapes with human commentary. Even a radical documentary film such as Chris Marker's *Sans Soleil* (1983) moves between personal and global environments, featuring, in one moment, footage of the video-game Pac-Man underscored by the commentary that Pac-Man "puts into true perspective the balance of power between the individual and the environment."[62] Perhaps what remains implausible about nature documentary as a pre-eminently tragic form of film is the often unacknowledged hand of the human editor and the overlay of human commentary. There is now, nevertheless, a substantial body of environmental film that mixes documentary forms with more dramatic forms to articulate contemporary tragedy. Bertolt Brecht, to cite one initially surprising example, suggested using contemporary newsreels as a backdrop for a production of *Waiting for Godot* so as to emphasize the revolutionary context of global struggle in the background of the play.

Brecht's provocative suggestion points to the dangers of literalism in imagining that the setting or *mise en scène* of a tragic performance might suture the gulf between tragic action and tragic context. After all, newsreels themselves are often constructed performances, not just in the editing but in their action. Nikolai Evreinov's mass action spectacle *The Storming of the Winter Palace* (1920), for example, recreated events in the Russian Revolution from three years earlier. The performance was staged outside the former Tsarist Winter Palace to an audience of some 100,000 spectators, involving hundreds of dancers, performers, and actors, along with tanks and armored cars. A celebration of the Russian Revolution, Evreinov's Proletkult spectacle sought to redefine the boundaries between performers and spectators, and, ironically, photographs and film footage of this spectacle are often mistaken for authentic photographs. This irony is compounded by Sergei Eisenstein's silent film *October: Ten Days That Shook the World* (1928), which recreated Evreinov's spectacle so successfully that Eisenstein's film is often mistaken for authentic newsreel footage of the events portrayed. From mass spectacle to film, the ecology of revolution as tragedy resists such dramatizations, even when dramatized using documentary techniques sited and performed in its literal context. Perhaps the most troubling and effective use of documentary footage to suggest the layering of different environments within an ecology of tragic film is that of Alain Resnais and Margaret Duras' *Hiroshima mon Amour* (1959). The film inter-weaves documentary footage with a fictional love story, a fragmented affair between a French actress and a Japanese architect. Using flashbacks and recursive narrative loops, the film moves between collective and personal tragedies to offer glimpses of the damaged ecology of a newly nuclear world.

The environmental horizons represented by global war, nuclear catastrophe, and climate breakdown necessitate radical new evaluations of the traditions and cultures of modern tragedy. For all that major cultural institutions have continued to reproduce forms of modern tragic performance, environmental challenges have combined with ongoing criticisms of Western imperialism, colonialism, slavery, and capitalism to create a crisis in the relevance of Western art-forms for twenty-first-century culture.

One cluster of potential resources is suggested by Wole Soyinka's "fourth stage," a radical rewriting of Yoruban drama in the light of Western tragedy:

> . . . man is grieved by a consciousness of the loss of the eternal essence of his being and must indulge in symbolic transactions to recover the totality of being. Tragedy, in Yoruba traditional drama, is the anguish of this severance, the fragmentation of essence from self.[63]

The emphasis on "man" appears all too traditional, and the hope for some shared totality of being, however much it remains open to a holistic environmental interpretation, appears secondary to the crisis of this existential "man." And yet, Soyinka's "fourth stage" dramatizes a rebellious vision of tragedy as a mythopoetic struggle with profound and traumatic conflicts, the writing and performance of an alternative stage of radical temporality, the "vortex of archetypes." This mythopoetic vision can scarcely be "grounded," but situates tragic poetry in a radical, post-colonial environmental poetics.[64] Olabode Iribonke nevertheless suggests that Soyinka's "fourth stage" can be read historically as Soyinka's attempt to capture "the unique and transformative character of the city of Ibadan."[65] Part of the fascination of Soyinka's poetics of tragedy is this attempt to finesse the weight of historical precedents—both knowingly globalized and post-colonial, both European and African—but written through a specific and yet imaginative, almost utopian ecology of Yoruban drama. Imagining new tragic forms capable of articulating ways through the conflicts and legacies of imperialism, colonialism, and slavery almost inevitably involves compounds that acknowledge and reject "Western" global ecology, while attempting to recycle and glean resistance movements out of a more local and specific ecology imagined differently. Samuel Beckett's imperative "imagination dead imagine" becomes the almost utopian imperative of tragic ecology: think again, out of the ruins of global ecology, so as to imagine acting locally.[66]

In *Decolonising the Mind*, Ngũgĩ wa Thiong'o writes of how British colonialism destroyed the traditions of drama in pre-colonial Kenya. Pre-colonial drama, in his account, was not performed in special buildings "set aside for the purpose. It could take place anywhere—wherever there was an 'empty space', to borrow the phrase from Peter Brook."[67] Out of the ruins of the history of colonial oppression emerged the Kamĩriithũ Community Education and Cultural Centre, a community theater and "an attempt at reconnection with the broken roots of African civilization and its traditions of theater."[68] Ngũgĩ describes the working ecology of this new kind of collective theater and its "peasant/worker-based language of African theatre" as being analogous with Augusto Boal's "theatre of the oppressed." The "neo-colonial" Kenyan government forcefully shut down the Centre, "razed the open-air theatre to the ground," thereby repeating the destruction of Kenyan drama initiated by British colonialism, but ensuring, as Ngũgĩ puts it, "the immortality of the Kamĩriithũ experiments."[69] The destruction of the Kamĩriithũ theater project is symptomatic of global historical processes, offering a metonym for the social and political forces against which sustainable ecologies of tragedy have to struggle. One antidote to the fate of the Kamĩriithũ project is the political fable of decolonization suggested by Aimé Cesaire's play *Tragedy of King Christophe* (1963, revised 1970). A variety of more recent antidotes and models are suggested by the Chilean artist, Cecilia Vicuña's *Spit Temple* (2012).[70] There are, nevertheless, no easy ways to reconcile the tragic legacies and ruins of ecocidal globalization with new ecologies of tragic performance.

CHAPTER THREE

Communities of Production and Consumption

Modernism and the Rebirth of Tragedy

OLGA TAXIDOU

Peter Szondi's somewhat aphoristic opening to his *Essay on the Tragic* ("Since Aristotle, there has been a poetics of tragedy. Only since Schelling has there been a philosophy of the tragic"[1]) has been very influential in establishing and theorizing the distinction—sometimes binary—between tragedy as a poetic practice and tragedy as a philosophical discourse. This reading of the tragic that German Idealism contributes to after Kant and through the crucial works of Schelling, Hölderlin, Hegel, and ultimately Nietzsche, is less of a break or a transition from poetics to metaphysics and more of a multiplying of the tragic, a radical reconfiguration of the relationship between aesthetics and metaphysics. As Miriam Leonard claims, "The philosophy of the tragic did not represent a departure from aesthetics and a refuge in metaphysics"; rather it proposed "the elevation of aesthetics to a new position within philosophy."[2] Tragedy, in this reading, is seen as adding an aestheticizing impulse to philosophy.

This chapter will trace some of the ways this fusion of philosophy and aesthetics that is inherited from German Idealism and in many ways both compounded and challenged by Friedrich Nietzsche's seminal work, *The Birth of Tragedy* (1872), is enacted and experimented with in modernist engagements with tragedy. For far from heralding the "death of tragedy,"[3] modernism represents some of the most articulate and passionate encounters with tragedy as both an idea and a practice. This practice is, of course, mostly through specific performances or attempts at performance. These performances are mostly formally experimental, and crucially are almost always accompanied by theoretical/philosophical writing, from essays to manifestos. From T.S. Eliot's attempts at creating Christian tragedies, to W.B. Yeats' and Ezra Pound's translations of Greek plays, to Bertolt Brecht's and Antonin Artaud's denouncing of tragedy in their formulations of Epic Theatre and Theatre of Cruelty respectively, to Edward Gordon Craig's and Isadora Duncan's calling upon the Greeks in their formulations of theories of acting and dancing, we could claim that modernism represents one of the most significant revivals of tragedy as both a poetics and a philosophy. Indeed, the emphasis that modernist theater makers place on performance as an embodied civic event may help to elide the binary between tragedy as a philosophy and tragedy as a poetics. Thus a specific modernist view of tragedy and the tragic is created that shapes the many afterlives that tragedy has had throughout the twentieth century and beyond.

The heightened position that tragedy occupies in the philosophies of modernity, this chapter claims, is mirrored on the stages of modernism. Sometimes proposing classical tragedy as a model to be emulated or at other times as the ultimate example of theater's failure to address contemporary predicaments, dramatists' encounters with tragedy proved crucial in helping modernist performance to articulate both its theoretical language and its performance practices. Indeed, we may claim almost counter-intuitively that the encounter with tragedy attests both to modernism's neo-Classicism and to its radical newness. In this sense the oldest form of theater in the European canon is called upon in order for modernist performance to stake a claim for its autonomy. Crucially, this quest for autonomy engages tragedy not solely in literary terms, responding to the plays of Aeschylus, Sophocles, and Euripides. Parallel to the concerns about translation and the overall poetics of tragedy, modernist theatrical experimentation also approaches tragedy as part of its quest for a non-naturalistic, non-psychological mode of performance. In this sense, the theatrical conventions of tragedy (like the mask and the chorus) offer modernist theater makers new modes of theatrical experimentation. These experiments are now forged not solely by philosophers, but by playwrights, directors, actors, stage designers, composers, choreographers, and dancers. And this may represent one of the most radical aspects of this modernist encounter with the tragic, what, following Jacques Rancière, we might call a "re-distribution of the sensible,"[4] where the conceptual, aesthetic, and political field of the tragic is opened up to include practicing artists.

Sometimes this quest for the autonomy of performance has been read as exclusively anti-textual, heralding a somewhat arbitrary "freedom" for the stage. However, the modernist dialogue with tragedy, both formal and thematic, also brings to the fore the issue of poetry on the stage. The poetry of tragedy is as central as the performative experiments it inspired. The relationships between the poetic word and the performing body forms one of the main concerns of the period. T.S. Eliot's essays on poetic drama, as he writes Christian tragedies, are very significant in this context, as are W.B. Yeats' experiments with poetic drama for The Abbey theater while he is translating *Oedipus the King*. Translation itself, crucial for literary modernism, is theorized and approached in new radical ways. Walter Benjamin's influential essay from the same period, "The Task of the Translator" (1923),[5] may offer ways of approaching translations like Ezra Pound's *Electra* (1949) and *The Women of Trachis* (1956), where the notions of faithfulness are drastically reworked, creating almost new works that we may say, following Benjamin, are premised on the principles of reproducibility and adaptability, rather than reproduction and faithfulness. This approach to translation could itself be read as continuing a tradition initiated by German Idealism, and particularly Friedrich Hölderlin (1770–1843), whose translations were attacked during his time for their errors and inconsistencies. The modernist translators, and particularly Pound, could be seen as continuing this tradition of Hölderlin, where the task of the translator is less about remaining faithful to the *letter* of the Greek plays, and more about using them as a channel for contemporary concerns and linguistic experiments.

These experiments are part of modernism's linguistic turn, but also part of its performative turn. This relationship with tragedy that this chapter sketches out also stresses the constitutive bind between linguistic and performative experiments. The fascination with the poetic word onstage is also paralleled by an equal concern with the performing body. The debates, manifestos, and essays about the presence or absence of the performing body also have a distinctly tragic dimension. Isadora

Duncan's experiments in dance are directly influenced by Nietzsche's *The Birth of Tragedy*. Edward Gordon Craig's manifesto "The Actor and the Übermarionette" (1908) is framed by two significant quotations on tragedy, from Aristotle and Plato, rehearsing the anti-theatricality debate about the representational efficacy of the performing body.

Craig and Duncan also typify another dominant modernist mode, where tragedy as a poetics, tragedy as an idea, and tragedy as a performance practice are all conflated under the general aura of "the Greeks." However, this analysis claims that calling upon "the Greeks" in this context, rather than expressing a general Romantic Hellenism, is itself more concrete and embodied precisely through this emphasis on the performance conventions of tragedy. Rather than relying on the great classical philological traditions of the reception of tragedy, or on the philosophical thinking that it helped inspire, Craig and Duncan, like Brecht and Artaud, are emblematic of the modernist turn to tragedy that seeks a mode of performance that is anti-illusionist, abstract, and collective in terms of its reception. In this sense, the turn to "the Greeks" rather than being nostalgic and somewhat regressive offers a license for more speculative experimentation in performance.

The emphasis on performance also brings to the fore an intense interest in and experimentation with the chorus. The philosophical entanglements with tragedy and its critical reception within modernity mostly focus on tragic subjectivity. Echoing Simon Goldhill, Miriam Leonard states that, "to be a modern critic of tragedy is to have a problem with the chorus."[6] But rather than posing a problem, the chorus becomes a site for some of the most innovative experiments in performance. The relationships between individual and group performance are infused by theories of acting and also dance. The emphasis on the chorus, its performative and communicative efficacy, almost always includes speculation about the audience. Again, whereas the so-called "German cast"[7] of tragedy is mostly focused on the individual subject, and also perhaps on the individual reader, the theatrical encounter with the chorus also ignites thinking and writing about a different kind of reception, one that is aimed at the theater audience and concerns spectatorship more generally.

This, too, stresses the fact that the split formalized by this "German cast" may contain its own complexity and ambivalence. We could claim that the principle of theatricality is already located within the somewhat schematic binary of the idea versus the aesthetic form of the tragic. From Hölderlin onwards the return to the Greeks and specifically to tragedy was not a form of nostalgia, but as Philippe Lacoue-Labarthe claims, a quest "for the grounds of theatricality."[8] So this idea of the tragic also engages the *praxis* of tragedy (Hölderlin's *mechane*, Schiller's introduction to *The Bride of Messina*, "On the Uses of the Chorus in Tragedy" of 1803, Nietzsche's championing of ritual and music, are some characteristic examples). In turn this idea of the tragic is heavily inflected by this revived theatricality.

In this sense calling upon "the Greeks" for modernist theater signals less of an evocation of the great philosophical ideas of the plays of tragedy, and more of a call for a re-theatricalization of the theater arts in general. Whether denouncing the "Greeks" (Brecht, Artaud) or praising them (Craig, Duncan, T.S. Eliot, Yeats), more often than not they offer a model for a kind of theater that we would call "total," bringing together the literary, performing, and visual arts and engaging the audience in innovative ways that radically rework notions of empathy, estrangement, and affect in general.

This expanded view of tragedy that includes literary, philosophical, and performative tropes is not solely "Greek." Although this chapter focuses on the Greek dimension of the modernist encounter with tragedy, for many of the central figures of modernist theater, their sense of the tragic and their experimental practices are also informed by their engagement with Shakespearean tragedy. T.S. Eliot writes adaptations of Greek tragedy while also writing essays on Elizabethan theater. Despite his multiple calls upon the Greeks, Craig does not stage a Greek play, but does design *Hamlet* for the notorious production directed by Konstantin Stanislavsky for the Moscow Art Theatre (1911–12).[9] A couple of years after Brecht adapts *Antigone* he starts work on his unfinished adaptation of *Coriolanus* (1951–3), both projects accompanied by detailed notes on Epic Theatre. In his famous essay "An End to Masterpieces" (1931–6),[10] Artaud denounces *Oedipus Rex* but also Shakespeare for the "decay" of modern theater. It is beyond the scope of this chapter to trace these intricate interactions. In most cases, however, and particularly regarding the quest for a non-naturalist, "total" theatricality, Greek and Shakespearean tragedy are almost conflated.

The absence of the divine or the "Death of God," has been hailed as one reason for the impossibility of tragedy within modernity, both as a motor for philosophical thinking *and* as a mode of performance. For the absence of the divine deprives tragedy both of its metaphysical dimension and its ritualistic discourses of performance. According to George Steiner this creates an insurmountable difficulty for modern playwrights, dooming all their attempts to failure. However, an aspect of the modernist encounter with Greek tragedy that this chapter addresses is precisely its attachment to the metaphysical and the divine (albeit in the shadow of the "Death of God"), sometimes in a heady fusion of Christianity and Greek tragedy, as in the work of T.S. Eliot, or through equally interesting fusions of Orientalism, Primitivism, and Hellenism.

The intriguing interface between Hellenism and Primitivism that we find in the theatrical works of T.S. Eliot, W.B. Yeats, in Ezra Pound's and H.D.'s (Hilda Doolittle) translations of Greek plays results both from the fascination with the theaters of South East Asia, Japan and China, and—in the case of H.D.—Egypt, and from the more direct influence of the group of charismatic Cambridge scholars, known as the Cambridge Ritualists. Although this grouping itself has been recently contested,[11] and although the validity of their theories is constantly re-assessed within classical studies, their impact on actual languages of performance is undoubtable and has recently received more critical attention.[12] Gilbert Murray's translations and his involvement with actual theatrical productions,[13] the works of Francis Cornford, Arthur Bernard Cook (with Sir James Frazer's *The Golden Bough*, providing a general theoretical context), and the work of Jane Harrison offer the modernist playwrights and theater makers ways of reviving notions of ritual and the sacred, that are at once part of an evolutionary trajectory of theater and quintessentially modern in their modes of production, and languages of performance. Within this group the centrality of Jane Harrison needs to be stressed both as a scholar and as a symbolic figure (and I would claim as a performer/lecturer as well). Harrison's impact on Sapphic and feminist modernism has been well documented.[14] Her work on Greek religion and art, drawing on the diverse influences of Durkheim, Darwin, nineteenth-century evolutionary anthropology, and theories of matriarchy, but also on modernist theories of time, like those of Bergson, and contemporary archaeological discoveries, helps to reconstruct a version of theater, closely linked with ritual, that does not see it as simply one amongst the arts, but as *the* foundational art-form itself; one that can provide both the lost links with the past, but also help her contemporaries to understand their modernity. Julie Stone Peters has recently claimed that "her work offered a model for modern theater historiography" and stresses "the consequences and meaning of her work not only for twentieth-century theater but also for the development of theater history and (eventually) performance studies as academic disciplines."[15] In positing theater center-stage again the Cambridge Ritualists and particularly Harrison seem to be reworking the *theatrum mundi* metaphor and their corollaries in the theater arts find, in their work, ways to enact this metaphor and materialize it on the stage. The Cambridge Ritualists offer methods of addressing the Platonic fear of *theatrocracy* and turning it into something positive, critical, and enabling, something that has always been part of the evolutionary trajectory of being human.

This humanity, however, despite its modernity or perhaps because of it, also entails a primitivist dimension. And in the ways that the Cambridge Ritualists reconfigure the classics, this Primitivism is not read in *opposition* to Hellenism or Classicism, but is seen to inhabit the same evolutionary trajectory. These are the Greeks as Primitives as Moderns. So, when Yeats utters his aphoristic proclamation: "After us, the Savage God" after viewing the dress rehearsal of Alfred Jarry's *Ubu Roi*, directed by Lugné-Poë in 1896, his Savage God is both primitive and modern. Significantly, this appears in an essay written years later in 1914 entitled "The Tragic Generation."[16] Of course, the use of the term "Tragic" is not coincidental here as the Greek model of theater is the form that receives a foundational refurbishment through these modernist experiments in performance. Through the impact of the Cambridge Ritualists and, of course, Nietzsche, that Savage God is allowed to wear the mask of Dionysus. And, as Yeats himself was later to find out, this mask does not even necessarily need to be Greek; it can also be found in the theaters of the so-called Orient or in what were termed as "primitive cultures." This fascination with Hellenist Primitivism does not only appear as a performance trope in the more metaphysical strands of modernist performance that can be found in the work of Yeats or Eliot, but also manifests itself in the more materialist traditions, as in Brecht's staging of *Antigone*. The interface between Hellenism and Primitivism creates enabling languages for the purposes of performance, ones that do not view the two terms in opposition but more often than not see them as interchangeable.

The "archeo-modern turn," as Rancière terms it,[17] is perhaps nowhere more prevalent than in the modernist encounter with tragedy. And it is a turn that at once revises and reconfigures the received understanding of classical tragedy as part of the past, reworks this in terms of its own present, and significantly, propels it into the future.

The rest of this chapter will look more closely at characteristic instances where modernist performance turns to Greek tragedy for thematic and formal inspiration. Experiments in the performing body, with the uses of poetry on the stage and new relationships with the audience are forged with direct reference to tragedy, as both a performance practice and a philosophical edifice. And through these a specifically modernist notion of tragedy begins to be articulated; one that may lay a claim to being faithful to the spirit of the Greeks, but these Greeks are now read primarily through Nietzsche and his radical vision for a modern Dionysus. In place of the tragic philosophical pose taken up by German Idealism and Romanticism, modernism proposes a specifically performative pose, where the tragic philosopher morphs into the actor, the dancer, the stage designer, the director, or the poet/translator.

THE DANCER, THE ÜBERMARIONETTE, AND THE CHORUS: ISADORA DUNCAN AND EDWARD GORDON CRAIG

Craig and Duncan, both iconic figures for modernist performance, have had a huge impact throughout the twentieth century and beyond, particularly regarding theories of acting and dance. Their conceptions of the performing body have sometimes been read in opposition: complete absence of physical and psychological embodiment at one extreme and absolute expressiveness at the other. Where Craig's Übermarionette might be read as a mechanized puppet, Duncan's experiments could be said to lack technique or even form. However, we should not read them as undiluted anti-theatricality at one extreme, and as pure theatricality at the other, but rather see them as folding into each other, addressing similar issues, and presenting themselves as both Greek and modern. We can thereby consider them as doubles rather than opposites in their complex encounters with the tragic. These encounters span the whole of their creative lives, starting at the turn of the twentieth century, and in the case of Duncan cut short by her tragic death in 1927. Although beyond the scope of this volume, the legacies that both Craig and Duncan helped to create reverberate throughout the twentieth century and are still debated today. These are legacies that share a distinct "Greek" dimension, where tragedy is approached primarily for its theatricality and not for its literary and philological inheritance. For both projects versions of Greek theater and art act as inspiration and template for their experiments. Craig finds in Greek tragedy a model for his Übermarionette and for his stage designs (and a theater without female performers) and Duncan is inspired by both archaeological objects (the Tanagra vases) and archaeological sites in her quest for a primal femininity that will create her modern dancer. Importantly both were also influenced by Nietzsche's reworking of Greek drama in his *The Birth of Tragedy*, as this was the book that Duncan was reading throughout her first tour of Europe (1900–4) and from the very term *Übermarionette* onwards the impact of Nietzsche reverberates throughout Craig's work.

From her account of her own family drama—"Like the family of the Atrides"[18]— through her early training in the Delsarte system, to her later stay in and engagement with modern and ancient Greece, this Hellenic dimension of Duncan's art and her identity as a dancer, is at once historicizing but also radical. It helps to "free" her as a dancing woman, but also to ground her in a tradition that she sees as ancient (Figure 3.1). It fuses romance, archaeology, travel narratives, philosophy, and gender politics in a gesture that could have come straight from her choreographies, remaining elusive and contradictory, almost impossible to notate.

Equally impossible to trace, other than the direct influence of *The Birth of Tragedy*, is Duncan's encounter with the texts of Greek tragedy. Rather than assessing this encounter in terms of its philological or archaeological correctness or accuracy, it might be more helpful to stress the kind of "license" to experiment that her view of the "Greeks" gave her as a female performer to radically rework her medium. This "license" marked a distinct break from the nineteenth-century "aestheticist" takes on staging the Greek plays. Gone were the cluttered costumes, the props, and the antiquarianism. Significantly, and tracing a reciprocal relationship with the Cambridge Ritualists, for Jane Harrison (who read texts from Homer and Theocritus during Duncan's London début on March 16, 1900) Duncan's vitalist, non-decorous dances would have chimed well with her own research into the relationships between religion and ritual, movement and rhythm. The

FIGURE 3.1: Isadora Duncan dancing. © Sovfoto/UIG via Getty Images.

fact that Duncan's work had a specific feminine perspective would also have been attractive to Harrison, whose reading of Dionysus and the *eniautos daimon* too has been read by contemporary scholars like Martha Carpentier as partaking in both the late nineteenth-century Bachofen-inspired vitalist quest for a primal matriarchy and in the more radical discourses of Sapphic modernism.

The Birth of Tragedy acts as an inspiration for both women. Nietzsche's emphasis on the power of ritual, rhythm, and collectivity, prioritizing ritual over narrative, and the chorus over the protagonist helps Harrison to radically re-conceptualize tragedy within the discipline of classics and Duncan's work, we can claim, may offer an aesthetic, performative parallel to the writing of the Cambridge Ritualists in general. Duncan called Nietzsche's first book "my bible,"[19] and in one of her early essays on dance she writes in terms that reverberated with echoes from that book, "To give back to the dance its place as the Chorus, that is the ideal. When I have danced I have tried always to be the Chorus . . . I have never once danced a solo."[20]

But, of course, she *did* dance solo. This idea of the performer, that Duncan creatively interprets from Nietzsche somehow aspires to override the gap between the individual protagonist and the chorus. Similarly, Craig's famous aphoristic call for the banishing of the actor from the stage cannot be read literally. And, it too, somewhat incongruously can be seen to have a distinct "Greek" or even specifically tragic dimension. For both artists and theorists of performance this "Greek" aspect introduces a highly experimental and significantly utopian aspect to their work. Duncan's dances are impossible to notate (or problematize the whole notion of notation), while Craig's Übermarionette remained unrealizable, a phantasmic creation, there to offer a locus for speculative experimentation, rather than a concrete example to be emulated.

Craig's essay, "The Actor and the Übermarionette" (1908),[21] hugely influential since it first appeared, is framed by three significant quotations that at once attest to its modernism and to its neo-Classicism. Firstly, the essay is prefaced by an aphoristic epigram by Eleanora Duse: "To save the Theatre, the Theatre must be destroyed, the actors and actresses must all die of the plague ... They make art impossible." This gesture of catastrophe is followed by Duse's equally demanding call for "a return to the Greeks." Craig's own designs for Duse's *Electra* (another project that was never realized) exhibit such a fusion of classical and modern.[22] The second quotation that appears in note form is the famous quotation from Plato's *Republic*, where through the guise of the rhapsode, Plato denounces mimesis in general.[23] How fitting that Craig uses this iconic passage— one that has generated so much philosophical reflection about mimesis—to frame and to also justify his own theories about the Übermarionette. Like Plato, he too is concerned about the power of the actor to distort reality and to *mesmerize*, to act as a kind of charismatic demagogue who threatens the political order. And as in Plato this power of the theater and theatricality is seen to be at the core of the problem of mimesis itself. To do full justice to the debate in the third quotation of his essay Craig also calls upon Aristotle in support of his manifesto for the actor, or more generally we could claim for a modern theater. The quotation, again in a note, he uses from Aristotle is the equally famous passage from *Poetics*, where the "spectacle" is denounced as the work of "the stage machinist" rather than the poet, and where tragedy "is felt even apart from representation and actors."[24] With Duse's epigram at the start they serve to frame his manifesto, to give it a historical lineage and to theatricalize it. So, when Craig calls upon the Greeks to help him construct and articulate his argument, he is not simply being nostalgic, calling upon a unifying and homogenizing rhetoric that would give his argument the aura of the classical. In many ways he is calling upon the Greeks as both a philosopher and a theater maker. Indeed, his own essay may be said to rehearse the ancient quarrel itself. As in Plato and Aristotle this quarrel is given shape and form through the workings of theater and in particular is located on the performing body.

Although Craig was Max Reinhardt's first choice of designer for his famous production of *Oedipus Rex* (1923),[25] that collaboration was not fruitful, and apart from his designs for Eleanora Duse's *Electra* Craig never worked directly on a Greek play. However, he did work on the famous production of Konstantin Stanislavsky's *Hamlet* (1911–12) for The Moscow Art Theatre. Looking at the designs in the *book beautiful* that resulted from that failed collaboration, *The Cranach Hamlet* (1930), and Craig's designs for theatrical characters (Figure 3.2) in his splendid collection entitled *Black Figures* (1989), it appears that his ideas of the tragic protagonist were indeed put to practice in the production of the Moscow *Hamlet*. Despite its received failure at the time, the Moscow *Hamlet* has since occupied an almost mythical position within twentieth-century theater historiography, as a quintessential modernist experiment in designing and acting Shakespeare.[26] The theatricality of this *Hamlet*, however, was heavily influenced by Craig's views of Greek tragedy.

Both Craig's and Duncan's work is somewhat plagued by discourses of failure and unperformability, and in Duncan's case the inability to reproduce and notate. It might be more critically and interpretatively helpful to see their work as more experimental and speculative, open to the liveness, risk, and ephemerality of performance. And this aspect of their work may be linked to its "Greekness," where the encounter with Greek tragedy

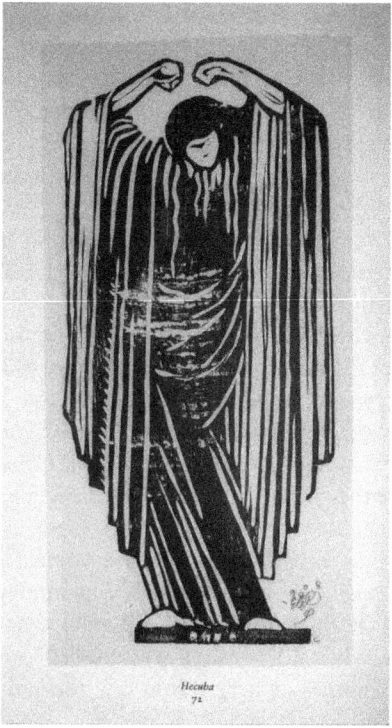

FIGURE 3.2: Edward Gordon Craig. *Hecuba*. 1908. © Edward Gordon Craig Estate.

rather than adding the aura, the cultural currency, the authenticity and monumentality that is traditionally associated with the classics, creates work that is more evocative, speculative, and utopian, work that intentionally or not celebrates its resistance to reproduction and notation.

POETRY AND TRANSLATION: T.S. ELIOT, W.B. YEATS, EZRA POUND

Greek tragedy as a source for modernist experimentation with the performing body (as protagonist or chorus), is also crucial in debates about poetry onstage. Usually the concerns about the representational efficacy of the performing body are parallel to the writing and thinking about the possibility of poetic drama. When central modernist figures, mostly poets, turn to the stage in their quest for both "poetry *in* the theatre" and "poetry *of* the theatre,"[27] they also turn to tragedy. However, this turn has now been informed by their exposure to the radical work of the Cambridge Ritualists and the Noh theater. T.S. Eliot, W.B. Yeats, and Ezra Pound all undertake translations and/or adaptations of Greek tragedy; in the process their attempts also gesture towards new notions of translation. All three leading modernist poets propose new ideas and practices about the function of translation itself. Problems of translating prosody and literary form are matched by equally challenging issues about performance.

Throughout his writing life Eliot was preoccupied with the issues of translating and adapting Greek tragedy and the possibilities this presented for poetic drama. Eliot's famous attack on Gilbert Murray's translations was primarily based on what Eliot considered appropriate use of poetry in the English language. He wrote "Greek poetry will never have the slightest vitalizing effect upon English poetry if it can only appear masquerading as a vulgar debasement of the eminently personal idiom of Swinburne."[28] For Eliot the path that Greek tragedy was to follow in order to have the required "vitalizing effect" on English poetry was primarily through experimentation. Crucially this experimentation was both linguistic and theatrical.

Eliot's forays into Greek tragedy as a form of contemporary poetic drama are paralleled by his equal interest in matters of staging, and particularly the staging of the chorus. After his attack on Murray (1920), Pound dared Eliot to translate the *Agamemnon*, a venture he was to take up himself, with both men eventually abandoning the task.[29] Perhaps this initial unsuccessful attempt shaped their later engagements with Greek tragedy; Eliot would write mainly heavily disguised adaptations and Pound would translate Sophocles. Before Eliot wrote his drawing-room adaptations of Greek tragedy, *The Family Reunion* (1939), *The Cocktail Party* (1949), *The Confidential Clerk* (1952), and *The Elder Statesman* (1954), he wrote the two fragments of *Sweeney Agonistes* (1926), as an attempt to combine Aristophanic comedy with music hall style-verse, and his early plays *The Rock* (1934) and *Murder in the Cathedral* (1935). Of these *Murder in the Cathedral* presents a fascinating attempt at a modernist Greek tragedy. It is an attempt that at once engages the idea of tragedy, reworking it through Christian theology, and the formal demands of training actors and chorus, while also dealing with audience reception. It presents what some scholars (including George Steiner) would consider an impossibility: a Christian tragedy.

Eliot's conflation of a Christian martyr (Thomas Becket) with the tragic protagonist, and the tragic chorus with the chorus of the women of Canterbury, can be read as a direct result of the influence of the Cambridge Ritualists and their ritualistic, evolutionary model of drama. He writes in *The Criterion* in 1923 in an article entitled "Dramatis Personae" in terms that echo the writings of the Cambridge Ritualists:

> Instead of pretending that the stage gesture is a copy of reality, let us adopt a literal untruth, a thorough-going convention, a ritual. For the stage – not only in its remote origins, but always – is a ritual, and the failure of the contemporary stage to satisfy the craving for ritual is one of the reasons why it is not a living art.[30]

Eliot was also familiar with the work of Craig and his writing on acting. He had read Craig's *The Art of the Theatre* (1905) while an undergraduate and was well versed in the debates about puppets and actors (he had defended Craig in an article in *The Dial* in 1921). The invitation from the Friends of Canterbury Cathedral to write a play,[31] allowed Eliot to bring together his experiments in poetic drama, with his interest in reviving Greek tragedy through both the prisms of Christianity *and* modernism. This attempt offered Eliot the opportunity to address the "problem of the chorus." Although it is viewed by most philosophical critics as the quintessential anti-modern aspect of Greek tragedy, modernist experiments in performance find in the Greek chorus a space (both conceptual and physical) to rehearse new theories of acting and audience reception. Here is Eliot, talking about the uses of the chorus in *Murder in the Cathedral*:

> In making use of [the chorus] we do not aim to *copy* Greek drama. There is a good deal about the Greek theater that we do not know, and never shall know. But we know that some of its conventions cannot be ours. The characters talk too long; the Chorus has

too much to say and holds up the action; usually not enough happens; and the Greek notion of climax is not ours. But the chorus has always fundamentally the same uses. It mediates between the action and the audience; it intensifies the action by projecting its emotional consequences, so that we as the audience see it doubly, by seeing its effect on other people.[32]

This is a sophisticated reading of the chorus both in terms of what it can offer theatrically and for the ways that Eliot considers it strange ("never shall know"). It posits the chorus as a mode of mediation that enables a kind of "double vision" in the audience. This metatheatrical, and quotational use of the chorus, as commenting both on the action and on the audience, is a trope that many modernist theater makers will employ (including Brecht and Artaud). For Eliot it marks the beginning of his experiments with the chorus, always parallel to those in poetic drama, that continued throughout his life. These choruses help create a modernist version of tragedy that is at once a Christian liturgical drama.

Eliot was well aware that he could not repeat the success of *Murder in the Cathedral* partly because he could not repeat these stylized, ritualistic choruses and partly because in his later ventures he could not have access to that "organic audience" that participated in the play as a religious experience, as the play was created specifically for the congregation of Canterbury Cathedral. He claims that "for a beginner . . . the path was made easy" and attributes this to three main factors: the subject matter was "generally admitted to be suitable for verse"; the play was produced "for a rather special kind of audience"; and "finally it was a religious play."[33] These three factors—heightened language, an "organic" audience, and the play as a religious experience—characterize Greek tragedy and present the most demanding challenges for modernist theater makers. As Eliot could not necessarily count on repeating this experience with his other Greek plays, he followed a slightly different path.

The Family Reunion (1939), Eliot's next play, which was to be his reworking of *The Oresteia*, offered him the opportunity to further experiment with modern tragedy. Unlike *Murder in the Cathedral*, henceforth Eliot deliberately chooses contemporary themes, drastically reworks the chorus, and continues his experiments with poetry on the stage. Indeed, the drawing-room dramas that followed (*The Cocktail Party*, *The Confidential Clerk*, *The Elder Statesman*), while all being adaptations of Greek plays, strive to carefully disguise their sources. This is so much the case that Eliot claimed in his apologia for poetic drama, *Poetry and Drama*:

> You will understand, after my making these criticisms of *The Family Reunion*, some of the errors that I endeavored to avoid in designing *The Cocktail Party*. To begin with, no chorus, no ghosts. I was still inclined to go to a Greek dramatist for my theme, but I was determined to do so merely as a point of departure, and to conceal the origins so well that nobody would identify them until I pointed them out myself. In this at least I have been successful; for no one of my acquaintance (and no dramatic critics) recognized the source of my story in the *Alcestis* of Euripides.[34]

His version of *Alcestis* morphed into *The Cocktail Party*. Despite Eliot's attempts to hide the source plays, and perhaps partly due to his "anxiety of influence," these engagements with tragedy throw up for him fascinating challenges regarding modern tragedy in general. Eliot departs from the original Greek dactylic trimeter in search of a rhythm that he deemed to be close to his contemporary speech, deciding to employ "a line of varying length and varying number of syllables, with a caesura and three spaces."[35] While this proved quite useful for expressing a heightened form of upper-class, drawing-room English, it also proved quite limiting. What was significant for Eliot, however, was the quest (*contra* Murray, as he believed) for a tragic language that would help revitalize the poetic aspects of English. He aspired "to bring poetry into the world in which the audience lives and to which it returns when it leaves the theatre" so "that the audience should find, at the moment of awareness that it is hearing poetry, that it is saying to itself: '*I* could talk in poetry too!'"[36] The function of poetry here is one of redemption and elevation. According to Eliot it should influence through rhythm in an unconscious manner, prompting the audience itself to speak poetry. In many ways this smacks of condescension, ignoring the fact that the audience might already speak in a form of its own poetry even before being initiated by Eliot's poetic dramas. And initiation was still on Eliot's mind, for despite the diminishing of the chorus, and the emphasis on quasi-poetic, everyday language, these plays still represent his ambitious attempts at creating Christian tragedies in a modernist cast. Characteristic of this fusion of Christianity and Greek tragedy is Eliot's highly evocative reflection about Harry's relationship (the Orestes character in *The Family Reunion*) to the chorus. As he states in a letter to E. Martin Browne who was about to produce the play, "he follows the Furies as immediately and as unintelligibly as the Disciples dropping their nets."[37] This extraordinary phrase conflates Christ and Dionysus, and reads the passion of Christ itself as a tragedy.

Such a conflation of Christ and Dionysus also appears in W.B. Yeats' play *Resurrection* (1927), which presents in the form of questions and answers (antiphones perhaps) a discussion about the nature of Christ among three emblematic figures: a Greek, a Hebrew, and a Syrian (or Egyptian in the *Adelphi* version). This debate is threatened by an offstage ecstatic chorus of Dionysus, which is performing horrific rituals. This brief play which combines prose and verse exhibits many of the traits that were to characterize Yeatsian drama: it features a chorus of musicians, it uses the mask, the folding and unfolding of the curtain, and it was specifically written for a small studio audience such as that of The Peacock Theatre (the smaller theater of The Abbey). Here is the opening song that, as Yeats states in his directions, is for "the folding and the unfolding of the curtain":

> I saw a staring virgin stand
> Where holy Dionysus died,
> And tear the heart out of his side,
> And lay the heart upon her hand
> And bear that beating heart away;
> And then did all the Muses sing
> Of Magnus Anus at the spring,
> As though God's death were but a play.[38]

All these formal aspects are borrowed from the Noh, and have parallels in Yeats' earlier *Four Plays for Dancers* (*At the Hawk's Well*, 1917; *The Only Jealousy of Emer*, 1919; *The Dreaming of the Bones*, 1919; *Calvary*, 1920). Yeats had spent considerable time with Pound in Sussex in 1913 familiarizing himself with the Fenollosa Noh manuscript, and witnessing performances by the Japanese dancer Michio Ito. *Resurrection* is dedicated to a Japanese admirer called Junzo Sato. However, Yeats' theater of this period is not solely influenced by the Noh tradition. While he is writing *Resurrection* he also returns to a project that he would pursue for many years: the translations of *Oedipus the King* and *Oedipus at Colonus*. (He had initially attempted and abandoned a verse translation of

Oedipus the King back in 1904.) The Greek translations allowed him to bring together his modernist concerns and his quest for a national literature. "I had three interests: interest in a form of literature, in a form of philosophy, and belief in nationality,"[39] he claimed later in *Explorations*, reflecting on this period.

The Oedipus plays offered Yeats the possibility of experimenting with poetic language and theatricality onstage as part of his quest for a national theater. This theatricality was a fusion of his inspiration from Noh combined with the ideas of ritual from the work of the Cambridge Ritualists. Yeats, too, had already worked with Edward Gordon Craig, who had designed The Abbey's production of *The Hour Glass* in 1911. The language that Yeats chose in his translations was a combination of prose and verse (prose for the protagonist and verse for the chorus). The quest for a language that could speak to the big national themes and attract large audiences fits in quite neatly with Yeats' fascination with the oral and popular tradition. Yeats, like Eliot and Pound, views the difficulty of reviving the poetry of the Greek plays as a general symptom of a modernist "malaise," a world where language has been debased and lost its "organic" links with a living community. Yeats finds the alternative, ideal audience on the Aran islands, and in line with many of the linguistic experiments of the Celtic Twilight (also undertaken by J.M. Synge and later Louise MacNeice who translates *Agamemnon* in 1937), uses rhythms and patterns that he considers to be part of an organic community, that somehow has not been marred by modernity. This approach to translation sees the Greek plays as a way of reviving an eternal and living popular culture. In this sense the difficulty that the use of prosody presents for translators of Greek plays is seen as part and parcel of a lost unity, one that perhaps the Greek plays may help to rejuvenate. So a nostalgic fantasy for what Yeats sees as the organic culture epitomized by Greek tragedy prompts him to turn to the popular Irish tradition, combining it with an intriguing fusion of Noh and classicism. The poetry and the theatricality of ancient tragedy find the possibility of resurrection (to borrow Yeats' title) in an energizing concoction of Orientalism and Primitivism.

This is a combination that proves useful for Ezra Pound too in his translations of Sophocles. He writes in his Preface to his *Women of Trachis*:

> The *Trachiniae* presents the highest peak of Greek sensibility registered in any of the Plays that have come down to us and is, at the same time, nearest to the original form of the God-Dance.
> A version for KITANO KATUE, hoping he will use it on my dear old friend Michio Ito, or take it to the Minoru if they can be persuaded to add it to their repertoire.[40]

Pound did not get the opportunity to put these ideas into practice as this translation was first performed on BBC radio's Third Programme. Although this translation appears much later than those of Eliot and Yeats it is still in dialogue with their projects, and continues to echo the terminology of the Cambridge Ritualists (God-Dance). In the same gesture Pound's hailing of Ito as the ideal performer for his *Trachiniae* (in the role of Hercules one presumes) underlines the parallels that were drawn between the *dromenon* of the Greeks and the ritualistic aspect of Noh drama. For Pound, it is this combination of a ritualistic reading of tragedy, as seen in the figure of the God-Dance, with the conventions of stylized embodiment presented by the Noh that offered ways of reviving Greek tragedy. A modernist theater aesthetic would combine all these sources in a manner that is clear, hard, concrete, and in all other ways imagistic.

This imagistic take is also evident in Pound's earlier attempt at translating Sophocles in his version of *Electra*, an extraordinary linguistic fusion of sources, references, registers, and dialects. Pound's version contains transliterated Greek, and uses various forms of English (African American, Scots, archaic English lyrics, Cockney, to name a few). This recourse to linguistic register and dialect can be read as part of the quest for an authentic and organic language. Pound's translations, however, may have the opposite effect, one of strangeness and distancing, where the categories of the "primitive" and the "classical," language and dialect are confused and interchangeable. An example of this modernist take on translation follows from the ending of the play with Orestes pronouncing, as he leads Aegisthus to his death:

> No, but you aren't dying for pleasure
> You've got to go thru with it ALL.
> It's a pity you can't all of you – die like this
> And as quickly, everyone like you
> It wd/save a lot of unpleasantness.
> Chorus (sings)
> O SPERM ATREOS
>   Atreides, Atreides
> Come thru the dark,
> (speaks)
> my god, it's come with a rush
> (sings)
> Delivered, Delivered,
>   TEI NUN HORMEI TELEOOTHEN
> Swift end
>   So soon.[41]

The way this sequence reads *and* looks on the page is parallel to Pound's imagist experiments in poetry, and particularly in the *Cantos*. The ways that Pound uses the transliterated Greek through this version creates a relationship with the original that raises more general questions about translatability. Several scholars have pointed out that Pound's use of Greek is more in a primitivist vein, where the Greek is used to "present mad or 'primitive' speech, curses or voices from the underworld,"[42] or in sequences that express the inability of Electra to mourn. This attitude towards the language of tragedy presents quite a departure from those of Eliot and Yeats. Here the linguistic variations used, including the transliterations, rather than reuniting Pound's present (and ours) with a reconciled, identified, and organic classicism, confront us with a Hellenism that is ritualistic, fragmented, savage, and strange. And possibly more so in Pound's versions than in Eliot's or Yeats', Greek tragedy emerges as at once primitive and modern.

The linguistic "difficulty" of Pound's translation is parallel to the issue of performability. His own references to the Noh present an attempt to address this, but may perhaps also raise the specter of unperformability that haunts most of these modernist encounters with Greek tragedy. David Wiles claims that, "it is exactly half a century since *Women of Trachis* appeared, and we are still waiting for a set of theatrical conventions to emerge that will make this modernist text finally playable."[43] Perhaps another way of reading the "unperformability" of these plays, is not so much as part of an empirical quest for more new and innovative stage conventions, but as a reflection on what Rancière considers endemic to the archeo-modern turn: the category of anticipation (still waiting, Wiles states above). Rancière claims that this "archaeomodern turn . . . is located at the core of the modern project" and "sets up two categories: that of figurative reason or of sleeping meaning, and the temporal category of anticipation."⁴⁴ So, this attitude towards the Greeks is possibly about the past but probably has more to say about the aesthetics of utopia. In this sense, these experimental, modernist takes on Greek tragedy, do not solely gesture towards their immediate chronological futures, but perhaps towards the category of the future in general, i.e., towards all futures. Rather than waiting for the stage to "catch up" as it were (although this too is possible), they may offer a kind of performative gesture in and of themselves, fusing the textual and the non-textual, and creating a relationship with Greek tragedy that is more like a laboratory for experiment than a programmatic declaration on how to write and perform modern tragedies.

BRECHT: ESTRANGEMENT AND HISTORY

Bertolt Brecht, modernist theater's chief proponent in approaching the stage as a laboratory for both aesthetic and political experiments, aligns his project in *opposition* to Greek tragedy, or at least what he understands as its Aristotelean theorization. "We know that the barbarians have their art. Let us create another," he blasts in aphoristic style in his manifesto for a modern, Epic Theatre, *A Short Organum for the Theatre* (1947–8).⁴⁵ And following the mode of epic rewriting and inversion, the "barbarians" here are "the Greeks" themselves. Rather than representing the spirit of critique and radical theatricality traced above, for Brecht the reception of Greek tragedy as part of the canonical neoclassical tradition is viewed as contributing to the failures of the project of the Enlightenment, its philosophy, its ideology, and its economies of representation. His own quest for an Epic Theatre is the counterpart or "cure" to the "failure" of tragedy to address the demands of modernity. Yet Brecht's relationship to Greek tragedy (and to Shakespearean tragedy for that matter) is more contradictory and nuanced than his own "crude" (to use his term) manifesto writings call for. His abhorrence of Greek tragedy ("Barbaric delights. Human sacrifices all round!")⁴⁶ is matched by an equally strong attraction to it, as can be evidenced in his first production after his exile and return to Europe after the Second World War. This was *The Antigone of Sophocles* based on a text by Hölderlin, with stage designs by Caspar Neher. Ruth Berlau was to photograph the process, formulating the first of what was to become the hallmark of the Brechtian project: the *model*. It is somewhat counter-intuitive that the first *model* for an Epic Theatre should be based on this iconic Greek tragedy. However, the play is radically re-visioned not only through Hölderlin, but also through the conventions of Epic Theatre. The *model* itself attests to Brecht's desire to address the issues of translatability and performability associated in a sense with every modern attempt to stage Greek tragedy. And Ruth Berlau's photographs creating the *model* may be read as addressing the whole issue of the reproducibility of performance itself (Figure 3.3). Almost against the grain of his own proclamations, Brecht's and Berlau's *Antigone-Model* highlights what I would claim is a fundamental characteristic of Greek tragedy: its adaptability.

In some ways Brecht's *Antigone-Model* could be seen as a reflection on and extension of Walter Benjamin's idea of translatability, where the encounter with the original always brings out a strangeness in the so-called target language. However, it also secures ways in which this original is reborn. "The life of the original" states Benjamin, "attains in them [the translations] to its ever renewed latest and most abundant flowering."⁴⁷ Like performability, Benjamin claims, "the translatability of linguistic creations ought to be considered even if men should prove unable to translate them." Of course, for him, the prime examples of this process can be seen in Hölderlin's translations of Sophocles,

FIGURE 3.3: Brecht. *Antigonemodel*. Photographed by Ruth Berlau. 1948. © Ruth Berlau/Bertolt-Brecht-Archiv, Akademie de Kunst.

ridiculed when they appeared for their inconsistencies and errors. "Hölderlin's translations are prototypes of their kind; they are even the most perfect renderings of their texts as a prototype is to a model."[48]

The model for Hölderlin, as it was for Pound, was Greek tragedy. And in this context we can view Hölderlin's translations as precursors to Pound's linguistic experiments *and* Brecht's theatrical ones. In many ways influenced by both Hölderlin and Benjamin, Brecht confronts the issues of translatability and performability in tandem. His model is neither simply a record of a performance nor is it a programmatic set of directions that are meant to be repeated. Rather, following Benjamin, it relies on the principle of *reproducibility* and not reproduction, in ways that echo the principle of *translatability* that does not simply transfer a Greek play (following Hölderlin) into a modern language, but creates it anew in a double movement that rewrites and estranges both the original and the target language.

Brecht's *Antigone-Model* presents one of modernist theater's most ambitious and far-reaching attempts to create a "text," both visual and linguistic, for performance. Significantly, Brecht approaches this endeavor through Sophocles' iconic play in a gesture that both relies on and radically reworks the legacies of German Idealism. The most classical of Greek plays becomes through Hölderlin, Brecht, and Berlau, the model for the most modernist of theaters: Epic Theatre. This use of tragedy presents at once a reflection on modernist neo-Classicism and challenges modernism's fascination with the "new." Brecht is very conscious of this function of the model as looking both back towards the past but also as questioning modernism's fixation on "newness." He writes in his Notes to *The Antigone-Model*, "The idea of making use of models is a clear challenge to the artists of a period that applaud nothing but what is 'original', 'incomparable', 'never been seen before', and demands what is 'unique.'"[49] And in this way, we can also claim that it, too, enacts the "archeo-modern turn," looking towards the past but also anticipating a potential future.

ARTAUD: RITUAL AND METAPHYSICS

Antonin Artaud can be seen as Brecht's counterpart in modernist performance. Where Brecht is in search of a political, historical form of theater to address the demands of the early twentieth century and its historical catastrophes, Artaud approaches those same demands through a theater that is ritualist and mythopoetic. Brecht's dialectic materialism is seen in binary opposition to Artaud's apocalyptic metaphysics. This is a binary that many contemporary performance theorists have challenged.[50] Significantly it has also been challenged in creative ways by many theater directors especially in their productions of Greek tragedy.

Like Brecht, Artaud conceptualizes his Theatre of Cruelty (1932) against the "masterpieces" of Greek tragedy. Specifically, in "An End to Masterpieces"[51] he chooses another iconic tragedy, *Oedipus Rex*, to help him articulate his aphoristic, apocalyptic, and eschatological vision of theater. It is a very specific view of Greek tragedy that Artaud is writing against. His critique focuses on the language of tragedy. He writes, "Sophocles speaks grandly perhaps, but in a manner that is no longer relevant to the age," and "in costumes and language which have lost all contact with the crude and epileptic rhythm of our time."[52] Like Brecht, Artaud identifies Greek (and Shakespearean) tragedy with tradition, regression, and conservatism. It is unable to speak to "a mass audience that trembles at train wrecks, that is familiar with earthquakes, plague, revolution, war."[53] And like Brecht, he had very little direct knowledge of the texts themselves. Still, the image of the "plague," such a potent metaphor for all of Artaud's writing, can be read as borrowed from *Oedipus Rex*.[54] Like Pound, Yeats, and Brecht, Artaud finds in the performance traditions of the "Orient" (in his case it is Balinese Dance) or in Primitivism (through his visits to the Aran islands and Mexico) conventions that allow for experimentation in non-psychological, non-mimetic acting. And this somewhat ambivalent and contradictory relationship with tragedy, that Artaud expresses, is addressed in performance by many visionary directors of the twentieth century and beyond. Artaud's Theatre of Cruelty has proved inspirational in approaching Greek tragedy as an embodied, ritualistic, and metaphysical mode of theater. His own formulations for a form of total theater that is collective, ritualistic, and relies on sacrifice and violence has been formative for theater makers of the late twentieth century and beyond, who view tragedy as a form of post-dramatic theater, a performance mode that does not rely on the play text, but opens up a liminal space to explore ideas of embodiment and collective experience.[55] This view of tragedy as a performance event that opens up metaphysical and mythopoetic but also political and historical themes through collective, sometimes immersive experiences for the audience has a distinct Artaudian genealogy. Ariane Mnouchkine, Jan Fabre, and Theodoros Terzopoulos are just a few of the contemporary directors who approach Greek tragedy through an Artaudian lens, sometimes also informed by Brechtian aesthetics. In their productions of Greek tragedies Brecht and Artaud appear as doubles, indeed almost in the way Artaud understands the function of the double in the theater.

Many of the projects we have approached in this chapter are haunted by the specter of failure. Brecht's *The Antigone of Sophocles* had a limited run in the theater;[56] Craig produced nothing after the received disaster of the Moscow *Hamlet*; apart from *Murder in the Cathedral*, Eliot's modern tragedies have been deemed unperformable by critics and performers alike; Pound's translations have only recently received the critical attention they deserve. Somewhat counter-intuitively considering their scathing attacks on tragedy, Brecht and Artaud have had the most impact on the postwar and contemporary reception of tragedy both in theoretical writings and in production.

Yet these modernist approaches to tragedy, however speculative and "unsuccessful," have helped to create an experimental, laboratory *topos* that radically re-conceptualizes our understanding of the form. The nineteenth-century figures of the classical philologist and the philosopher are augmented by the figure of the theater maker who is both a poet of the theater and a poet in the theater. The aestheticizing impulse that tragedy adds to the tradition of primarily German Idealism is continued throughout all these modernist encounters with tragedy, and the dominating figure of the philosopher is shadowed, or doubled by the figures of the actor, the dancer, the scenographer, and primarily by the director. In this way, modernism's encounter with the oldest form of theater in the European tradition contributes to the articulation of theater's quintessentially modernist ideal: the autonomy of performance.

These approaches have helped to create a genealogy in the reception of tragedy that may allow us to read late twentieth-century adaptations of Sophocles like *The Gospel at Colonus* (1983) by Lee Breuer as a continuation of T.S. Eliot's attempts at a Christian tragedy, or Yukio Ninagawa's Noh- and Kabuki-inspired productions of Greek tragedy, like *Medea* (1985), as elaborating on the work of Pound and Yeats, Heiner Müller's *machines* as versions of Brecht's models, and Theodoros Terzopoulos' and Jan Fabre's radical performances of tragedy as a conflation of Epic Theatre and Theatre of Cruelty. Perhaps equally importantly for a cultural history of tragedy these modernist encounters have helped to expand the critical vocabulary of tragedy and have created a laboratory space for experiments in tragedy as performance.

CHAPTER FOUR

Philosophy and Social Theory

DAVID KORNHABER

To speak of tragedy and philosophy in the twentieth and twenty-first centuries is to arrive rather late to the play. The philosophical investigation of tragedy in the Western tradition is at least a three-act drama, one that reaches back to the early years of the German Idealist movement in the late eighteenth century and then moves through that tradition's transformation in the nineteenth century before arriving at twentieth-century modernity. For Peter Szondi, whose book *An Essay on the Tragic* (1961) set the standard for most later investigations of the topic, the engagement between tragedy and European philosophy begins with Friedrich Schelling at the very end of the eighteenth century and includes significant contributions from G.W.F. Hegel in the early nineteenth century before being revised in the later nineteenth century by Søren Kierkegaard, Arthur Schopenhauer, and Friedrich Nietzsche, among others. If act one, covering the span from Schelling's *Philosophical Letters on Dogmatism and Criticism* in 1795 to the publication of Hegel's *Lectures on Aesthetics* in 1835, was dominated by the aesthetic and ethical theories of Kant and Hegel, then act two, extending to the end of the First World War, saw that lineage complicated and refigured by the likes of Nietzsche and Sigmund Freud, whose *Birth of Tragedy* in 1872 and formulation of the Oedipus complex in *The Interpretation of Dreams* in 1899, respectively, would give shape to much of the twentieth century's most important thinking about tragedy.

Act three has no such break-out stars, figures whose theories of the tragic are able to dominate the conversation for generations. Rather, the philosophical engagement with tragedy after 1920 is marked by a diversity of critical voices working through and working past the monumental theories that emerged around the turn of the century, as well as those voices offering new directions altogether. Across these manifold thinkers, a few common themes and approaches emerge, and it is around these themes that the present chapter will unfold. Organized roughly in order of their chronological waxing and waning, these include the view of life as inherently tragic; the exultation of tragic drama as a wellspring of philosophy; the philosophical rejection of tragedy and the tragic; the figuration and refiguration of Oedipus and Antigone as tragic emblems; and the rehabilitation of tragedy as a viable philosophical position. To construct any history of philosophy's relationship to tragedy is inevitably to offer an incomplete picture of the philosophies described, most of which, particularly in the twentieth century, intersect with concepts of tragedy and the tragic but only very rarely take them as their primary and core concerns. Likewise, to do so in the condensed format of a book chapter is inescapably to elide certain intellectual and methodological differences, to place in relative proximity thinkers and ideas that in full development may seem more distant, and to only imperfectly capture evolutions and revisions within any given thinker's own development over time. With those caveats in mind, let the curtain rise.

LIFE AS TRAGEDY

Freud's *Civilization and its Discontents*, first published in 1930, treats tragedy as such almost not at all. Unlike his earlier works from before 1920 that examined tragic heroes like Oedipus and Hamlet at length, here Freud attaches no figural representative to his story of the psychic struggle between the will to life embodied in *Eros* and the countervailing urges of the death drive. "The meaning of the evolution of civilization is no longer obscure to us," he writes. "It must present the struggle between Eros and Death, between the instinct of life and the instinct of destruction, as it works itself out in the human species. This struggle is what all life essentially consists of, and the evolution of civilization may therefore be simply described as the struggle for life of the human species."[1] Yet the idea of tragedy would never be far from Freud's thoughts in this work, so much so that the treatise's entire outlook might be regarded as tragic. Paul Gordon goes so far as to argue that Freud's construction of the relationship between *Eros* and the death drive is explicitly derived from Nietzsche's articulation of the Apollonian and Dionysian dimensions at work in classical tragedy, those forces of individuated order and passionate destruction whose unresolved interplay first gave rise to the genre of tragedy according to *The Birth of Tragedy*. "Freud's theory of civilization as tragically conflicted between the libidinal id's 'death wish' and the societal individual's life-preserving ego corresponds exactly to Nietzsche's theory of the conflict between Dionysian and Apollonian drives," Gordon writes.[2] Nietzsche, of course, was speaking specifically of the theater when he posited the dichotomy of Apollonian and Dionysian drives as being the engine behind Greek tragic performance. In *Civilization and its Discontents*, Freud expands that tension to encompass the very experience of human existence under the strain of social organization. He speaks of the "fatal inevitability" of psychic conflict, "of the eternal struggle between Eros and the instinct of destruction or death. This conflict is set going as soon as men are faced with the task of living together."[3] For Freud, civilized life is inherently tragic insofar as it is bound up inescapably with a struggle of organizing and disorganizing impulses that can achieve no resolution and whose very tension is constitutive of the civilized experience. As he writes, "A good part of the struggles of mankind center round the single task of finding an expedient accommodation . . . between this claim of the individual and the cultural claims of the group; and one of the problems that touches the fate of humanity is whether such an accommodation can be reached by means of some particular form of civilization or whether this conflict is irreconcilable."[4] In this vein, Freud would be among the first thinkers of the twentieth century to take Nietzsche's postulations on the originary dynamics of Greek tragic drama and expand them into a way of reading the psychic experience of life itself. Nietzsche had foretold such a project, in broad outline at least, when he spoke late in his career of being not just a philosopher of tragedy but indeed "the first *tragic philosopher*."[5] He would hardly be the last, with any number of thinkers in the early half of the twentieth century vying to assume that mantle as well.

Foremost among these inheritors was Martin Heidegger, for whom Nietzsche's views on tragedy were a necessary origin point to his own worldview. "*Incipit tragoedia*. The tragedy begins. Which tragedy? The tragedy of beings as such," he writes in his treatise on Nietzsche. In his forebear's philosophy, Heidegger explains, "*the tragic as such becomes the fundamental trait of beings.*"[6] The particular experience of being human—what Heidegger calls *Dasein*—thus begins in a sense of tragic dislocation, of being cut off from the world around us and left without a sense of stable home. As he writes in the *Introduction to Metaphysics*, "The extent to which humanity is not at home in its own essence is betrayed by the opinion human beings cherish of themselves as those who have invented and who could have invented language and understanding, building and poetry. How is humanity ever supposed to have invented that which pervades it in its sway, due to which humanity itself can *be* as humanity in the first place?"[7] Heidegger originally developed his views on the dislocation of human experience apart from his readings of tragedy, but he nevertheless found in classical tragedy an important source of articulation for the conditions he meant to describe. Like Freud before him but to different intellectual ends, he appropriates the figure of Oedipus as being emblematic of a certain human universal. Here it is the figure of Oedipus wholly exposed and expelled from his home that captures the philosopher's attention: "Oedipus, who at the beginning is the savior and lord of the state ... is hurled out of this seeming. This seeming is not just Oedipus' subjective view of himself, but that within which the appearing of his Dasein happens. In the end, he is unconcealed in his Being...."[8]

The argument that this experience of dislocation and exposure transcends Oedipus himself and encompasses the core of the human condition forms the crux of Heidegger's most famous engagement with tragic drama, his reading of Sophocles' "Ode to Man," the first choral ode from *Antigone*, which begins in Heidegger's somewhat idiosyncratic translation as follows:

> Manifold is the uncanny, yet nothing /
> uncannier than man bestirs itself, rising up beyond him. /
> He fares forth upon the foaming tide /
> amid winter's southerly tempest /
> and cruises through the summits /
> of the raging, clefted swells.[9]

The ode is typically taken as an exultation of human kind's mastery of the natural environment and its dominion over the earth. Yet Heidegger sees underneath this seeming celebration an admission of a fundamental separation and unresolvable estrangement from the world. Focusing on the idea of the uncanny in the ode's opening line, Heidegger insists that "we understand the un-canny as that which throws one out of the 'canny,' that is, the homely, the accustomed, the usual, the un-endangered. The unhomely does not allow us to be at home."[10] In Heidegger's reading, the verse tells us that "to be the uncanniest is the basic trait of the human essence, into which every other trait must always be drawn."[11] Human kind is condemned from birth to feel ill at ease in the world, to mistake and misuse our environment, and to wander without home: to begin from that low place of tragic dislocation to which so many classical heroes fall, unable to reconcile themselves to the world around them.

Heidegger's thought would have a substantial influence over the development of existentialism in France towards the middle of the century and that philosophy's own engagements with the classical tragic tradition. The existentialist philosophy of Jean-Paul Sartre, Albert Camus, and Simone de Beauvoir takes as one of its guiding premises a sense of fundamental disjunction between human and world not unlike that which undergirded Heidegger's worldview, here articulated in terms of an irreducible interplay of freedom and necessity and its paralyzing effects on human experience. "I am condemned to exist forever beyond my essence, beyond the causes and motives of my act. I am condemned to be free," Sartre famously writes in *Being and Nothingness*.[12] Indeed, Sartre explicitly refers to this condition as tragic, describing a hyperarticulated form of the confrontation with freedom as "the tragedy of the absolute Creator," who is faced with "the impossibility of getting out of himself, for whatever he created could be only himself."[13] Liberty, in the Sartrean view, is not ultimately liberating so much as it is horrifying, leaving human beings with no stable recourse in the world. Musing on a world of total freedom in which "everything is permissible," Sartre observes that "man is consequently abandoned, for he cannot find anything to rely on—neither within nor without. . . . That is what I mean when I say that man is condemned to be free."[14] Set adrift by unbounded freedom and left without any stable mooring in the world, the Sartrean individual, infused with Heidegger's vision of the alienated human condition, confronts a tragic predicament in which he is fated to be free.

For many of Sartre's commentators, such descriptions of the existentialist position as fundamentally tragic would take an even more central role. Cerness Moran describes the whole of Sartre's philosophy under the banner of "a tragic ontology of freedom," while Maurice Natanson would likewise sum up Sartre's thought under the aegis of tragedy: "If the more than seven hundred closely printed pages of Sartre's *L'etre et le neant* [*Being and Nothingness*] could be reduced to a single sentence, that sentence would perhaps be this: the tragedy and the dignity of man lie in the dictum, to be is to be free."[15] In his own writings outside of *Being and Nothingness*, Sartre similarly made clear the fundamental debt he owed to Greek tragic drama in conceptualizing the human experience as a negotiation between freedom and necessity. Cognizant of the apparent discord between classical notions of fate and his conceptualization of absolute agency, he argues that the ideas of freedom and fate are in fact coterminous, even synonymous. "Tragedy is the mirror of Fatality," he argues in a 1943 edition of *The Flies*. "The ancient Fatum is simply an inverted freedom."[16] In the essay "For a Theater of Situations," he offers an even more aggressive articulation of that stance. "The chief source of great tragedy—the tragedy of Aeschylus and Sophocles, of Corneille—is human freedom. Oedipus is free; Antigone and Prometheus are free. The fate we think we find in ancient drama is only the other side of freedom."[17] If for Heidegger certain odes taken from Greek tragedy offered a useful means of articulating a tragic view of life that paralleled his own philosophy, for Sartre the whole of classical tragedy could be seen as reflecting the basics of his thought.

This connection between the philosophy of existentialism and the drama and myth of Greek antiquity comes even more to the fore in Albert Camus' "The Myth of Sisyphus," perhaps the most famous expression of the existentialist position. Camus makes clear in his text that the myth of Sisyphus, as he sees it, is undoubtedly tragic: "If this myth is tragic, that is because its hero is conscious," he writes.[18] He even goes on to liken the condition of Sisyphus directly to that of Oedipus. "Oedipus at the outset obeys fate without knowing it. But from the moment he knows, his tragedy begins."[19] Like Sartre, Camus saw the existentialist project as harkening back to and building upon a view of the human condition first articulated in the Western tradition by the Greek tragedians, even as positing a response to the ancient challenge of that tragic view. "One must imagine Sisyphus happy," Camus argues—seeing such happiness first as a temporary response to absurd suffering in the moment when Sisyphus returns to his rock and then ultimately as a permanent rebuttal to it.[20] "Sisyphus," Camus writes, "teaches the higher fidelity that negates the gods and raises rocks"; ultimately, he explains, "the absurd man says yes and his efforts will henceforth be unceasing."[21] For Camus, the utter impossibility of achieving lasting meaning in the world indicated both in classical conceptions of the tragic and in his own ideation of the absurd necessitates such willful, imaginative acts of revolt. It is a revolt that is actually already prefigured in Greek tragedy itself, he claims. "Oedipus," Camus writes, "gives the recipe for the absurd victory," drawing attention to the character's supposed remark that "Despite so many ordeals, my advanced age and the nobility of my soul make me conclude that all is well."[22] Thus Sisyphus must fashion himself after the model of "a blind man eager to see who knows that the night has no end"—that is, after Oedipus.[23] For Sartre and Camus both, existentialism was conceived in no small part as a dialogue enacted across millennia, an interlocution with the tradition's tragedian forebears in the ancient world. "Ancient wisdom confirms modern heroism," Camus writes of the great Greek dramatists.[24]

This deep connection to the world of classical tragedy likewise explains much of de Beauvoir's work in existentialism and her articulations of a feminist position from within that tradition. In de Beauvoir's accounts of the existentialist project, what exists in Sartre as a question of absolute freedom and in Camus as a confrontation with the universal absurd becomes something closer to a negotiation between human choice and contextual social circumstance. In her telling, "one of the fundamental ideas of existentialism" is that "man is not given once and for all, and the qualities that can be attributed to him . . . are actually the result of certain choices. He chooses himself and he finds himself afterward to be such as he chooses himself."[25] De Beauvoir opens a position from within existentialism that will allow for the investigation of the contexts that create gender norms and expectations and the constraints these will impose on the exercise of freedom. Notably, the question of sexual difference in de Beauvoir serves to heighten the tragic experience for all parties, to redouble and echo the basic tragedy of existence that lies at the foundation of existentialist thought. In *The Second Sex*, she describes the sense of disjunction between man and woman as both a source of alienation and as an opening to transcendence of those differences: "Man wants to affirm his individual existence and proudly rest on his 'essential difference,' but he also wants to break the barriers of the self and commingle with water, earth, night, Nothingness, with the Whole. Woman who condemns man to finitude also enables him to surpass his own limits: that is where the equivocal magic surrounding her comes from."[26] If the human condition is tragic in its origins, defined by separation and dislocation, then so too are gender and sex amplifying factors in this originary estrangement; yet gender difference for de Beauvoir also offers a means of recognizing and thus possibly overcoming such limits. In introducing questions of gender and sex into the rubrics of existentialist thought, De Beauvoir played a significant role in grounding the abstractions of the movement in the conditions of social reality, a move that she proved could be made without sacrificing the program's tragic ethos or universalist aspirations. The unequal conditions of modern life, gendered and otherwise, served to compound rather than dilute the limitations on human freedom and the struggle toward happiness that the existentialists believed were part of the shared tragic condition of human kind.

TRAGEDY AS PHILOSOPHY

For Heidegger and the existentialists, the close proximity that they felt between many of their philosophical positions and the historical insights of the Greek tragedians opened the possibility of a new intellectual pathway that bridged the divide between the philosophical and the artistic: if they might be able to derive philosophical insight from dramatic tragedy, then the opposite position—that philosophy might also become the basis for dramatic tragedy—proved an intriguing possibility. Attendant to their philosophies proper, then, came a deep and relatively unique investment in examining the world-making power of art in general and tragic theater in particular—theoretical in the case of Heidegger but practical in the cases of Sartre, Camus, and de Beauvoir.

For Heidegger, the revaluation of art as a means of philosophical production proved an important part of his overall intellectual project. Heidegger viewed the philosophy of aesthetics as a symptom of human kind's estrangement from the world—part and parcel of the tragic condition that grounded his approach to metaphysics. "Aesthetics," he writes in *The Origin of the Work of Art*, "takes the work of art as an object, the object of *aisthēsis*, of sensuous apprehension in the wide sense."[27] Yet art's proper purpose, according to Heidegger, was not aesthetic but ontological—not the construction of beauty but the production of meaning. "Art is the setting-into-work of truth," he writes. "Art lets truth originate."[28] For Heidegger, "great art" always functions in this way, either consolidating and articulating meaning as it was already known in a particular cultural moment or else, in exceptional cases, advocating new formulations that in time might meaningfully shift a culture's understanding of the world.[29] "To be a work means to set up a world," he writes of history's masterpieces. "Towering up within itself, the work opens up *a world* and keeps it abidingly in force."[30] To Heidegger's mind, there were few finer examples of art that functioned in this vein than the work of the great Attic tragedians—his two key examples of the category of "great art" in *The Origin of the Work of Art* are the Aegina sculptures and Sophocles' *Antigone*.[31] In fact, Greek tragedy was for Heidegger an especially potent case for his theory insofar as the conflict between existing and emergent values and positions was in many cases the actual substance of the drama. "In the tragedy nothing is staged or displayed theatrically, but the battle of the new gods against the old is being fought," he explains.[32] Hence his reading of the nature of tragic conflict such as that between Antigone and Creon, wherein "every living word fights the battle and puts up for decision what is holy and what unholy, what great and what small, what brave and what cowardly, what lofty and what flighty, what master and what slave."[33]

Set within the historical context of Heidegger's involvement with the Nazi party, the philosopher's views on the role of art in constructing the values and perspectives of a particular historical community take on a dark tenor. Yet the analogs between Heidegger's views on the practice of tragedy and those of the anti-fascist existentialists in France demonstrate the degree to which these perspectives need not be tied to particular political commitments and might rather be adapted to differing historical and political circumstances. With Heidegger, the existentialists shared a belief in the philosophical potency of the theater and its connection to value formation: but where Heidegger proved content to merely articulate a philosophy of art as such, Sartre, Camus, and de Beauvoir each took steps to actively construct new works for the stage modeled at least in part on the example of Greek tragedy. For many critics, the plays of the existentialists are didactic vehicles first and foremost, tools for disseminating a pre-conceived existentialist worldview the substance of which can be found only in the philosophical prose writings of the group. Yet de Beauvoir took pains to contradict such a viewpoint, insisting that the stage was in fact the philosophical wellspring of the movement and not merely a vehicle for spreading their ideas. In this regard, the theatrical activity of the existentialists appears much closer than otherwise appreciated to the philosophy of art articulated by Heidegger as being philosophically generative, ontological in purpose rather than aesthetic. As de Beauvoir explains, the writing of plays offers "the concrete meditation on a particular individual side of the human drama [that] might very well lead the philosopher to clarify his thought even on a theoretical plane."[34]

And as with Heidegger, the model of Greek tragedy proves for the existentialists to be the superlative example of art properly conceived. The theater of the existentialists, Sartre writes, grew from "the theatre of Antiquity" wherein "each character represents *one* pole of the contradiction, never two. Here you have on the one hand the family, on the other the City State." In his view, "what's new today in the theatre ... is that now contradiction can belong to one individual character."[35] The model is perhaps most clearly seen in those plays that draw explicitly on classical sources, as in Sartre's rewriting of the Orestes myth in *The Flies*. There, according to the explanation provided by de Beauvoir, the central story of the drama follows a movement from meaninglessness to action, which serves as a bulwark against humanity's inescapably tragic condition (Figure 4.1). In de Beauvoir's reading, Orestes' purpose in Sartre's play "was to find himself by saving his people," with "this link between subjective salvation and the objective motivation of an act" being "the most important thing in the play, as well as in Sartre's general theory of freedom."[36] It is notable that this same explanation of the play's dramaturgy applies equally well to non-mythological works like Sartre's famous *No Exit*, wherein decision-making likewise constitutes the pinnacle of dramatic action and thereby reveals the play's own indebtedness to the tragic tradition. Though the play deals with imprisonment rather than freedom, it displays, as Peter Norrish has observed, "a classical economy of structure, with a tightness in action, time and place" that enables the audience to "identify with the characters to the extent that they are suffering from one inescapable part of the human plight"—entrapped by their concern with social judgment and their

FIGURE 4.1: Jean-Paul Sartre's *The Flies*, directed by Juergen Fehling, at the Hebbel Theater, Berlin, 1955. © Charlotte Willot/ullstein bild via Getty Images.

own inability to fully accept or even recognize their freedom.[37] "Each character will be nothing but the choice of an issue and will equal no more than the chosen issue," Sartre writes of his new "theatre of situations," *No Exit* included. "An issue is invented. And each one, by inventing his own issue, invents himself."[38] If one considers choosing an issue to be a concrete action as the existentialists would, then Sartre's explanation of his dramaturgy neatly parallels Aristotle's famous dictum in the *Poetics* that action take precedence over character in the construction of a proper tragedy.

Yet perhaps the most potent example of the linkage between existentialist drama and tragic drama comes not in Sartre's plays but in de Beauvoir's sole work for the stage, *The Useless Mouths*—a play that seems to fit easily alongside any classical tragedy as an exemplary modern parallel, even though it makes no specific classical allusions. Set in Flanders during a period of siege, the play concerns the decision of a city's governing council to sacrifice the women, children, and elderly by placing them outside the city walls, the better to allot resources to the able-bodied men leading the defense (fig 4.2). With its focus on collective peril and collective responsibility situated in terms of inclusion in or expulsion from the city-state, the play reformulates the central concerns of tragedies like Aeschylus' *The Suppliants* or Euripides' *The Trojan Women* and *Children of Heracles*. Though it ends in reconciliation and escape rather than destruction and thus disrupts a certain view of the inevitability of tragic demise (and in this regard is not unlike Euripides' *Iphigenia at Tauris*), the play's tight focus on deliberative decision-making and its

FIGURE 4.2: Simone de Beauvoir's *The Useless Mouths*. Theatre of Carrefours, Paris. October 1945. © Lipnitzki/Roger Viollet/Getty Images.

THE REJECTION OF TRAGEDY

The existentialist moment of the 1940s and 1950s marked a high point in the relationship between philosophies of the tragic and the actual practice of tragedy in the theater. Never again in the twentieth century would a philosophical movement be so closely aligned with the stage. Instead, there emerged outside of and after existentialism a counter-tradition in Western philosophy that explicitly rejected ideas of tragedy's universal appeal or modern applicability. Grounded originally in the cultural Marxism of the Frankfurt School (though also extending far beyond that basis), this anti-tragic philosophical tradition would in many ways become one of the dominant schools of thought in relationship to tragedy in the later twentieth century.

Walter Benjamin's *The Origin of German Tragic Drama* was among the earliest texts of this counter-school in the era after the First World War. Closely reading the works of relatively obscure dramatists of the German sixteenth and seventeenth century, Benjamin argues that these violent, rhetorically ornate, heavily plotted, and thinly characterized quasi-tragedies—roughly analogous to the bloody plays of the later Jacobean period in England—are not so much failed tragedies conceived in poor imitation of Aristotle's dictums as a separate species of drama, the *Trauerspiel*, wholly unique to the dawning of modernity. "The history of modern German drama has known no period in which the themes of the ancient tragedians have been less influential," Benjamin claims. "This alone testifies against the dominance of Aristotle.... No one looked to the Greek author for serious instruction in matters of technique and subject matter."[39] Discourses on Aristotle and dramaturgy notwithstanding, for many today the lasting importance of Benjamin's treatise on the *Trauerspiel* lies in its early demonstration of a historical-materialist mode of literary criticism. Equally remembered is the work's important distinction between the symbol and the allegory, which remains theoretically viable well beyond its immediate application in this work. But in the context of the philosophy of tragedy specifically, Benjamin's text is especially important for its early articulation of the view that tragedy in its classical conception has little place in modernity. In contrast to those thinkers of the early twentieth century who sought to use tragedy toward the understanding of a universal human experience, Benjamin sees the idea of the tragic as inapplicable even to a body of plays from the early modern period supposedly conceived on Aristotle's model.

The reason, Benjamin argues, has to do with questions of divinity and questions of action and the ways in which these two themes become refigured in modernity. The bloody *Trauerspiels* Benjamin considers are conceived for a world where the divine is not expected to actively operate, a world whose God is not dead *a la* Nietzsche but who is perhaps more removed from the terrestrial realm than has ever been the case before—what Benjamin describes as "a world which was denied direct access to a beyond."[40] It is a world, post-Luther, where the Catholic notion of good works has lost its currency and individual human action has therefore lost its most immediate potential for meaning. Thus Benjamin speaks of the "insuperable despair which seems necessarily to be the last word of the secularized Christian drama."[41] It is a world, in other words, deeply out of touch with the experience of the eternal and disabused of the idea that action can create meaning: a world where history replaces theology and economic exchange replaces divine interaction. "Historical life, as it was conceived at that time, is its content, its true object," Benjamin writes. "In this it is different from tragedy. For the object of the latter is not history, but myth."[42] Tragedy, which for Benjamin necessitates an idea of community shaped by a shared mythology, simply cannot be said to operate in any meaningful way in the fragmented and alienated world of early modernity. "The German *Trauerspiel* is taken up entirely with the hopelessness of the earthly condition," Benjamin writes. "The rejection of the eschatology of the religious dramas is characteristic of the new drama throughout Europe; nevertheless the rash flight into a nature deprived of grace, is specifically German."[43] To group such dramas under the rubric of tragedy, in Benjamin's view, significantly misapplies the term.

Much of the material in *The Origin of German Tragic Drama* is specific to Benjamin's unique subject of study, but the deep skepticism as to tragedy's utility in the modern era seen in that work would find echoes across a variety of other philosophers in the years following its publication. Among the most prominent of these thinkers would be Hannah Arendt, whose political commitments were different than Benjamin's but who was likewise skeptical of tragedy as a form applicable to the modern world. For Arendt, the inapplicability or even danger of tragedy in the context of modernity had to do with the ways in which it might stifle or misdirect meaningful political action. Arendt's most extended engagement with classical tragedy comes at the end of *On Revolution*, which concludes with a meditation on the challenge to human action posed by the chorus of Sophocles' *Oedipus at Colonus*: "Not to be born prevails over all meaning uttered in words; by far the second-best for life, once it has appeared, is to go as swiftly as possible whence it came," per Arendt's own translations.[44] In drawing attention to this passage, Arendt is arguing for the importance of political action as a source of meaning in the modern world. Most of modern life has been rendered hopeless in her view, overcome in the postwar world by "the 'nightmare of reality' before which our intellectual weapons have failed so miserably" and by a general "spiritual nakedness."[45] For Arendt, politics is one of the few realms where meaning might yet be made. She thus rejects the tragic as politically inert in a moment when political action is more fervently important, even necessary to human experience, than ever before. Her choice of plays in *On Revolution* is telling: *Oedipus at Colonus* ends not with the isolated, exiled death of its tragic hero but rather his transcendent ascension to the status of cult hero, achieved by way of a political negotiation with the leader and citizens of Athens. It is one of the few extant plays in the classical tradition where politics answers and overcomes the tragic condition, where rather than going "as swiftly as possible" to death, instead life is made meaningful via political engagement. For Arendt, *Oedipus at Colonus* is the play where Sophocles "let us know . . . what it was that enabled ordinary men, young and old, to bear life's burden: it was the *polis*, the space of men's free deeds and living words, which could endow life with splendor."[46] If Benjamin regards tragedy as inapplicable to modernity, Arendt regards it instead as inadmissible, something to be rejected lest one of our last vestiges of meaningful action in the world be denied.

Writing only a few years later, Edward Said would offer an important instantiation of Arendt's general skepticism towards tragedy in his writings on the politics of the ongoing Israeli-Palestinian conflict, wherein, he observes, "the word 'tragedy' turns up with cloying frequency."[47] Like Arendt, Said views the idea of tragedy as being dangerously opposed to political action. "The tragic vision is a static one," he writes, "unsuited to the dynamics of political action currently enacted and lived through. . . . The reality of Palestine remains, however, and that requires action, not tragic suffering."[48] Part of the problem with applying ideas of tragedy to the realm of the political, Said argues, is that it invariably aestheticizes and makes abstract that which requires engagement and specificity. "It would be just as silly to try to convince a refugee living in a tent outside Amman that he is the daily victim of a tragedy, as it would be to tell an Israeli that he is a tragic hero."[49] While the idea of tragedy aestheticizes suffering and places political situations in the realm of the unresolvable, for those who are actually enmeshed in those situations "life must go on. Reason, and negotiation, ought now to prevail."[50] Equally problematic is the degree to which tragedy is an intellectual and cultural imposition from what Said views as a very particular Eurocentric tradition. Tragedy, he writes, "is an imposition of an occidental aesthetic model on what is in large measure a non-occidental political situation. . . . Tragedy is not a Semitic idea, much less a universal one."[51] Far from the universal category of experience as seen by philosophers from Heidegger to Camus, tragedy is here rejected as both culturally specific and, as in Arendt, politically deadening.

Another variation on the anti-tragic impulse can be found in the work of Theodor Adorno and Max Horkheimer, for whom tragedy is neither intellectually inapplicable (as with Benjamin) nor politically inadmissible (as with Arendt and Said) but simply inert as a means of approaching modernity. Adorno and Horkheimer in fact find the idea of tragedy as a rather useful metaphor for understanding what they call the dialectic of enlightenment—the long, desultory history of rational thought in the West wherein the contradictions of the rationalist project eventually become too great for the tradition to bear. In writing on this theme, they turn pivotally to the figure of Oedipus to describe the genesis of the Enlightenment position:

> According to enlightened thinking, the multiplicity of mythical figures can be reduced to a single common denominator, the subject. Oedipus' answer to the riddle of the Sphinx—"That being is man"—is repeated indiscriminately as enlightenment's stereotyped message, whether in response to a piece of objective meaning, a schematic order, a fear of evil powers, or a hope of salvation. For the Enlightenment, only what can be encompassed by unity has the status of an existent or an event.[52]

Importantly, though, any interest in tragedy that Adorno and Horkheimer have is by way of metaphor only. As a practical matter, they align closely with Benjamin in viewing the form as incompatible with the conditions of modernity, though for Adorno and Horkheimer this is less the result of its metaphysical assumptions than the product of a deliberate process of political-aesthetic "liquidation" by forces bent on minimizing social unrest.[53] "Existence in late capitalism is a permanent rite of initiation," they observe. "Thus is tragedy abolished. Once, the antithesis between individual and society made up its substance. . . . Today tragedy has been dissipated in the void of the false identity of society and subject."[54] One might think that in the wake of the horrors of the Holocaust and the Second World War—which by any vernacular definition are the very epitome of tragedy—the form could be rehabilitated. But Adorno in particular insists otherwise, viewing the impossibility of tragedy as a sub-dictum to his famous statement that "it is not possible to write poetry after Auschwitz."[55] The scale of historical tragedy has so overwhelmed the tenets of dramatic tragedy as to make the form seem utterly irrelevant: "Tragedy evaporates because the claims of the subjectivity that was to have been tragic are so obviously inconsequential."[56]

After Benjamin, Adorno, Horkheimer, and Arendt, tragedy frequently becomes seen not as an ally of philosophy as it was once configured but rather as an enemy, a tool of intellectual constriction and social enforcement, as in Said. Such is the position of Gilles

Deleuze and Felix Guattari in *Anti-Oedipus*, where tragedy is explicitly figured as a tool of ideological policing and a means of controlling and stifling desire. "Myth and tragedy," they write, "are systems of symbolic representations that still refer desire to determinate exterior conditions as well as to particular objective codes ... and that in this way confound the discovery of the abstract or subjective essence."[57] This view of tragedy as being primarily a means of alienating desire from itself applies not only to the idea of tragedy as an intellectual artifact but also to the actual practices of theatrical presentation; one of the great goals of the anti-psychoanalytic approach to understanding desire that Deleuze and Guattari pioneer is to succeed at "undoing theater, dream and fantasy."[58] The problem, Deleuze and Guattari argue, is that theater in general and tragedy in particular as they are practiced in the culture serve to contain and organize the experience of desire rather than to liberate it, which for them is the goal towards which art and culture must properly strive. Against the tradition running from Freud to Heidegger to the existentialists that saw in tragedy a means of understanding human experience even to the point of writing new tragedies for the modern stage, a counter-tradition of politically-charged thinkers has gone from skepticism to outright hostility at the incursions of the tragic into a modern age where it does not fit and can only be misused. Where once the stages might be filled with tragedies anew, now the theaters must be emptied.

OEDIPUS AND ANTIGONE

Running alongside the broad story of philosophy's enchantment and subsequent disenchantment with tragedy over the course of the twentieth century lies another narrative that recapitulates its basic moves in miniature: it is the story of two figures from tragedy—Oedipus and Antigone—who became detached from larger questions of tragedy and the tragic per se and came to take up their own intellectual space in twentieth-century thought. The philosophical employment of these figures is not synonymous with the theorization of either tragedy or the tragic insofar as the specific conditions of the plays in which they appear or the stories they help tell are often considered in a deeply abridged or highly abstracted form, if at all. Yet they represent an inheritance bequeathed to twentieth-century thought and passed down through the generations as objects of study in themselves, and they arguably carry vestiges of the tragedies from which they come that partly inform the responses to which they have been subject. Most importantly, perhaps, the debate around these figures helps in many ways to presage and prepare for a return to the philosophy of tragedy that comes about in the later decades of the twentieth century and the first decades of the twenty-first.

The process of detaching certain tragic heroes from the plays in which they appear so as to use them in figural form in connection with a separate set of ideas extrinsic to the plays themselves originates before the period considered here, specifically in Freud's early and middle works and especially in his development of the Oedipus complex in *The Interpretation of Dreams*. Thus the Oedipus encountered by most of the thinkers of the twentieth century is a figure already severed from dramaturgy, narrative, and theater, a figure taken as a classical alibi for a psychoanalytic process the contours of which were discerned from Freud's clinical practice more than from any play text. Here Oedipus stands for the better part of the century, used occasionally to other purposes (as in Heidegger's metaphors of human estrangement or Adorno and Horkheimer's writings on the dialectic of enlightenment) but difficult to disassociate from Freud. In fact, the first substantial attempt to do so would come from outside the disciplinary boundaries of psychoanalysis, philosophy, or theory—in Jean-Pierre Vernant's groundbreaking 1967 essay "Oedipus without the Complex," which offered a historically and politically grounded reading of the play that focused not on Oedipus' sexual transgression and psychic stain but on his contested relationship with the *polis* of Thebes based on "the social thought peculiar to the fifth-century city."[59] (The space for such a reading, it bears noting, was itself at least partly opened by Benjamin's own materialist approach to the far less canonical tragic dramas of the German sixteenth and seventeenth centuries.)

Vernant's essay is itself not concerned with questions of philosophy or social theory except insofar as the piece loosens the psychoanalysts' grip on the figure of Oedipus, but it bears mentioning here for the degree to which it presaged an important breakage in philosophical figurations of tragedy in the twentieth century and the liberation of figures like Oedipus from the specific meanings to which they had long been attached. Jacques Derrida in fact specifically cites Vernant's essay in his own important reconsideration of the Oedipus character in *Dissemination*, writing that Vernant's work "seems to confirm our hypothesis" regarding "the clear necessity of bringing together the figures of Oedipus and the *pharmakos*," what he calls the "magician, wizard, poisoner; the one sacrificed in expiration for the sins of a city."[60] For Derrida, the liberation of Oedipus from the complex to which Freud had semi-permanently affixed him reveals the degree to which the figure is himself unfigurable. Derrida speaks of Oedipus as one of three concepts, along with the Christian trinity and Hegelian dialectics, that "have always governed metaphysics" but that now, detached from a seemingly permanent sense of meaning, can be used to disabuse "the West of all its fantasies of mastery (including the mastery of its fantasies)."[61] Derrida's liberated Oedipus is more than just another signifier revealed to be in free play in his works; to unchain Oedipus from the intellectual positions previously ascribed to him is to unsettle the Western metaphysical tradition. While Derrida is circumspect in articulating the case, certain of his followers have been more triumphalist in declaring a newfound deconstructionist role for Oedipus in particular and tragedy in general. "*Oedipus Rex* is a paradigm of the deconstructive form of tragic drama," writes one critic. "The sequence of action in *Oedipus* deconstructs not only the situation and the protagonist, but also the narrative movement, the process of deconstruction itself."[62]

Derrida's interest in the figure of Oedipus would point to a larger recuperation of tragedy to come in postmodern thought. But before that recuperation could be fulfilled, some other transformations would need to be worked through first. On one level, there is the explicit rejection of the Oedipus figure proposed by Deleuze and Guattari in the appropriately titled *Anti-Oedipus*. "Oedipus is a requirement or a consequence of social reproduction," they write. "We have evolved in Oedipus, we have been structured in Oedipus."[63] Thus the rejection of Oedipus and the entire system of psychoanalytic thought he represents "must devote itself with all its strength to the necessary destructions. Destroying beliefs and representations, theatrical scenes."[64] But one irony of the move that Deleuze and Guattari make in articulating a grounding for an anti-Oedipal philosophy is that the overcoming of Oedipus they demand had in fact already largely been achieved—not via direct confrontation as they advocate in that book but rather through subtler tactics of avoidance and escape. (Not unlike the ultimate strategy employed in de Beauvoir's *The Useless Mouths*, in fact.)

Starting with the work of Jacques Lacan in *The Ethics of Psychoanalysis*, many twentieth-century thinkers have come to see Antigone rather than Oedipus as the central figural representative of the tragic tradition. For Lacan, the turn to Antigone instead of Oedipus was a necessary and much delayed update to psychoanalytic thinking. If the Oedipus complex was the driving intellectual force of Freud's middle years, Antigone was the belated emblem of Freud's later thought, the era that produced *Civilization and Its Discontents* and that focused on the animating tension between *Eros* and death. Antigone's unflinching, almost inhuman embodiment of the death drive is what makes her so fascinating for Lacan. Antigone, he writes, "pushes to the limit the realization of something that might be called the pure and simple desire of death as such. She incarnates that desire."[65] She is for him an emblem of pure desire, but desire as destruction, and she has a kind of splendid beauty in that unflinching commitment to death. Lacan's interest in Antigone is not Hegelian: he is not interested in her argument with Creon or her position inside any rational dialectics, as Hegel once was; he is instead interested in her position outside those dialectics, as an emblem of what Julian Young would call the Kantian "experience of a state of being in which one overcomes the pain and finitude of life"—the sheer splendor of her impulse to annihilation and her existence beyond the realm of language and the symbolic.[66] She is a figure, Lacan writes, who demands "an invocation of something that is, in effect, of the order of law, but which is not developed in any signifying chain or in anything else."[67]

Following Lacan, Antigone would become arguably the pre-eminent tragic figure of late twentieth-century thought. And though the Lacanian focus on Antigone as an emblem of radical transcendence would persist, much of the discourse around her would in fact return her to a position of Hegelian argument: the liberation she represents would be as much political as psychic. Hence Luce Irigaray's insistence on a vision of the character who "in no way resembles the hot-headed, impatient character with no regard for rights and laws who is proposed to us in a choice between subjective despair or decadent nihilism, with those corrupted by power on one side and suicidal young anarchists on the other." Instead, she argues, "The true Antigone has nothing to do with these pathetic theatrical exhibitions.... Antigone respects the natural and social order by genuinely (not metaphorically) respecting the earth and the sun, respecting maternal ancestry as a daughter, respecting oral law rather than a written law which is becoming established and which claims to know nothing of the oral."[68] Irigaray argues for an Antigone whose political position cannot be eclipsed by the impossibility of her situation; for others, however, Antigone's merger of the impossible and the politically specific is part of her unique power. Such is the case with Giorgio Agamben's positioning of Antigone in relationship to the figure of *homo sacer*, the political outcast both sacred and profane whose unique ability to illuminate the nature of political power and concomitant inability to affect or alter that power is encapsulated for the philosopher in a phrase from Sophocles' play, "the oxymoronic *hypsipolis apolis*, literally: 'superpolitical apolitical.'"[69]

This notion stands behind Judith Butler's own approach to the figure of Antigone as representing a political stance outside of politics, one that prefigures "various utopian projects to revamp or eliminate family structure" and undo the assumptive political and social power of biological kinship ties.[70] "One might reapproach Antigone's 'fatality,'" she writes, "with the question of whether the limit for which she stands, a limit for which no standing, no translatable representation is possible, is not precisely the trace of an alternate legality that haunts the conscious, public sphere as its scandalous feature."[71] Slavoj Žižek seeks to reconcile the Hegelian-political view of the character with the Lacanian-Kantian vision of her sublime rejection of meaning, arguing that Antigone represents a position beyond politics: "One should pin down neither the position from which (on behalf of which) Antigone is speaking, nor the object of her claim," he writes, allowing her to enact a revolt beyond politics as "an uncanny figure who disturbs the harmony of the traditional universe."[72] In point of fact, Žižek reminds us, Antigone is in this regard precisely her father's daughter. The Oedipus of the Oedipus complex was always the Oedipus of *Oedipus Tyrannus*, which tells only one half of the character's story. In contrast to Freud's Oedipus, the Oedipus of *Oedipus at Colonus* was always a figure who escaped rather than upheld the structure of meaning, a precursor to what Antigone would become. Žižek, building on Lacan, implores that we remember "what the standard version of the Oedipus complex leaves out of sight: the first figure of what is 'beyond Oedipus,' which is *Oedipus himself* after he has fulfilled his destiny to the bitter end: the horrifying figure of Oedipus at Colonus," a figure already "beyond the Law."[73] Oedipus himself was always already anti-Oedipus.

RECOVERING TRAGEDY

In the various moves made by Derrida, Agamben, Butler, and Žižek in reconfiguring and reconceptualizing the status of figures like Oedipus and Antigone, one begins to sense a narrowing of the divide between philosophy and tragedy that took hold after the era of the existentialists. Is there not something still recoverable in tragedy, these thinkers seem implicitly to ask. That the prevailing idea of tragedy would need in some way to be transformed before such recuperation could be complete is beyond question. As Miriam Leonard notes, philosophies of tragedy have long tended towards "universalizing metaphysical abstractions" even as they claim to abjure such conceits.[74] The question asked by later theorists in the twentieth and twenty-first centuries is what form or forms might tragedy properly take in philosophical thought if it is not to assume the essentializing and universalizing characteristics of its earlier manifestations? One possible answer is suggested in the title of Žižek's 2009 treatise on the first decade of the twenty-first century, *First as Tragedy, then as Farce*—an appropriation of Marx's dictum about the repetitions of history in his 1852 essay *The Eighteenth Brumaire of Louis Napoleon*. The citation, a common enough reference for anyone versed in Marx's work, takes on particular meaning when placed in the context of Žižek's speculations elsewhere about the possibilities that exist between the polarities of tragedy and comedy. Žižek posits the possibility of the "non-tragic" to describe the unique familial circumstances of the biblical Abraham and classical Antigone, beset by complicated kinship situations that neither receive tragic treatment in themselves (Antigone being ultimately a side character in *Oedipus Tyrannus* and *Oedipus at Colonus*) nor yet fall easily into comedy.[75] Žižek in essence proposes the possibility of a form between tragedy and farce, even the idea of a tragedy repeated not as tragedy but as farce, as part of an answer as to how the tragic might be recovered for contemporary thought.

Here we might return to Adorno's central aesthetic question of whether art must be lighthearted and wonder whether the idea of a lighthearted tragedy might not be entirely a contradiction in terms, a form perhaps analogous to Žižek's non-tragic. Adorno argues for the fundamental light-heartedness of art, claiming that "art is a critique of the brute seriousness that reality imposes upon human beings. Art imagines that by naming this fateful state of affairs it is loosening its hold. . . . As something that has escaped from reality and is nevertheless permeated with it, art vibrates between this seriousness and lightheartedness."[76] On the one hand, one can think of being lighthearted as connected to the idea of being spectral, ethereal, lighter than air. The idea of a spectral tragedy is given particular currency by Derrida in his 1994 *Spectres of Marx*, in which he positions Europe's relationship to Marxism as one that has moved from waiting to mourning, undoubtedly aware of the connection to be drawn to Benjamin's exposition of the German mourning-play. Derrida speaks of the contemporary left as being beset by "a politico-logic of trauma and a topology of mourning. A mourning in fact and by right interminable, without possible normality, without reliable limit. . . ."[77] He makes clear that he sees this position as tragic, but tragic in a way that vacillates with comedy. "Between the spirit and the specter, between tragedy and comedy, between the revolution on the march and what installs it in parody, there is only the difference of a time between two masks." In the end, he writes, Marx "is perhaps as aware as we are of the essential contamination of spirit (*Geist*) by specter (*Gespenst*)" and therefore of the essential cross-contamination of tragedy and comedy.[78]

Although maybe the lighthearted tragedy is not so much spectral as fragile. Here one thinks, in a very different vein from Derrida, of Martha Nussbaum's turn to an ethical engagement with tragedy in *The Fragility of Goodness*, first published in 1986 and revised and reissued in 2001. Here it is not Marx but Hegel who haunts the philosopher's reading of ethical quandaries in Aeschylus, Sophocles, and Euripides. But Nussbaum offers Hegel with a difference, a Hegel content to let tensions hang unresolved: which is to say, no Hegel at all. Great tragedy, she writes, "shows us not so much a 'solution' to the 'problem of practical conflict' as the richness and depth of the problem itself. . . . 'Solutions' do not really solve the problem. They simply underdescribe or misdescribe it." That is to say, she writes, "the only thing remotely like a solution here is, in fact, to describe and see the conflict clearly and to acknowledge that there is no way out."[79] The ethical power of tragedy, in Nussbaum's view, lies specifically in the form's ability to acclimate us to conditions of profound uncertainty and radical contingency, to hold both sides of an ethical quandary in abeyance indefinitely. "The best the agent can do is to have his suffering," she writes. "The best we (the Chorus) can do for him is to respect the gravity of his predicament . . . and to think about his case as showing a possibility for human life in general."[80] Nussbaum's vision of tragedy as rooted in the ethically insoluble is undoubtedly a far cry from Žižek's observations on the proximity of tragedy and farce or Derrida's connections between tragedy and spectrality. But what all three thinkers share, despite their manifold differences, is an investment in understanding tragedy as something other than the vehicle of somber certainty that so many previous thinkers held it to be, a genre synonymous with fate and finality. For Nussbaum, the power of tragedy lies not in its demonstrations of inexorable fate but its exposition of the delicacy of our ethical positions and the inevitable insufficiency of any attempts to create a firm moral order.

This is a position both adopted and transformed by Cornel West in his writings on the philosophy of prophetic pragmatism. West acknowledges that tragedy has long been a problem in the philosophical pragmatist tradition. For him, the ways in which pragmatists have historically "formulated the relation of human powers and fate, human agency and circumstance, human will and constraints made it difficult . . . for subsequent pragmatists to maintain a delicate balance between excessive optimism and exorbitant pessimism regarding human capacities."[81] West, drawing on the work of figures from Hans-Georg Gadamer to W.E.B. Du Bois, proposes a prophetic pragmatism that "tempers its utopian impulse with a profound sense of the tragic character of life and history," acknowledging that "tragic thought is not confined solely to the plight of the individual; it also applies to social experiences of resistance, revolution and societal reconstruction."[82] Like Derrida's suggestion of a mode that vacillates between the tragic and the comic, West argues that "the relation of tragedy to revolution (or resistance) is intertwined with that of tradition to progress (or betterment)," the two antipodes being irreducible and inseparable.[83] For West, this means there is a strange potential for joy embedded in the acknowledgment of tragedy. "Like both Russian novelists and blues singers," he writes, "I also stress the concrete lived experience of despair and tragedy and the cultural equipment requisite for coping with the absurdities, anxieties and frustrations as well as the joys, laughter and gaiety of life."[84]

In this acknowledgment of the gaiety held within tragedy, West brings us back to Deleuze. Perhaps lighthearted tragedy is neither spectral nor fragile but simply affirmative: positive where classical tragedy is negative, engaged where classical tragedy is detached. Perhaps it is simply transfigured into something like the opposite of itself, tragedy come first as tragedy and then literally as farce. Deleuze points us toward this view in his statements on tragedy in his 1962 treatise *Nietzsche and Philosophy*. "The tragic is not to be found in this anguish or disgust, nor in a nostalgia for lost unity," he writes. "The tragic is only to be found in multiplicity, in the diversity of affirmation *as such*. . . . *The tragic* is the aesthetic form of joy, not a medical phrase or a moral solution to pain, fear or pity. It is joy that is tragic."[85] Deleuze's views here seem to stand in contrast with those articulated just a few years later in *Anti-Oedipus*, where tragedy is a literal constraint and form of psychic burden. Arguably, though, the two texts are speaking of different forms: the latter a culturally determined form serving established intellectual and psychic ends, the former a Nietszchean transvaluation of the same, a mode of tragedy manifested as a tool of affirmation rather than repression—a lighthearted form of tragedy rather than a solemn one. In Deleuze's reading, Nietzsche's version of tragedy—*contra* Freud's rendition of the form—does not repress and confine but affirms, allows, and opens. "Multiple and pluralist affirmation—this is the essence of the tragic," he writes. "This will become clearer if we consider the difficulties of making *everything* an object of affirmation. Here the effort and the genius of pluralism are necessary, the power of transformations."[86] A tragedy that exalts in and celebrates the destruction it unfolds, that affirms the ethical uncertainty Nussbaum identifies, that welcomes the ability to haunt more than the responsibility to take place: such is the sketch of a tragedy beyond tragedy toward which so much of postmodern thought seems at least dimly to point, a recuperation of tragedy that stands apart from its older and ossified forms. Such might someday be the opening of a new fourth act in the story of philosophy's relationship to tragedy, one wherein the prophesies and intimations of the last portion of the third act are perhaps at last fulfilled and one wherein an intellectual enterprise that can trace its roots back to the eighteenth century can find cause to begin anew once again.

CHAPTER FIVE

Religion, Ritual and Myth

BEN QUASH

This topic is potentially vast, and I propose in what follows to speak from my own disciplinary vantage point, as a Christian theologian with a particular interest in the arts (in all their forms; the visual and the literary especially). While this will not yield total coverage or even a representative overview of the relation of religious beliefs and practices to the idea of tragedy in the modern period it will nevertheless—I hope—serve to identify some important tendencies and recurring themes in the last century. If I manage to fix some useful pegs to the wall, then a variety of hats may be hung on them, supplied by readers with specialisms in other religious traditions or other forms of ritual practice, and a discerning eye for other examples of relevant art. If more pegs are needed, then at least mine will be a start.[1]

There are two common assumptions that this chapter will seek to challenge. The first is that the secularizing momentum of modern Western societies has more or less banished religious (and especially Christian) reference points from any significant role in public discourse and contemporary culture. This is surprisingly untrue. Recent studies of the vibrant and often unpredictable role of religious themes and imagery in modern and contemporary visual art show the abiding appeal of theological ideas and questions in the artistic mainstream of the twentieth and twenty-first centuries.[2] A subset of this first assumption can sometimes be that tragedy is not a modern art form. There are several possible reasons for this. As David Kornhaber points out in his chapter in this volume, it may be because the actual horrors of recent decades so greatly eclipse what can be presented in the medium of a stage production that the tragedy of an individual subject is "out-tragedied" by modern history, and thereby rendered inconsequential (Adorno).[3] It may be that tragedy's inevitably aesthetic "construction" of human suffering turns things that properly require political engagement and specificity into abstractions (Said).[4] It may be that we no longer have the community-shaping shared mythologies that were once the condition of tragic performance, such that they can no longer "operate in any meaningful way in the fragmented and alienated world of early modernity" (Benjamin).[5] And I would add to this last suggestion the closely-allied one that, to many moderns, tragedy's age-old connections with ritual practice (especially in ancient Greece), and with what might seem to be its concomitant Dionysian irrationality, now seem ill-suited to express the deepest concerns of the hyper-rational, technocratic societies we inhabit. A world which believes that everything can in principle be managed or solved may be inclined to view tragedy—like religion—as a hangover from a more primitive and excitable past. Here, a link between tragedy and religion is reinforced precisely in the dismissal of both.

The other common assumption that I will seek to challenge is the idea that Christianity is intrinsically anti-tragic by virtue of its emphasis on hope. That hope is grounded in a narrative of resurrection in which a grisly death is interpreted as a redemptive divine gift whose powerful ramifications can effect the eventual reconciliation of all things to each other and to God.[6] The idea that Christianity is opposed to tragedy, I will argue, demonstrates both a misunderstanding of certain elements of what tragedy has been (and is), and a caricature of religious hope as a kind of immunization against the uncertainty and pain of historical existence.

THE END OF HEROISM

One key plank in the argument that tragedy is not a modern art form is the longstanding link that endures between the idea of tragedy and the idea of the dramatic hero. We no longer seem to believe much (in serious-minded art) in the idea of heroes. Thomas Hardy's central characters are bellwethers for this deposition of the heroic agent in the twentieth century. The plots have many of the features of traditional tragic drama: the idea that fateful forces override the best-laid plans of human beings, who inadvertently find themselves colluding in their own destruction, and the apparently final sovereignty of death over human life. But a character like Jude Fawley in *Jude the Obscure* inhabits a world in which it is precisely the fantasy of a great destiny that is the deadly illusion that will destroy him and those around him. His romantic attachments to "mediaevalism" will, the novel suggests, inevitably lead to a life in which "at best only copying, patching and imitating" go on.[7] Jude when we first meet him is not yet fully cognizant of "[t]he deadly animosity of contemporary logic and vision"[8] to his personal aspirations, the industrial-scale forces that will make of him a merely superfluous man. Dostoevsky masterfully explores similar dynamics of the modern condition through his nameless civil servant in *Notes from Underground*, and (earlier) the petty, increasingly invisible, and finally replaceable Golyadkin in *The Double*.[9] Arthur Miller's Willy Loman takes the type forward into the twentieth century, and paradigmatically displays how much more we feel our modern selves represented by the shabby and self-doubting bit-player than by any world-shaking protagonist.[10] "Do I dare to eat a peach?" says T.S. Eliot's Prufrock.[11] With the retreat of heroes to a great distance it can seem that the more representative dramatic form of the twentieth century is the tragi-comedy, and perhaps especially the theater of the absurd.

Contemporary atrocities in the name of religion are perhaps, as Pankaj Mishra has argued, forms of mutiny against such superfluousness. Resentment is the mood of great swathes of the world's semi-Westernized population (especially those not actually living in the West): "educated into a sense of hope and entitlement, but rendered adrift by . . . limited circumstances, and exposed to feelings of weakness, inferiority and envy." We might think of Hardy's Jude once again, marked by a distinctly modern condition of "unrest." The sense of whether or not one can be "at home" in the world—whether, indeed, the world is set up in such a way that this is even a reasonable question to ask—seems one of the besetting anxieties of the modern period, and an intensifying sense of personal irrelevance, and the impossibility of fulfilling activity, is what fuels the humiliated rage of the frustrated "actor" in search of a "play."[12] This is what Mishra calls "the gap between the noble ends of individual liberation and the poverty of available means." This is why, as he puts it:

> [I]ndividuals, trained to believe in a lofty notion of personal freedom and sovereignty, and then confronted with a reality that cruelly cancel[s] it, [can] break out of paralysing ambivalence into gratuitous murder and paranoid insurgency.[13]

But inasmuch as both the obscure resignation of Arthur Miller's salesman and the senseless lashing out of the religious militant are equally a witness to the inhospitality of the modern world to human visions of meaningful belonging, they both equally point to something that has not conventionally been a mark of tragedy as an art form: the specter of nihilism. It is not that the gods "kill us [or at least some of us] for their sport";[14] it is that there are simply no gods watching at all, rendering "man's organic need for self-expression"[15] merely ludicrous.

Two extraordinarily successful contemporary American novelists help to frame the issue here in their contrasting outlooks. Marilynne Robinson, in her intensely-observed, slow-paced novels (*Gilead* above all, perhaps) displays how modern human lives may still be lived (and surrendered in old age) in ways that issue in a "yes" to the world and to God. Her concentration on place, habit, and the discreet fruits of human reciprocity, on patterns of attention and abiding, assert that fundamental human aspirations to community and to stability ought not to be despised, and are not always doomed to fail. Cormac McCarthy's *The Road*, on the other hand, describes a post-apocalyptic future in which the world has shrunk down "about a raw core of parsible entities [that are] [i]n time to wink out forever."[16] The man and the boy who are the story's main characters meet an old man on the road who declares that "[t]hings will be better when everybody's gone."[17] In this world, what the narrator calls the "sacred idiom" has been "shorn of its referents and so of its reality." Ritual persists but it signals no higher metaphysical realm. The man's rubbing dry of his son's hair before a fire is "like some ancient anointing," but is a flimsy bulwark against the void:

> Evoke the forms. Where you've nothing else construct ceremonies out of the air and breathe upon them.[18]

Strikingly, Robinson's vision seems to provide better soil for tragic themes to be explored than McCarthy's. Even if her novels are not best described, in the end, as tragic in character or tone, the affirmative world of the *Gilead* trilogy is nevertheless replete with incidences of hurt, failure, betrayal, frustrated striving, and deep sorrow which are acutely and movingly communicated to her readers. McCarthy's world, meanwhile, has all but abandoned the measure by which human loss and disintegration can be evaluated, and thus it also makes these things hard to mourn. One might say that there is something more tragic about a situation when people are shut off from a happiness, a justice, an "at-homeness" that they *might* have reached but for some cruel stroke of fate or some mistake of their own, than about a situation where there is no happiness, justice, or plausible "at-homeness" to be shut off from in the first place. Likewise, Edith Hall's claim that tragedy, in its classical forms, explores "the gross unfairness of human pain" must surely presume a context in which the idea of fairness has some foundation.

Moreover, despite what we have noted above about the difficulties of identifying the "superfluous man" as a tragic figure, Robinson's novels place a question mark against the notion that obscurity or liminality is in itself a bar to any particular *mise en scène* being a locus for the exploration of tragic themes. Marginality may not be the same as superfluity. Not every provincial drama is ludicrous or nihilistic simply because it is low-key and domestic. The key criterion seems to be that it must convince us that it matters. We have to care about the feelings and the fates of the characters whose words and actions are played out before us, with a sense that something is at stake in our recognition of their struggle (and that they have a worth that does not merely subsist in how readily they permit us to project our own self-regard onto them, or how easy it *could* be simply to ignore them).

In a less mundane context, but one that is often just as easily marginalized by mainstream Western consciousness, it has been an achievement of photographers like Larry Burrows to resist the way that the victims of war can also—very easily—be perceived as superfluous (as nameless statistics, for example) when viewed from a distance. Although not heroes, they are held up for our focused contemplation in this form of photographic art; we are made to countenance their bodies and also (if they are not already obliterated) their faces, and are summoned to recognize the call they make on our moral attention (Figure 5.1).

The deposition of heroes in the various dramas that might otherwise, potentially, claim the status of tragedies in the modern period may curiously make them rather "christic," in that the figure of Christ, whose goodness seems to necessitate his destruction, is also of low birth and from an obscure province of a great empire.[19] There is a recalibration of the idea of heroism in Christianity's legacy, which plays through Marilynne Robinson's novels or conflict photography as it does in numerous novels, plays, photographs, and films in our purportedly post-Christian era. This recalibration of heroism may not have heralded an end to tragedy, but it has—arguably—had some significant modifying effects on the virtues whose glories and vulnerabilities tragedy began to probe once the ancient Greek world was a thing of the past. It might be that the protagonists of modern dramas like Samuel Beckett's *Waiting for Godot*, or *Endgame* are part of this recalibration, descendants of the "holy fools" whose strange experiments in what sanctity might look like are generally a long way from Aristotle's great men.

The foregoing sortie into the decline of a heroic paradigm in modern tragedy has led to a set of reflections on the specter of human superfluity that haunts the twentieth and

FIGURE 5.1: Larry Burrows' photograph of a grieving widow crying over the remains of her husband killed by the Viet Cong during the Tet offensive the previous year. Vietnam, 1969.
© Larry Burrows/Time magazine/LIFE picture collection/Getty images.

twenty-first centuries, and to my proposal that a world in which it is ludicrous to think that we even *could* be at home will no longer be a tragic world in any critically-useful sense of the term. Such a world would somehow be more flattened, sterile, and numbing than the worlds of tragic drama and literature have typically been. Reflections like these seem to make a dialogue between tragedy and theology an obvious one to have, in that claims about the goodness, the badness or the sheer arbitrariness of the structures of the world (from a human, or any, perspective) are not only claims that are pressed in tragic art, but have a long history of discussion in religious thought.

In the next section, I will look in greater detail at what some key theologians in the twentieth century, and the first years of the twenty-first, have had to say about tragedy. And, in light of the above, it should be no surprise that most theological discussions of tragedy open onto discussions that are about just the issues I have just noted: discussions about the goodness, badness, or sheer arbitrariness of the structures of the world. They ask whether it is possible to invoke categories like fairness or unfairness (as Edith Hall does) without facing the question of whether there is a loving or unloving deity. And this in turn introduces the question of Providence, and (as a subset of that) the related problems of evil and of suffering. Theological responses to these questions often take the form of theodicies—in other words, attempts to justify God's character and actions in the face of the human experience of wrong. So, in this next section, we must address the relationship between theodicy and the theological treatment of tragedy.

TRAGEDY AND THEODICY

The two world wars of the first half of the twentieth century—and especially the unprecedentedly clinical mass barbarism of the Shoah—had vast effects within Christian theological discourse as in nearly all other areas of thought and cultural life. One of its key effects was to make a certain kind of theological liberalism—with its benign view of human moral capabilities and historical progress—seem bankrupt. Allegedly civilized human societies had conspicuously failed to live up to any such ideals, and the darkness of the human heart had been exposed as more intractable than ever. The return of former liberals like the Swiss theologian Karl Barth (1886–1968) to a renewed engagement with the Bible and pre-modern traditions of doctrinal thought changed the face of subsequent theology. It had the odd effect of returning theology to what could sound like a more triumphalist account of God's sovereignty over history precisely under the impetus of a human experience of devastation. A radically transcendent God was affirmed as sovereign despite, not because of, appearances; affirmations based on appearances were, so Barth proposed, the wishful constructions of human minds wanting to make the evidence for God stack up on the basis of a smoothly narratable historical plot.

Smoothly narratable plots are in key respects profoundly anti-tragic. In this respect, Barth and others whom he influenced (and still does) cleared a space for a new theological attention to what tragedy might have to say in judgment on our epistemological pretensions and our moral complacency. Theological liberalism, as the tradition most inclined to try to explain evil away, emerges here as a more insidious opponent of tragic insight than theological (neo-)orthodoxy. However, Barth's own theology is not interested in paying any great attention to tragic themes. His explicit references to tragedy are consistently dismissive; he characterizes tragic outlooks as a form of resistance to the revealed truth that (again, *despite* all appearances) God in Jesus Christ has conquered sin and brought all creatures back into fellowship with himself. Thus he writes:

> [W]e can no longer try to experience and bear ... an as it were divine, eternal, irremovable weight of sorrow. ... [A] divine pain of that kind is not only taken away from us, but forbidden to us as something presumptuous – a tragic consciousness to which we may not pretend.[20]

Even Judas' act of betrayal is emphatically not tragic, according to Barth. The kiss in Gethsemane is a moment that might seem to approach very near indeed to tragedy not just because it sets in train the sequence of events by which the world extinguishes the very light from which all its life is derived, but (as though mirroring this at a personal level) because a deep intimacy between friends is the locus for the cruelest "othering" of one by the other, and because this expulsion (in a classic tragic irony) is an act in which Judas proves the deadliest enemy not of Christ but of *himself*. But of this Barth declares:

> The act of Judas cannot ... be considered as an unfortunate episode, much less as the manifestation of a dark realm beyond the will and work of God, but in every respect (and at a particularly conspicuous place) as one element of the divine will and work.[21]

Barth's antipathy to tragic "presumption," as he puts it, is of a piece with his wider opposition to giving too great a weight to general experience as a normative source of theological insight and judgment. Neither positive nor negative experience—neither happiness nor pain—may reliably be appealed to as a basis for the knowledge of God and God's ways. Revelation may not be summoned to the bar of general human experience to give evidence, as though to defend itself from prosecution. It is human reason, in its uncertain struggle to interpret its own experience, that must be brought to judgment by revelation, and the overwhelming content of that revelation, on Barth's account, is that Christ has been victorious over the powers of this world. This is revealed to those with the eyes of faith, and will be fully revealed eschatologically.

A number of Christian theologians later in the century, both Protestant and Catholic, have followed Barth in rejecting both the possibility and the desirability of a theodicy (in the sense of a justification of the ways of God to humanity in terms that humanity already has at its disposal). However, they have not shared his brisk dismissal of tragedy. These include, for example, Barth's fellow Swiss, the Roman Catholic theologian Hans Urs von Balthasar, as well as Balthasar's great admirer and early advocate the Scottish philosophical theologian Donald MacKinnon, and a number of MacKinnon's pupils, including Nicholas Lash, Rowan Williams, and David Ford.

A dismissal of tragic experience, so Balthasar argues throughout his five-volume *Theodrama*, risks "drawing the teeth" not only of human suffering, but also of the once-for-all character of the person and work of Christ.[22] God's affirmation of his world—demonstrated in the historical death and resurrection of Jesus—rules out Nietzschean doctrines of "eternal recurrence," just as much as it forbids any idea that the world is evolving towards a progressively better state propelled only by resources internal to itself. God's pledge in Jesus Christ is a free, personal commitment to the finite, which interrupts and transfigures the vain strivings and frequent self-mutilations of finitude. As Balthasar points out on numerous occasions, God's covenant cannot be recast as some kind of impersonally valid natural law. Moreover, this free commitment—this unreserved self-giving which is an absolute yes to humanity—requires with absolute acuteness a response. The absoluteness of the "word" addressed by God to humanity suggests that the reply—if one believes that humanity is given space and freedom to reply—will have an absoluteness about it too. Christ's crucifixion is a central part of God's address to humanity. One of the areas in which Balthasar and MacKinnon are most at one is in their conviction that there are real and not simply illusory outcomes at stake in the harsh necessity that makes the cross a central part of the divine self-disclosure; of the divine "speech." This is not make-believe, or the "ballet dance of ideas."[23] Judas having one moment slipped out into the night slips all the way into the oblivion of an agonized death. Jerusalem finds its daughters warned to weep for themselves, suggesting a freedom that has resulted in an *actually* "irretrievable disaster";[24] that the city's refusal to accept what Jesus represents will have actually irretrievable consequences. As Donald MacKinnon puts it:

> [I]n a certain sort of idealist theological tradition, the category of the decisively significant is ... replaced by the vague concept of a developing spiritual tradition which somehow plays down the heights and depths of human existence, mutes the cry of Jesus in Gethsemane, turning his agony into a kind of charade.... We have ... to resist the drift into a state of mind which regards all that passes before it as a kind of play ... empty in itself of deep and drastic significance.[25]

Supporting the idea that the attempted sterilization of the idea of evil is a spiritual error, David Ford points out that the tragic is not negated by Christ, but taken into a transformation that sharpens it (though the category of the tragic is also revealed not to be adequate by itself).[26] Those who preach Christ can, as Paul indicates in 2 Corinthians, be to some "a fragrance from death to death."[27] What is at stake is an eternal Yes or No.

On these accounts, the revelation in Christ seems to require a rejection of the suggestion that Christianity is post- or anti-tragic. If one believes that Jesus Christ in some way defines the human situation, and reveals its real dimensions, then part of what he defines is its harshly constraining realities. MacKinnon identifies the danger of an idolatry of our own human powers of explanation against which the tragedy-like qualities of the Christian founding narrative can help to defend us. He thus introduces an important counterpoint to Barth's worries about that different sort of idolatry: the indulgent worshiping of ourselves as tragic victims and as sufferers of an infinite sorrow with no recompense; the exaltation of misery as a condition from which in principle we are *certain* we could *never* be sprung.

At this point, it is important to note the presence of a forceful alternative strand of thought about suffering in twentieth-century Christian theology—although I would argue that this strand can boast less of a fertile legacy than we see stemming from Barth, Balthasar, MacKinnon, and others. It might be argued that this strand exemplifies that idolization of our human powers of explanation which is so roundly condemned by MacKinnon. The work of the British philosophical theologian John Hick made concerted attempts to revive the early Christian theodicy of Irenaeus of Lyons, for whom—even if only from a God's eye perspective (though Hick exerts himself to attain such a perspective for himself and his readers)—worldly suffering can be interpreted as a positive stimulus to moral growth and full self-realization. This is a contemporary version of the idea that the world, with all its apparent tragedy, is ultimately a "vale of soul-making."[28] Hick thought he discerned in the Irenaean tradition something that might productively be married with a modern evolutionary (and also voluntarist) outlook in which human striving in the face of adversity is a condition of progress towards perfection: a sanctifying struggle. This is to hallow (or at least absolve) the adversity itself.

The most controversial issue here is not so much the ontological claims that this approach may or may not imply.[29] It is an epistemological hubris that is the problem. Hick's modern attempts at theodicy seek a vantage point on historical experience that can seem quite inappropriate to ways that the lived traumas of this past century rebuff our explanatory resources. A well-worn anecdote in theological circles recalls how Donald MacKinnon was asked what he thought of John Hick's project, and how he replied, obliquely but pointedly, "some theologians seek clarity at all costs; other wrestle with reality at its darkest points." It is in just this tradition that Rowan Williams writes that "human disaster does not submit itself to a calculus of perceivable necessities in this or any imaginable world."[30]

Terrence Malick's much-anticipated 2011 film *The Tree of Life* was characteristic of his previous ambitious, metaphysically-questioning treatment of unabashedly-theological subjects. One of its main concerns is how the violence of nature and the affliction of human loss might be compatible with a belief in beauty and grace—themes already present in *Badlands* (1973) and *The Thin Red Line* (1998). The film sets the domestic tragedy of the loss of a child, and the pressures of this loss (as well as of various frustrated ambitions, creative and professional) on a Texan family in the 1950s against a vast, cosmic backdrop in which life at the microbial as well as the planetary level is tracked with a loving and beautifying directorial lens. At one stage, Malick shows us the encounter of two dinosaurs—one a predator and one a wounded potential victim—and imagines a spark of compassion awakening as the predator seems to feel an empathy for the helpless creature under his claw: this is presented as though it were the beginning of morality, long before the arrival of humanity. In a very long sequence set on a vast beach, Malick strives to evoke what he conceives of as a heavenly context so capacious, so free of the immediate concerns and struggles of earthly existence, and so visually rewarding that it will help us imagine how we might find ourselves reconciled with all the losses, sufferings, and failures of our finite lives. He does not deny these losses, sufferings, and failures, and he certainly does not explain or excuse them; he strives instead for a vision in which they are not absolutized, and do not have the last word. The linking of this long sequence with earlier meditations on evolutionary process does, however, suggest an affinity between *The Tree of Life* and a Hickian theological outlook. With enough time and enough space we will see that our travails are part of a bigger plan.

By way of a contrast, one might turn to the BBC's drama *Rev.* (broadcast in three series, between 2010 and 2014), in which a struggling parish priest (Adam Smallbone) eventually faces ostracization, the closure of his church, and both marital and personal breakdown because of a moment of indiscretion in which he kisses a female friend, a kiss that is witnessed (and reported) by a colleague. The act is an unforced and senseless expression of misdirected desire (in a truly Augustinian tradition) whose consequences are nevertheless dire. With all liturgical activity in his church suspended, the priest undertakes his own all-night *via dolorosa* through the streets of his parish during Holy Week, carrying a cross and receiving the taunts and ridicule of passers-by, until at dawn he finds himself on some shabby raised ground above the council estates where he has served, and begins to sing. A vagrant appears and joins in; they sit down and the vagrant—having discovered that Adam is in crisis—offers him some hard-won advice. What follows is a string of completely useless platitudes ("you can't make an omelette without breaking eggs"; "what doesn't kill you makes you stronger"; "never parachute into an area you've just bombed") until Adam pleads with his interlocutor to stop, whereupon the interlocutor looks as though into his soul, and speaks his name (when he could not have known it) and says "I understand; I will always be there for you." This powerful scene is an adroit critique of all theodicies which suppose that some sort of *explanation* will resolve the problem of sin and suffering. It reduces the theodicy to the level of the platitude, and exposes its pastoral inefficacy. The one thing that reaches Adam in his despair is not an argument for why his suffering means something, but the reawakened conviction that he can be empathized with; that he is not alone.

The fact that explanatory meanings cannot easily be assigned to every event in our historical experience need not issue in resignation, nor in a negative evaluation of our finitude. This is what Balthasar—to turn back again from the Hickian strand of twentieth-century theology to his more "theo-dramatic" one—is keen to insist upon. His emphasis on the momentousness and irreversibility of historical action in the theo-drama (both Christ's and ours) has much in common with the scene of personal encounter in *Rev*. God is met with in the I–Thou encounter; as a presence in the midst of the world's turmoil, not in a theoretical construction that floats above it. Because of this presence, the tragic lineaments of experience do not necessitate despair; the dramatic sensibility given its acutest expression in tragedy is "very different from the mood of tired impatience which finds nothing new under the sun."[31]

Controversies other than those with Hick (and his style of approach) haunt recent theology, however, and introduce further points of contrast with the attitudes of MacKinnon et al. For example, we might turn to the North American theologian David Bentley Hart at this point, whose Eastern Orthodox theological stance is not as pessimistic about the vitiating effects of the Fall as most Western traditions are, and who suggests that theologies which over-assert the intractability of tragic experience make an idol of suffering. The similarity of this position to Karl Barth's will already be evident, and it is also convergent with the British theologian John Milbank's occasional suggestion that if one declares, following Adorno, there can be no poetry after Auschwitz then the Holocaust has become one's God. Hart's version of this claim is that Christianity's framework of committed hope—resting on and licensed by the proclamation that Christ has risen—makes it more open to historical surprise. To be in the middle of history also means to be in a position to be surprised by it—and tragedy is *not* surprising, according to Hart. Tragedy is what world-weary minds have come to expect all too readily, and sometimes to venerate. Much more truly surprising is the resurrection—a genuine novelty irrupting within history as the disclosure of history's good origins and glorious end. On the basis of the resurrection, Christianity is equipped with a capacity to question the tragic "givens" of situations or world-descriptions with which it is presented.

Hart claims that a concern with tragic experience (especially tragic experience that is modeled on the Attic tragedies) usually indicates a whole way of life and thought: a tragic worldview, a tragic aesthetic, a desire to propagate "tragic wisdom."[32] He argues that these perspectives and commitments are intrinsically antipathetic to Christianity's own. And they are, paradoxically, a sort of consolation to those who hold them: "the most narcotic metaphysical solace of all."[33] Why? Because a tragic outlook defers all attempts to understand the origins of evil, and to answer ultimate questions about the moral intelligibility of the universe, and looks simply for an accommodation with evil's perceived *nature*. It is in a sense a sort of cosmic pragmatism, claiming a "realism" that knows how the world goes, even if it does not know why. It sees the world's basic logic as a sacrificial one, and then sets about making whatever offerings need to be made to keep existence's various forms of violence in balance, precisely by joining in with them, and working with their forces. The wisdom tragedy imparts is one of "accommodation":

> resignation before the unsynthesizable abyss of being, a willingness on the part of the spectator to turn back towards the polis as a refuge from the turmoils of a hostile universe, reconciled to its regime and its prudential violences, its martial logic.[34]

Death in particular will always be part of this dark economy with its pretensions to exhaustively define the world; the resurrection meanwhile, according to Hart, serves no economy at all—it simply surprises, and does so wholly on its own terms. Death is an economy which God's infinity can pass through as though it were nothing, breaking its limits as it does so. Evil is thereby shown to be incidental: "the superscribed text of a palimpsest, obscuring the aboriginal goodness of creation."[35]

The position Hart advances is not necessarily as much at odds with that of (say) Balthasar as it might initially seem. Both are concerned to avoid a generalized metaphysical outlook (*tragic*, for Hart, and *undramatic*, for Balthasar) that adopts a false repose, and expects no disruptions in the form of particulars that are unassimilable to its preconceptions. Both Hart and Balthasar desire to show how "all the sober verities by which we measure the nature of the world, our common lot, and our place in the order of things" is in fact "overturned and inverted" in Christ.[36] For Balthasar, it is that God enters the world's drama and reveals that even a real and horrific death may be part of God's self-gift such that a road-block is placed in the way of our comforting narratives of historical melioration. For Hart, it is that the resurrection denies us the right to absolutize specific examples of tragic failure (even when aggregated) in the service of an unshakable, dogged theory of the human lot as only suffering and finitude. Balthasar is against presumption; Hart is against resignation. What both have in common is that history matters, and its contingencies must be allowed to unsettle any premature (and false) universalizing theories about it.

EXCESS AND LAMENT: TWO THEOLOGICAL CONVERSATIONS WITH TRAGEDY

Rowan Williams' *The Tragic Imagination* considers the violence of the late Sarah Kane's plays (as earlier, in *Grace and Necessity*, he explored the dark themes of Flannery O'Connor's novels). Williams' treatment of this material seeks to show that he does not regard anything, however extreme, as beyond the concern of Christian theology, precisely because theology may not regard anything as beyond the reach of grace.[37] To quote *Grace and Necessity*: "The tightrope that the [Christian] must walk is to forget or ignore nothing of the visually, morally, humanly sordid world . . ., while doing so in the name of a radical conviction that depends on that world being interrupted and transfigured by revelation." The wager here is that "God is possible even in the most grotesque and empty or cruel situations."[38]

Underlying Williams' wager is, perhaps, a sense that tragic excess might in many cases be a better propaedeutic to the theological conceptualization of divine excess than some more tame appeal to "all the blessings of this life."[39] Grace, in Christian terms, is wild, disproportionate, wholly resistant to any predictable calculus of just desert. The human desire to reduce all people, actions, and artifacts to precisely costed commodities of exchange (a desire ever more assertive in capitalist modernity) is—theologically speaking—a refutation of the Christian logic of grace. At a more modest level than market capitalism, even the benign reasonableness (in art, politics, or education) that seeks to enshrine and transmit good sense, good morals, and good taste hinders a proper appreciation of the full radicalness, the full prodigality, of the Christian gospel. So, to the playwright Sarah Kane and the novelist Flannery O'Connor one might add the Danish filmmaker Lars von Trier, whose works are drenched in theological allusions, but whose themes are unfiltered by any customary proprieties. Von Trier's holding up of the excesses of violence, of sexual lust, and of many other horrifying forms of self-serving libido, alongside the terrifyingly widespread human ability to embrace or to tolerate these excesses, means that at the same time that his films tear at the complacency of modern, liberal, rational, technocratic social order he also opens a door to the contemplation of what a redemption that could deal with our unaccountable natures would have to be like. It would have to be beyond accounting. At the end of *Breaking the Waves* (1996), the brutal killing of a young woman with severe learning difficulties who is prostituting herself in the belief that it will miraculously heal her abusive husband's paralysis is followed by the sudden disclosure of bells ringing in heaven—and the husband's recovery.[40] In *Dogville* (2003), a woman (appropriately named Grace) who has sought to serve a small and remote community "for nothing" and whose acts of service (and eventually also whose body) have progressively been commodified for the community's purposes under the rationalizing rhetoric of what is "costly" to them and what is "fair" to all, returns with her gangster father at the end of the film to wreak a wholly unrestrained and ruthless vengeance on the town. Both endings model excess in their rejection of "what would normally be expected," and *Dogville*'s denouement in particular—in its portrayal of what "grace" would look like if inverted (as Grace herself "turns")—may offer useful resources for thinking theologically about *divine* grace in its positive guise.

Unfazed by such horrors, Rowan Williams is encouraged by the fact that tragic genres of writing (and, we may suppose, films like von Trier's) are nevertheless "forms": they are formulations in language of atrocities that have been, or might be, undergone; they are communicative acts. In this respect, they encode a certain hope that human communication (in a shared medium) outruns and outlasts what threatens to sunder all meaningful connection between human beings. The shared acts of witness that have an ancient, and still lively, embodiment in theatrical performances are rituals of a sort. They ritualize the durability and vigor of the medium in which we share what we most suffer. On this basis, Williams counterintuitively but cogently shows how the Christian Eucharist is like Attic tragedy. (Liturgy, as a wholly bodily, performative medium is one of his principal analogs for tragic drama.)

In this regard, Williams' thought may have parallels with the linkage of tragic drama to religious ritual practice that was a mark of the work of the twentieth-century Nigerian playwright Wole Soyinka. Soyinka, like Williams, does something fundamentally affirmative in making such a link, though in both cases the affirmation is at a collective and even cosmological level that does not deny the more immediate bitterness of individual mortal suffering. Having studied English Literature in the UK, and been profoundly influenced in his upbringing by Christian parents,[41] Soyinka returned to Nigeria and found himself exploring new dramatic possibilities by conjoining Western tragic forms with the myths and rites of his native Yoruba tradition. In a way that is politically-engaged and contemporary while yet metaphysical in its claims,[42] Soyinka's plays explore how the destructive confrontation of his protagonists with inimical forces in their environments, resulting often in their individual disintegration, have at the same time a communal benefit, which is underwritten by the intimate involvement of divinities which (as he observed) bear close comparison with Nietzsche's Apollonian and Dionysian principles. The god Obatala suffers dismemberment; the god Ogun is a force of destructive reconfiguration. But the Obatala figure has a redemptive power precisely in the quality of his suffering endurance:

> Obatala is symbolically captured, confined and ransomed. So at every stage he is the embodiment of the suffering spirit of man, uncomplaining, agonized, full of the redemptive qualities of endurance and martyrdom.[43]

The human being who suffers disintegration in this way comes "to the very edge of consciousness when he feels completely isolated from the environment and from other people." Soyinka continues: "He undergoes intense suffering, after which he may be able 'to reassemble himself' through an act of will, or he may die." However, (and here we see the analogy with Williams' own argument that a larger communicative community can gainfully "hold" and "share" tragic loss and rupture):

> Whether the protagonist is alive or dead at the conclusion of the drama, his tragic experience itself is profitable both for his self-knowledge and for his people. Society benefits in different ways – the hero can bring the community to a new knowledge of itself, or he can display an exemplary moral courage in the face of social injustice.[44]

Soyinka's redefinition of tragedy in terms of an African worldview demonstrates how it can function as "a productive genre in the modern African world because of a definite, living tradition of myth and ritual,"[45] serving what he calls "the spiritual consolidation of the race," not least through its opening up of an affirmative attitude to death as in some respect a god-like experience.[46] His plays are examples of art *as*, rather than merely *about*, ritual.

Ritualized art is not, however, the preserve of the theater. In contemporary Detroit, for example, some remarkable initiatives have brought artists and people of various religious backgrounds together to give expression to collective mourning over what could be described as a "failed city."[47] The continuities with the ancient biblical genre of lamentation (and, in particular, laments over the destruction of Jerusalem after the Babylonian exile) are not lost on those involved in Detroit's crisis. Prominent as they are in Scripture, such texts of lament have a lively afterlife in liturgy and other ritual forms: they are, for example, frequently intoned during the stripping of the altars in Christian Holy Week rites.

FIGURE 5.2: *A Requiem for Douglass* (2015) by Oren Goldenberg. Photo credit: P.D. Rearick.

Lament may, then, be proposed (alongside excess) as a point of conversation between tragedy and modern religious thought. Lament is both a well-established tragic mode of utterance, and a religious one too. This demonstrates that there is nothing intrinsically inimical in religious practice to the adoption of a tragic register. One of the Detroit activists writes that although the "rebirth" of the city is often proclaimed in the name of a "concerted boosterism" that would be impatient of sounding a tragic note, the fostering of shared forms of lamentation helpfully foregrounds "the loss and suffering—the mourning and grieving, the demolition and displacement—underway as communities and lives dissipate and dissolve in the process [of such alleged 'rebirth']." The ritualizing of this tragic note re-binds some of what is under threat of dissolution, and thus—paradoxically—gives better grounds for hope than the assertively-optimistic bravado of the "boosters":

> Laments are ritual enactments of mourning and grief that admit more than what one individual or collective can comprehend. They frame events that we struggle to narrate or tell on our own. As such, they enable communities to name incalculable loss and to hope that a new way forward will be found. They instill resiliency by providing communities with resources for weaving new agency, identities and networks.[48]

The ritual of lamentation thus seems to offer a potentially rich locus for exchange between theological thinkers and a range of contemporary artists. The Latin Americans Doris Salcedo and Teresa Margolles are just two from among many recent examples of visual artists who are testing possibilities in this area. Margolles, a Mexican, has used her work *Plancha* (2010) to commemorate and mourn the anonymous victims of organized crime in her native country: the water used to wash their murdered bodies in the morgue (where she also works) drips from the ceiling onto hotplates which sends them disappearing with a sharp hiss into thin air (Figure 5.3). This acute evocation of their ephemerality (so that "their place shall know them no more"[49]) becomes paradoxically a holding them in being, because it is a focusing of attention on their passing. Salcedo, meanwhile, is a Colombian, and was the first artist to alter the physical fabric of the Turbine Hall at Tate Modern in London with her work *Shibboleth* (2007), a long concrete crack in the floor which sought to provoke reflection on the social, economic, and political fissures in modern global society (Figure 5.4). Much of her work, like that of Margolles, evokes the nameless victims of violence (often, in her case, of Colombia's long civil war). Works like *Unland: The Orphan's Tunic* (1997), *Atrabiliarios* (1992–2004), and *Plegaria Muda* (2008–10, in which living blades of grass "individualize" an array of superficially identical coffin-like structures by growing differently from within each one of them) are deliberately fashioned as "acts of memory" and thus—perhaps—as having some reparative potential in resisting a despairing amnesia. *Plegaria Muda* can be translated "silent prayer."

In parallel with such artistic explorations, there has been a burgeoning of scholarly interest in biblical forms of lament in recent years,[50] and in assessments of their theological importance.[51] Some scholars explicitly invoke the genre of tragedy as an aid to understanding and interpreting certain biblical texts,[52] like the Books of Kings (especially the narrative of Saul) and the Book of Job, as well as parts of Genesis[53] and (in the New Testament) of the Gospel of John.[54] Rebekah Eklund points out in her book *Jesus Wept* that even though the New Testament may proclaim an "inaugurated eschatology," in which God's vindication of his suffering people takes more concrete shape than before, the role of lament is "by no means diminished."[55] Indeed, in his utterances Christ himself (often echoing forms of lament in the Old Testament/Hebrew Bible) "embodies the full

FIGURE 5.3: Teresa Margolles. *Plancha (Hotplate)*, 2010. Installation: 10 heated steel plates, 1 dripping system, and a mix of water from the morgue used to wash corpses after their autopsy. Courtesy the artist and Galerie Peter Kilchmann, Zurich. Photo: Nils Klinge.

FIGURE 5.4: Doris Salcedo. *Shibboleth*. Turbine Hall, Tate Modern. 2007. Photographer: Gilberto Dobon/Wikimedia Commons.

pattern of lament." This is lament as "primarily ... a form of longing"—even of "protest."[56] The laments of Jesus ("in Gethsemane, at the tomb of Lazarus, and from the cross") "are the most significant form that lament takes in the New Testament." They are premised on the belief that there is a faithful God who listens, even in the face of terrible creaturely adversity. Lament is thus a mode in which human creatures "grasp and live into the reality of the new age."[57] This emphatically does not entail that grieving or sorrow has been eliminated by the resurrection; on the contrary, lament is "a Christian practice" as a form of perseverance and longing in the face of persistent suffering and evil.

To recall the discussion in previous sections of this chapter, one might say that, in Christian terms, a desire rapidly to assimilate loss to a greater good refuses either to take evil or in fact *goodness* seriously. Goodness in such cases becomes a function of human beings' powers of "making sense" and "moving on" rather than being something manifested supremely on Christ's cross—something which should more properly elicit from believers an attitude of penitential mourning as well as gratitude (and this being why, perhaps, Christian worship includes grief within its joy). Far from being anti-tragic, and concerned with the evasion or denial of tragic experience, the Christian narrative (including both Old and New Testaments) is about a full entry into such experience, in order then to suggest it might have a "beyond"—thus refusing to make an idol of the tragic moment.

Though she does not appeal explicitly to Christian doctrine in her essay "The Sublime and the Good," Iris Murdoch (writing in 1959) argues for a closely comparable outlook in the course of a double critique of Kant and Hegel. Kant's approach admits that humans find themselves confronted with an ungraspable excess in being (the infinite), but fails to locate this confrontation in the complex particularity of historical experience. Hegel locates all human knowing in the complex particularity of historical experience, but is so confident of its reconcilability in thought that he underplays the very ungraspability that Kant recognized. For Murdoch, a theory of *tragedy* would have served Kant much better than the theory of the sublime that he chose to develop. The problem is that he was too "afraid of the particular... afraid of history" to embrace it.[58] Tragedy is always concerned with "the most individual thing" (though in overwhelmingly ramifying networks of such "things," in which each "thing" has its own agency and there is "no prefabricated harmony") and for this reason, says Murdoch, tragedy is "the highest art."[59] It acknowledges the reality of what is other and unassimilable to one's own ends more faithfully than Kant's theory of the sublime, and it is thus also closely linked with the experience of love (in which in like fashion we encounter the reality of what is immeasurably other but in definite and particular forms). Once again, an affirmative note is struck here. As the cousin of love, tragedy's lessons presume an otherness in the face of which we ought not to give up with a sigh, as though all struggle is vain and pointless. The moments of defeat that are everywhere in history are not grounds for surrender, any more than they are susceptible of being bypassed or denied.

Murdoch is alive to the fragility of goodness, but argues that we must open ourselves to learning about its exaltedness from its very fragility. This will only happen if we give it our best attention. Those who resolutely countenance tragedy, she proposes, will learn something profound about what love is too. In analogous vein, the contemporary US theologian Andrew Prevot argues that precariousness is a necessary companion of praise. Precariousness, he shows, attends all *precation* (i.e., prayer in the form of supplication and entreaty)—and even doxology. The challenge here is to seek to contemplate and glorify "the divine wellspring of eternal freedom and love" without manifesting either hubris in one's "own conceptual formulations" or imperviousness to reality's horrors. Prevot asserts that the proper disposition of any Christian who seeks to glorify God is

> [A] doxology that is shot through with a piercing cry from the depths, a thunderous roar that bears the weight of the world's anguish and raises it up to God, as Jesus' psalmic voice does on the cross and as countless other sufferers have done throughout the ages.[60]

I set two goals for myself at the start of this chapter. The first was to challenge the widespread assumption that Christianity is intrinsically anti-tragic. This challenge is well opposed by Prevot's concept of "precarity" and the tradition of thought that undergirds it—for he speaks for a host of contemporary religious thinkers for whom the conversation of theology with tragic theory is a live one. My second goal was to challenge the idea that theological ideas are absent from modern and contemporary works of art. This, too, I hope to have combated with some measure of success. Towards the beginning of this chapter we looked at the fiction of Marilynne Robinson and Cormac McCarthy, noting how despite their differences both novelists exemplify the way in which religious concerns still animate very recent literature, perhaps especially when it asks large questions about the nature of suffering, the destiny of humanity, and what human beings ultimately owe to one another, to the planet, to the future (and, for some authors, to God). Ritual or ritual-like practice is a central theme in both novelists' work, as is the language of divinity (even if, as in *The Road*, it is apparently rendered hollow).

This presence of religious concerns, images, and language in two singularly successful mainstream novelists is not a freak event. As we have seen, it has a longer history in novelists of the late nineteenth century like Hardy and Dostoevsky, and the earlier twentieth century like O'Connor. It is widespread in other strands of the arts too. We have observed it in the poetry of Eliot, the plays of Beckett, Soyinka, and Kane, the films of Malick and von Trier, and the art of Goldenberg, Margolles, and Salcedo. It should barely need saying that these artists are not the servants of a niche religious market, nor are they glaringly anomalous in their concerns. It is more truthful to describe them, taken together, as the tip of a much larger iceberg. The concerns they both express and address have been widespread concerns in the modern period, and look likely to continue. Though variously indexed to existing religious discourses—sometimes more, sometimes less—the work of these artists is at multiple points susceptible to engagement with such discourses, and capable of both enriching and being enriched by them. In themes of resignation, consolation, excess, lament, and ritual, tragic consciousness and theological thought seem persistently to gravitate towards dialogue with one another, and the widespread presence of religious concerns, images, and language in the modern period seems typically to intensify when tragedy's themes of suffering, sin, and loss (whether of others or of oneself) are most the focus of exploration.

CHAPTER SIX

Politics of City and Nation

Tragic Politics and the Incommunicable Experience

TONY FISHER

Nothing could be more at odds with the spirit of tragedy than the forms of rationality that came to regulate the political experience of the twentieth century. It was this influential claim that George Steiner developed in his essay of 1961, announcing the "death of tragedy." "Tragedy," he wrote, "can occur only where reality has not been harnessed by reason and social consciousness."[1] Where one encounters the logistics of mass production and consumption, or the calculative rationality of the bourgeois individual, one will not find the tragic. Nor will one be able to locate the conditions necessary for the development of tragic drama in a culture predicated on a strict separation between the domains of private and public life—fertile ground for the novel, to be sure, but not the tragic stage. Still less can it be found in the totalitarian state, in the culture of austere uniformity laid bare by the horrors of both communism and fascism. It is with the advent of modernity that triumphant reason, with its espousal of secularism and materialism, first poisoned the socio-political ground where once tragedy found its spiritual home in the European *polis*, according to Steiner. In this sense, not even Christianity could kill off tragedy. What it took was the power of enlightenment, with its eviscerating light of reason, and the dispersal of every superstition and myth upon which the old cosmology that gave birth to tragedy was constructed.[2]

All the same, there is something quite counter-intuitive, not to say perverse, about Steiner's argument when one considers the political context of the twentieth century and what its political formations—liberal, corporatist, fascistic, or communist—unleashed.[3] Terry Eagleton's skepticism is entirely justified when he observes, rather witheringly, that for "obituarists of tragedy like George Steiner, only tragic world-views can finally sustain legitimately tragic works of art."[4] The circularity in the argument, pinpointed here by Eagleton, through which Steiner presented dogma as though it were an iron-clad law of poetic history, reveals not just a fallacy in his thinking but more importantly demonstrates the reductive nature of every exercise that pronounces a decision on what tragedy "really" is. "Tragedy is . . . not a single and permanent kind of fact," Raymond Williams once declared; one should reject the assumption that it possesses an "unchanging nature."[5] That said, I would like to hold onto the central motif of his argument, that in order to understand the place of the tragic within the twentieth century, one must also understand in what way it has "died." Or, if I may repurpose this idea by expanding on it a little: in order to understand the *politics* of the tragic during the last century, it is imperative to grasp in what sense the "tragic" belonged to the experience of the twentieth century as well as how that experience led theater to a rejection of "tragedy" or at least a certain conception of it.

Let us return briefly to the way in which Steiner understands tragedy. It is not in terms of the rules of its poetics that the concept finds its proper place in his argument but in light of a certain kind of experience that informs the development of its *Weltanschauung*. To understand tragic drama one "must start from the fact of catastrophe" because "Tragedy is irreparable."[6] However, this is not because tragedies "end badly." From Steiner's perspective, the reverse is true: they end badly because tragic experience trades in *what is fundamentally irreparable about our experience of the world*. To associate tragedy with the irreparable is to say that it resides in events that admit ultimately of no rational explanation: tragedy delivers us, not to the certitude of some pacific state of justice, but, at best, offers only momentary respite from the political turbulence that constantly assails us, our society, and our world. What irreparable tragedy discloses is that "the spheres of reason, order, and justice are terribly limited and that no progress in our sciences or technical recourses will enlarge their relevance."[7] It is not without irony, however, that we may remark on how, in proclaiming the death of tragedy, Steiner came closer than most to describing the "spirit of tragedy" insofar as it was realized through the radical experimentation that characterizes the twentieth-century theater. At the very moment he recoiled from it, the tragic nature of that theater loomed most vividly into view for him, and no more so than through the work of Samuel Beckett: "There are moments in *Waiting for Godot* that proclaim with painful vividness the infirmity of our moral condition: the incapacity of speech or gesture to countenance the abyss and horror of the times."[8] This "anti-drama," as he not entirely incorrectly described it, produced a "crippled and monotonous" theater: a "metaphysical *guignol*, a puppet show made momentarily fascinating or monstrous by the fact that the puppets insist on behaving as if they were alive."[9]

My approach in this chapter will strive to maintain a degree of fidelity with the rhetorical figure of the "death of tragedy," then. I do so, however, in order to redeploy Steiner's insight into the irreparable nature of the tragic, by directing it away from his narrative of cultural decline, towards understanding the political aspect of twentieth-century theater's refusal of tragedy. It is in the attempt to frustrate or circumvent its intended effects; to deny its overweening sense of cultural supremacy, promoted by tragic discourse of previous centuries; or to wrangle from tragedy and its poetics, or whatever it is that constitutes its internal law, an arguably less prescriptive and more open dramaturgical form, that I suggest radical modernity, to employ Williams' expression, is able to retain its own fidelity to the experience of the tragic in its own century. Only through the "death" of tragedy was the twentieth-century stage able to discover a relation to the tragic. Granted, it is by no means obvious that such a relation should be understood as a *political* relation. But it is a question of discerning in what way political experience of the twentieth century might be said to animate a range of theatrical responses, and how, in so doing, theater reconfigured the proper place, character, and meaning of "tragic experience" so that it was able to reflect the age of consumerist society, the global mobilization of productive forces, mechanized warfare, and mass slaughter on a previously unimaginable industrial scale, the trauma of the Holocaust, the violent struggles that were to reverse European colonial rule across the globe, and the dropping of the atomic bomb on Nagasaki and Hiroshima. Where "tragedy" permeated the experience of the century's various catastrophes, political crimes, and power struggles, theater responded not by producing "tragedies"—at least, not any constructed on the basis of past models. It sought instead to transform tragedy, to render it commensurate with a truth that had hitherto never confronted human beings before. What it discovered, through harrowing and ghastly lessons, was that the category of experience could itself unite with tragedy in enduring a kind of "death." This, I conclude, is one of the profoundest lessons that the theater of the twentieth century would teach its auditors about their own tragic experience.

TRAGIC EXPERIENCE AND TRAGEDY'S CLASSICAL "DISCOURSE"

A cursory glance at the copious literature on the subject shows that when it comes to understanding the term "tragic experience" there is no settled critical consensus on what is meant by it. Nor is there any agreement over what kind of event the term should be applied to. There are, as most critics would accept, such things as tragic experiences. We are all likely to have them at some point in our lives; we all get to know "tragedy" for ourselves. We do so either directly through some dolorous personal chapter or other we would rather forget, involving injury to ourselves or to a loved one, or we experience tragedy indirectly by acquaintance, or more distantly still through our mediated encounter with terrible misfortune, occurring in another part of the world, but transmitted straight into our homes and our lives. The news draws us, with inexorable predictability, into tragedy's dismal radius every time we turn it on. Tragedy is, in common parlance, the term we use to designate tumultuous events in which anyone might be unfortunate enough to get caught up. "For most people," Eagleton writes, "tragedy means an actual occurrence, not a work of art."[10] It can include events that possess historic breadth and scope, such as wars, famines, natural disasters, and revolutionary upheavals; but also, and more typically, it refers to a range of experiences that appear to us in rather more intimate and sequestered ways, those painful episodes that we call "private tragedies." The perennial question, particularly regarding the latter, is whether or not tragic *meaning* can be imputed to such everyday calamities. As harrowing as they may be, are those agonizing events that insinuate themselves into the experiences of common men and women properly-speaking tragic? Or do such events only become tragic once they have been "shaped" into art. More acutely still: can they ever attain that status or should certain experiences be discounted for failing to meet the criteria we assign to events that are tragic? Is it not the case that tragic experience is in fact rare? It is a moot point, indeed, whether common and quotidian suffering exhibits *any* of the sort of hubris whereby the actions of an average individual might reliably qualify as significant enough to be *staged* as a "tragedy." But this, as Eagleton points out, is to indulge another kind of fallacy: "that only in art can the value released by destruction be revealed; that real-life suffering is passive, ugly, and undignified, whereas affliction in art has an heroic splendour or resistance."[11] According to one viewpoint, in other words, it is the creative act that confers upon an event a "tragic sense" it does not possess in itself; according to another, tragedy implies something that transcends everyday experience altogether.[12]

It was in an attempt to tease apart the tangled threads of controversy, knotted together in this hoary dispute, that Raymond Williams wrote his book *Modern Tragedy*, describing at its outset, how we "come to tragedy by many roads. It is an immediate experience, a body of literature, a conflict of theory, an academic problem."[13] Williams' rejoinder to those who opted for a strict separation between "tragedy" and non-aesthetic forms of tragic experience was to observe that not only is it impossible to distinguish between an event and our "response" to it—by which he meant the transformation of the event into some "communicable form" by the act of conferring a tragic "meaning" upon it—but, more critically, that any attempt to do so is already to enact some form of exclusion.[14] There are, he argued, always ideological motives at play in such exclusions. But what exactly is put in play "ideologically" whenever the "habitual" distinction is made between tragedy and everyday suffering? For Williams, it is an ideology whose subtle effects conceal the power of those granted the right, by virtue of the privileges of education, or social standing, to decide what kind of suffering is "significant" (and thereby countable as worthy of the appellation "tragedy") and what should be set aside as "mere" common-or-garden suffering. What is concealed in such choices is, of course, implicitly a political decision since it points to the "deeper exclusion of all that suffering which is part of our social and political world, and its human relations."[15] The purposes behind such acts of concealment are never simply reducible to the niceties of "aesthetic" choices, since ultimately their effect, if not always explicit intent, is to separate "human agency from our understanding of social and political life."

The same ideological mechanism is discernible in the distinction of tragedy and accident. For to mark that discrepancy one must invoke "some conception of a law or an order" whereby one event can be described as the result of blind fate or chance, whereas the other designates a significant action through which an exceptional individual is destined to immortalize himself heroically in a valiant if futile struggle with the gods or whatever forbidding power he confronts. The problem is that this "law" of tragedy is wholly partial and always founded on the "alienation" of some aspect of social existence.[16] It provides the criterion for distinguishing the kinds of subject matter that are considered most appropriate to tragedy, apportioning worth to an honored few among us, while consigning the rest of humanity to the meritless drudgery of insignificant life. It is this law that makes tragic experience intelligible for the "*classical* discourse" on tragedy, as I shall call it here, and specifically insofar as its precise discursive function is to make legible such a division. According to classical discourse, tragedy derives its legitimacy directly from its dependence on the pre-assigned rank, reputation, and social prestige of the tragic hero. It is "rank" that acts as the discursive filter dividing "mere" suffering from the "tragic" kind of suffering. The classical law of tragedy is itself inscribed in a long history of social distinction, promoted first during antiquity, then forcefully reasserted during the neoclassical period, extending right up to the end of the nineteenth century, when it finally began to loosen its grip over the stage. To be sure, were one to trace in detail a comprehensive genealogy of this discourse, no doubt one would discover the different ways in which it responded to singular historical, economic, and political exigencies, that it is not "one thing" but rather more nuanced than I have implied here. Nevertheless, through its shifting emphases, one would still be able to discern what it was that the classical discourse on tragedy remorselessly sought to demonstrate to the theatrical public: that an immutable moral order lay behind tragedy's hierarchical distribution of social roles.

In this sense, what Eagleton condemns as the "far right wing of tragic theory" might be seen as the anachronistic extension of this older, more classical discourse. If tragic theory itself is otiose in the twentieth century, it is because tragic discourse had already been invalidated by tragic experience at its very outset. After all, as early as 1917, the convulsive tremors of war, reverberating across the battlefields of Flanders and crashing through the gates of the Winter Palace in St. Petersburg, had violently swept away the conventional presuppositions of the social order that underlay the dramaturgical apparatus that was central to the symbolic regime promoted by classical tragic discourse. That "hardly a word" of its definition of tragedy was "true" is in some senses irrelevant, although Eagleton is quite right to point out that it is demonstrably contradicted in practice.[17] Rather, what is decisive is how that classical discourse insinuated a politics into the very heart of tragedy; or, to be more specific, how it constructed a tragic "politicity"—a term derived from the French *politicité* and used here to specify the social dimension of art, rather than an inherent or explicit "politics" any work might promote. To understand the classical discourse of tragedy is to understand how that discourse sought to articulate tragedy through a complex of discursive relations, determined by wider social and political norms. For instance, to the guardians of tragedy in the classical age, it is quite unconscionable to think of endowing the common man with the power of persuasive or elevated speech. To give him the power of articulate "speech" would signify—culturally and politically—an act of leveling that would risk the collapse of all social distinction, threatening the very foundations of existing societal order. Thus, regardless of the actual politics promoted in any given play (and even in those cases where there is an apparent absence of politics) classical tragic discourse nevertheless ensured the playwright's conformity to the prescribed norms of tragedy, reflecting existing political considerations of theater and its social purpose. To simplify matters, let us say, broadly, that for the classical discourse, the social function of the tragic stage, and thus that which makes theater acceptable within a political community, was determined by the belief that it can influence the conduct of its auditors. Theater instructs by means of the moral deterrent. By showing the consequences of errant behavior tragedy produces a spectator who, having drawn a vicarious lesson after watching a dramatic representation in which some transgression is punished, will consequently be more likely to comply with the wider aims and norms of a well-governed state. To understand tragedy's "politicity" during the classical period is to understand how aesthetic experience was co-opted by a kind of governmental agenda that sought to press tragedy into the service of the state. How it did so was precisely through evolving an extended discourse that regulated tragedy both through its internal laws of construction, its "poetics," and in respect of its intended social effects: through both its *composition* and its *disposition*.[18]

THE TRAGIC EXPERIENCE OF THE COMMON MAN

In contrast, twentieth-century theater would seek to expurgate from the stage what it saw as the insipid moralizing infection spread by classical tragic discourse. Now, everything was to be redefined in an explicitly critical relation to what was considered most problematic about tragedy, changing not only how tragic experience was to be understood, but as a consequence, theater's approach to tragic form as a mode of representation. One of the century's most politically radical theater makers, Bertolt Brecht, would write: "It is not only moral considerations that make hunger, cold and oppression hard to bear."[19] For Brecht, theater's function would now no longer be simply to "arouse moral objections to such circumstances . . . but to discover the means for their elimination."[20] This critical process necessitated a fundamental reclassification of the category of the political in its relation to tragedy. In the first place, it is evident that twentieth-century theater marks an absolute break with the notion of the politicity of the tragic, as advocated by the classical discourse on tragedy. And with this break, the categories of order, rank, and hierarchy, previously often taken as invulnerable facts of life, would be viewed as not only belonging to a reactionary social edifice but also as contingent products of the historical process. It is not that the theater of the twentieth century no longer had an interest in questions of morality—as Brecht himself confirms—but that in order to emancipate itself from the constraints of bourgeois "discourse," those questions could no longer be posed in terms of an uncritical acceptance of the status quo. The consequences of this would be far-reaching, entailing not just the rejection of a discourse, but along with it, the nullification of the framework of laws and conventions that had previously governed tragedy, now viewed as being wholly inadequate to the new conditions of life. This is not to say that theater turned away from tragic experience, but rather that it discovered "tragedy" afresh; or rather, what it discovered as "tragic" now began to animate a novel critical spirit that stirred within tragic experience. Experience itself would testify to the profoundly irreconcilable nature of modern life. It is experience that speaks, after all, directly and with lived immediacy, of the contradiction between public morality and the values of the new age, but above all—and for this very reason—it is the experience of the common man that would finally come to the fore.

In his essay "Tragedy and the Common Man," Arthur Miller demanded precisely this kind of fundamental revision of tragedy, pointing to its anachronistic character for a democratic age: "It is time . . . that we who are without kings, took up this bright thread of our history and followed it to the only place it can possibly lead in our time—the heart and spirit of the average man." For Miller, such a reappraisal of tragic discourse would open up the way to an altogether different kind of tragedy, not its wholesale rejection: "I believe that the common man is as apt a subject for tragedy in its highest sense as kings were."[21] Had Freud, after all, not brought Oedipus the king down to the level of the everyman, insofar as each and every person (at least if he was male) was seen to embody him in the form of a "complex"? Still, how are we to reconcile the claim that the common man is fit for tragedy in its *highest* sense" if the criterion of rank, which conferred that status upon it in the first place, is to be dismissed? It is here that the radicalism that permeates Miller's reworking of tragedy begins to emerge. To pinpoint that radicalism more precisely: if Miller's plays retain, at least in outward appearance, the semblance of classical tragic form, they do so in quite a deceptive sense, for there is little that is "classical" about them. What they reject are the two basic axioms of classical discourse: the idea that tragedy ennobles by virtue of the status or rank of the hero and the purpose to which tragedy should be put in punishing the hero's transgression.

Willy Loman, the hero of Miller's *Death of a Salesman*, for example, is neither a man of noble birth, nor does his "tragic" fate act as a moral exemplar to the audience. Miller has no desire to influence the audience at the level of individual moral conduct as, say, George Lillo did when justifying his use of a common apprentice as the hero of his tragic drama *The London Merchant* (1731).[22] So, in what sense can such a play be classified as a "tragedy"? I would like to suggest two possible ways of addressing this question. The first is to say that Miller discards notions of criteria, as inadequate to the experience of tragedy, choosing instead to derive his own tragic theater from a different kind of authority—one that I think in many ways reflects the approach of twentieth-century theater makers in general. Tragedy on stage derives its power not from the conventional instruction of aesthetics, or from a "poetics," but from the existential dimension of lived tragic experience itself—an experience that explodes the prescriptions of poetic form and releases the stage from its domination by "discourse." Thus to speak of the tragedy of the *common* man is precisely to place his *actual* experience *above* that of aesthetic experience. Tragic feeling has nothing to do with rank per se, but with "the disaster inherent in being torn away from our chosen image of what or who we are in this world."[23] The disaster that Miller writes about here is one that invokes our profoundest existential fears: it threatens who we are and how we are perceived by others in the world. It is not the nobleman but "the common man who knows this fear best."[24]

In this way, tragic experience, which once evoked an immutable moral order, now becomes associated with constantly shifting and uncertain values that undercut the subject; it appears in the form of an experience of what is incommensurable and ambiguous about our lives and it attests to our inability to reconcile ourselves to its contradictions. It is this incommensurability that Loman embodies, appearing in the play in the form of an overwhelming subjective crisis, which will lead him down the path of eventual suicide. Loman, as Miller puts it at one point, is "looking for his selfhood."[25] And what prevents him from finding it is the world he inhabits—the contemporary world of the salesman. Loman's fantasy encounters during the play with his (now-deceased) brother Ben reveals just to what extent Loman is an internally divided subject. Ben represents what might have been if only Loman, at least in his own mind, had been a "better" version of himself and therefore he appears as an alienated part of Loman, a troubling manifestation that reinforces the sense of incoherence into which he has descended. This is not, however, reducible to a psychological state, or "inner" conflict, but is a function of Loman's social alienation. In this first exchange, Loman is told the story of how his brother, seeking his fortune in the new frontiers of Alaska, ended up (by traveling south rather than north) in the jungles of Africa. "William," Ben intones, in a supercilious reflection on his own success, "when I walked into the jungle, I was seventeen. When I walked out I was twenty-one. And, by God, I was rich!"[26] Where Willy admires his brother's exploits, and measures his own failure in relation to the wealth his brother apparently acquired, what he fails to appreciate—owing to this state of ideological misrecognition—is that he too has entered a jungle, and it is one that is far more barbaric and cruel than any found in Africa. Ben's tawdry advice to Loman's son, Biff, never to "fight fair with a stranger" as "[you'll] never get out of the jungle that way,"[27] is advice Willy is himself incapable of hearing or following. If he is a tragic figure, it is because he is very much a victim of the cut-throat, treacherous world he inhabits.

A different relation of the tragic to the political emerges in Miller's reworking of tragedy. Loman stands before us not as a cautionary tale to be avoided, but as an allegorical reflection of our own alienated being, our entrapment within the systemic processes of work, value, and consumption that we are incessantly compelled to participate in, in order to survive. It is precisely because he is not a political figure, but man represented in a kind of pre-political state of self-alienation, only partially aware of his actual economic condition, that Loman—in all his ferocious yet inchoate fury and frustration—comes to possess political significance for us. In a symposium on the play, held in 1958, Martin Dworkin described *Death of a Salesman* as a "frightening social criticism" without thereby being "propaganda."[28] It is "political" not because it openly advertises its political affiliations or acts as a vehicle for propagandistic slogans but because of what Loman reveals about our own condition. The figure of the salesman, after all, enshrines the ambiguous position of the everyman under late capitalism. The salesman, as Dworkin remarks, exists "out in space, completely divorced from the fundamental productive processes which manufacture the merchandise that he is selling, not quite the friend and not quite the enemy, and not quite the instrument of the people to whom

FIGURE 6.1: Dustin Hoffman (as Willy Loman) and John Malkovich (as Biff Loman) in a staged-for-television version of *Death of a Salesman*, 1985. © CBS Photo Archive/Getty Images.

he is selling; somehow, this strange intermediary must sell himself in order to sell things."[29] In confronting his own inevitable prospect of defeat, Loman brings into view the facticity of the world that fundamentally limits any notion we might entertain of possessing an unconditional freedom of choice. In this sense, the optimism or "positive value" that Miller himself ascribes to the play is itself somewhat misplaced, or at least belied by his own anti-hero. When Biff, in his confrontation with his father toward the end of the play (Figure 6.1), insists: "I am not a leader of men, Willy, and neither are you ... I'm one dollar an hour," crushing reality finally breaks into the world of the play; its dramaturgical effect is to invert the traditional priority that dramatic action has over the event that theater stages, as a crisis to be resolved in the world.[30]

Or rather than inverted, let us say, instead, that the order of the event is itself displaced "dramaturgically," and in its place what rises to prominence is the insuperable *fact* of the non-event: it is the fact of the world that is *lived* and in being lived is transformed into a facticity that no tragic hero can either master or escape. On the contrary, it renders him prostrate, perpetually at its disposal; he is indisposed by it in his very being. The German philosopher Martin Heidegger once provided a description of the peculiar existential condition of modern man that captures this tragic dimension of experience as it emerged with the modern consciousness of facticity. "Man," he wrote, "is that inability to remain and is yet unable to leave his place."[31] In being "thrown" into the possibilities of existence, our very being (what Heidegger termed our "Dasein"—literally our "being there" in the world) is constantly "exiting from itself" yet can only exit into the world as it is given to us.[32] The very word "experience" covertly signals this act of being a "thrown-project" (*ex*-perience), through which we are "destined" as finite beings to "ex-ist" *out there in the world*, as Heidegger describes it; what we are not, according to this definition of experience, is that autonomous subject, as imagined by the classical discourse of the Enlightenment, possessed of "free will." In being destined to the world, man is inescapably *"subjected* to what is actual." Yet even here, at the very heart of our subjection to the world, incommensurability threatens to rent our experience of being-in-the-world; let us say, it takes the tragic form of an irrelationality that opens up as the contradictory space we are compelled to inhabit between what "is there" and what we believe is *possible*.[33] Loman himself cuts a strangely intoxicated figure, prey to a kind of delirium, which to Biff appears to be nothing more than a "phony dream."[34] The problem for Loman is that he is held suspended in the impossible state of being both possessed and dispossessed simultaneously by the dimension of his own factical situation, in his being *disposed of* by a world that renders him nothing but a "contemptuous, begging fool."[35] The tragic aspect emerges in the underlying sense of "wrong" that has rendered Loman so supine in the face of incommensurable experience; or rather it is in this *consciousness* of having been wronged that Loman fully reveals the tragic dimension of incommensurable experience: that it is *irreparable*. What Loman endures, or profoundly suffers—as Miller describes it—is the "wound of indignity," where the tragic sense arises as "the consequence of a man's total compulsion to evaluate himself justly."[36] In other words, for Loman, it is in his dogged pursuit of realizing that subjective compulsion that he is ultimately defined as a tragic character insofar as it is this very compulsion that puts him at odds with the world; his self-evaluation is utterly incommensurable with the objective reality he faces, which remains coldly indifferent to the fact of his existence.

The second *reclassification* of tragedy at work in Miller pertains to the wider purpose of the theater. This is revealed in Miller's response to criticisms leveled at *Death of a Salesman*, and in particular that Willy Loman could not be construed as a "tragic character." John Beauford remarked: "I think that [Loman] is a sad character. I think that he is a vicious character. The trouble with Willy Loman . . . is that he never starts with any ideals to begin with . . . He has no moral values at all." Those values are "love of country, religious principles, and ethical values." It is for this reason, Beauford concludes, "I just can't accept Willy Loman as the average American citizen."[37] What Beauford fails to appreciate—and in this way he misapprehends the play—is that those established values are exactly what *Death of a Salesman* opposes itself to, just as Loman, in refusing to "accept his lot," finds himself eventually opposed to the values that constitute the "stable cosmos" that so degrades him. Miller remarks: "From this total questioning of what has previously been unquestioned, we learn. And such a process is not beyond the common man. In revolutions around the world, these past thirty years, he has demonstrated again and again this inner dynamic of all tragedy."[38] This is not to say that "tragedy must preach revolution" but that the "tragic view" concerns man's need "to wholly realize himself" in the face of intransigent reality. It is not the audience's moral edification that Miller's tragedy aims at but to critically disclose for them those forces that prevent the common man from achieving his full human potential—and it is for this reason that Miller asserts that "drama . . . is not so much an attack but an exposition, so to speak, of the want of value."[39] Tragedy's function, in other words, is not to prescribe a form of behavior or influence the conduct of men so that they might be better citizens, but to *expose* the forms of power that lie behind such prescriptions in the first place.

IRREPARABLE EXPERIENCE AND THE CRISIS OF THE SUBJECT

Where Miller locates tragic experience in the form of a subjective crisis, experienced as the incommensurability that exists between man's ideals and his factical world, a more radical dramaturgical response to the unfolding catastrophe of the twentieth century discovers the "tragic" in the crisis of the subject as such. In marked contrast to Miller, here we encounter a profoundly skeptical attitude to the question of whether human freedom amounts to anything more than a cruel deception—a "swindle," in the words of the German philosopher Theodor Adorno, perpetrated on "humanity" by the Enlightenment. For this more radical viewpoint, "tragic experience" cannot be rendered adequate to that which is irreparable, traumatic, and cataclysmic, without first acknowledging the very inadequacy of the category of experience itself, with its foundation in the bourgeois concept of the individual. Writing in the decades immediately following the Second World War, Adorno would argue that, while "[m]odern history begins with the discovery of the individual," nevertheless that history has "its shadowy side, namely the *crisis* of the individual."[40] Moreover, it is a crisis that had, with the arrival of the twentieth century, "assumed extreme forms."[41] What modernity produces is a counterfeit freedom, a masquerade for what is in fact a real lack of freedom. Through ever-increasing processes of bureaucratization, whose objective effect is to reduce people to "the status of functions," and through a correlative subjective process, under conditions of modern consumerism—where our "addiction to consumption" leads to mass conformism—what grows is an *indifference* to freedom.[42] Both processes give the lie to the bourgeois notion of the autonomous individual. More fundamentally, after Auschwitz, Adorno contends, "not only every positive doctrine of progress but also even every assertion that history has a meaning has become problematic and affirmative." And he goes on to add: "[e]ven if the murder of millions could be described as an exception and not the expression of a trend (the atom bomb), any appeal to the idea of progress would seem absurd given the scale of the catastrophe."[43] Where once philosophers such as Kant and Hegel could argue that history moved in the "direction of freedom," the holocaust(s) of the twentieth century "[make] all talk of progress towards freedom seem ludicrous. The concept of the autonomous human subject is refuted by reality."[44] The political, aesthetic—and indeed fundamental *human*—task confronting us is, for Adorno, to fully penetrate the nature of this crisis and its catastrophic consequences, since not to do so is to become complicit in reproducing the same conditions that made it possible in the first place: "A human being who is not mindful at every moment of the potential for extreme horror at the present time must be so bemused by the veil of ideology that he might as well stop thinking at all."[45]

In a similar vein, the German political philosopher Hannah Arendt would argue that "[u]nthinking men are like sleepwalkers."[46] Reflecting on the trial in Jerusalem of Adolf Eichmann, she would write, evil is the result "not [of] stupidity but thoughtlessness." It is unthinking men who are responsible for the political evils of the age. "Bad people," Arendt wrote, "are *not* 'full of regrets'" for a person who is incapable of examining himself in "silent intercourse" is someone quite capable of "committing any crime, since he can count on its being forgotten the next moment."[47] Although Eichmann's "deeds were monstrous," the man himself was "quite ordinary, common place, and neither demonic nor monstrous."[48] This thought gives rise to the troubling question posed by recent history, according to Arendt: "Is evil-doing . . . possible in default of not just 'base motives' ... but any motives whatever, of any particular prompting of interest or volition?"⁴⁹ Hence, it is the utter absence or relinquishment of any critical, independent consciousness that lies behind the "banality of evil," in Arendt's famous expression.

The task for radical art, confronted by such barbarity—a task simultaneously political and aesthetic—revolves around the question of how to resist this tendency of modernity toward murderous "thoughtlessness." For this same reason, it becomes imperative for art to bear witness to the "extreme, unprecedented, exorbitant horror," as Adriana Cavarero has recently described it, that modernity unleashes and thus to the "ontological crime[s]" of our age.⁵⁰ Indeed, we can begin to understand how the intolerable violence perpetrated during the twentieth century, with its concentration camps, genocides, and industrial-scale slaughter, relocates "tragic experience" within the experience of the *victims* of that violence. What is unique to this "scene" of horror is that it is "entirely tilted toward unilateral violence. There is no symmetry, no parity, nor reciprocity"—only an omnipotent power, dedicated to the production of the total degradation of the living being.⁵¹ But it is also precisely because it aims at the total destruction of the victim that any talk of "tragic experience" now runs up against an apparently insuperable paradox, which Cavarero draws out in a discussion of Primo Levi's autobiographical account of the Holocaust, *The Drowned and the Saved*: "The only real witness, whom Levi calls the integral witness, is he who has gone to the heart of the horror. But 'those that did so, those who saw the Gorgon, have not returned to tell about it or have returned mute'. . . ."⁵² Recalling from Greek mythology that whoever saw the Gorgon was immediately turned into stone, we can begin to understand how paradoxical representation is in its relation to what is truly "irreparable" about the tragic experience of the twentieth century—for irreparable experience is an experience that lies beyond the reach of the consolations of philosophy or art, and which communicates the relinquishment of hope and the abandonment of man whose shattered subjectivity attests only to a state of utter desolation and ruin. In this sense, we would have to draw a critical limit in relation to Williams' understanding of tragedy, for whom the "irreparable" was seen as a step too far.⁵³ While for him, the concentration camp could indeed provide "an image of an absolute condition, in which man is reduced, by man, to a thing," nevertheless, he objected to the idea that it *should* be used as such an image, particularly in defining tragedy, since to do so amounted to a form of blasphemy: "For while men created the camps, other men died, at conscious risk, to destroy them . . . ."⁵⁴ For such a bleak viewpoint, all that tragedy can reveal "is the fact of evil as inescapable and irreparable,"⁵⁵ thereby negating a more "optimistic" vision of tragedy based on the idea that the very fact of human agency meant that it was always possible to change the course of events. After all, where evil arises, men and women are (and have always been) prepared to die in order to defeat it. While the latter is of course true, it is a moot point whether, in denying the dimension of the irreparable, Williams did not also deny himself the possibility of fulfilling his ambition to try to "understand and describe . . . the tragic experience of our time"⁵⁶—and not least because in so doing he was led precisely to overlook the lacuna of experience as revealed by the century's production of that utterly forsaken figure, the "total victim" of the camps. These were those starving and forsaken figures—the "husk-men," of whom Levi wrote, when describing the camp's "drowned [who] form the backbone of the camp, an anonymous mass, continually renewed and always identical, of non-men who march and labor in silence, the divine spark dead in them, already too empty to really suffer";⁵⁷ Italian philosopher Giorgio Agamben designates them "the non-living . . . the being whose life is not truly life."⁵⁸ Reflecting on the disquieting ontological status of the extreme figure of the victim—of those whose descent into horror meant crossing the "threshold between the human and the inhuman"[59]—Agamben also describes the tragic paradox lying at the heart of irreparable experience (as revealed by the extermination camps) when he writes, in reference to Primo Levi's account:

> The "true" witnesses, the "complete witnesses", are those who did not bear witness and could not bear witness ... They have no "story", no "face", and even less do they have "thought." Whoever assumes the charge of bearing witness in their name knows that he or she must bear witness in the name of the impossibility of bearing witness.[60]

If we wish to understand the emergence, within twentieth-century theater, of a radically distinct concept of the tragic, we must attend to the paradox raised by Agamben. How does a representational art form such as the theater "bear witness" to that which escapes experience? To be sure, this lacunary problem of experience, as Agamben describes it, is not exclusively revealed by the Holocaust. Walter Benjamin had already observed the fundamental impoverishment of experience in the aftermath of the First World War: "Was it not noticeable," he wrote, "at the end of the war that men returned from the battlefield grown silent—not richer, but poorer in communicable experience."[61] What those men had seen, and endured on the killing fields of Western Europe, could no longer be conveyed in speech. Yet what had contradicted experience so fundamentally really owed its existence to the temperament of modernity itself: it was produced by those forces that had, by the beginning of the twentieth century, thoroughly infiltrated all aspects of social life, and revealed themselves brutally on the battlefields of Ypres and the Somme:

> Never has experience been contradicted more thoroughly than strategic experience by tactical warfare, economic experience by inflation, bodily experience by mechanical warfare, moral experience by those in power. A generation that had gone to school on a horse-drawn streetcar now stood under the open sky in a countryside in which nothing remained unchanged but the clouds, and beneath these clouds, in a field of force of destructive torrents and explosions, was the tiny, fragile human body.[62]

The annihilation of experience, then, is not limited to—and still less is it *causally explained* by—the catastrophe of the Holocaust, or the traumas of the First World War, or the dropping of the atomic bomb on Hiroshima—albeit the incalculable degree of barbarism characterizing those events represent the extreme threshold by which the phenomenon becomes most visible. Indeed, Agamben would go so far as to argue that today "humdrum daily life in any city will suffice. For modern man's average day contains nearly nothing that can still be translated into experience."[63] What is implied here is by no means meant to equate the horrors of war or genocidal murder with the banalities of quotidian life; it is simply to point to the general tendency of modernity and its fundamentally expropriative character—in other words, that it is precisely in the expropriation of experience that everyday alienations (see, for example, Figure 6.2) reveal the subtle effects of modernity's *impoverishment* of experience:

> Modern man makes his way home in the evening wearied by a jumble of events, but however entertaining or tedious, unusual or commonplace, harrowing or pleasurable they are, none of them will have become experience. It is this non-translatability into experience that now makes everyday existence intolerable—as never before—rather than an alleged poor quality of life or its meaninglessness compared with the past (on the contrary, perhaps everyday existence has never been so replete with meaningful events).[64]

FIGURE 6.2: Japanese salarymen. Tokyo, 1980s. © Robert Wallis/Panos Pictures.

Nevertheless, it is, without doubt, in relation to the appearance of the total victim, more than anywhere else, that the paradox of the incommunicability of experience, of its fundamental irreparability, most starkly discloses itself as a *problem for tragic art*. In other words, if the specific character of tragic experience for radical modernity can no longer be said to be appropriately represented by the actions of a hero, but instead takes its orientation from the appearance of modernity's anonymous victims, then how is it possible to represent tragic experience at all? It was this problem that Adorno had in mind when he asserted that it was "barbaric to continue to write poetry after Auschwitz."[65] What he meant by this, as he went on to explain, was that literature must "not surrender to cynicism merely by existing after Auschwitz."[66] On the contrary, for art to be possible in the wake of such barbarism, it required the kind of radical wakefulness, mentioned earlier, to the ever-persistent possibility of horror. Adorno makes the point by citing Pascal's aphorism, "On ne doit plus dormir" ("Sleeping is no longer permitted"), which—he says—should be "secularised." Only art works of "uncompromising radicalism" are able to attest to the suffering of the victim—indeed, "hardly anywhere else does suffering still find its own voice, a consolation that does not immediately betray it."[67] The problem remains—and once again the paradox reasserts itself—that the "awareness of affliction ... also demands the continued existence of the very art it forbids."[68] The dangers of inattentiveness, at this historical conjuncture, Adorno writes, is that "the victims are turned into works of art, tossed out to be gobbled up by the world that did them in."[69] For such works, the victim becomes a victim twice-over: in being produced in the first place as an object to be disposed of, and then in being reproduced as a victim in art as an object for the consumption of the spectator. What this paradox invokes, more specifically, is a crisis *for* representational art, for the very reason that mimetic art, as Adorno designates it, cannot but hover over the "abyss of its opposite."[70] This is not the same thing as saying that one *cannot* represent the horrors or atrocities of war, but only that in mimetically reconstructing them, one cannot assign to such images any ethical injunction, no matter how much one wishes them to affirm "humanity" in the face of evil, or to invest those images with a sense of moral outrage. In reproducing horror, the mimetic image confers, once again, a "meaning" on that which should be unthinkable. In so doing, what was once unthinkable becomes transfigured into that which can be thought and countenanced; and thus through the mimetic reproduction of atrocity, "something of its horror is removed."[71] There is, for this reason, something fundamentally heteronomous about the mimetic image that threatens art with complicity in the production of possible future victims. This is one of Adorno's fundamental objections to what the French philosopher, Jean-Paul Sartre, had termed "committed" literature—those works that wear their political affiliations on their sleeve, but whose "dreary metaphysics ... affirms the horror." Adorno writes: "when even genocide becomes cultural property in committed literature, it becomes easier to continue complying with the culture that gave rise to the murder."[72]

The solution to this dilemma, for Adorno, if one dare put it in such terms, can only be adequately developed by a different, non-appropriative, and non-representational approach to the experience of the victim. It is encapsulated in what he called the "autonomous" work of art. An autonomous work stands in a twofold relation to the reality it problematizes: first, insofar as it embodies a critical detachment from the social world from which it distances itself, through an "ahermeneutic" gesture that frustrates "meaning." In frustrating meaning, or what we might call "armchair readability," it becomes "autonomous" in its refusal to be co-opted at the level of aesthetic form, where instead it appears to be "difficult" or "obscure." It derives its power, in other words, from formal intransigence in the face of society's demand that it reveals its "message" with all the self-evidence and facileness of an advertising catchphrase. Second, an artwork is autonomous insofar as it remains "detached from empirical reality" at the same time as it is "mediated by [that] reality." In other words, to understand the autonomous work is to see it precisely *in relation to* the world of which it is still a "part," even if it is a part that introduces a "negation" into the domain of what would otherwise constitute a totalization of meaning—the tendency to totality characterizes what Adorno termed the "administered world." It is in its very gesture of refusing meaning, something that fundamentally differentiates it from the committed work, that the autonomous work of art reveals its critical relation to such an administered world. By means of rejecting "the gesture of addressing the listener" with a "message," the autonomous work enacts a kind of political refusal, while the committed work, despite being politically radical, cannot but find itself "accommodated" to the world, and in that accommodation, complicit in its illusions.[73] Thus, although Adorno wrote that "[now is] not the time for political works of art," this statement does not entail that autonomous works are somehow "apolitical." On the contrary, "politics," he observed, "has migrated into autonomous works of art, and it has penetrated more deeply into works that present themselves as politically dead."[74]

In his *Aesthetic Theory*, Adorno was to expand on this rejection of an explicitly political approach to art by arguing: "The acute reason today for the social inefficiency of artworks—those that do not surrender to crude propaganda—is that in order to resist the all-powerful system of communication they must rid themselves of any communicative means that would perhaps make them accessible to the public." Artworks take effect not "by haranguing" their audiences, but rather more subtly, through the "scarcely apprehensible transformation of consciousness."[75] One can see the distance that autonomous art takes from works that adhere to the Aristotelian vision of tragic catharsis—the social effect of art as promoted by classical tragic discourse, described by Adorno as "an ally of repression."[76] With Adorno's theory of the autonomous work, what one finds is the articulation of a new "politicity" of the tragic image. Such works refuse to offer the "surrogate satisfaction[s]" served up to the public by the culture industry, and in that refusal, a distinct kind of antagonism can be discerned that testifies to what Adorno described as the "social truth content" of the work.[77] It is important to note that, according to Adorno, one finds this social truth content not in the work of explicitly political theater makers such as Brecht, who at best "preaches to the converted," but in the work of Beckett. In Brecht's theater, what Adorno calls the "process of aesthetic reduction"—the experimental attitude of Brecht's aesthetics that permits him to oppose the "illusory stance of empathy and identification" associated with the bourgeois stage—itself suffers from the limitations imposed by the dictates of "didactic *poésie*." The very process he "undertakes for the sake of political truth works against political truth."[78] For Adorno, Brecht oversimplifies reality, "disdaining" its complex play of mediations. His attempt to distill the essence of social contradiction in a kind of abridged dialectical image or social gesture falsifies the social truth it aims to reveal. Thus, Brecht's acerbic attack on fascism in his "parable" *Arturo Ui* (1941), for instance, overlooks the historical fact that German fascism was a "conspiracy of the highly placed and powerful" in order to trivialize it in the comically digestible form of a "silly gangster organisation." In this way, writes Adorno, the "true horror of fascism is conjured away; fascism is no longer the product of the concentration of social power but rather an accident, like misfortunes and crimes."[79] Brecht's attempt to ridicule fascism leads him to distort the experience of fascism. The paradoxical effect of this technique is that it suspends the "efficacy" of the political theater precisely at the level of its message by presenting an oversimplified image of reality in which no one can believe.

What plays such as Beckett's *Endgame* or *Happy Days* practice is a rather different kind of "aesthetic reduction." Think, for example, of the bleakly absurd and unforgiving landscape of *Happy Days*, and the "scorched grass" of the mound in which Winnie is buried, trapped beneath a remorselessly blazing sun. It is not just that such an image seems to pre-empt the threats of global warming, but rather that it presents, in reduced form, the spiritual desolation of a denuded humanity whose struggle is merely to survive (Figure 6.3). Beckett's characters all seem to follow a path that leads to a "survival minimum as the minimum of existence remaining."[80] Certainly, to describe these plays as tragedies or comedies would seem inappropriate. Beckett defies categorization. In offering a vision of the tragic destitution of humanity in the twentieth century, his plays—at least according to Adorno—"bear witness to a state of consciousness that no longer admits the alternative of seriousness or lightheartedness, nor the composite tragi-comedy."[81] As such, Beckett's plays testify to the irreparable experience of modernity in ways that overtly political theaters, such as Brecht's or Sartre's, cannot hope to convey.

We find Adorno's imperative to be ever mindful of the possibility of extreme horror in the images of "worldlessness" which Beckett's theater invokes.[82] What Beckett marks is a startling point of convergence where a new kind of aesthetic experience, neither obviously political in its discourse, nor emptily formalist in its aesthetic reductions, was able to

FIGURE 6.3: Beckett's *Happy Days*, directed by Deborah Warner at Bam Harvey Theater, New York City. January 2008. © Hiroyuki Ito/Getty Images.

testify to the disintegration of the sovereignty of the subject. It was in the most radical drama of the twentieth century that the "crisis of the subject" was recognized in a new kind of "tragic" theater, which—in embracing the irreparability of the category of experience—captured thereby the "tragic sense" of the irreparable. While it is an approach that has been identified with the theater of Samuel Beckett—perhaps Beckett first and foremost—it can be discerned also in the theater that came after Beckett: in the theater of Peter Handke, Heiner Müller, or Sarah Kane, for instance. In his short theatrical text *Waterfront Wasteland Medea Material, Landscape with Argonauts*, Müller borrowed not only from Euripides but also from T.S. Eliot's modernist masterpiece *The Wasteland*, from both its desolate vision of modern life and its technique of textual fragmentation and quotation:

> The theatre of my death
> Was opening as I stood in between the mountains
> In the circle of dead companions on the stone
> And above me the airplane appeared as anticipated
> Without thinking I knew
> This machine was
> What my grandmother had called God
> The air pressure swept the corpses from the plateau
> And shots rang out into my tottering escape
> I felt MY blood flow out of MY veins
> And MY body metamorphose into the landscape of
> MY death.[83]

It is in this kind of radical "anti theater," I think, that the "tragic sense" of the age is perhaps most fully realized. To be sure, what the irreparability of experience signifies for dramatists such as Beckett and Müller is thus irreducible to "tragedy" as such, although not indifferent to it. What their radical experiments in dramaturgy uncover and make painfully apparent, I would suggest, is a different kind of "tragic sense." It is a sense of the "tragic" that can only be disclosed *beyond* tragedy, and where the "death of tragedy" is transfigured, as in Müller's "theatre of my death," into a theater capable of testifying to the death of the category of the subject. This is how we might read these lines of Müller's, and his "post tragic theatre"—as attesting to the tragic paradox of a subject who can no longer bear witness to the horror of the obliteration of his or her own experience.

CHAPTER SEVEN

Society and Family

Vibrant Affiliations

KÉLINA GOTMAN

The marriage industry today is estimated to be worth £10 billion ($13 billion) annually in the UK alone and, according to some estimates, $300 billion worldwide, employing 500,000 businesses and 750,000 people in the United States. Much of this economy is increasingly attributed to web platforms and digital apps, aiding in the colossal task of family and social organizing.[1] At the same time, activists across the LGBTQIA spectrum have championed legal recognition of trans partnerships and gay marriage, while couples of all sexes are finding an ever wider array of methods for delaying and otherwise reorganizing the biological matter of childbirth, from pronuclear transfer, enabling a "three-parent" baby to be born from the fertilization of a mother and a donor's egg with a father's sperm, to the now widely practiced, though still expensive, process of embryonic cryopreservation (egg freezing). Egg sale for stem cell research is wrapped into a wide neocolonial network of trans-border exploitation typically involving women from poorer backgrounds.[2] Added to this, sizable expenditures and inheritance disputes regarding pets and other companion species, especially dogs, complicate any perceived primacy of the "human" in the familial realm.[3] "Family" and "society" have never, it seems, been more intricately intertwined—legally, affectively, and culturally—nor have they been so open to renegotiation.

This chapter proposes to interrogate some of the ways family and society have been and continue to be imagined in the cultural history of tragedy in the twentieth and twenty-first centuries. Tragedy, after all, is an art form that has long taken the "family" as its core unit for organizing and disorganizing power politics. Family is at once the conservator of normality and the site within which practices of normality are splayed apart. In the modern age, roughly from 1920 to the present, tragedy is also increasingly mapped onto a cultural history of warfare and the daily display of "tragic" death and disorder across media. With unprecedented migration, worldwide retrenchment of social services disproportionately affecting women and men at the end of life, as well as children and young people; and ever widening wealth inequalities, involving the systematization of untenable employment precarity, we have to account for and to imagine new biosocial configurations—and new forms of "tragedy"—better to protect and honor the most vulnerable.

These are what I call vibrant affiliations: affiliations, within and beyond the nuclear family, that enable vibrant life. Not only do these affiliations reconfigure the Greek legacy of "tragedy" on the theatrical stage, reimagining a system of representation some critics have seen as elitist and non-democratic.[4] Vibrant affiliations also reawaken what may be broadly construed as the Dionysian foundations of ancient tragedy. According to Terry

Eagleton, Dionysus is "Janus-faced," a "principle of unity and individuation, identity and difference, breaching boundaries in the name of communal bliss yet also, as the god of progress and evolution, summoning us to autonomous existence." The Dionysian is at once destructive and world-bearing. And while the Dionysian may be structured dramaturgically by Apollonian principles of harmony, Dionysianism ultimately represents an effervescent force of life.[5] In this view, the "family" is not only a microcosm of hierarchical society or a universal principle of law and order but a pliable and complicated form continually reconfiguring "society." The "family" represents a tragic principle of Dionysianism: it refuses to be contained just as it operates as a container. Thus it is at this border zone—between the "family" and "society"—that discourses on modern tragedy meet what philosopher Gilles Deleuze and activist anti-psychiatrist Félix Guattari have described in terms of the *socius* or "social body." The *socius* is a complex system of political, institutional, and affective flows; and it is a daily practice concerned with what to do (or not to do) with the fragility of everyday life.[6]

This poststructuralist approach reconfigures the concept of the "nuclear" family cemented in a 1950s Cold War culture of "nuclear" family values, described by Natalia Sarkisian and Naomi Gerstel as "consisting of a mother, a father and their young children still living at home"—a cultural fabrication operating to the detriment of the real lives of extended families (grandparents, aunts, uncles, cousins) or monoparental homes or homes without children, including among gay couples.[7] Writing in *Intimacies: A new world of relational life* (2013), Alan Frank, Patricia Ticineto Clough, and Steven Seidman further describe the "solid" and "fluid" intimacies that characterize myriad ways of being together among life partners, partners in love, adopted children, half-siblings, and networks of friendship not always mappable onto socially sanctioned heterosexual love. Destabilizing a century of psychoanalytic work pioneered by Sigmund Freud, for whom the father/mother/child trio sat inalienably at the center of a bourgeois sphere of repressed desires, new generations of activist scholars are rethinking what it means to be vulnerable together, to care, and to share in the work of relational life.

OF NUCLEAR FAMILIES AND NUCLEAR WARS: GOVERNING LIFE

The past hundred years have witnessed waves of cultural upheaval transforming every aspect of sociality. After the suffragist movements and flapper culture of the 1920s and economic austerity of the 1930s, the Second World War further transformed the economic and affective structures of family lives. With fathers, husbands, and sons ready to regain a place at home, a new familialist discourse emerged to prioritize family structures in systems of care over government intervention. Women, who had worked successfully during the war years as nurses, drivers, etc., were folded back into a domestic sphere now characterized more than ever as being inalienably theirs. With the increasing availability of dishwashers, Tupperware (first sold in 1946), and various electric appliances, the "home economy" of the family household came to represent a sacrosanct backbone of postwar life. This was especially true in America, soon the "leader of the free world."[8] With its wholesome appearance, carefully cultivated in cinema, glossy magazines, and comics, America in the postwar period conquered the imaginations of nations worldwide still struggling to rebuild after wartime devastation and fighting a tide of anticolonial wars. Simultaneously, as the Cold War raged between the United States and the USSR, nuclear bombs figured at the center of everyday life. This marked a new era of fear-mongering, social and economic protectionism, and isolationism. The "nuclear" family and "nuclear" war symbolized a life of retrenchment (Figure 7.1): in Aldous Huxley's terms, the "brave new world"[9] of perpetual surveillance and eventually of planetary bio- and techno-power.

In this context, the cultural concept of "tragedy" gains ascendency as a trope signaling cultural and political upheaval, marking a number of competing claims and imperatives. First, the "tragedy" of the world wars was met by the equally colossal inflation of military arsenals designed to prevent further disasters of this scale. Yet ongoing wars in Korea, Vietnam, Central America, Northern Ireland, Turkey, Lebanon, Iraq and Iran, Somalia, Rwanda, the Balkans, the Democratic Republic of the Congo, Israel, Afghanistan, and Syria, as well as continued fall-outs from the Cold War among member countries of the former Soviet Bloc, have entrenched a culture of near-perpetual warfare over the past seventy-five years, escalating—and normalizing—a climate of fear capitalized on by political regimes eager to maintain what Giorgio Agamben has termed a "state of exception."[10] In this view, citizens give up autonomy to a paternalistic regime putatively in return for protection from a continuous threat to the integrity of social borders and bodies. The ongoing contention over practices of displaying one's body in public reveals the perpetuation of race and sex-based exceptionalisms: it is not the same for a black or brown man or woman to walk down the street as it is for a white man or woman. We know this from the spate of police murders of unarmed black men in recent years.

Indeed, this century has given rise to a tidal wave of activism and theoretical interest in women's bodies, queer, trans, black and brown bodies, and the "public" and "private"

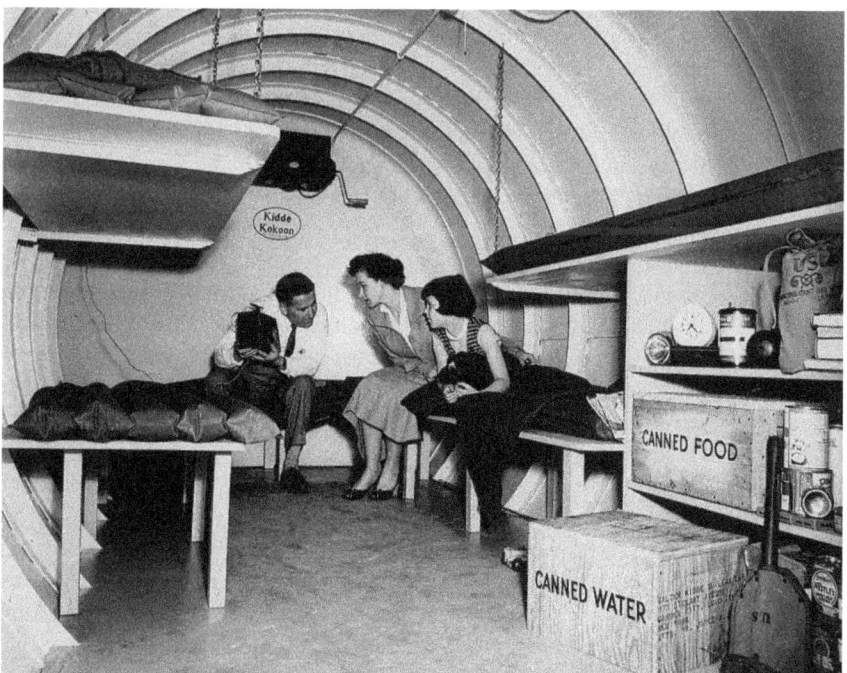

FIGURE 7.1: An American family in a backyard bomb shelter. Garden City, New York. 1955. © Granger Historical Picture Archive/Alamy Stock Photo.

spheres within which these move (or may be impeded from moving). Theater, specifically tragedy, models ideal forms of life, normative and non-normative. As I note below, for Judith Butler, normality and abnormality are learned, via Oedipal tragedy, "through the breach," through the ways normality is contravened and continually reasserted in Greek tragic drama and perpetuated in its turn in the structures of psychoanalysis. Perversion in this view is the special purview of the Greeks; repeating those perversions brings us at once closer to the myth of their exceptionalism and reasserts a modern distaste for the (sexual) taboo. This "Greek" model of tragic exceptionalism, miniaturized on the naturalistic stage, places the perversions of the family and governance of the household at the center of social and political debates on the structures of relational life. A breach at the level of the family represents a violation of social norms. In Michel Foucault's analysis, since the eighteenth century the "conduct" of bodies has been regulated by the family.[11] These codes of conduct are enacted in modernity everywhere the "family" comes to be represented: in advertising, in courts of law, in school, at the cinema, on television, and at the theater. Yet tragedy in particular articulates a manner of being familial that reaches mythopoetically "back" to the Greeks and serves as a heightened space of familial imagining. Tragedy is at once further removed from "modernity" chronologically than these other genres of biosocial "conduct," and yet, as such, it works all the more intensely as a site within which "modernity" shapes itself.

As theater scholar Julie A. Carlson notes, nothing seems further from the elevated realm of tragedy than the mundanity of the domestic sphere. Yet tragedy is unthinkable without the concepts of home and family—realms typically marked as feminine.[12] Indeed, the household, quintessentially a model for political government, as I discuss at the end of this chapter, becomes a space for negotiating hierarchies, gender roles, and social systems. For Hannah Arendt, writing in the late 1950s, modernity is characterized by "the rise of the social," marked in turn by its opposition to the "private."[13] Society is conservative in that it upholds conformism to a societal norm that was previously upheld by the head of the household. With the rise of the science of economics in a market system, the household becomes dispersed into the social realm, and management of private affairs becomes a public and a national concern. Yet the border between "public" and "private" is continually open to abuse. Thus notions of "home" (and of homeland) are sites of ideological war, and "domesticity" represents all that the head of a household—as of a ruling party—is meant to govern and protect. The legacy of paternalism in tragedy as in government thus represents a question of border protection. This is as true in the postwar period as in an allegedly borderless era of global capital, in which multinationals (and states increasingly redesigned to serve them) take on the role of managing biopolitical processes—through access (or restricted access) to pharmaceuticals, reproductive technologies, or end-of-life care. Thus while this century of cultural renegotiations has decisively put questions of reproduction, care, and community affiliation into new light, the cultural politics of the "family"—and its relation to a social norm—remain fraught.

Indeed, while the intersection between family and society may be summed up in the late 1960s feminist adage, "the personal is political," a new wave of feminist writing articulated by, among others, feminist scholar Sara Ahmed further suggests "[t]he personal is theoretical": it is a daily practice of articulation, a manner of seeing what remains invisible. What Ahmed calls "sweaty concepts" move through our bodies, often with effort; they come from and return to relations with our aunts, sisters, mothers, fathers, brothers, our workplaces, the street. The "homework" of feminism, Ahmed submits, is never done. Feminism continues to take place at the dining room table.[14] We may call this a theatrical space: it is a space in which we are meant to see—to make appear—and to theorize. (The *theatron*, after all, is the "seeing-place": theater is in this sense a theoretical space. It is the space within which a particularly heightened form of *seeing*, of taking stock, takes place. Significantly, this *seeing* is not just intellectual but also affective, moving.) Thus although questions of gender are considered specifically elsewhere in this volume, it is impossible to write about family and society in tragedy without talking about gender and politics since the notion of the "family" is inextricably bound up in issues of gender normativity, affect, and affiliation and with different political communities and forms of social arrangement.

DISRUPTIVE KINSHIP: ILLIMITABLE TERMS FOR ANALYSIS

The language we employ to describe the messy ways family and society may play out has to be rewritten. Alternative ways of imagining family and society include, in Avital Ronell's terms, "disaffiliation, kinship outside of blood or race, new socialities, affinities minus families, affiliation by adoption, subcultures."[15] The list suggests not only the complexity of relations that shape (or, as Ronell suggests, misshape) our familial (and non-familial) affiliations, but also the racial and sexual violence of "blood ties." These are the ties that gave way to mid-twentieth-century fascisms, and the language of racial and sexual purity that the family was meant in that context to uphold. As Butler suggests, "if kinship is a way of ordering relationships," perhaps what we need is a little bit of "kinship trouble." Rather than prioritize contractual marriage and blood relations, "elective affinities," she offers, describe what it means to choose with whom and how we live. Queer kinship takes neither conjugality nor reproduction as a determining force.

The legacy of Greek tragedy, wrapped up into a history of psychoanalysis, has to be re-examined. It is exemplary for Butler of a kinship myth according to which kinship relations come to be learned "through the breach." Oedipus stands as the primary (dis)ordering principle of all family relations, in a Freudian conception, as Antigone (his sister and daughter) stands for rebellious sisterly love. Kinship thus can be understood to precede and to supersede family, potentially infinitely expanding and reconfigurable. It is also contradictory. When does kinship begin? Simultaneously at the point one discovers "I cannot live without this person, and I must absolutely live without this person; or, that this person loves me madly, and that I will surely be killed by this person." These paradoxical structures signal the intensity of a bond that is neither only nurturing nor merely destructive, but both. It is where kinship begins, and it is where we begin to exceed ourselves, to become community; it is where politics begin. Thus, at the source of kinship trouble for Butler is "a sudden swing that belongs, we might say, to the absolutes of affective life: intense adulation and the fear of death converging at the site of ordinary life. I belong here; I will die if I stay here. This is one form the knot of kinship takes." If kinship is a "knot," it is also for Ronell a "tightrope," a series of "fissures." "Without," she remarks, "is connected unstoppably to with."[16]

Thus we are with and without those who make our lives worth living and unlivable. The ordinary and the extraordinary forces of such relations create a scenario within which we are—at the site of our "elective affinities"—embroiled in alterity. We are inextricably composed of the particular others we have and have not chosen to let in. This is the "tragedy" of the family as a site of unending ("illimitable") negotiation and rupture.

HERSTORIES AND VILLAGES

The 1960s feminist adage, "the personal is political," resounded through feminist liberation and gay pride, black power and indigenous rights protest (Figure 7.2). But this insertion of what has been termed identity politics into the public sphere in the latter half of the twentieth century belies what has also stayed ("tragically") true in the twenty-first: the extent to which sexism and racism continue to be elided in political practice if not cultural policy. The #BlackLivesMatter campaigns, inheritors of the Black Liberation and civil rights movements, highlight the systematic abuse of police violence against black men, and the consequences of these abuses in family homes. As black men are disproportionately represented in the carceral system, black women are disproportionately left to do the work of managing the economic and social structures of their families and homes. Yet, perhaps because of this what underpins the recent protest movement is also a model of "sisterhood" and a black queer stance that claims a "Herstorical" counter-narrative privileging intergenerational solidarity and extended family "villages." These seek to disrupt the heteronormative nuclear family model.[17] In this view, the "personal" is not only "political"; the entire structure of family alliance is reconfigured.

For British-Danish theorist, playwright, and performer Mojisola Adebayo, the aim is to "[mess] with form," creating structures of recognition that "[expose] the mythical norm," reimagining sexuality, race, family, and trans-border genealogy.[18] Rather than integrate herself into a "Western" canonical structure and mode (dominated by returns to the "Greeks"), she perverts canonicity to represent her (other) selves. *Muhammad Ali and Me* (2008) is a semi-autobiographic and semi-fantastical tale of (anti-)familialism between "a queer dyke kid and the Muslim man, physically impaired by Parkinsonism," their relationship further mediated by a Sign Language interpreter.[19] Although not strictly

FIGURE 7.2: A group of women, under a Women's Liberation banner, march in support of the Black Panther Party. New Haven, Connecticut, November 1969. © David Fenton/Getty Images.

"tragic" either in tone or genealogy, Adebayo's work acknowledges a "mythical norm" which it playfully subverts, effectively laying bare a whole set of "tragic" biases requiring families to be constituted a certain way, socially to perform domesticity as an oikological, archetypal historicity—even transhistoricity—a sort of (classical) atemporality inscribed onto the figure of the familial triad, translated or transposed into the holy trinity—one that it is (as Butler points out) the special purview of the Greeks to transgress. It is as if the entire cultural history of contemporary returns to Greek tragedy required us to perform *again and again* a myth of Greek exceptionalism, by which we may only transgress inasmuch as we repeat earlier transgressions, themselves imagined to be constitutive or even pre-constitutive of what has come to be enshrined as nuclear normativity. History, historicity, transhistoricity, are posited as normative structures (even feelings) whose exception *and* preservation "tragedy" has as its special purview to enact. We will never get "out" of tragedy until we get—fully—"out" of this familialism. At the same time, tragic drama enables us to play other family models out.

OF DISTANCE AND PROXIMITY: OTHER MUTUALITIES

Writing in *Notes Toward a Performative Theory of Assembly* (2015), Butler argues that with the proliferation of protest movements and remote wars in the last decades, we are compelled to work at reconciling the bodily proximity of people, objects, and architectures—ecologies as well as communities—around us with the mediatized representation of violent events taking place every day often far away. Thus we may submit that what Jean-François Lyotard, after Immanuel Kant, described as the "sublime enthusiasm" experienced by spectators of the French revolution (as of the May 1968 upheavals in France) becomes today an ethical call and site of "local and global" questioning.[20] What is the boundary of our society? Where does our "household" begin or end? Who must we care for? Drawing on the work of Emmanuel Levinas and Arendt, Butler argues that "cohabitation"—by which, via Arendt, she means a worldwide, planetary scale of cohabitation—trumps the discourse of "chosenness" by which some people claim to be more entitled to a place on this earth than others, and which can, as we know from the world wars, ultimately lead to genocide. Substituting this genocidal logic with an imperative to recognize that we are all *unchosen*, and must all therefore *learn to live alongside others, of whatever sort*, Butler argues for an ethics hinging on care, specifically care for the socially vulnerable—by which she means potentially *all of us*. This claim posits humanity as a global sphere within which, against the trappings of state- or private-run paternalism (not necessarily associated with paternity), which would tend toward redressing injury, we understand ourselves to be mutually entangled. We are vibrant social beings inasmuch as those around us may thrive too.

The "tragedy" of vulnerability, and the mutual responsibility of care, thus becomes, with the gradual disassembly (typically, the privatization) of social networks and health care systems, an urgent space for thinking about mutual dependence. In Romeo Castellucci's hour-long dramatic performance *On the Concept of the Face, Regarding the Son of God* (2010), Antonello da Messina's round-faced Jesus, projected as large as the theater's entire back wall, stares out at the viewer, impassive, it seems, nearly, or quietly and benignly watching, as an aging and incontinent father shits brown liquid, and a son mops it up, again and again. The father is also God, the son is also Jesus, perhaps; more immediately, the father is playing tricks on the son. He knows that he has the power to make the son act in this way, again and again. The father is vulnerable, but this is his power. The power to make others act. And to make images. As Joe Kelleher remarks, the father is addressing us in his role as actor—as holder and enactor or embodier of images—pouring a container of liquid brown paint onto his white clothes, his son's white house.[21] In this pouring, the father is tainting the domestic sphere, perverting the relationship of care the son demonstrates. The son seems on the cusp of exiting the domestic enclosure. But he does not, and in the incessant repetition of this shitting and cleaning, we find ourselves engrossed in a tender and violent show of filial piety, hovering between voluntary and involuntary: the involuntary shitting; the voluntary showing of the involuntary shitting (Figure 7.3). What we discover is an experience of theater as a space where images appear to us, and yet, in this act of appearance, a tender relation is *also* staged. The image is not merely a representation of reality, but an invitation to reality to step into the frame. The reality we experience is intimately our own, an affect hovering somewhere between our seats and the stage.

In the tragic relation—the son becoming beholden to this repetition, not really able to escape, finding that he cannot because he does not want to, that he is trapped in his own desiring to be there, to help (not only because Jesus is looking, but because something within him is awoken, again and again, to the necessity of *staying there*)—we discover an opening, an address. We discover that in performing the repetition, the white wall fixed to a black wall behind it, and behind that, whatever may be taking place in "real" life, we are also engaging in a series of choices. We are being interpellated: what would you do, if this were you? And in finding ourselves surprised at the father's furtive, insubordinate act, we realize that we are also *not* surprised. We perhaps knew this all along, that this was *theater*: that the actor is there pouring paint; that the son is there mopping up paint. We are engrossed in a

FIGURE 7.3: Romeo Castellucci's *On the Concept of the Face, regarding the Son of God*, for Socìetas Raffaello Sanzio. Barbican Theatre, London. April 2011. © Christophe Raynaud de Lage/Festival d'Avignon.

complicit relation, one that suggests that, in theater, what we see is the seeing. That *seeing* is the most formidable thing, the thing that can break the mold of our lives; that can help us discover that this is not necessarily the way that things are, or have to be.

As Rachel Fensham has pointed out, the Socìetas Raffaello Sanzio operated for many years as an "extended family," with husband and wife duo Claudia and Romeo Castellucci joined by Romeo's sister Chiara Guidi and their various children.[22] Their magisterial *Genesi: The Museum of Sleep* (1999), part of the *Tragedia Endogonidia* trilogy, rendered what Castellucci called "an organism on the run," an event that unfolds organically. "Endogonida" refers to the "biological term for an organism possessing both male and female gonads and therefore capable of ceaseless self-reproduction," Daniel Sack notes in his review of the cycle's American premiere.[23] This *endogonidic* theater is neither male nor female, neither before nor after; it refutes generation and genealogy, familialism and heredity. By blurring the lines of "tragedy" as an organizing principle designed to show stakes or take sides, favoring instead a disorienting and disquieting opera of scenes and tableaux responsive to every new site, the Raffaello Sanzio "society" produces an alternative familial economy that never spars or resolves. Thus the company does not only *represent* alternative ecologies onstage; their very production process enacts this.

QUEER SPACE, TRAGIC ACTS

Though tragedy enacts a representation of suffering, it also constitutes an occasion to reorganize affective relations. Reprising Raymond Williams' approach to "tragedy" as a disordered *experience* of disorder, one that nevertheless performs a "revolutionary" overturning of a whole set of "structures of feeling," queer theorist David Román notes that the conjunction of sights of suffering in the wake of the 9/11 events and the tragic onslaught of deaths among gay men in the 1980s and 1990s AIDS epidemic compels a reconsideration of the role "tragedy" plays in our critical thinking about theater.[24] For Román, suffering comes to be experienced as meaningful when it is transformed into action. This can be as simple as a discussion with students and other attendees following a play. He describes the palpable emotion following an outing to Terrence McNally's *Corpus Christi* (1998), the passion play that, in staging a Texan Jesus living as a gay man among gay men, gave rise to violent uproar, often discussed alongside the nearly contemporaneous death of the gay Wyoming university student Matthew Shepard, an event itself widely heralded as tragic.[25] Shepard's death, now understood to be associated with a complex scenario involving drug trafficking more than simply the redneck hate crime it has come to represent, nevertheless became a rallying cry for anti-homophobic resistance and gave rise to anti-hate crime legislation (known as the Matthew Shepard Act [2009]) and *The Laramie Project*,[26] by Moisés Kaufman and the Tectonic Theater Project. "One of the most performed plays in America today," which was also made into an award-winning film starring Peter Fonda and others, *The Laramie Project* (1998) is based on hundreds of interviews with inhabitants of Laramie, Wyoming. Styling itself a call to action by theater makers responding within weeks to the murder, the play heeds Bertolt Brecht's call to the dramaturgy of the "street scene," effectively creating a genre of epic theater that seeks to transcend the nineteenth-century legacy of realism and naturalism.[27] What Kaufman and his collaborators sought instead was to produce "moments," juxtaposing found text (interviews and journal entries) in scenes that would call the audience to self-reflection and ultimately to action. The Far West rural setting earned this a designation as a "pastoral elegy," akin to the genre of the western, according to Amy L.

Tigner, a long-time resident of Laramie. She attributes the hero's "tragic" death to a nostalgic return to nature depicted in the mythic setting by which a "real" town attempts to come to terms with violence in its midst.[28] As docudrama and Brechtian metatheatre, this project is hardly standard "tragic" fare; yet its quaint didacticism suggests a more insidious transposition of biography onto a tragic frame: one that presents Matthew's story as a singular event, standing for a broader principle, and that singularizes Matthew himself, away from the complex web of interrelations he acted within.

The arguably even more tragic epic of the latter part of the twentieth century is Tony Kushner's *Angels in America: A Gay Fantasia on National Themes*, first performed in 1991, recently revived for production at London's National Theatre, and also now a film and TV series. Its close association with the 1980s AIDS epidemic and the disintegration of the social fabric under rampant Reaganite economics has branded it a classic tale of American outrage and overcoming and, significantly, as Jennifer Wallace notes, an extended portrait—at the cusp of the new millennium—of a radically reimagined American family. "Family" in Kushner's work is "queer," composed of gay couples, among many others, but also of non-familial relations of alliance, including between nurses and patients. Proximity to death in this work compels a "tragic" reckoning with the structures of care—with what sustains life.[29]

Suffering comes to signal a turn in contemporary approaches to the "tragic" loss of life endured by all those engaged in war *and* in the banality of everyday life. Every death is a tragic death. Mourning does not become more or less right, in this new humanist conception, depending on *who* is doing the mourning or who is being mourned. This radical horizontalism overturns the hierarchies of life posited in saying one life is worth, and another not worth, mourning, such as Bonnie Honig argues colors debate on Iraq war veteran parents, or close relations of AIDS victims not associated by blood but acquired kinship.[30] With the universality of grieving supplanting the question of sovereignty (who grieves, where, and for whom), flattening kinship to include close friends and acquired relations, "tragedy" comes to signal another sort of unexpected event: loss of life so intense and untimely as to *throw* off its axis the life-world of a person. All losses impel reconfigurations, calling the status quo into question, so that it oscillates.

From a biopolitical (and necropolitical) perspective, the organization of death and life into *grievable* events signals the meaning-making possibility of otherwise inexplicable loss. And there is no more efficacious space for doing this than theatre or performance. A ceremony at a gravesite, a funeral oration, or a play may serve similarly to reorganize the way loss is experienced, life invited in. By seeing the world as an infinite set of movable parts, we may understand tragedy to disorient and disorganize what had been oriented or organized in this or another way, *not necessarily forever*. The open-endedness of this approach suggests "tragedy" as a space for reassessment, in other words, for opening onto (mutual) transformation rather than folding in onto the intractable authority of received opinions, or the singularity of a pre-agential individual fate.[31]

SUFFERING TOGETHER: FEMINIST SORORITY IN THE UNDERCOMMONS

Family is not just parental but sororal and fraternal as well. It may lead to birth and new generation, but it may also open onto the horizontal affiliations that may *stop there*. There is not always life after a brother or sister. That sort of love is not (normally) progenitive. Honig reminds us that for Lee Edelman, Butler's appropriation of Antigone as a (moderately queer) heroine betrays the monstrosity Antigone may also be said to represent. Edelman argues that Antigone marries death and is thus *not* open onto the future. Her inability to marry (in life) is not just a refusal of heteronormative social and kinship structures, but of all progeny.[32]

Antigone is *anti-gōne*, the end point to futurity, generation, genealogy; after Antigone, there is nothing except what reorganizes itself around the void she leaves behind. Except that, as Honig points out, Ismene is left behind, cared for, in Antigone's self-burial act. And in this, *sorority* may be posited as an alternative kinship and social model, one that does not quite equate to *fraternity* nor to maternity, but reorients the modern reception history of *Antigone*—adopted in the twentieth century as the political play *par excellence*—towards a politics of complicity by which Ismene is not apolitical, passive, and risible. On the contrary, she is half of a politico-ethical engine of resistance operating, Honig writes, "beneath the radar of Creon's sovereignty."[33] What feminist critic Mary Rawlinson calls Ismene's this-worldliness, in contrast to Antigone's sacrificial impulse, may serve feminism best, particularly when it is poised to continue what the other sister commenced.[34] The duo, in this regard, straddle life-death (or death-life), as Ismene will also live a life-in-death, in her uncle Creon's house. Following Antigone's sacrifice—which can be read thus not *only* for the dead brother or the dead father, but also co-conspiratorially for her sister—Ismene's "subtle agency" performs, more quietly, half of the total act that buries Polynices *twice*.[35] "*Two sisters, two burials*," Honig muses, showing that Sophocles' play does not entirely account for the two burials, except, as she shows, if we surmise that Ismene also did it. Ismene's sororal love for Antigone "*calls* for" her continued working-through what to do, and strengthens her resolve, and their solidarity.[36] Averse to reckless disobedience, but not necessarily to a disavowal of this act, Ismene performs the burial first, under the cover of night; Antigone will go back and finish the job, more loudly, later. What's more, Honig remarks, Ismene admits to it. "Why has no one for hundreds of years or more taken her at her word?"[37] Standard readings after Hegel that have seen Antigone as a sort of man, asexual, virginal, tending-toward death, obviated the possibility that the quieter woman could be equally rebellious, and perhaps cleverer, more strategic and life-loving. Ismene's affirmation of life *and* her successful disobedience of Creon's edict enable her to survive her act, to come off (relatively) free. This is the more intolerable reading, even on the borderline of unthinkable.[38]

Antigone, then, in sacrificing herself to let Ismene go on in life, is more a hero, and less a hero than we thought.[39] She is also, significantly, less exceptional, less individuated, and more imbricated in sorority. This sorority is a relation not dependent on (love for) men, though men may be part of it; as such, it is even more counter- (or para-) hegemonic than Butler's reading showed, and radically reconfigures our understanding of individuation in tragedy. As Deleuze noted, following Nietzsche, tragedy is joy in multiplicity, plural joy.[40] What if we take this injunction to plurality and against individuation seriously, in order to consider tragedy's radical intervention into social and political life as that which intensifies rather than severs bonds—and not always those we may expect? "Family" is, like Antigone, at once stronger and less strong than we may have thought; its contours more unsure; and the symbolic structures of kinship it represents subject to even more radical complexities, even stronger and more potentially revolutionary bonds. What may still counter modern individualism is a structure of sociality that shares agency in the act. In this regard, Antigone standing up to Creon is less radical than Antigone and Ismene conspiring to speak and to act, under his radar, in the "undercommons," together.[41]

THE PERSISTENCE OF GREECE: OF ANARCHISM, ASSEMBLIES, AND THE PUBLIC SQUARE

Freedom of assembly constitutes the right to revolution, Butler notes. It constitutes the right to move about in an unregulated fashion, to be unfettered by "public," "private," or state-regulated laws and law enforcement. To move about as one wants in public space is also, one might argue, a positive anarchic right (Butler elides this term, claiming that the right to assembly falls *just short* of anarchism).[42] The civic, public square in this anarchic sense is not only analogous to the agora, the space of encounter and exchange; it is prior to discussion or debate. It serves as the symbolization of the possibility for debate—not just between two (not just agonistically), but according to any unspecified number and sort of combinations and recombinations, involving modes of sitting, walking, talking, etc. Is this the space within which "tragedy" plays out? Effectively, "public" "assembly" only makes sense if it is conjugated with (and *as*) a zone that makes apparent what it leaves out, the family, the home, the "private"; when we are coming into a public space to assemble, to trade, to debate, to watch, to feel others' bodies brushing against ours in the ecstatic solidarity of the crowd, or the irritation of a busy market, we are in effect translating ourselves between fictionalized realms, "in" and "out," hidden and seen (Figure 7.4).

When the pensioner Dimitris Christoulas took his life outside Parliament in Syntagma Square in Athens in April 2012, at the height of the austerity debacle, his gesture was heralded as an act of martyrdom for the sake of revolution, a call to arms; he argued that

FIGURE 7.4: A young couple dance with joy in Athens' Syntagma Square during a political demonstration to celebrate the "No" result in a popular referendum over the EU bailout and austerity measures. The result was overturned a week later. May 2015. © Kostas Pikoulas/ Pacific Press/LightRocket via Getty Images.

he was not committing suicide, but that the state—in slashing his meager pension and ability to buy medication—was killing him. Although his public, performative act gained substantial media attention, recalling the Vietnamese Buddhist monk Thích Quảng Đức's public self-immolation in Saigon in 1963, an act symbolic of Vietnam War-era protest, Christoulas, like Quảng Đức, was not acting alone. More than 500 men have been reported killing themselves as a more or less direct result of unlivable austerity measures in the years immediately following the fiscal meltdown; calling this a "modern Greek tragedy," Nikolaos Antonakakis and Allan Collins, in the journal *Social Science and Medicine*, argue that the global recession from 2008 and sovereign debt crisis from 2009 catalyzed a sharp peak in debt, migration, and unemployment-related suicides.[43] Playwright and novelist Petros Markaris, in *Termination* (2011), the second novel in his "crisis trilogy," describes four female pensioners taking their lives, less in this case directly and publically to protest austerity measures than almost privately to extract themselves from a body politic they felt was burdened by their presence. What sort of tragedy does this set of austerity stories represent? What is the tragic space of public *enactments*, performative assertions of bodily presence in the face of death? If the language of "tragic" theater bleeds out of the theater hall into a public space marked by the banality and intimacy of everyday life, is such a theatricalized life more than—or is it *as much as*—this intimate banality? Tragedy today may describe more than ever before the banality and the intimacy of the "domestic." Yet what defines such domesticity is also an urgent call for widening the public space within which structures of care come into play.

Eagleton argues that "tragedy," following Williams, is a combination of features, and this includes the "very *very* sad" often reserved for awful newsworthy events sadder than merely "very sad."[44] But the spectrum of "sadness" that makes of "tragedy" a special recipe—most frequently (and sometimes exclusively) mapped onto the ancient Greeks and derivative works relating back to them—does little to assuage our sense that beyond Greece, and beyond sadness, there is something of "tragedy" or the "tragic" that might aptly describe a process of making deep discontentment, unsettlement, and social problems *public*. In making public (making a theater of) questions that startle us into a process of self-questioning, we articulate a form of collective being that is also "historical" (rather than mythical): it prompts "history" to move along. Although "tragedy," as Eagleton somewhat wryly laments, may have to do with gods and heroes and other unfashionable things supposedly at odds with the anarchic flows of poststructuralist philosophy (a surprising comment, if we note that the gods and heroes were themselves perpetually changing, multiple, impossible to pin down), tragedy is also implicated in the very process of historical unfolding that makes the staging of the *present* moment agonistic, filled with struggles, debates, and competing belief systems brought to light. What defines "tragedy," we may say, is the rift that comes to light between one and another manner of living one's life. "Tragedy" stages a conflict between systems of understanding and power. This yields a heightened moment of observation (and self-observation) within which we may find ourselves, as audiences, provoked to *see* and to *hear* the shape of another possible world.

For Butler and Athanasiou, to stand one's ground in public is already to present a body as worthy of being present, in the presence of others. This mutual space-taking (and space-making) constitutes a space of politics where individual bodies, aggregated together, claim a social right to being here, a right to constitute a social body, one that can then, perhaps, become political. Returning to Butler's reflections on Antigone, might we not imagine that the *prepolitical* space Antigone represents is less that of kinship, today, than of social solidarity?[45] In *Ce ne andiamo per non darvi altre preoccupazioni* (*We Decided to Go because We Don't Want to Be a Burden to You*) (2014), Italian duo Daria Deflorian and Antonio Tagliarini attempted to stage the collective suicide imagined by Markaris, to understand what moments, what intimacies, the pensioners shared. As actors in crisis-poor Italy, they sought to understand how their lives are little more valued than they are in Greece; how difficult it is to go on every day in the face of want and humiliation. What does it mean to be alone together (in Honig's terms, to "conspire"), the duo asked. What private space do we have left, and what intimacy? How can we reconstitute the public/private binary so that it is not an *either/or* situation, the distinction between them dissolving with increasing surveillance? How can the secretive language of co-conspiracy come out into a broader light so that the already weaving solidarities we nurture in the "undercommons" may constitute a vibrant "public"? For what is a "public" if it is not comprised of proliferating mutualities, of deepening intimacies, which may form, inform, and *re*form it?

In this sense, my reading of the assembly—as a public but also an intimate sphere, a sphere *also* composed of zones of intimacy or the possibility of a movement toward intimacy—slightly reconfigures Butler's, in that it suggests with Honig that structures of "sorority" (not necessarily attributed to women) condition the *showing* of bodies assembled together. Bodies standing together in public space, showing themselves alongside one another, of course may help to move politics along; but multiple affiliations, none necessarily attributed to "blood," compose the sorts of kinship relations that make politics possible. This is not to suggest that there is no place for the "family" (composed of mother, father, child; mother, mother, child; brother, sister, uncle; etc.) but that affective groupings—those that matter—tend to be intimate in number, to be based on the repetitive action of touch, words shared, languages co-created. That in sharing these intensities, we become greater than the sums of our parts, and thus make way for a "social" sphere that *makes* biopolitical affective life *worth living*, worth struggling for; worth—if we follow Ismene, arguably the most modern heroine—*not* dying for. If we refuse dying for the state or religion, and affirm life together beyond the strictures of authoritarian power, we must do so with the strength and resilience of *other* bonds, bonds that are close at hand. This is a chosen family; family that becomes constituted again and again, perhaps as we travel and grow; it may also be "blood" family, if we equate "blood" with birth.

But we may, following Achille Mbembe's analysis of *necropolitics*, equate it with death.[46] Here, what I am positing is that those we choose to be alongside when we die—to care for and to share our lives with—are also those with whom we are most complicit, with whom our life extends most intensely into futurity. In recognizing those special persons with whom we share time, we constitute a network of affiliations that does not replace politics or the nation but becomes itself a *form-of-life* whose power is to exceed the fiction of singularity, the anomic "one."[47] This is to practice vibrant affiliation.

OIKOLOGIES: OF HOMES, HOMELANDS, AND RETURNS

Two brothers reunited: Syrian refugees. Their story is one of war, loss, and overcoming. In the mediatized version, luck plays little part; readers, listeners would rather hear of perils and hope. The intensity of the family as a site of rupture and return is always first to be deployed to universalize affect, to help us feel the pain of millions, metonymized in just this one—typically, just these two, or three, or four, but not more. Children washed up are the children *of someone*; they represent futurity (and its loss), but also the inconsolable mourning of those who should have died before them; those who nurtured, who cared. As if we could not possibly feel for millions, even dozens; we can only extend a hand to the one (at a time) before us. This last section asks what is the work of giving—of nurturing—in the "tragic" space of today's mass migrations and displacements; today's border wars? What is the space of hospitality, of hosting? What is the imaginary homeland, the home, the house into which one might set foot again? And how does this affective and figural notion of the (lost) home come to epitomize not just the sense of (extended) family, historicity, and right; but also the notion of a transgenerational and transnational space of rest?

Giorgio Agamben, writing of the development of a "theological genealogy of economy" emerging in the early Christian church between approximately the second and sixth centuries CE, describes a shift in the use of the term *oikonomia*, the ancient Greek science by which a household is governed. As Agamben notes, the analogy with the state is almost immediate. The term *oikonomia* comes to be integrated into church discourse as the church Fathers are wrestling with the imposition of the Holy Trinity. Father, son, and Holy Spirit are opposed to the pagan proliferation of deities, *but also*—in their multiplicity—opposed to the singularism of the "monarchians," "promoters of the governance of a single God." They operate in an *oikology*, a system of household governance. God, then, is one, but "administers his home, his life, and the world he created" *like a good father* able to entrust his son with the execution of duties without losing his own power. Christ is "the man of the economy," according to the Gnostics, *ho anthrōpos tēs oikonomias*; he rules over the "administration and government of human history."[48] This principle in effect separates the material conditions of historical and administrative life from pure being, the first principle. It also ousts Mary from the immediate *oikonomical* equation, except inasmuch as she becomes, as Andrew Parker notes in his study of *The Theorist's Mother* (2012), a "constitutive absence," "an inassimilable body," and a "foreign native tongue." She is too busy to do the public work of (administered) thinking, conception, and governance, though the figures of speech by which these terms enter into public discourse are first of all, basically, maternal.[49] Significantly, this tangle of praxes and concepts extends to the sphere of domestic "help," to the governess who supplements the mother: tending and attending to children while she oversees the rest of the domain.

Foucault notes that from the sixteenth to the eighteenth centuries, the "government of the family" comes to be conflated with the "economy," a system (and art) of governance that extends through the domains of morality, partially supplanting religion, and politics, embedded in the state.[50] Childbirth is increasingly regulated, just as are hospitals, all tending to the proper management of future generations, given implicitly (sometimes explicitly) to the state—more so, to its economy (largely overwhelmed by the military). In particular, Foucault emphasizes the "medicalization of the family," by which "the problem of 'children' (that is, of their number at birth and the relation of births to mortalities [i.e., population control]) is now joined by the problem of 'childhood' . . . ." The life of the adult is inextricably tied to a system of operations designed to "manage" this extended phase of life (childhood) resulting in "new and highly detailed rules to codify relations between adults and children." Thus, population control mechanisms meant that "[t]he family is no longer to be just a system of relations inscribed in a social status, a kinship system, a mechanism for the transmission of property; it is to become a dense, saturated, permanent, continuous physical environment that envelops, maintains, and develops the child's body."[51] But not only children's bodies are enveloped, maintained, controlled. By the mid-twentieth century, school education comprises "Home Economics," including sewing, baking, and the like; similarly, a proliferation of handbooks for wives appear, instructing them in the proper management of their households, from table-setting and cutlery alignment to storage and preserves. Systems of household management are taught through a mediated system of handbooks regularizing modes of conduct in the implicitly public-facing home (one that can be socially judged according to administrable, regularized, and broadly recognizable standards), just as these handbooks and curricula distribute the site for instruction away from maternal genealogies.

The oikonomical realm is of the mother and it exceeds the mother; it is a realm that trades in the symbolism of excess expenditure, frugality, and care. But the affective link between the home and the state remains strong; more than that, the state becomes a space for framing the feeling of safety one has under one's own roof: it represents the place, in modernity, par excellence, from which one comes, and to which one may return—if not now, then some day in the future. Svetlana Boym, in *Another Freedom: The Alternative History of an Idea* (2010), suggests: "Contrary to the poetic dictum that philosophy is about homecoming, there could be a different way of inhabiting the world and making a second home, not the home into which we were born but a home that we freely choose for ourselves, a home that contains a palimpsest of world culture."[52] Similarly Jacques Derrida, in *Monolingualism of the Other; or, The Prosthesis of Origin* (1998 [1996]) suggests that we might replace the nostalgic notion of "roots" and "origins" with a place of arrival: in this view, we might substitute the proposition "from" (as in, where are you from?) with a movement towards. . . where are you going. . . where have you chosen to be. Where do you most desire to end up (even, to die). In this view, migrants, "rootless cosmopolitans," asylum seekers, as well as those "rooted" nationals happy to remain where they were born might be identified culturally with the place they are now, perhaps the place they end up; our adopted homes are those we have chosen, perhaps freely, and perhaps at great cost.

"Home," then, more than family, is the great concept and question of the twentieth and twenty-first centuries, the site of Dionysian and Apollonian reconfigurations. A home is not only a place of shelter; it is also a place of cultivation, of birth and death. Though we may have many homes—divided families, itinerant and precarious professional lives, forced displacements, vacations, temporary and transient accommodations, foreclosed properties, mansions, and squats—we become ourselves in the homes that mark our passage, and which constitute *oikologies* that reflect and intensify our relations to something "outside" their walls, to the passages and the translations by which we imagine our movements. A "family" is a daily practice of care that may reside within the four walls of a "home." But it may also be that which passes between and across properties, states. It is not merely a monadic replica of the state, governable inasmuch as it is constituted by proper "model" citizens. It is also an *ungovernable* force; a practice of insubordination, a freedom by which our chosen and shared co-compositions are made, only secondarily sanctioned by governing policies. It is that *ground* of care and love on which the "house" lies that enables us to organize ourselves across relations of affiliation that are complex, multiple, some transient, others stable yet growing and transforming, becoming reconfigured all the time. That ground requires protection, if the "tragedies" of the twentieth and twenty-first centuries are to give way to an era of greater generosity and care. So too the language of borders, the protectionism of the isolationist tendencies have to be loosened, out of tenderness for the neighbors and friends who also co-compose "our" social bodies: bodies that are always in relation. To attempt legally, culturally, to purify the *socius* of its own alterities is to risk falling into the violent brittleness, the mean purism, of a self-proclaimed body politic without ground or hospitality.

Bodies, moving in and out of borders, back to remembered, or barely remembered homes, constitute their own freedoms, their own *lines of alliance*, to borrow from Guattari and Antonio Negri.[53] If we are to imagine the twenty-first century as a century of reconstitution, after the traumas of war in the twentieth century, the financial collapse that characterized the start of this one, and the ongoing struggles for control against "terror," then what remains are less the agonisms of society and family, state and clan, but friendships, families constituted by choice as well as by sanguine affiliation; families that take all sorts of shapes: same-gendered, singular, multiple, nuclear, recomposed. Adopted, artificially inseminated, naturally birthed. The affective biopolitics of these "families" are schizological, that is to say, they are perpetually reconstituting themselves; and that includes in their dreams of moving, of returning; of moving as freely as it is possible to move across borders. Not to be punished by inequalities of wealth or opportunity, nor to be punished for "difference."

If the twentieth century was a century of public differentiation—from feminist and queer to black power—then will the twenty-first be one of re-affiliation? The blurring of racial or gender boundaries into a new communitarianism? This is not only "intersectional," taking for example race *and* class or gender *and* race into consideration, but perhaps illimitably composite. "Tragedy," in this scenario, has a role to play: it is the canvas on which we continue to reflect dreams and desires. Antigone, if we return to her, is with Ismene a force of alliance, a reconstitution of power; not against the state, but beside it. In this view, the state becomes itself, we might say, through its own disappearance: that is not to say that there are not organisms, organizations to support the most vulnerable (and what better organism to do this than the state, rather than private capital?), but that in these protective organisms, there are also real representations, in other words, real and complex citizens with multiple belongings, multiple relations of alliance, looking out for one another, helping one another, lending a hand, showing themselves without fear in the agora, debating, speaking, playing. The perpetual oscillation tragedy *shows others* becomes the dramatic space of reconfiguration by which one can—oneself—become foreign to oneself *again* and thus, in this regard, "free" to nurture kinships and alliances, ruptures and continuations, generations and genealogies. Free to continue to recompose who it is that we may become along with others.

CHAPTER EIGHT

Gender and Sexuality

Watching as Praxis

P.A. SKANTZE

FOR WHOM THE TRAGEDY OCCURS

In the past the word most likely to be yoked to the word tragedy was genre: the genre of tragic literature, the genre of tragic drama. Yet, intriguingly, in two important recent works discussing the tragic and theater the word yoked to tragic is "experience." Both Hélène Cixous in "Enter the Theatre" and Hans-Thies Lehmann in *Tragedy and Dramatic Theatre* write of the "tragic experience." Why? I would suggest this shift has to do with an understanding of where tragedy occurs. In a time when our common usage of the word tragedy seems to be rendered banal by its ubiquitous appearance across every electronic form of media, what forms of art actually awaken us to the consequences of our actions and the actions of those in power? What forms of art reveal how the daily saturation of "disaster porn" threatens to freeze all sensory perception leaving only overwhelming powerlessness and its attendant anxiety?

First and foremost, a spectator's experience of tragedy in the theater, which indeed can be intense and provoke profound change in understanding and potentially in behavior, remains protected from the everyday experience of tragic catastrophe: war, famine, death, loss, and the sudden reversals life seems to delight in. But as all artists and audiences for artistic productions know, recognition, sensory understanding, and personal or political change often can only occur at a distance from the living out of tragic circumstances. In Hans-Thies Lehmann's figuring of the "tragic experience":

> The tragic cannot be conceived either as a manifestation of dialectic or as an intellectual paradox; it also cannot be conceived as an insoluble conflict or "insight" into subjective or world-historical collapse . . . if tragic experience were really thus, then tragedy . . . would merely illustrate relations that concepts can grasp more deeply and fully.[1]

When my students explore practice as research methods, often I find myself inviting them to move beyond "illustration," a paint-by-number rendering of the idea into the performance. So with Hans-Thies Lehmann, I argue that the spectator who is practicing, who is in the midst of a partnership with the theatrical art before her or him, becomes the locus for the transformation from illustration to experience, to recognition and beyond.

The scope of Lehmann's book makes it impossible to do justice to his arguments, particularly about post-dramatic theater, in this chapter. However, with the emphasis of my work on the particularities of the bodies in the theater, their gender, race, nationality, sexuality, I hope to augment our understanding of where tragedy happens. Reception cannot be separated from the bodies we bring into the theater, and simultaneously we shift fluidly between our various states in the course of a theatrical production, just as we do in the course of a lifetime. By thinking with Catherine Clément, Hélène Cixous, and Sylvia Wynter alongside Lehmann's predominantly white, male European considerations, I hope to suggest that in performance the tragic experience can also allow us to see the tragedies inherent in the systems that have blinded us one to another.

Coping with tragedy then requires the spectator to theorize, and here let's be clear—to theorize is not to analyze, not to be caught in the perversely cool pleasures of the always already known dialectic. To theorize practically is to become the crucible for the mixing of the reception of the work before one and the decisions about how and when to accept the propositions theatrical performance presents: shall I "accept the unacceptable," that mistaken messengers and parents unrecognized set the course for baffling disaster? And what to do with the aftermath of the disaster, when the spectator leaves her seat, picks up his coat, wanders out of the theater? As Cixous writes, the tragic is "the irreconcilable as ineluctable, the situation in which I must accept the unacceptable, or renounce what is most dear and most necessary to me because there is no right answer or happy ending."[2] Cixous and Ariane Mnouchkine, the collaborative writer/director team who make theater with the Paris-based Theatre du Soleil, "dream" as do many makers of theater "of telling in such a way that something will move in reality. If not change—which would be enormously presumptuous—then at least be recalled, resuscitated, delivered from silence."[3]

In this chapter I join Lehmann in querying the strange arc of the philosophical/literary ideas of tragedy which have so often drawn only upon the printed literary work even while the mask of tragedy appeared first above a stage, the theater as locus of tragedy. Instead as Lehmann writes, "the European intellectual opinion has held that something about theater 'gets in the way.'" What Lehmann does not explore in this old prejudice beyond the knee-jerk anti-theatricality of the "feelings cloud reason" intellectual is how this distrust has always been gendered.[4] What is valued in patriarchy is the fixed, the solid, the evident, and the evidence. One might reflect here on the basic masculine fear of generation and paternity, as Hortense Spillers wonderfully reminds us in her title "Mama's Baby, Papa's Maybe." Performance has most often been associated with Mama to Papa text, the printed dramatic work resting in the fixed pantheon of the canon.[5] The distrust goes both ways in the sense of the medium itself and of those who make and watch it: the ephemeral can reinvent itself and the sensual responses of our bodies in a theater are unruly. Unruly women, unruly people of color, unruly queer people, all those theatrical types whose effect on the audience mars the pristine, ordered, and hegemonic world.

Much has been written on anti-theatricality, and Lehmann has a section on the prejudice in his book, but the patriarchal, white supremacist, homophobic systems underpinning the distrust of theatricality are not just theories, they are engines that drive the creation of character and as crucially engines that make and mar the reception of character.[6] The joy of the ephemeral is its ability to reinvent itself and in this chapter I argue that new forms of performance production reorient our experience of tragedy. Though most of us (who are not straight white males) by necessity have learned to borrow a straight white male character's sorrow and make it our own, many of the traditional stories fueling the downfall or the mistake or the misfortune of the hero are so sexist, so racist as to bar the female, queer, black/brown spectator from inhabiting the reversal and the recognition.[7] Yet through performance intervention the tragic experience can occur by way of the spectator's recognition of injustice. In ancient tragedy that injustice might have been set firmly at the gates of Olympus with meddling gods and implacable fate; as we come to understand the cost of inequality across the lines of gender, class, race, and sexuality, the spectator potentially receives old stories with a new sense of what fuels the cruelty, of how our own social configurations of power are as arbitrary and cruel as any slighted mythological deity. As spectators, the tragic experience occurs in time and in *our* times where the understanding of the human as what Sylvia Wynter terms a "genre" might reorientate our reception. Wynter's call to discard disciplinary, bourgeois categories in order to reinvent as praxis the genre of human potentially offers us as spectators in the midst of the tragic experience an understanding as profoundly moving in its complexity and in the praxis of its fluidity as the traditional teleological catharsis. Where the theatrical understanding of catharsis generally moved through the flaw, fall, and re-establishment of masculine power, potentially we in the praxis of being human spectators understand ourselves in the multiplicity and fluidity that is enacting contemporary citizenship.[8]

Let me pause for a moment to note how the emphasis I place in this chapter on the performance itself as crucible confronts Wynter's conception of the staleness of where we are now in our inability to move beyond bourgeois binaries and her positing of the human being not as a noun but as a verb—"being human as praxis." According to Katherine McKittrick, Wynter posits a collective "rewriting of knowledge as we know it,"[9] and according to Sarah Trimble, Wynter's ideas pose

> a challenge that asks us—thinkers, creators, knowledge-makers, storytellers—to accept disorientation in exchange for the possibility of exercising "dazzling creativity" (p17) as we recalibrate our sense of who "we" are. Wynter's project of completely transforming Western ways of knowing derives from her argument, following Frantz Fanon, that humanness is hybrid. We are, in Wynter's terms, both *bios* and *mythoi*; flesh-and-blood organisms that also (re)invent ourselves by telling stories of where we came from and what we are.[10]

In the theater, the performance made by bodies for bodies hosts the very hybrid potential Wynter wants to suggest will open the space for the "dazzlingly creativity" of encounter, of *bios* and *mythoi*, the reanimation of storytelling that is the live performance with auditor. Cixous articulates her similar approach directly in terms of tragedy:

> My plays ... present the tragic in a performative manner by asking questions about the tragic, calling into question the tragic, trying to interrupt the end, the teleological, trying to write History in which "there is still some blank space"—still some indetermination ... a theatrical writing which overflows tragedy—it possible?—to write understanding the tragedy and at the same time overflowing it and asking in the play itself the question about the overflowing of tragedy.[11]

Calling the tragic into question in terms of gender, sexuality, and race requires interruption and reconfiguration of time and space. Space configures the theatrical situation of tragedy. As Cixous notes, "to begin with there is the *Place*."[12]

The spatial theatrical setup for Western tragedy depends on patriarchal notions of gender. To have one exit from the stage in a Greek amphitheater understood to be the port and the other understood to be the city is to mark a difference between who travels away and who stays at home. In fact thinking as a director, I have always wanted to draw a stark and simple image for the remarkably durable notion of the need for a steadfast non-moving woman (or love object of whatever gender) to anchor our hero, our protagonist.[13] If there were a cord running from a wife—to use a conventional term—to her husband which remains slack while she stays faithfully in her place, quite literally the tragedy would begin when she shifted out towards something more than home, be it lover or another sort of passion than her domestic duties. As the protagonist, our hero, feels the tug on the line, he is literally pulled into an inevitable disorientation: she who has provided the stable ground from which he can always depart now herself departing. Needless to say, in many tragic theatrical narratives the cord does not even actually ever become taut; simply a whiff of suspicion that the woman has dislodged herself as trusty anchor and faithful home is enough to darken the mind of the protagonist as the spectacle of betrayal begins its relentless repetition on the stage of his imagination.

A short review of how this works in tragedy might begin with *Macbeth* following through to domestic tragedies by Ibsen to the most recent instance of an oddly traditional tragedy, *Hir* by Taylor Mac. In *Macbeth* Shakespeare diagrams for us the attribute of the fluid as feminine and the fixed as masculine, but does so in a way that delineates how much the genders borrow from one another in times of crisis. Lady Macbeth while an anchor at home awaiting her returning husband must consistently reinforce for her husband the value of fixity, "screw your courage to the sticking place" in contrast to his fretful indecision. Intriguingly she might be "unsexed" which on the one hand renders her masculine but perhaps on the other allows for a dual role as keeper and protector of the hearth. Quite palpably in word and act when she becomes unfixed, wandering in wit and disturbing the household by her constant movement, Macbeth, almost martinet-like, becomes the masculine killing machine he never was until now.

Other Shakespeare plays like Cymbeline as well as many tragedies in the repertory of European drama turn on the trick of proving a wife's infidelity. Here too as with Othello's demise the idea of infidelity is enough to undo our protagonist. Unmoored by suspected infidelity, he wants revenge or loses his sense of who he is in the world. As with Othello these men, pondering the moved and therefore inconstant wife, find their "occupation" gone. Century after century mobile women undo male certainty in Ibsen (*The Doll's House*, *Hedda Gabler*), in Wedekind (Lulu), in Lorca (*Yerma*) (Figure 8.1), in Tennessee Williams (*Streetcar Named Desire*). Even contemporary tragic work often repeats the trope. In Taylor Mac's *Hir*, as with work by Sarah Kane (*Blasted*) and Mark Ravenhill (*Shopping and Fucking*), the dramatic story remains remarkably traditional even while the characters move out of the realm of heteronormativity. In *Hir* it is the mother who becomes a kind of scapegoat for the sons at war at home and abroad. One son, an ex-soldier returned from Afghanistan, comes home to find his sister Maxine has transitioned into Max, a second son, a change that sees his soldier brother escalate in masculinity in response. The failure of the mother to create stability for the children fuels the play; she is at once unreliable because her instability has made the ground on which the children stand unsafe and also ridiculed for her lack of easy mobility in understanding the choices made by her transsexual child.

The above paragraphs demonstrate how tediously recurrent is the use of a female character as a tool to make a narrative unfold. Incredible as it might seem, the theatrical roles women—and those queer characters who also play under the sign of the heteronormative woman to man—inhabit on the contemporary stage *still* consist for the most part as roles of reaction. Virginia Woolf's astute assessment of women's role at home in a world at war in *Three Guineas* as that of a mirror magnifying the frightened recruit to ten times the size of his training or ability applies equally to the theatrical world of tragedy.[14] And it's exhausting magnifying men all the time. It results in characters

FIGURE 8.1: Billie Piper in Lorca's *Yerma*: Young Vic, London, August 2016. © Johann Persson/ArenaPAL.

onstage who by turns are hysterical, whiny, and suddenly violent.[15] None of these responses represent actions of a protagonist but rather the reactions of a necessary component to the main story. To see the consequences of the heteronormative and patriarchal in theatrical production is to see the waste of (female/queer) energy necessary to drive the old stories. Here we might disrupt the weariness with Wynter's "genre" of the *human narrans*, the storytelling that gets us from one day to the next, from fear to a willingness to try again. To think about tragedy and gender, sexuality, and race is not to replace the white male face with the white female or the black male or the transsexual protagonist. Arguments can and have been made for *Antigone*, to take only one example, as a tragedy with a woman protagonist.[16] But the see-saw of "now you are the subject, now I am" leaves the underlying power relations intact, whoever is wearing the costume. Instead of a universal human subject, being "human as praxis" means we must invent with "dazzling creativity" stories or performative interventions in stories that undo the fixedness, even in resistant philosophies, of gender, race, and sexuality. If we enter the theater practicing such creativity in reception, it is clear that as spectators we play a double role as auditor of a story moving across the space between players and audience and as spectators who refashion the story in the immediate moment as well as in memory.

Thus one way to redress or reimagine gender in terms of tragedy is surely to write new work, create new forms of contemporary tragedy as does Caryl Churchill (see below). Another is to take Lehmann and Cixous at their words and let the theater do its work to reveal, remember, and to offer more than an illustration, to offer a way for the spectator to know the tragedy differently, to expand the field of tragedy beyond the individual. Illustration draws the crude lines of binaries and dialectic, limiting the exits to port or city. A modern rendering of the tragic experience instead addresses the spectator as the third term, not illustrating but theatricalizing, letting space exist between representation and consequences. Thus a space emerges that the spectator might theorize in and make room to reconfigure the tired dichotomies, accumulating through the time of performance new interpretations arising from what has been offered in the experimental space of the tragic experience.

PACIFIC OVERTURES (CLASSIC STAGE COMPANY 2017)

Two instances of performative intervention in the last years will allow us to see how the space that invites the spectator to discern and inhabit the theatrical conditions for the tragic experience occurs whether the text comes under the category of tragedy or whether the production awakens the spectator to tragic conditions newly understood in the context of gender and sexuality played out against politics of race and colonial violence. In her brilliant *Opera, or the Undoing of Women* Catherine Clément dissects the sacrifice at the heart of tragic opera in her pithily titled chapter "Dead Women": "All the women in opera die a death prepared for them by a slow plot woven by furtive, fleeing heroes . . . ."[17] Writing specifically of Puccini's *Madame Butterfly* Clément reminds the reader of the centrality of the figure of a pinned creature, held motionless in order to be collected by the American who fixes "the butterfly woman to the board of the white Occident."[18] Even those who barely know opera have at some time or another seen a representation of the little geisha girl and the American naval officer. For Sondheim's *Pacific Overtures* this tragedy of the naïve Orient and the betraying invader lingers in the shadows.

Intriguingly the production history of *Pacific Overtures* includes a twist in the aesthetic genealogy. In 1988 David Henry Huang premiered his play *M. Butterfly* in which the geisha turns out to be a man who plays a woman so well that the American lover professes never to have known him to be male. The much-acclaimed play brought to the New York stage a work that revealed the Occident in all its homoerotic glory. The actor B.D. Wong who played the title role in *M. Butterfly* appeared in the 2004 revival of *Pacific Overtures* as the reciter/narrator in a lavish revival on Broadway. As Marvin Carlson reminds us, the theater is always haunted by past productions and the manner in which this musical could be understood to realign sexuality, race, and imperialism transformed over the years.[19] We arrive then at 2017 with director John Doyle to ask the question: now in this moment what conditions "of the theatrical situation must be fulfilled in order for tragic experience to occur"?[20]

If, as I have suggested, traditional (and not so traditional) narratives of tragedy in theater often rely on women and their im/mobility, the opening of Doyle's production enigmatically presents us with just such a vision. A beautiful, young, curious Asian actor (Megan Masako Haley) dressed in white wanders across a platform stage set between two blocks of bleacher seating on either side, making me at once intrigued and wary. Intrigued because a woman moving on stage alone is not what one expects to open a production of Stephen Sondheim's *Pacific Overtures*; wary because a young, very innocent looking woman wandering onstage in a musical about Japan courts not only the dangerous territory of orientalism but of the sexism/colonialism that refers to a nation as a "she" to be taken, most particularly the Western sexism that includes fantasies of the submissive services of an exotic geisha.

The audience witnesses this dicey opening from either side of a small runway of a stage in Doyle's production at Classic Stage Company in New York. The small orchestra only partly visible in an alcove to the back of the action underscores our watching with Sondheim's deliberate musical opening in a Japanese key, or at least a key that Western musical ears hear as Japanese, the "mystery" of the lone young woman looking curious, looking excited, and a bit wary. In her excitement and wariness she embodies a potential state of spectatorship one might have at the beginning of any production. The stage setup becomes a conduit for the "tragic experience" that theater constructs in part because of the deliberate address the actors employ through asides to us as this work is narrated. The asides are neither coy nor are they a bid for the entanglement beloved of immersive theater makers, but delivered coolly and deliberately in a reminder of how theater traditionally calls its audience to attend to the history it tells. This musical tragedy works as a tragedy visited on a country by entering us into the daily human costs of occupation and the coming of modern industrialization.

What happens to the civic of tragedy, the city state devastated by plagues caused by incest, in a global world? The original production of *Pacific Overtures* in 1976 asked this question lyrically in a moment in which in the United States all the books on business were about the Japanese miracle, the boom that was Sony and Toyota. The musical unfolds—and I mean that verb to suggest a physical unfolding as in a series of screens—the story of the invasion of Japan by the West (and the East in the persona of Russia). Sondheim uses all sorts of tropes, often foregrounding every form of stereotype, but particularly ones about nation, to re-enact the shifting moment for an agrarian, ritualistically controlled society whose territories once sovereign become porous and available for trade and exploitation. There are few women characters, and they were played by men in the original production in an imitation of Kabuki. Sondheim has always been clear that the work is Japan seen from a U.S. perspective. Despite the elegiac key of the late songs like "A Bowler Hat" in which the main character Kayama sings his transformation from Japanese fisherman to anglophile administrator, the finale "Next" combined a sorrow for loss with a rhythmic pounding that could not help but convey admiration for the ambition and scope of a capitalism unstoppable.

While capitalism has not been stopped—a reminder of our own tragic incapacity to create a just, economic system—the "boom" in Japan certainly has, and more pertinent to this production in 2017, the question might be reframed: "what happens to the civic of tragedy when the devastation is global?" In Doyle's production, the young woman who plays a kind of spectatorial doppelganger steps into the story to play the young wife who commits suicide as instructed by her husband Kayama, though the disaster he predicts as he sings to her that "there is no other way" but to kill themselves in shame at his failure does not in fact happen. Kayama returns in triumphant joy only to find Tamate dead. After that episode in the play the player returns to the role of a wandering listener, auditor, spectator (Figure 8.2). Only once more will Masako Haley enter the fictional world of *Pacific Overtures*. During the creepy song "Pretty Lady" she doubles as the innocent figure of Japan onstage and the menaced young woman surrounded by sailors who begin in beseeching and end in the barely restrained violence of spurned occupiers. Having seized the "land" by force, these sailors are outraged that their advances are not met with admiring submission.

FIGURE 8.2: Sondheim's *Pacific Overtures*, directed by John Doyle. Classic Stage Company, New York, May 2017. © Joan Marcus.

I would argue that the figure of the young woman onstage as performance intervention changes the relation of spectator to the work in ways that create exactly the conditions for the tragic experience, the sensory dimension of *being together in the same time as others* in Lehmann's terms borrowing from Walter Benjamin.[21] More importantly this sensory relation of spectator to the work occurs in ways that place gender, sexuality, and indeed race at the center of the question of tragedy. Or more precisely at the center of the contemporary challenge of our time to unfix the patriarchal, white central tragic figure not by substitution but by exploring the tragic experience as it offers reflections on the genres of human we narrate and inhabit.

We might think of singing as a form of aesthetic exploration of the tragic experience not simply because the history of tragedy begins in the sung/spoken oral of myth and narratives of community that become narratives of nation. In contemporary theater in the practice that is spectating, music changes the time and space of our reception, guiding us by rhythm and lyric and allowing for pauses underscored by orchestration. The crescendo of tragedy, the denouement of discovery, offers the composer of opera or musical theater an already prepared ground for the intervention of sung language. For those who find the moment in musicals when a character moves from speaking to singing absurd, the genre of opera exceeds that absurdity matching tragic expression note for note. What's intriguing about how *Pacific Overtures* works in Doyle's production is that what is heightened is not only the plot exposing the slow and inevitable encircling by larger powers of the small islands that form Japan, but the way in which we see two layers at once: the action of history, the action of the telling of the action of history. The theatrical nature of the tragic experience as Lehmann reminds us is "not simply a reflection, it is a pause in reflection."[22]

By continuously returning the story to us as spectators, the players enact forms of reporting history that make us reconsider how we recollect the stories we *think* we know about the past. Sylvia Wynter's positing of being human as praxis in the exercise of reinvention through story aligns with a contemporary understanding of tragedy which moves away from the static philosophical concept illustrated by literary genre to the fluid shifting of experience, an experience created from the "theatrical situation—corporeal play on the stage and the mode of spectatorship unique to the theatre."[23] As Wynter argues for the dissolution of disciplinary boundaries, so the denotation of a work as a tragedy no longer works according to a list of plays in categories labeled tragic.[24] Lehmann quoting Olga Taxidou admonishes us away from genre and literature towards "the spectacular, physical, collective, physiognomic (as Benjamin would call it) dimension of tragedy."[25] In considering the works I chose to write about in this chapter on gender, sexuality, and race, I bore in mind my response to a question posed by my partner, "are there tragedies where a woman actually plays a protagonist?" My answer surprised me, "I don't know; I would have to see a production."

So I found myself not scanning a bookshelf for titles but thinking through memory towards the works I had seen. For example, Ivo van Hove's 2015 production of *Antigone*, I would argue, entered the spectator into the tragic experience via Creon, an unexpected turn particularly for those of us hanging on to the few plays with forceful tragic heroines. Alternatively, his production of Arthur Miller's *A View From the Bridge* employed a closely drawn square for a set in which incest was not at all a mystery to be revealed but rather an engine of narrative destruction for young women, in which homoerotic longing flashed across the masculine order disturbing the status quo and the conflicted men who labored to hide their desires.

Performance interventions in two version of *King Lear* in recent years opened out the philosophical weight behind the "love of old men" that underpins everything from Eliot's *Romola* to depictions of St. Jerome in Renaissance painting. While Shakespeare exposes Lear's folly, no one can doubt the pathos of the mad Lear and blinded Gloucester which works to erase our memory of the impossible fathers to daughters and sons that they have been. Both Ruth Maleczech in 1990 and Glenda Jackson in 2016 inhabited the theatrical space in a way that transformed the work of tragedy in the play. In the Mabou Mines version with Maleczech, the director Lee Breuer decided to change the pronouns to suit the gender reversals in the casting.[26] Lyric memory opened out to sensational discovery as Maleczech spat out "what a poor, bare forked thing is woman." With Glenda Jackson the transformations were just as startling while not being made by way of language. In Deborah Warner's production the combination of Jackson's extraordinary instrument, her body and voice, together with her age (eighty), created the conditions for tragedy across one of the few universals humans can share, namely becoming old. To cite just one example, Jackson implied that the character of Lear deployed the mad dementia Shakespeare's lines suggest: in her sing-songy voice she lulled her listeners into dismissing her as a demented old man only to drop into that vocal register exclusively her own to skewer her auditors with her clarity and her power.

A MIDSUMMER NIGHT'S DREAM (2017)

So here's a comedy, yes? Mismatched lovers, forest fairies, implacable patriarchs, a stolen Amazon who magically melts into her conqueror's arms. Heteronormativity, patriarchy, imperial rapine usually costumed in productions of this play so prettily that the spectator with the actors passes over the narrative bumps, the fact that true love wins out in the end only because one lover remains under the influence of a drug. Even more cynical versions of *Midsummer* like the brilliant late twentieth-century production in New York directed by Liviu Ciulei, where Hippolyta is stripped of her Amazonian motorcycle leathers and the leathers are burned onstage, still let some things come around right by the end. In Joe Hill-Gibbins' production at the Young Vic in April 2017, however, the theatrical conditions for the tragedy in the comedy render this play a bewildering parable for our times with barely concealed violence and loss at the center of every love match.

If space conjures meaning again and again in the context of the corporeality that awakens the practicing spectator to her task, the set for this *Midsummer* established quite literally the impossible grounds on which we stand these days. The entire stage filled with dirt—not a dusting of notional gravel but dirt deep and loose enough to demand constant effort on the part of the actors to get from one place to another. On the back wall a mirror the length and height of the stage in which we saw ourselves. This is not a new trope in the theater but I would suggest in this performance the mirror rather than representing a gentle nudge of "see how silly we are and how our behavior looks when it is revealed to us" became as unforgiving as the ground on which the characters trudged (Figure 8.3). Its surface reflected back to us our participation in the recognition of the proximity between "happily ever after" and "mourning what we have lost" ever after.[27]

At the heart of this production was a reinvention of the centrality of the lovers, characters too often relatively dreary and boring when compared with the drama of Titania and Oberon or the class warfare manifested in the representation of those silly,

FIGURE 8.3: *A Midsummer Night's Dream*, directed by Joe Hill-Gibbins. Young Vic, London, February 2017. © Geraint Lewis/Alamy Stock Photo.

uneducated mechanicals led by the ever-diverting Bottom. The dirt meant that all encounters marked the actor and changed her/his appearance and none more so than the confusion in the woods near Athens. The actors varied in race and stature as the text requires given the fight between Hermia and Helena over "being low." Though the women had real physical power, as they needed to if they were to run about in the dirt, the men alternated between lovers and spurners with casual physical menace. The enactment of the mistaken love scenes, the anger of the sudden spurned, the overenthusiasm of the newly devoted shifted swiftly to a real violence in the voice and gesture which demanded the audience see the vulnerability of the female bodies to the male potential to overpower. Thinking back to the production in this moment of public acknowledgment of the abuse of power available to men in theater and film makes me admire even more how much the production made us as spectators understand the different stakes in the woods for men and for virginal young daughters. The tussle before Hermia asks Lysander to sleep farther off is no cute "let's wait until we are married" fumble, but a very near rape.

Overall grief reigned. Even after the return of Bottom to himself, the Duke watched him warily, Hippolyta looked back over her shoulder in longing for her former assheadman as if his bestial nature promised more affection than any coming from Oberon or the Duke he transformed into. As for the lovers, no freedom occurs despite the very end of the play when we are supposed to free them with our "hands" as Puck asks us—a Puck that embodied the kind of vicious British masculinity furious in subservience and ripe for taking it out on others. Instead Demetrius wanders about re-establishing the tragic, repeating forlornly, again and again, "Are you sure that we are awake?" He thus refuses the spectators the handy forgetting we are encouraged to enact of the fact that he alone does not have his eyes touched or the drug removed, and therefore we are aware that his supposedly true love is the product of manipulation and interfering magic.

At the point of the mechanicals' play when all is supposedly returned to equilibrium, fathers no longer promising to kill their daughters, and Dukes accompanied by decorative Duchesses, the actors take up huge paint rollers and paint the mirror black, the one that has until now reflected us continually within the action. Small lights come up on the edge of the stage and a theater of sorts is established, one still full of the unforgiving earth, of mud made by water here and there. The refusal of participation that marks the erasing of the audience heightens the sense of what would in tragedy be a descent into the inevitable denouement. The "deus ex mechanicals," instead of providing a point of convergence where aristocrats can remind themselves of the bond between them by way of ridiculing the working class, unleashes instead more confusion. Even as the spectators get caught up in the giddy glee of the fabulous foolishness of Piramus and Thisbe, the commentary from the lovers is acidic enough to bounce back on themselves. Meanwhile the Duke and Hippolyta respond with something between bravado on the Duke's part and an unseemly desire still in Hippolyta's voice and gaze as she practices a different kind of spectating than we are accustomed to see in the finale. She creates the conditions for the most lamentable tragedy watching with a doubled gaze, longing to move back to freedom even as she is returned fully to the limited motion afforded an ex-Queen and now consort only.

In the end all are dirty, bewildered, ranting with unnameable loss and sadness.[28] This production made of *Midsummer* a contemporary form of tragic telling: these are Wynter's humans as praxis and the praxis demands we as spectators face consequences rather than remain above the difficult ground. When still in the woods Titania narrates the out-of-jointness of nature due to her greedy fight with Oberon over a small Indian boy, born of a woman clearly evoked as Titania's lover as well as friend. Titania's description of the earth's instability, the weather gone awry in response to the bickering pair sounds not unlike the evening weather on the BBC. The set cannot be separated from the ravages of global warming, ravages rendered here in lyric. The strange thing about this form of production that demands our attention is that though surely one leaves the theater sad, the catharsis happens in the pleasure of being awakened, of being called to account both as spectators and as humans who might with "dazzling creativity" revisit our stories first to clarify what is at stake and then to ask questions about where we go from here.

NO EXIT: *ESCAPED ALONE*

As I have argued, performative interventions make for one way to redress and reimagine gender in terms of tragedy. Another intervention comes when a playwright writes new work and creates new forms of contemporary tragedy as does Caryl Churchill. In fact, she writes a form of deceptive tragedy, against the grain of the single protagonist. In *Escaped Alone* the revelation appears with characters in a garden, four women aged "at least seventy" as the dramatis personae directions dictate.[29] The deception invites us into a summer garden somewhere, most probably England. The spoken polyphony of lines winding round one another—something Churchill invented early on in her play writing— she has now reduced to sonic hieroglyphs, rather as if her earlier plays *Cloud Nine* or *Serious Money* were written by Walt Whitman and these late works written by Emily Dickinson. Her signature dialogue—broken, overlapping, intertwining—sets the quotidian scene, the content of the talk as normal as the garden party.

Like *Pacific Overtures* the performance intervention of *Escaped Alone* snaps the audience to attention. Few writers are clearer about what I suggested earlier is our own tragic incapacity to create a just, economic system, and the question now reverberating: "what happens to the civic of tragedy when the devastation is global?" With Doyle's direction of the Sondheim musical this happened both by the actors' direct address and by the doubled sense of seeing the platform on which the work unfolded and the people sitting opposite us watching, watching the stage, watching us watching them. In Churchill's new interventions in tragedy (including *Here We Go*: see below) a form of violent proscenium arch establishes both separation and entrapment. The "fourth wall" is surrounded by neon red lights in *Escaped Alone* that announce something like a barrier and a new dimension in time. For the audience member, the character speaking in that vicious frame clearly directly addresses us but from a place and time both yet to be and horrifyingly near.

Such dilation in the nonstory of the play becomes a kind of emotional promenade theater where, every time our guide steps out of the action to speak the consequences of the way we live now, the tragic experience accumulates as we move on our next stop towards the apocalyptic outcome. First, though, we don't know what Mrs. J (Mrs. Jarret) will say. All we know is that she is our "I" narrator, moving us into the scene with the barest of indications: "I am walking down the street and there is a door in the fence open and inside there are three women I have seen before."[30] Economical and effective, she sets the scene for us before the percussive, wandering, fragmentary chatter of the women begins. Then that segue, that sudden shock of red and light and a frame; Mrs. J steps away from the garden, stands alone and begins: "Four hundred tons of rock paid for by senior executives split off the hillside to smash through the roofs, each fragment onto a designated child's head."[31] And so we enter the horror of the monologue, the dimension of an unimaginable, all too imaginable future. Churchill's deftness in brevity establishes so much in just that one sentence: Class, money, power, and planned murder of the innocents. With the word "child" she shifts the stakes; this will happen often in the play. The tragic neglect of the next generation becomes intergenerational war (note the word "designated") again and again as these monologues hammer at the heart and the ear of the spectator. What's so remarkable is that here we meet what I spoke of at the beginning of this chapter, the relentless everyday evocation in media of tragedies in the world, but rather than having them reiterated as "what we all know," the spectator is laid bare to the descriptions so casually imparted by Mrs. J. The monologues are spoken matter-of-factly by a woman, without actorly intervention. The horror of the content then is harder to escape, not just initially when we have no idea what this relatively benign-looking woman in her seventies is going to say to us, but even further on as a spectator might begin to anticipate the next monologue.

Churchill's is a fine-tuned attention to the work of the spectator, to where tragedy occurs. Surely one possible response is to retreat, flinch away from the next speech, but the small bits of information forming something like a story in the women's talk when all four sit in the garden creates a traditional theatrical narrative of tragedy pulsing behind the violent interventions framed for us to hear (Figure 8.4). The dribble of words, "been away six years," begins to accumulate around the idea of "Vi" who murdered her husband, perhaps in self defense. The mystery of her actions, the potential of her as a tragic figure keeps being eroded by the suspicion of her interlocutors. A Churchillian suspicion this, nothing as demarcated as true doubt growing and becoming performed for the audience but rather a suspicion in passing, as everything seems to be in passing in this world. Even the monologues.

FIGURE 8.4: Caryl Churchill's *Escaped Alone*. Directed by James Macdonald. Royal Court Theatre, London. January 2016. © Geraint Lewis/Alamy Stock Photo.

All male presence comes by report through the mouths of the woman speaking. Vi might have murdered her husband; she did only get six years. Murdering one's husband might be a response to violence or to boredom or to both. The tragic figure however is not the middle-class woman but the scores of people just beyond the frame drowning and dying from thirst, becoming desperate in the search for the bare necessities as against the women in the garden. It is not that the women are posh or snooty, though they are all white, but that the price paid for gardens with power and light and running water occurs just beyond the threshold of that frame. The anxiety and confusion of middle-class life plays out against the desperation, reflecting for the spectator the peculiar modern condition we experience now where we fret about haste and the burden of commitments virtual and real within the context of the disasters, knowing that we inhabit a life that a small percentage of the world lives which is unavailable to most. So the tragic experience paradoxically is then heightened; the quiet calm of the monologues delivered as if nothing matters enough to speak forcefully or demand answers leaves the audience with work to do.

HERE WE GO

Neither death from old age nor the fall into dementia that occurs as part of aging can be designated tragic. While being born to die has its disadvantages, it is the condition under which we exist. So when do the theatrical conditions of tragedy obtain in the context of the natural conditions of death?

As with *Escaped Alone* one enters the Churchillian world of *Here We Go* by way of fragmented chatter. A party, people speaking semi-vapidly among themselves just loud enough for us to overhear. Then a figure steps out of the party setting. Lit by a spot she says, "I die in ten years from cancer" and then she returns to the chatter. This happens several times until Susan Engel, a veteran Churchill actor, steps out and says, "I die the next day, I see the bus but I think I can outrun it."[32] Many things happen for the spectator as we hear the narration of future death. One of the most profound is the sense of loss when Engel tells us she will die the next day; suddenly I realize how I assume these fictional characters have some sturdiness, that they will go on (as they will of course for the duration of the run of the show at the National Theatre—barring tragic catastrophe). But the title does not contain "we" for nothing. "We" are going, sooner or later. During the party scene we come slowly to understand this is a wake for a man involved in politics.

The second scene brings the new form of proscenium arch we see in *Escaped Alone* before us. Harshly lit, this time with white light perhaps in honor of the snippets of supposed knowledge about passing over to the afterlife where everyone seems to see "a white light." In the middle and looking a bit like a pinned bug, the man whose wake we have been attending considers his life. The brightly lit frame holds him before us figuratively paused between life and death. We hear the musings of the corpse from the wake.

The third scene, however, makes more demands on the spectator than any scene I have witnessed in the theater. Without violence, amplification, choreographed murder, savage beating, this scene grabs the watchers by the throat by way of silence and a relentless repetition of care for the elderly person incapable of caring for himself. For twenty-one minutes (on the night I saw the play that was the duration) a black woman helps the man we last saw in the passageway between death and life get out of bed, dress and sit in the armchair that sits close to the bed. After he sits up dressed, she begins to undress him and then help him back into bed. This takes place in absolute silence. Whereas John Cage made people uncomfortable for four minutes and thirty-three seconds, Churchill requires her audience to sit for twenty-one minutes together witnessing a very possible future if we live long enough to see it. As with *Escaped Alone* the tragedy comes in the form of the bargains made for the lives we live. It is no accident that the carer is a woman of color, no accident that the subscriber base for the National Theatre go to those wakes for friends and watch friends become enfeebled in precisely the same way as Churchill requires us to witness. At the party a young woman steps out to say, "I die of an infection five years from now; due to the overuse of antibiotics." Telegraphic and to the point, Churchill pinpoints the conditions of our collective tragedy. She makes equally clear the distance between those with the money to make the ending easier and those upon whom they depend to care for them.

Intriguingly in both the Churchill plays the female characters demarcate the terrain of the tragic. With Mrs. J in *Escaped Alone*, we look out onto a plausible and terrifying future. In *Here We Go*, the casually announced deaths come mostly through the mouths of the women and the final silent action of the woman caring for her elderly employer demarcates class, race, and the return of the domestic, but a domestic made possible by a precarious labor force and one even more vulnerable than the household where a wife might stray and destabilize a hero's world. As we watch and it is excruciating to watch the dull repetition, no talk, no easing of the shame and embarrassment of the suddenly incapacitated, we can see clearly that should that carer decide to leave, the man will be stranded, left to die in bed, alone.

A recent article in *The Guardian* with the cloyingly familiar title "Scientists Confirm What Women Always Knew: Men Are the Weaker Sex" details the finding that women live longer than men, i.e., they endure.[33] The tragedy that Churchill invents, the tragic experience that I am suggesting occurs between active spectator and performers, understands endurance as a quality as well of witnessing, of interpreting, of acknowledging. The fierceness with which Churchill deploys these characters to show how we live now comes from an artistic perspective dedicated for years to unmasking patriarchy in works that honor the "dazzling creativity" Wynter urges us to employ. A "counter poetics" of the tragic on the part of the writer and the spectator might move us towards a future imagined by Jennifer Nash in the context of black feminist love politics as

> the idea that the radical future requires certain kinds of very hard work, pushing beyond our investments in selfhood and sameness, and reaching toward collectivities and possibilities. Nor does this vision neglect the host of ways that power and structures of domination work on and against bodies in quotidian and spectacular ways. It is a critical response to the violence of the ordinary and the persistence of inequality that insists on a politics of the visionary.[34]

NOTES

Introduction

1. Trudi Tate, *History, Modernism and the First World War* (Manchester: Manchester University Press, 1998), 133–60.
2. Historians continue to debate whether Winston Churchill authorized the world's first use of chemical weapons on rebellious Iraqi Kurds in 1920. It seems likely that he *authorized* the use but in the end the weapons were not available and the bombs were not dropped. Instead a tactic of aerial bombardment and punitive village burning was adopted. See Niall Ferguson, *The War of the World: History's Age of Hatred* (London: Allen Lane, 2006), 412.
3. F.R. Leavis, *Mass Civilisation and Minority Culture* (Cambridge: The Minority Press, 1930), 5, 12.
4. Walter Benjamin, "The Work of Art in the Age of Mechanical Reproduction" (1936), in *Illuminations*, trans. H. Zorn (London: Fontana, 1992), 211–44.
5. John Carey, *The Intellectuals and the Masses: Pride and Prejudice among the Literary Intelligentsia, 1880-1939* (London: Faber and Faber, 1992).
6. Terence Rattigan, *After the Dance* (London: Nick Hern Books, 1995), 28.
7. George Steiner, *The Death of Tragedy* (London: Faber and Faber, 1961), 241.
8. Bertolt Brecht, "The Modern Theatre is the Epic Theatre," in *Brecht on Theatre: The Development of an Aesthetic*, trans. and ed. John Willett (London: Methuen, 1964), 37.
9. Augusto Boal, "Aristotle's coercive theory of tragedy," in *Theatre of the Oppressed*, trans. Charles A. and Maria-Odilia Leal McBride and Emily Fryer (London: Pluto Press, 1979; new edn, 2000), 1–50.
10. Friedrich Nietzsche, *The Joyous Science ("La Gaya Scienza")*, trans. R. Kevin Hill (London: Penguin Books, 2018), 134.
11. See Albert Camus, *The Myth of Sisyphus and Other Essays*, trans. Justin O'Brien (New York: Vintage Books, 1991), 23.
12. A.D. Nuttall, *Why Does Tragedy Give Pleasure?* (Oxford: Clarendon Press, 1996), 54.
13. Miriam Leonard, *Tragic Modernities* (Cambridge, MA: Harvard University Press, 2015), 122.
14. Christopher Hamilton, *A Philosophy of Tragedy* (London: Reaktion Books, 2016), 10.
15. Edith Hall, "Why Greek Tragedy in the Late Twentieth Century?" in *Dionysus since 69: Greek Tragedy at the Dawn of the Third Millennium*, ed. Edith Hall, Fiona Macintosh, and Amanda Wrigley (Oxford: Oxford University Press, 2004), 2.
16. Peter Szondi, *An Essay on the Tragic*, trans. Paul Fleming (Stanford, CA: Stanford University Press, 2002); Joshua Billings, *Genealogy of the Tragic: Greek Tragedy and German Philosophy* (Princeton: Princeton University Press, 2014).
17. Helene P. Foley and Jean E. Howard (eds.), "The Urgency of Tragedy Now," *PMLA*, 129.4 (2014): 618.
18. Terry Eagleton, *Sweet Violence: The Idea of the Tragic* (Oxford: Blackwell, 2003), xvi. See also Arthur Miller, "Tragedy and the Common Man," in *The Theatre Essays of Arthur Miller*, ed. Robert A. Martin (London: Penguin, 1978), 3; Raymond Williams, *Modern Tragedy*

19. Williams, *Modern Tragedy*, "Foreword," 9.
20. Ibid., 47.
21. Eagleton, *Sweet Violence*, p. 99.
22. Irving Wardle, "Comedy of Menace," *Encore*, 5 (September–October 1958): 28–33.
23. Jan Kott's interpretation of Shakespeare as speaking to "a post-war, absurdist world" was inspired by seeing Peter Brook's touring production of *Titus Andronicus* in 1957. His essay, "King Lear or Endgame," comparing Shakespeare and Beckett, which appeared later in *Shakespeare our Contemporary* (1964) was read by Peter Brook in 1962 and influenced Brook's 1962 production of *King Lear* in Beckettian minimalist fashion. See Dennis Kennedy, *Looking at Shakespeare: A Visual History of Twentieth Century Performance* (Cambridge: Cambridge University Press, 1993), 164–75.
24. Andrea J. Nouryeh, "Shakespeare and the Japanese Stage," in *Foreign Shakespeare: Contemporary Performance*, ed. Dennis Kennedy (Cambridge: Cambridge University Press, 1993), 254–69. The changing appreciation of the "problem plays" can be attributed to A.P. Rossiter's *Angels With Horns: Fifteen Lectures on Shakespeare* (London: Longmans Green, 1961) which influenced the work of director John Barton. Jonathan Bate's Arden edition of *Titus Andronicus* (1995) was to influence Julie Taymor's film *Titus* (1999) and Lucy Bailey's production at the Globe Theatre (2014). Ivo van Hove's *Roman Tragedies* premiered at the Holland festival in 2007 and was first staged at London's Barbican theatre in November 2009.
25. Anne Carson, *Antigonick (Sophokles)* (New York: New Directions Books, 2012).
26. In this respect, I disagree with the assumption of Hans-Thies Lehmann, in his recent *Tragedy and Dramatic Theatre*, trans. Erik Butler (London and New York: Routledge, 2016), that "no tragic experience can exist without theatrical experience" (3) and that somehow to consider tragedy beyond theatre in literature or wider historical experience is to "reduce" it.
27. Rita Felski (ed.), *Rethinking Tragedy* (Baltimore: The Johns Hopkins University Press, 2008), 14.
28. See, for example, Williams, *Modern Tragedy*, 121–38; Jeanette King, *Tragedy in the Victorian Novel* (Cambridge: Cambridge University Press, 1978); Jennifer Wallace, *The Cambridge Introduction to Tragedy* (Cambridge: Cambridge University Press, 2007), 168–72.
29. Primo Levi, *If This Is a Man* and *The Truce*, trans. Stuart Woolf (London: Abacus, 1987), 120.
30. Felski (ed.), *Rethinking Tragedy*, 6. However the bibliography of writing on tragedy and film is growing: see Elizabeth Bronfen, "Femme Fatale—Negotiations of Tragic Desire," and Heather K. Love, "Spectacular Failure: The Figure of the Lesbian in *Mulholland Drive*," in Felski (ed.), *Rethinking Tragedy*, 287–301, 302–18; Wallace, *The Cambridge Introduction to Tragedy*, 172–6; Rebecca Bushnell, *Tragic Time in Drama, Film, and Videogames: The Future in the Instant* (London: Palgave Macmillan, 2016), 47–64. Drew Milne contributes to this discussion in his chapter in this volume.
31. Sergio Leone's *A Fistful of Dollars* (1964), *For a Few Dollars More* (1965), and *The Good, the Bad and the Ugly* (1966); Clint Eastwood's *The Unforgiven* (1992).
32. For example, Britten's *Billy Grimes*; Berg's *Lulu* and *Woyzzeck*; Poulenc's *Dialogues des Carmelites*. See Philip Rupprecht, *Britten's Musical Language* (Cambridge: Cambridge University Press, 2001); Mervyn Cooke (ed.), *The Cambridge Companion to Twentieth Century Opera* (Cambridge: Cambridge University Press, 2005).
33. Paul Gordon, *Tragedy After Nietzsche: Rapturous Superabundance* (Urbana and Chicago: University of Illinois Press, 2001), 92.

34. Gotthold Ephraim Lessing, *Laocoon, An Essay on the Limits of Painting and Poetry*, trans. Edward Allen McCormick (1962; 2nd edn, Baltimore: Johns Hopkins University Press, 1984).
35. Simon Critchley, *Very Little ... Almost Nothing: Death, Philosophy and Literature* (Routledge, 1997), 141–80. Critchley does not discuss Giacometti in his book, but the friendship in Paris between the artist and Samuel Beckett is well known.
36. Roman Vishniac, *Vishniac: Children of a Vanished World*, ed. Mara Vishniac Kohn and Hartman Flacks (Berkeley and Los Angeles: University of California Press, 1999). For Khmer Rouge portraits, see Figure 0.3 and also the Yale University Cambodian Genocide Program's important photographic database: https://gsp.yale.edu/case-studies/cambodian-genocide-program/cgp-photographs
37. Susan Sontag, *On Photography* (New York: Farrar, Strauss, and Giroux, 1977), 109–10. See, for example, Figure 0.4 and also James Nachtwey, "A Hutu man who did not support the genocide and was attacked by machetes" in his *Inferno* (New York: Phaidon Press, 2003), 256–7.
38. Ian Patterson, *Guernica and Total War* (Cambridge, MA: Harvard University Press, 2007).
39. See my *Tragedy since 9/11: Reading a World Out of Joint* (London: Bloomsbury, 2019).
40. Christopher Clark, *The Sleepwalkers: How Europe Went to War in 1914* (London: Penguin, 2013).
41. This inverted tragic sacrifice is brilliantly articulated again by Wilfred Owen in "The Parable of the Old Man and the Young."
42. Aleksandr Solzhenitsyn, *One Day in the Life of Ivan Denisovich*, trans. Ralph Parker (1962: London, Penguin, 1963).
43. The photograph of the assassination of Martin Luther King by Joseph Louw (Figure 0.6) draws attention to the tragic lack of justice by focusing on the pointing fingers of King's companions, who gesture towards a hidden figure, the obscured cause of his death. Again the power of this photograph is derived from what can or cannot be seen.
44. A.W. Schlegel, *A Course of Lectures on Dramatic Art and Literature*, trans. John Black (London: Henry G. Bohn, 1846), 45–6.
45. *OJ: Made in America*, directed by Ezra Edelman (ESPN Films, 2016).
46. For the "erasure" of Nicole Brown, admittedly read as trauma rather than tragedy, see Shoshana Felman, *The Juridical Unconscious: Trials and Traumas in the Twentieth Century* (Cambridge, MA: Harvard University Press, 2002), 77.
47. Theodor Adorno, *Prisms: Cultural Criticism and Society*, trans. Samuel and Shierry Weber (London: Neville Spearman, 1967), 34.
48. Adorno, *Negative Dialectic*, trans. E.B. Ashton (London: Routledge, 1973), 362.
49. Hamilton, *A Philosophy of Tragedy*, 57.
50. Steiner, *The Death of Tragedy*, 351–5; Robert Nozick, "The Holocaust," in *The Examined Life: Philosophical Meditations* (New York: Simon & Shuster, 1990), 236–42; Jean Améry, *At the Mind's Limits: Contemplations by a Survivor on Auschwitz and its Realities*, trans. Sidney and Stella P. Rosenfeld (Bloomington, IN: Indiana University Press, 2009); Hamilton, *A Philosophy of Tragedy*, 57–70.
51. Donald Mackinnon, "Atonement and Tragedy," in *The Borderlands of Theology and Other Essays*, ed. G.W. Roberts and D.E. Smucker (London: Lutterworth Press, 1968), 97–104; Juergen Moltmann, *The Crucified God: The Cross of Christ as the Foundation and Criticism of Christian Theology*, trans. R.A. Wilson and John Bowden (London: SCM Press, 1974).

52. Hannah Arendt, *The Human Condition* (1958; Chicago: University of Chicago Press, 2nd edn, 1998), 6.
53. Richard Brody, "The Inadequacy of Berlin's 'Memorial to the Murdered Jews of Europe,'" *The New Yorker*, July 12, 2012.
54. Human "shadows" were found in both Hiroshima and Nagasaki after the bombs. Figure 0.7 is an archive picture of the Nagasaki aftermath.
55. The picture of a watch retrieved after the Nagasaki bombing with its hands stuck at 11:02 is part of a landmark series of photographs of the bomb's aftermath by Shomei Tomatsu entitled *11:02 Nagasaki* (1966).
56. Critchley, *Very Little . . . Almost Nothing*, 167.
57. Karl Jaspers, *Tragedy Is Not Enough*, trans. H.A.T. Reiche, H.T. Moore, and K.W. Deutsch (London: Victor Gollancz, 1953), 31.
58. Ch'ien Chung-Shu, "Tragedy in Old Chinese Drama," *T'ien Hsia Monthly*, 1 (Aug. 1935); repr. in *Renditions* (Spring 1978): 85. See also Chu Kwang-Tsien, *The Psychology of Tragedy*. Diss. (Strasbourg: University of Alsace, 1933), 216–23.
59. See Jennifer Wallace, "Tragedy in China," *Cambridge Quarterly*, 42.2 (2013): 99–111.
60. Lu Xun, *The Real Tale of Ah-Q , and Other Tales of China: The Complete Fiction of Lu Xun*, trans. Julia Lovell (London, 2010), xxiv.
61. Steve Odin, *Tragic Beauty in Whitehead and Japanese Aesthetics* (New York and London: Lexington Books, 2016), 284–6.
62. John W. Dower, *Ways of Forgetting, Ways of Remembering: Japan in the Modern World* (The New Press, 2012); David McNeill and Lucy Birmingham, *Strong in the Rain: Surviving Japan's Earthquake, Tsunami, and Fukushima Nuclear Disaster* (London: Palgrave Macmillan, 2012).
63. See, for example, Sylvia Rupani Smith, "Japanese artists respond to Fukishima," *New York Times*, June 26, 2014; Justin McCurry, "Fukushima's radioactive wasteland turns into art gallery," *The Guardian*, November 16, 2015.
64. Erin B. Mee and Helene P. Foley (eds.), *Antigone on the Contemporary World Stage* (Oxford: Oxford University Press, 2011).
65. Wole Soyinka, *Death and the King's Horsemen*, ed. Simon Gikandi (New York: Norton & co., 2003), 3.
66. The play was first performed in America in 1976 (Chicago) and in Britain in 1990 (Manchester). Olesegun Ojewuyi directed a production at the St. Louis Black Repertory Theater, Missouri, in 2008 and also a Yoruba-language version in Lagos in 1994. See Christiane Fioupou, "Variations on Wole Soyinka's *Death and the King's Horseman*," in *New Theatre in Francophone and Anglophone Africa*, edited by Anne Fuchs (Amsterdam: Rodopi, 1999), 229–40.
67. For more on apocalyptic narrative in the twentieth century, see Ursula K. Heise, *Sense of Place and Sense of Planet: The Environmental Imagination of the Global* (Oxford: Oxford University Press, 2008).
68. Maurice Blanchot, *The Writing of the Disaster*, trans. Ann Smock (Lincoln, NB: University of Nebraska Press, new edn, 1995), 1.
69. Stephen Gardiner, *A Perfect Moral Storm: The Ethical Tragedy of Climate Change* (Oxford: Oxford University Press, 2011), 24–32, and *passim*.
70. See Roy Scranton, "Learning to Die in the Anthropocene," *New York Times*, November 10, 2013. For climate change as a new type of tragic narrative, see my *Tragedy since 9/11*, chapter 7.
71. Francis Fukuyama, *The End of History and the Last Man* (New York: Free Press, 1992).

72. Hamilton, *A Philosophy of Tragedy*, 57–8.
73. Martha Nussbaum, "Compassion and Terror," *Daedalus*, 132 (2003): 26, 11.
74. Judith Butler, *Precarious Life: The Powers of Mourning and Violence* (London: Verso, 2004) and *Frames of War: When is Life Grievable?* (London: Verso, 2009). See also Rowan Williams' prescient short book, *Writing in the Dust: Reflections on 11th September and its Aftermath* (London: Hodder and Stoughton, 2002).
75. See, for example, Bonnie Honig, *Antigone, Interrupted* (Cambridge: Cambridge University Press, 2013).
76. Williams, *Writing in the Dust*, 16.
77. See, for example Ann Keniston and Jeanne Follansbee Quinn (eds.), *Literature after 9/11*, (London: Routledge, 2008); Richard Gray, *After the Fall: American Literature after 9/11* (Oxford: Wiley-Blackwell, 2011); Clare Finburgh, *Watching War on the Twenty-First Century Stage: Spectacles of Conflict* (London: Bloomsbury, 2017).

Chapter One

1. Luk Van den Dries, "Mount Olympus/24H," http://mountolympus.be/about.
2. See Michel Beistegui, "Hegel: or the tragedy of thinking", in *Philosophy and Tragedy*, ed. Michel Beistegui and Simon Sparks (London: Routledge, 2000), 11–37.
3. Friedrich Nietzsche, *The Birth of Tragedy And Other Writings*, ed. Raymond Geuss and Ronald Speirs, trans. Ronald Speirs (Cambridge: Cambridge University Press, 1999), 98.
4. David Wellbery, "Form und Funktion der Tragödie in Nietzsche," in *Tragödie. Trauerspiel. Spektakel*, ed. Christoph Menke and Bettine Menke (Berlin: Theater der Zeit, 2007), 203.
5. See the following: David Lenson, *Achilles' Choice. Examples of Modern Tragedy* (Princeton: Princeton University Press, 2015). Jeanette King, *Tragedy and the Victorian Novel. Theory and Practice in the Novels of George Eliot, Thomas Hardy, and Henry James* (Cambridge: Cambridge University Press, 1978). Ilya Kliger, "Dostoyevsky and the Novel-Tragedy: Genre and Modernity in Ivanov, Pumpyansky and Bakhtin," *PMLA*, 126, No. 1 (January 2011): 73–87.
6. David Baldick, "Tragedy," *Online Oxford Dictionary of Literary Terms*, accessed February 15, 2017. http://www.oxfordreference.com/view/10.1093/acref/9780198715443.001.0001/acref-9780198715443-e-493?rskey=e4LEC5&result=499
7. J.A. Cudden, *The Penguin Dictionary of Literary Terms and Literary Theory*, 3rd edn (London: Penguin, 1991), 984.
8. Julie Orlemanski, "Genre," in *A Handbook of Middle English Studies*, ed. Marion Turner (London: John Wiley & Sons, 2013), 208.
9. Susan Sontag, *Against Interpretation and Other Essays* (New York: Dell, 1969), 138.
10. George Steiner, *The Death of Tragedy* (London: Faber & Faber, 1961), 292.
11. See Arthur Miller, "Tragedy and the Common Man," *The Theater Essays of Arthur Miller* (New York: Vintage, [1949] 1978), 3–7. And see Raymond Williams, *Modern Tragedy* (London: Chatto & Windus, 1966), 13–15.
12. Williams, *Modern Tragedy*, 80–1.
13. Williams, *Modern Tragedy*, 83.
14. Lionel Abel, *Tragedy and Metatheatre*, ed. Martin Puchner (New York: Holmes & Meier, 2003), 183.
15. See John L. Styan, *The dark comedy: The development of modern comic tragedy* (Cambridge: Cambridge University Press, 1962).
16. Rita Felski, "Introduction," in *Rethinking Tragedy*, ed. Rita Felski (Baltimore: Johns Hopkins University Press), 14.

17. Samuel Beckett, *Endgame* (London: Faber and Faber, [1957] 2009), 6.
18. Jonathan Kalb, *The Theater of Heiner Müller* (New York: Cambridge University Press, 1998), 15.
19. Heiner Müller, *Hamletmachine and Other Texts for the Stage*, ed. and trans. Carl Weber (New York: PAJ Publications, 1984), 53.
20. David Barnett, "Resisting the Revolution: Heiner Müller's Hamlet/Machine at the Deutsches Theater, Berlin, March 1990," *Theatre Research International* 31, No. 2 (2006): 190.
21. Walter Benjamin, *Illuminations*, ed. Hannah Arendt (London: Fontana Press, 1992), 249.
22. Howard Barker, *Arguments for a Theatre*, 3rd edn (Manchester: Manchester University Press, [1989] 1993), 53.
23. Barker, *Arguments*, 18.
24. Charles Mee, *the (re)making project*. http://www.charlesmee.org/index.shtml (accessed April 5, 2017).
25. Mee, *(re)making*.
26. Mark Chou, "Postmodern Dramaturgy, Premodern Drama: The Global Resurgence of Greek Tragedy Today," *Journal for Cultural Research*, 15.2 (2011): 43.
27. Mee, "Big Love," *(re)making*.
28. David Mamet, "The Art of Theatre II," interviewed by John Lahr, *The Paris Review*, Issue 142 (1997). https://www.theparisreview.org/interviews/1280/davidmamet-the-art-of-theater-no-11-david-mamet (accessed March 20, 2017).
29. David Mamet, *Oleanna* (New York: Vintage Books, 1992), 14.
30. Ibid., 53.
31. David V. Mason, "The Classical American Tradition: Meta-Tragedy in Oleanna," *Journal of American Drama and Theatre* 13.3 (2001): 57.
32. Pantelis Michelakis, "Theater Festivals, Total Works of Art, And the Revival of Greek Tragedy on the Modern Stage," *Cultural Critique*, Number 74 (Winter 2010): 151.
33. Erika Fischer-Lichte, *Tragedy's Endurance: Performances of Greek Tragedies and Cultural Identity in Germany since 1800* (Oxford: Oxford University Press, 2017), 348.
34. See Erika Fischer-Lichte, *Tragedy's Endurance*. See also: John L. Styan, *Max Reinhardt* (Cambridge: Cambridge University Press, 1982).
35. For a more detailed exploration of the role of performance in constituting modern tragedy, see Chapter 3 in this volume.
36. Hans-Thies Lehmann, *Tragedy and Dramatic Theatre*, trans. Erik Butler (London and New York: Routledge, 2016), 443–4.
37. See the following: Erika Fischer-Lichte and Matthias Dreyer, "Antike Tragödie heute," in *Antike Tragödie Heute. Vorträge und Materialien zum Antikenprojekt des Deutschen Theaters*, ed. Erika Fischer-Lichte and Matthias Dreyer (Berlin: Henschelverlag, 2007). See also: Edith Hall, "Why Greek Tragedy in the Late Twentieth Century?" in *Dionysus Since 69: Greek Tragedy at the Dawn of the Third Millennium*, ed. Fiona Macintosh, Amanda Wrigley, and Edith Hall (Oxford: Oxford University Press, 2004). See also Simon Goldhill, "Greek tragedy: setting the stage today," Cambridge University Website (February 1, 2008). http://www.cam.ac.uk/research/news/greek-tragedy-setting-the-stagetoday (accessed March 6, 2017).
38. Finley as Dionysus in Richard Schechner, ed., *Dionysus in 69* (New York: Farrar, Straus & Giroux, 1973), n.p.
39. Richard Schechner, *Environmental Theatre*, 1973 (New York: Applause, 1994), xx.
40. See Chapter 3, pp. 71–3, in this volume, and Figure 3.3.

41. Bertolt Brecht, "Masterful Treatment of a Model," in *Brecht on Theatre. The Development of an Aesthetic*, ed. John Willett (New York: Hill and Wang, 1964), 211.
42. Bertolt Brecht, *Journals 1934–1955*, trans. Stephan S. Brecht (London: Routledge Chapman & Hall 1995) 386–91
43. René Girard, *Violence and the Sacred*, trans. Patrick Gregory (Baltimore: Johns Hopkins University Press, 1977), 4.
44. See Peter Iden, *Die Schaubühne am Halleschen Ufer 1970–1979* (München: Carl Hanser Verlag, 1979).
45. Simon Goldhill, "The Greek Chorus: Our German Eyes," in *Choruses, Ancient & Modern*, ed. Joshua Billings, Felix Budelmann, and Fiona Macintosh (Oxford: Oxford University Press, 2013), 51.
46. For a more detailed discussion of the modernist chorus, please refer to Chapter 3 in this volume.
47. Helene P. Foley, "Modern Performance and Adaptation of Greek Tragedy," *Transactions of the American Philological Association*, 129 (1999): 2.
48. Suppliant Women, "Teaser Trailer," YouTube, posted October 3, 2016, https://www.youtube.com/watch?v=2FdLq_vRKmE (accessed February 2, 2017).
49. The Wooster Group, "Hamlet," The Wooster Group Company Website, accessed April 1, 2017, http://thewoostergroup.org/hamlet
50. W.B. Worthen, "Antigone's Bones," *TDR—Deb Margolin: I'm Just Sayin*, 52.3 (2008): 28.
51. Williams, *Modern Tragedy*, 121.
52. Emile Zola, "Naturalism on the Stage," in *Playwrights on Playwriting: From Ibsen to Ionesco*, ed. Toby Cole (New York: Cooper Square Press, 2001), 6.
53. Jeanette King, *Tragedy and the Victorian Novel*, 39.
54. David Lenson, *Achilles' Choice*, 1–23.
55. Stanley Corngold, "Sebald's Tragedy," in *Rethinking Tragedy*, ed. Rita Felski (Baltimore Johns Hopkins University Press, 2008), 236.
56. Max Frisch, *Homo faber. A Report*, trans. Michael Bullock (Orlando, FL: Harvest Books, 1959), 179.
57. David Desser, "The New Eve: The Influence of Paradise Lost and Frankenstein on Blade Runner," in *Retrofitting Blade Runner: Issues in Ridley Scott's Blade Runner and Philip K. Dick's Do Androids Dream of Electric Sheep*, ed. Judith B. Kerman (Bowling Green, OH: Bowling Green State University Popular Press, 1991), 55. See also Decio Torres Cruz, *Postmodern meta-narratives: Literature in the Age of the Image. Scott's Blade Runner and Puig's novels*. PhD Diss. State University of New York Buffalo: Proquest Dissertations Publishing, 1998.
58. Elizabeth Bronfen, "Femme Fatale—Negotiations of Tragic Desire," in *Rethinking Tragedy*, ed. Rita Felski (Baltimore: Johns Hopkins University Press, 2008), 288.
59. Jennifer Wallace, *The Cambridge Introduction to Tragedy* (Cambridge: Cambridge University Press, 2007), 158.
60. Susan Sontag, *Against Interpretation*, 20.
61. Richard Mosse, "Artist Statement," http://richardmosse.com/projects/artist-statement#home (accessed July 30, 2017).
62. For an extensive discussion of tragic sites and the relationship of tragedy and ecology, please refer to Chapter 2 in this volume.
63. John Torpey, *Making Whole What Has Been Smashed* (Cambridge, MA: Harvard University Press, 2006), 24.

Chapter Two

1. Will Eno, *Tragedy: A Tragedy* (London: Oberon Books, 2001), 2–3.
2. Young Jean Lee, ed., *New Downtown Now: An Anthology of New Theater from Downtown New York* (Minneapolis: University of Minnesota, 2006).
3. Richard Schechner, "9/11 as Avant-Garde Art?" *PMLA* 124, no. 5 (2009): 1820–9.
4. See also Samuel Adamson (and others), *Decade: Twenty new plays about 9/11 and its legacy* (London: Nick Hern, 2011).
5. Ruby Cohn, *From Desire to Godot: Pocket Theatre of Postwar Paris* (Berkeley, CA: University of California Press, 1987).
6. Raymond Williams, "Drama in a Dramatised Society" (1974), in *Writing in Society* (London: Verso, 1983), 11–21.
7. Guy Debord, *Society of the Spectacle* (Detroit: Black & Red, 1977) and Guy Debord, *Comments on the Society of the Spectacle*, trans. Malcolm Imrie (London: Verso, 1990).
8. Edward S. Hermand and Noam Chomsky, *Manufacturing Consent: The Political Economy of the Mass Media* (New York: Pantheon Books, 1988).
9. Nick Kaye, *Site-Specific Art: Performance, Place and Documentation* (London: Routledge, 2000); Mike Pearson, *Site-specific Performance* (Basingstoke: Palgrave Macmillan, 2010); Anne Birch and Joanne Tompkins, eds., *Performing Site-specific Theatre: Politics, Place, Practice* (Basingstoke: Palgrave Macmillan, 2012); and Hans-Thies Lehmann, *Tragedy and Dramatic Theatre*, trans. Erik Butler (London and New York: Routledge, 2016).
10. See, for example, Wyatt Bonikowski. *Shell Shock and the Modernist Imagination: The Death Drive in Post World War I British Fiction* (Burlington: Ashgate, 2013); Walter A. Davis, *Deracination: Historicity, Hiroshima, and the Tragic Imperative* (Albany: State University of New York Press, 2001) and *Death's Dream Kingdom: The American Psyche Since 9-11* (London & Ann Arbor: Michigan University Press, 2006).
11. Catharine Arnold, *Pandemic 1918: The Story of the Deadliest Influenza in History* (London: Michael O'Mara Books, 2018).
12. T.W. Adorno, "Cultural Criticism and Society" (1949), trans. Samuel and Shierry Weber, in *Prisms* (London: Neville Spearman, 1967).
13. John Turpin, "Monumental Commemoration of the Fallen in Ireland, North and South, 1920–60," *New Hibernia Review / Iris Éireannach Nua*, 11, No. 4 (Winter, 2007): 107–119.
14. James E. Young, *The Texture of Memory: Holocaust Memorials and Meaning* (New Haven: Yale University Press, 1993).
15. Frank O'Hara, *What's With Modern Art: selected short reviews & other art writings*, ed. Bill Berkson (Austin, TX: Mike and Dale's Press, 1999), 27.
16. Philip Auslander, *Liveness: Performance in a Mediatized Culture* (Abingdon: Routledge, 2008).
17. Sean Carney, *The Politics and Poetics of Contemporary English Tragedy* (Toronto: University of Toronto Press, 2013).
18. David Palmer, ed., *Visions of Tragedy in Modern American Drama: from O'Neill to the Twenty-First Century* (London: Bloomsbury, 2018).
19. Joe Kelleher and Nicholas Ridout, *The Theatre of Societas Raffaello Sanzio* (London: Routledge, 2007). See Kélina Gotman's further discussion of this theater company later in this volume.
20. See Bill McKibben, *The End of Nature* (New York: Random, 1989); and Timothy Morton, *Ecology without Nature: Rethinking Environmental Aesthetics* (Cambridge, MA: Harvard

University Press, 2009). See also Carolyn Merchant, *The Death of Nature: Women, Ecology and the Scientific Revolution* (San Francisco: Harper & Row, 1980).
21. Stephen M. Gardiner, *A Perfect Moral Storm: The Ethical Tragedy of Climate Change* (Oxford: Oxford University Press, 2011).
22. Jason M. Moore, ed., *Anthropocene or Capitalocene?: Nature, History, and the Crisis of Capitalism* (Oakland, CA: PM Press. 2016).
23. Franz J. Broswimmer, *Ecocide: A Short History of the Mass Extinction of the Species* (London: Pluto, 2002).
24. Baz Kershaw, *Theatre Ecology: Environments and Performance Events* (Cambridge: Cambridge University Press, 2007); and Gabriella Giannchi and Nigel Stewart, eds., *Performing Nature: Explorations in Ecology and the Arts* (Bern: Peter Lang, 2005).
25. Elle Carpenter, ed., *The Nuclear Culture Sourcebook* (London: Black Dog, 2016); and Lucy Neal, ed., *Playing for Time: Making Art as if the World Mattered* (London: Oberon, 2015).
26. Royal Court, "Environmental Policy" (2012–18), website mission statement: https://royalcourttheatre.com/about/environmental-policy/ (accessed August 5, 2018).
27. Raymond Williams, *Modern Tragedy* (London: Chatto and Windus, 1966), 87–105 and *passim*.
28. Elizabeth Kolbert, *The Sixth Extinction: An Unnatural History* (London: Bloomsbury, 2014).
29. Bradon Smith, "Staging Climate Change: the last ten years" (2014), http://bradonsmith.com/wp-content/uploads/2014/04/Staging-climate-change-the-last-ten-years.pdf (accessed August 8, 2018).
30. Steve Waters, *The Contingency Plan* (London: Nick Hern Books, 2009).
31. Mike Pearson, *Site-specific Performance*; Anna Birch and Joanne Tompkins, *Performing Site-specific Theatre*; Katia Arfara, Aneta Mancewicz, and Ralf Remshardt, eds., *Intermedial Performance and Politics in the Public Sphere* (Basingstoke: Palgrave Macmillan, 2018).
32. T.W. Adorno, *Minima Moralia: Reflections from Damaged Life*, trans. E.F.N. Jephcott (London: Verso, 1974), 144.
33. Jan Selby, Omar S. Dahi, Christiane Frölich, and Mike Hulme, "Climate change and the Syrian civil war revisited," *Political Geography*, 60 (September 2017): 232–44.
34. Duncan Ackerley, Ben B.B. Booth, Sylvia H.E. Knight, Eleanor J. Highwood, David J. Frame, Myles R. Allen, and David P. Rowell, "Sensitivity of Twentieth-Century Sahel Rainfall to Sulfate Aerosol and CO_2 Forcing," *Journal of Climate*, 24.19 (2011): 4999–5014.
35. Mohamed Osman Akasha, *Darfur: A Tragedy of Climate Change* (Hamburg: Anchor, 2013).
36. Raymond Williams, *Modern Tragedy*, 2nd edition, 207.
37. Michael Marder, *The Chernobyl Herbarium: Fragments of an Exploded Consciousness* (London: Open Humanities, 2016).
38. Marder, *The Chernobyl Herbarium*, 50.
39. Serhii Plokhy, *Chernobyl: The History of a Tragedy* (London: Allen Lane, 2018).
40. Eva Urban, *Community Politics and the Peace Process in Contemporary Northern Irish Drama* (Bern: Peter Lang, 2010).
41. Rustom Bharucha, "Between Truth and Reconciliation: Experiments in Theatre and Public Culture," *Economic and Political Weekly*, 36.39 (2001): 3763–73.
42. Steve Waters, "The truth behind the facts," *The Guardian*, February 11, 2004.
43. Downing Cless, *Ecology and Environment in European Drama* (New York: Routledge, 2010).
44. Lucien Goldmann, *The Hidden God: A Study of Tragic Vision in the Pensées of Pascal and the Tragedies of Racine*, trans. Philip Thody (London: Routledge & Kegan Paul, 1964).
45. Randall Martin, *Shakespeare and Ecology* (Oxford: Oxford University Press, 2015).
46. Peter Brook, *The Empty Space* (London: Penguin, 1972).

47. David Wiles, *Tragedy in Athens: Performance Space and Theatrical Meaning* (Cambridge: Cambridge University Press, 1997).
48. David Wiles, *A Short History of Performance Space* (Cambridge: Cambridge University Press, 2003), 259.
49. Frederic Spotts, *Bayreuth: A History of the Wagner Festival* (New Haven and London: Yale University Press, 1994).
50. Vanessa Lacey, "The History of the Cambridge Greek Play" (2015), http://www.cambridgegreekplay.com/the-history-of-the-cambridge-greek-play (accessed August 5, 2018).
51. Christie Carson and Farah Karim-Cooper, eds., *Shakespeare's Globe: A Theatrical Experiment* (Cambridge: Cambridge University Press, 2008).
52. Graham Ley, "Modern Visions of Greek Tragic Dancing," *Theatre* Journal, 55.3 (2003): 467–80. See Olga Taxidou's discussion later in this volume and Figure 3.1.
53. Lynn Garafola, *Diaghilev's Ballets Russes* (New York & Oxford: Oxford University Press, 1989); and Jane Pritchard and Geoffrey Marsh, eds., *Diaghilev and the Golden Age of the Ballets Russes 1909–1929* (London: V. & A., 2010).
54. Nurit Yaari, "Myth into Dance: Martha Graham's Interpretation of the Classical Tradition," *International Journal of the Classical Tradition*, 10.2 (2003): 221–42.
55. Yvonne Rainer, "Some retrospective notes on a dance for 10 people and 12 mattresses called 'Parts of Some Sextets,'" *The Tulane Drama Review*, 10, No. 2 (Winter, 1965): 168–78.
56. Royd Climenhaga, *Pina Bausch* (London: Routledge, 2009) and Royd Climenhaga, ed., *The Pina Bausch Sourcebook: The Making of Tanztheater* (London: Routledge, 2013).
57. T.W. Adorno, *Aesthetic Theory*, trans. Robert Hullot-Kentor (London: Continuum, 2002), 199.
58. Claude Lanzmann, "Why Spielberg has distorted the truth," *The Guardian Weekly* (April 3, 1994): 14.
59. David Ingram, *Green Screen: Environmentalism and Hollywood Cinema* (Exeter: Exeter University Press, 2000).
60. Sean Cubitt, *Ecomedia* (Amsterdam: Rodopi, 2005); and Sean Cubitt, Stephen Rust, and Salma Monani, eds., *The Ecocinema Reader: Theory and Practice* (London: Routledge, 2012).
61. Gregg Mitman, *Reel Nature: America's Romance with Wildlife on Films* (Cambridge, MA: Harvard University Press, 1999).
62. Chris Marker, *Sans Soleil* (1983): translation of the spoken script: https://www.markertext.com/sans_soleil.htm (accessed August 5, 2018).
63. Wole Soyinka, *Myth, Literature and the African World* (Cambridge: Cambridge University Press, 1976), 144–5.
64. Biodun Jeyifo, *Wole Soyinka: Politics, Poetics, and Postcolonialism* (Cambridge: Cambridge University Press, 2003).
65. Olabode Ibironke, "The Fourth Stage: Wole Soyinka and the Social Character of Ibadan," *History Compass*, 13/11 (2015): 541–9.
66. Samuel Beckett, *Imagination Dead Imagine* (London: Caldar Publications Ltd, 1966). An adaptation of Beckett's four-page prose work was staged by Mabou Mines, directed by Ruth Maleczech, and shown at the Performing Garage, New York, June 1984.
67. Ngũgĩ wa Thiong'o, "Language of African Theatre," in *Decolonising the Mind: The Politics of Language in African Theatre* (London: Heinemann, 1986), 37.
68. Ngũgĩ wa Thiong'o, *Decolonising the Mind*, 42.
69. Ngũgĩ wa Thiong'o, *Decolonising the Mind*, 59.
70. Cecilia Vicuña, *Spit Temple: the selected performance of*, trans. Rosa Alcalá (Brooklyn, NY: Ugly Duckling Presse, 2012).

Chapter Three

1. Peter Szondi, *An Essay on the Tragic*, trans. Paul Fleming (Stanford, CA: Meridian: Crossing Aesthetics, Stanford University Press, 2002), 1.
2. Miriam Leonard, *Tragic Modernities* (Cambridge, MA: Harvard University Press, 2015), 43.
3. George Steiner, *The Death of Tragedy* (London: Faber & Faber, 1961).
4. Jacques Rancière, *The Politics of Aesthetics: The Distribution of the Sensible*, trans. and ed. Gabriel Rockhill (2004; London and New York: Bloomsbury Academic, 2013), 7–15; also see *Aisthesis: Scenes from the Aesthetic Regime of Art*, trans. Paul Zakir (London and New York: Verso), ix–xii.
5. Walter Benjamin, "The Task of the Translator," in *Illuminations*, trans. H. Zohn, ed. and intro. Hannah Arendt (1923; London: Fontana, 1992), 70–82.
6. Leonard, *Tragic Modernities*, 132.
7. See Stephen Halliwell, *The Aesthetics of Mimesis: Ancient Texts and Modern Problems* (Princeton: Princeton University Press, 2002), 99.
8. Philippe Lacoue-Labarthe, "Hölderlin's Theatre," in *Tragedy and Philosophy*, ed. Miguel de Beistegui and Simon Sparks (London: Routledge, 2000), 118–19.
9. Laurence Senelick, *Gordon Craig's Moscow Hamlet: A Reconstruction* (Westport, CT: Greenwood, Praeger, 1982).
10. Antonin Artaud, *Collected Works Vol. 4*, trans. Victor Corti (London: Calder and Boyars, 1968), 252–9.
11. Mary Beard, *The Invention of Jane Harrison* (Cambridge: Harvard University Press, 2000).
12. Robert Ackerman, *The Myth and Ritual School: J. G. Frazer and the Cambridge Ritualists* (1991; London: Routledge, 2002).
13. Fiona Macintosh, "From the Court to the National: The Theatrical Legacy of Gilbert Murray's *Bacchae*', in *Gilbert Murray Reassessed: Hellenism, Theatre, and International Politics*, ed. Christopher Stray (Oxford: Oxford University Press, 2007), 145–65.
14. Martha Carpentier, *Ritual, Myth and the Modernist Text: The Influence of Jane Ellen Harrison on Joyce, Eliot and Woolf* (London: Routledge, 1998).
15. Julie Stone Peters, "Jane Harrison and the Savage Dionysus: Archaeological Voyages, Ritual Origins, Anthropology, and the Modern Theatre," *Modern Drama* 51, no. 1 (2008): 1–41.
16. W.B. Yeats, "The Tragic Generation," in *Autobiographies* (1914; London: Macmillan, 1955), 279–348.
17. Jacques Rancière, "The Archaeomodern Turn," in *Walter Benjamin and the Demands of History*, ed. Michael P. Steinberg (Ithaka: Cornell University Press, 1996), 24–40. This argument is developed in Vassiliki Kolocotroni, "Still Life: Modernism's Turn to Greece," *Journal of Modern Literature* 35, no. 2 (2012):1–24.
18. Isadora Duncan, *My Life* (1927; New York: Liveright, 1996), 5.
19. Ibid., 35.
20. Ibid., 69.
21. Edward Gordon Craig, "The Actor and the Übermarionette," in *The Mask* 1, no. 2 (Florence: The Arena Goldoni, 1908), reissued with index by Lorelei Guidry (New York: Benjamin Blom, 1967).
22. L.M. Newman, *Edward Gordon Craig, Black Figures: 105 Reproductions with an Unpublished Essay* (Wellingborough: Christopher Skelton, 1989).
23. Plato, *Republic*, III, 395. Qtd. in *The Mask* 1, no. 1, 5.
24. Aristotle, *Poetics*, VI, 19 and XXVI, 1–4. Qtd. in *The Mask* 1, no. 1, 11.

25. L.M. Newman, "Reinhardt and Craig?," in *Max Reinhardt: the Oxford Symposium*, ed. Margaret Jakobs and John Warren (Oxford: Oxford Polytechnic, 1986), 6–15, 8.
26. Senelick, *Gordon Craig's Moscow Hamlet: A Reconstruction.*
27. Jean Cocteau, "Preface to *The Wedding on the Eiffel Tower*," in *Modern French Plays: An Anthology from Jarry to Ionesco*, trans. Michael Benedikt (1922; London: Faber and Faber, 1964), 96–7.
28. T.S. Eliot, "Euripides and Professor Murray," in *The Complete Prose of T. S. Eliot, Vol. 2: 1919-1926*, ed. Anthony Cuda and Ronald Schuchard (1920; Baltimore: Johns Hopkins University Press, and London: Faber and Faber, 2014), 195–201, 201.
29. Ezra Pound, *Guide to Kulcher* (1938; New York: New Directions, 1970), 93.
30. T.S. Eliot, "Dramatis Personae," in *Complete Prose of T. S. Eliot, Vol. 2*, 430–4, 434.
31. E. Martin Browne, *The Making of T. S. Eliot's Plays* (Cambridge: Cambridge University Press, 1969), 34–79.
32. T.S. Eliot, qtd in David E. Jones, *The Plays of T. S. Eliot* (London: Routledge & Kegan Paul, 1960), 52.
33. T.S. Eliot, "Poetry and Drama," in *Selected Prose of T. S. Eliot*, ed. Frank Kermode (1951; New York: Farrar, Straus and Giroux, 1975), 132–47, 139.
34. Ibid., 144.
35. Ibid., 141.
36. Ibid., 141.
37. T. S. Eliot, qtd in Browne, *The Making of T. S. Eliot's Plays*, 108.
38. W.B. Yeats, *The Collected Works of W. B. Yeats, Vol. II The Plays*, ed. David R. Clark and Rosalind E. Clark (New York: Scribner, 2001), 481–2.
39. W.B. Yeats, *Explorations* (London: Macmillan, 1962), 263.
40. Ezra Pound, *Women of Trachis, A Version by Ezra Pound* (London: Faber and Faber, 1956), ii.
41. Ezra Pound and Rudd Fleming, *Sophokles, Electra, A Version by Ezra Pound and Rudd Fleming*, ed. Carey Perloff (New York: New Directions Books, 1990), 73.
42. Katerina Stergiopoulou, "'And a Good Job'? Elektrifying English at St. Elizabeth's," *Journal of Modern Literature* 39, no. 1 (2015): 87–111, 100.
43. David Wiles, "Sophoclean Diptychs: Modern Translations of Dramatic Poetry," *A Journal of Humanities and the Classics* 13, no. 1 (2005): 9–26, 17.
44. Jacques Rancière, "The Archaeomodern Turn," 28–9.
45. Bertolt Brecht, "A Short Organum for the Theatre," in *Brecht on Theatre*, trans. and ed. John Willett (1957; London: Methuen, 1964), 180.
46. Ibid.,189.
47. Walter Benjamin, "The Task of the Translator," 72.
48. Ibid., 82.
49. Bertolt Brecht, "Texts by Brecht," in *Brecht, Collected Plays Vol 8*, ed. Tom Kuhn and David Constantine (London: Methuen, 2003), 209.
50. Anthony Tatlow, *Brecht, Shakespeare and the Intercultural Sign* (Durham, US: Duke University Press, 2001); Hans-Thies Lehmann, *Postdramatic Theatre*, trans. Karen Jürs-Munby (London: Routledge, 2006).
51. Antonin Artaud, *Collected Works Vol. 4*, 252–9.
52. Ibid., 252.
53. Ibid., 252.
54. Brian Singleton, "Plague," in *Le Théâtre et son double* (London: Grant & Cutler Ltd, 1998), 23–31.

NOTES   173

55. Hans-Thies Lehmann, *Postdramatic Theatre*; *Tragedy and Dramatic Theatre*, trans. Erik Butler (London: Routledge, 2016).
56. Olga Taxidou, "Machines and Models for Modern Tragedy: Brecht/Berlau, *Antigone-Model 1948*," in *Rethinking Tragedy*, ed. Rita Felski (Baltimore: The Johns Hopkins University Press, 2008), 241–62.

Chapter Four

1. Sigmund Freud, *Civilization and Its Discontents*, trans. James Strachey (New York: W.W. Norton and Co., 1961), 82.
2. Paul Gordon, *Tragedy after Nietzsche: Rapturous Superabundance* (Champaign, IL: University of Illinois Press, 2001), 55.
3. Freud, *Civilization and Its Discontents*, 95.
4. Ibid., 50.
5. Friedrich Nietzsche, *Ecce Homo*, *The Genealogy of Morals and Ecce Homo*, trans. Walter Kaufmann (New York: Vintage Books, 1989), 273.
6. Martin Heidegger, *Nietzsche*, vol. 1, trans. David Farrell Krell (San Francisco: Harper San Francisco, 1979), 28. Emphasis in original.
7. Martin Heidegger, *Introduction to Metaphysics*, trans. Gregory Fried and Richard Polt (New Haven: Yale University Press, 2000), 174.
8. Heidegger, *Metaphysics*, 117.
9. Ibid., 156.
10. Ibid., 161.
11. Ibid.
12. Jean-Paul Sartre, *Being and Nothingness: An Essay on Phenomenological Ontology*, trans. Hazel E. Barnes (New York: Philosophical Library, 1956), 439.
13. Ibid., 590.
14. Jean-Paul Sartre, "Existentialism is a Humanism," in *Existentialism is a Humanism*, trans. Annie Cohen-Solal, ed. John Kulka (New Haven: Yale University Press, 2007), 29.
15. Cerness Moran, *Jean-Paul Sartre: A Tragic Ontology of Freedom* (Washington D.C.: Catholic University of America, 1978); Maurice Natanson, "Jean-Paul Sartre's Philosophy of Freedom," in *Sartre and Existentialism: Existentialist Ontology and Human Consciousness*, ed. William L. McBridge (New York: Routledge, 1997), 30–46, 46.
16. Jean-Paul Sartre, jacket copy for *Les Mouches* (Paris: Gallimard, 1943); translated in *Sartre on Theater*, ed. Michel Contat and Michel Rybalka (London: Quartet Books, 1976), 186.
17. Sartre, *Sartre on Theatre*, 328.
18. Albert Camus, "The Myth of Sisyphus," in *The Myth of Sisyphus and Other Essays*, trans. Justin O'Brien (New York: Vintage Books, 1991), 23.
19. Ibid.
20. Ibid., 24.
21. Ibid.
22. Ibid.
23. Ibid.
24. Ibid.
25. Simone de Beauvoir, "Existentialist Theatre," in *"The Useless Mouths" and Other Literary Writings*, ed. Margaret A. Simons and Marybeth Timmermann (Champaign, IL: University of Illinois Press, 2011), 125–50, 146.

26. Simone de Beauvoir, *The Second Sex*, trans. Constance Borde and Sheila Malovany-Chevallier (New York: Vintage Books, 2011), 158.
27. Martin Heidegger, "The Origin of the Work of Art," in *Basic Writings*, trans. David Farrell Krell (San Francisco: Harper San Francisco, 1993), 139–212, 204.
28. Ibid., 202.
29. Ibid., 166.
30. Ibid., 170, 169.
31. Ibid., 166.
32. Ibid., 168–9.
33. Ibid., 169.
34. De Beauvoir, "Existentialist Theatre," 139.
35. Jean-Paul Sartre, *Un théâtre de situations* (Paris: Gallimard, 1992), 139. Translated in Christina Howells, *Sartre: The Necessity of Freedom* (Cambridge: Cambridge University Press, 2009), 80.
36. De Beauvoir, "Existentialist Theatre," 140.
37. Peter Norrish, *New Tragedy and Comedy in France, 1945–1970* (Lanham, MD: Rowman and Littlefield, 1988), 29.
38. Jean-Paul Sartre, *"What is Literature?" and Other Essays*, trans. Bernard Frechtman (Cambridge: Harvard University Press, 1988), 235.
39. Walter Benjamin, *The Origin of German Tragic Drama*, trans. John Osborne (New York: Verso, 1998), 60.
40. Ibid., 79.
41. Ibid., 78.
42. Ibid., 62.
43. Ibid., 81.
44. Hannah Arendt, *On Revolution* (New York: Penguin Books, 1990), 281.
45. Hannah Arendt, "Nightmare and Flight," in *Essays in Understanding, 1930–1954: Formation, Exile, and Totalitarianism* (New York: Schochen Books, 1994), 133–5, 133.
46. Arendt, *Revolution*, 281.
47. Edward Said, "The Palestinian Experience," in *The Edward Said Reader*, ed. Moustafa Bayoumi and Andrew Rubin (New York: Vintage Books, 2000), 14–37, 34.
48. Ibid.
49. Ibid.
50. Ibid.
51. Ibid.
52. Max Horkheimer and Theodor W. Adorno, *Dialectic of Enlightenment: Philosophical Fragments*, ed. Gunzelin Schmid Noerr, trans. Edmund Jephcott (Stanford: Stanford University Press, 2002), 4.
53. Ibid., 124.
54. Ibid.
55. Theodor W. Adorno, "Is Art Lighthearted?" in *Notes to Literature*, vol. 2, ed. Rolf Tiedemann, trans. Shierry Weber Nicholsen (New York: Columbia University Press, 1992), 247–56, 251.
56. Ibid., 252.
57. Gilles Deleuze and Felix Guattari, *Anti-Oedipus: Capitalism and Schizophrenia*, trans. Robert Hurley, Mark Stern, and Helen R. Lane (Minneapolis: University of Minnesota Press, 1983), 330.
58. Ibid., 417.

59. Jean-Pierre Vernant, "Oedipus Without the Complex," in Jean-Pierre Vernant and Pierre Vidal-Naquet, *Myth and Tragedy in Ancient Greece*, trans. Janet Lloyd (New York: Zone Books, 1990), 85–112, 88.
60. Jacques Derrida, *Dissemination*, trans. Barbara Johnson (New York: Continuum, 1981), 131, n. 56; 132, n. 59.
61. Ibid., 352.
62. David McDonald, "The Trace of Absence: a Derridean Analysis of 'Oedipus Rex,'" *Theatre Journal* 31.2 (May 1979): 147–61, 147.
63. Deleuze and Guattari, *Anti-Oedipus*, 13, 312.
64. Ibid., 314.
65. Jacques Lacan, *The Ethics of Psychoanalysis, 1959–1960*, vol. VII, ed. Jacques-Alain Miller, trans. Dennis Porter (London: Routledge, 1992), 282.
66. Julian Young, *The Philosophy of Tragedy: From Plato to Žižek* (Cambridge: Cambridge University Press, 2013), 265.
67. Lacan, *Ethics of Psychoanalysis*, 278.
68. Luce Irigaray, "Civil Rights and Responsibilities for the Two Sexes," in *Luce Irigaray: Key Writings* (New York: Continuum, 2004), 203.
69. Giorgio Agamben, *The Use of Bodies: Homo Sacer IV, 2*, trans. Adam Kotsko (Stanford: Stanford University Press, 2016), 236.
70. Judith Butler, *Antigone's Claim: Kinship Between Life and Death* (New York: Columbia University Press, 2002), 73.
71. Ibid., 40.
72. Slavoj Žižek, *Antigone* (London: Bloomsbury, 2016), xxi.
73. Slavoj Žižek, "Psychoanalysis in Post-Marxism: The Case of Alain Badiou," *The South Atlantic Quarterly* 97.2 (Spring 1998): 235–61, 253.
74. Miriam Leonard, *Tragic Modernities* (Cambridge: Harvard University Press, 2015), 161.
75. Žižek, *Antigone*, xiii.
76. Adorno, "Is Art Lighthearted?" 248, 249.
77. Jacques Derrida, *Spectres of Marx: The State of the Debt, the Work of Mourning, and the New International*, trans. Peggy Kamuf (New York: Routledge, 1994), 97.
78. Ibid., 113.
79. Martha Nussbaum, *The Fragility of Goodness: Luck and Ethics in Greek Tragedy and Philosophy*, rev. ed. (Cambridge: Cambridge University Press, 2001), 49–50.
80. Ibid., 50.
81. Cornel West, "On Prophetic Pragmatism," in *The Cornel West Reader* (New York: Basic Books, 2000), 149–74, 164.
82. Ibid., 166.
83. Ibid.
84. Ibid., 13.
85. Gilles Deleuze, *Nietzsche and Philosophy*, trans. Hugh Tomlinson (New York: Continuum, 2005), 16.
86. Ibid.

Chapter Five

1. Some parts of this chapter were published in an earlier form in the following works: Ben Quash, "Real Enactment: The Role of Drama in the Theology of Hans Urs von Balthasar," in *Faithful Performances: The Enactment of Christian Identity in Theology and the Arts*, ed.

Trevor Hart and Steven Guthrie (Aldershot: Ashgate, 2007); "Christianity as Hyper-Tragic," in *Facing Tragedies*, ed. Christopher Hamilton, Otto Neumaier, Gottfried Schweiger, and Clemens Sedmak (Wien-Berlin-Münster: LIT Verlag, 2009); "Four Biblical Characters: In Search of a Tragedy," in *Christian Theology and Tragedy: Theologians, Tragic Literature, and Tragic Theory*, ed. Kevin Taylor and Giles Waller (Aldershot: Ashgate, 2011).
2. See in particular Aaron Rosen, *Art + Religion in the 21st Century* (London: Thames and Hudson, 2015).
3. Theodor W. Adorno, "Is Art Lighthearted?" in *Notes to Literature*, vol. 2, ed. Rolf Tiedemann, trans. Shierry Weber Nicholsen (New York: Columbia University Press, 1992), 252.
4. Edward Said, "The Palestinian Experience," in *The Edward Said Reader*, ed. Moustafa Bayoumi and Andrew Rubin (New York: Vintage Books, 2000), 14–37, 34.
5. David Kornhaber, in this volume, p. 84; summarizing Walter Benjamin, *The Origin of German Tragic Drama*, trans. John Osborne (New York: Verso, 1998), 81.
6. A recent example of this point of view is Edith Hall's testy review in *Prospect Magazine* of Rowan Williams' *The Tragic Imagination*, bolstered by a blog post entitled "Why Greek Tragedy and Christianity Don't Mix." Oddly, Hall objects on two seemingly incompatible grounds, claiming both that Christianity is inclined "to subject tragedy to cosmetic surgery to reduce its ferocity" and that Williams' problem is that he doesn't acknowledge tragedy's beauty, its various upbeat endings, and its celebration of ennobling stoic resilience—in other words, Williams is *too* caught up with tragedy's "ferocity." http://edithorial.blogspot.co.uk/2016/11/why-greek-tragedy-and-christianity-dont.html (accessed November 2, 2017).
7. Thomas Hardy, *Jude the Obscure*, ed. Patricia Ingham (Oxford World's Classics; Oxford: Oxford University Press, 1985 [1895]), 85.
8. Hardy, *Jude the Obscure*, 85.
9. The continued power of this fable to speak to early twenty-first-century experience is attested to by Richard Ayoade's reworking of the novella in filmic form in his *The Double* of 2014.
10. Arthur Miller, *Death of a Salesman* (1948) (London: Penguin Books, 2000).
11. T.S. Eliot, "The Love Song of J. Alfred Prufrock," in *The Complete Poems and Plays of T.S. Eliot* (London: Faber and Faber, 2004), 16.
12. David Kornhaber also identifies the importance of this consideration in his chapter, noting how for Heidegger and, later, the French existentialists "estrangement" and "dislocation" are aligned with tragic experience.
13. Pankaj Mishra, "How to Think about Islamic State," *The Guardian*, July 24, 2015. https://www.theguardian.com/books/2015/jul/24/how-to-think-about-islamic-state (accessed January 22, 2018).
14. William Shakespeare, *King Lear*, Act 4, Scene 1.
15. Robert Louis Jackson, "Introduction: Vision in Darkness," in Fyodor Dostoevsky, *Notes from Underground* and *The Double* (London; New York: Penguin Classics, 2009), xi.
16. Cormac McCarthy, *The Road* (London: Picador, 2006), 88–9.
17. McCarthy, *The Road*, 183.
18. McCarthy, *The Road*, 77–8.
19. Burrows' photograph of a Vietnamese woman crying over the remains of her husband (Figure 5.1) echoes the characteristics of a traditional Pietà. We will return to a discussion of the theme of lament in the closing part of this chapter.
20. Karl Barth, *Church Dogmatics* 2.1 (Edinburgh: T&T Clark, 1957), 374.
21. Karl Barth, *Church Dogmatics* 2.2 (Edinburgh: T&T Clark, 1957), 502.
22. Hans Urs von Balthasar, *Theo-Drama: Theological Dramatic Theory*, 5 vols (San Francisco: Ignatius Press, 1988–98).

23. D.M. MacKinnon, *Explorations in Theology 5* (London: SCM, 1979), 68.
24. MacKinnon, *Explorations in Theology 5*, 194.
25. MacKinnon, *Explorations in Theology 5*, 58–9.
26. David Ford, "Tragedy and Atonement," in *Christ, Ethics and Tragedy: Essays in Honour of Donald MacKinnon*, ed. Kenneth Surin (Cambridge: Cambridge University Press, 1989), 117–30; see especially 123.
27. 2 Corinthians 2:16 (NRSV).
28. The phrase itself is that of John Keats in a letter of 1819. See *The Letters of John Keats, 1814–1821*, ed. Hyder Edward Rollins (Cambridge MA: Harvard University Press, 1958), 100.
29. In other words, whether you claim that evil has substantial being, or manifests a lack of being, is not necessarily the key index of how seriously you take it. The Augustinian suggestion that all apparent evil is, ultimately, a mere privation or distortion of being (and that all being has one ultimate source in an absolutely good God), is not in itself a panacea for the acuteness of tragic experience—you can, after all, *die* from a lack of something. Augustine's privative model of evil, in other words, is very serious about evil.
30. Rowan Williams, "Trinity and Ontology," in Surin, *Christ, Ethics and Tragedy*, 78.
31. MacKinnon, *Explorations in Theology 5*, 6.
32. David Bentley Hart, *The Beauty of the Infinite: The Aesthetics of Christian Truth* (Grand Rapids: Eerdmans, 2003), 374.
33. Hart, *The Beauty of the Infinite*, 375.
34. Hart, *The Beauty of the Infinite*, 383.
35. Hart, *The Beauty of the Infinite*, 384.
36. Hart, *The Beauty of the Infinite*, 392.
37. Kane herself was deeply indebted to Jacobean revenge tragedy, with its theological interests. See Graham Saunders, *"Love Me or Kill Me": Sarah Kane and the Theatre of Excess* (Manchester: Manchester University Press, 2002), for example, 18–23.
38. Rowan Williams, *Grace and Necessity: Reflections on Art and Love* (London: Bloomsbury, 2005), 100.
39. See the "Prayer of General Thanksgiving" in The Book of Common Prayer of the Church of England.
40. The film, and the ending in particular, are perceptively discussed by Slavoj Žižek in relation to the category of excess (and modernity's problems with certain sorts of excess) in "Femininity Between Goodness and Act," *Lacanian Ink* 14 (1999): 26–40. I am grateful to my graduate student Rebecca Ver Straten-McSparran for discussions about von Trier's work.
41. "I consider myself very fortunate. I was raised in a Christian environment in Abeokuta, but another side of me was very much enmeshed in African values." According to Soyinka, this enabled him to gravitate towards "what I saw was a cohesive system of a certain relationship of human beings to environment, a respect for humanity in general." Peter Godwin, "Wole Soyinka: 'If religion was taken away I'd be happy'", *Telegraph*, October 12, 2012. https://www.telegraph.co.uk/culture/hay-festival/9600954/Wole-Soyinka-If-religion-was-taken-away-Id-be-happy.html (accessed July 11, 2018).
42. "[P]owerful natural or cosmic influences are internalized within the protagonist" and this casts their passions onto a "titanic scale." Ketu H. Katrak, *Wole Soyinka and Modern Tragedy: A Study of Dramatic Theory and Practice* (Westport CT: Greenwood, 1986), 25; citing Wole Soyinka, *Myth, Literature and the African World* (Cambridge: Cambridge University Press, 1976), 43.

43. Wole Soyinka, "The Fourth Stage," in *The Morality of Art: Essays Presented to G. Wilson Knight by his Colleagues and Friends*, ed. D.W. Jefferson (London: Routledge, 1969), 128.
44. Katrak, *Wole Soyinka*, 19.
45. Katrak, *Wole Soyinka*, 40.
46. Soyinka, *Myth, Literature and the African World*, 56.
47. For example, Oren Goldenberg's *A Requiem for Douglass* (Figure 5.2), which ritualizes the destruction of the first public housing built primarily for African Americans in the U.S. from 1935–55. In the description of William J. Danaher Jr., the Douglass Towers were "once home to celebrated cultural icons like Diana Ross and Joe Louis"; their "degradation and dereliction," and eventual demolition in 2014, have therefore come to symbolize Detroit's catastrophic decline. *Requiem* is an interactive installation that creates "a ritual composed of many rituals." Entering a dark room, viewers are invited to deconstruct a sculpture of bricks salvaged from the Douglass towers. Moving each brick initiates a series of videos documenting both the destruction of the towers by massive machines and multiple rites of mourning—by church choirs, jazz funeral bands, modern and African dancers, indigenous ritualists, slam poets, and artists—filmed during the demolition. In this way, Goldenberg brought "not only the documentation of ritual to the viewer, but the act of ritual as well." William J. Danaher Jr., "Lamentation in Art: On Art, Ritual and Religion in Detroit"; paper delivered at the conference of the Society for the Study of Theology, University of Durham, 2016; citations from Oren Goldenberg, "Artist Statement," http://www.artxdetroit.com/art-x-detroit-2015/artists/oren-goldenberg/ (accessed January 19, 2018).
48. Danaher, "Lamentation in Art."
49. Psalm 103:16; Job 7:10.
50. Ellen Charry is an important voice in this regard, whose work has explored parallels between ancient Greek tragedy and the Psalms; both are collective exercises in resolutely facing the extremes of human experience without falling into a despairing silence. See Ellen T. Charry, *Psalms 1–50: Sighs and Songs of Israel*, Brazos Theological Commentary on the Bible (Grand Rapids MI: Brazos, 2015).
51. See, for example, Johann Baptist Metz's discussion of *Leiden an Gott* and the consequences of this for the imitation of Christ by his disciples, in *Followers of Christ: The Religious Life and the Church*, trans. Thomas Linton (New York NY: Paulist, 1978) and *passim*. See also the fine discussion of Metz in Andrew Prevot, *Thinking Prayer: Theology and Modernity Amid the Crises of Modernity* (Notre Dame IN: Notre Dame University Press, 2015).
52. See Cheryl J. Exum, *Tragedy and Biblical Narrative: Arrows of the Almighty* (Cambridge: Cambridge University Press, 1992).
53. See Søren Kierkegaard's famous treatment of Genesis 22 in *Fear and Trembling: Dialectical Lyric by Johannes De Silentio*, trans. Alastair Hannay (Harmondsworth: Penguin Classics, 1985) as well as George Steiner's philosophical-poetic response to the *Akedah* in *Proofs and Three Parables* (London: Granta Books, 1992).
54. See Rowan Williams, *The Tragic Imagination* (Oxford: Oxford University Press, 2016), 119–27.
55. Rebekah Eklund, *Jesus Wept: The Significance of Jesus' Laments in the New Testament* (London: Bloomsbury T&T Clark, 2015), 2.
56. Eklund, *Jesus Wept*, 14.
57. Eklund, *Jesus Wept*, 165.
58. Iris Murdoch, "The Sublime and the Good," *Chicago Review* 13.3 (1959): 50.
59. Murdoch, "The Sublime and the Good," 52.
60. Prevot, *Thinking Prayer*, 331.

Chapter Six

1. George Steiner, *The Death of Tragedy* (London: Faber & Faber, 1961), 342.
2. Ibid., 193.
3. Admittedly, not even Steiner would deny the enormity of the calamities of the twentieth century: "We are still waging Peloponnesian wars" (6).
4. Terry Eagleton, *Sweet Violence, The Idea of the Tragic* (Oxford: Blackwell Publishing 2003), 10.
5. Raymond Williams, *Modern Tragedy* (London: Chatto & Windus, 1966), 45–6.
6. Steiner, *The Death of Tragedy*, 8.
7. Ibid., 8–9.
8. Ibid., 350.
9. Ibid., 350.
10. Eagleton, *Sweet Violence*, 14.
11. Ibid., 15.
12. Williams, *Modern Tragedy*, 47.
13. Ibid., 13.
14. Ibid., 48.
15. Ibid., 48.
16. Ibid., 49.
17. Eagleton, *Sweet Violence*, 7.
18. For a fuller account of the historical development of a governmental discourse on the theatre, see my *Theatre and Governance in Britain 1500-1900: Theatre, Disorder and the State* (Cambridge: Cambridge University Press, 2017).
19. Bertolt Brecht, "Theatre for Pleasure of Theatre for Instruction," in *Brecht on Theatre: The Development of an Aesthetic*, trans. John Willett (London: Methuen Drama, 1964), 75.
20. Ibid., 75.
21. Arthur Miller, "Tragedy and the Common Man," in *The Theater Essays of Arthur Miller*, ed. Robert A. Martin. (London and New York: Penguin, 1978), 3.
22. Lillo wrote in his dedication: "Plays founded on moral tales in private life may be of admirable use by carrying conviction to the mind with such irresistible force as to engage all the faculties and powers of the soul in the case of virtue by stifling vice in its first principles." George Lillo, *The London Merchant* [1731] (Nebraska: University of Nebraska Press, 1965), 4.
23. Miller, "Tragedy and the Common Man," 5.
24. Ibid., 87.
25. Arthur Miller and Phillip Gelb, "Morality and Modern Drama: Interview with Arthur Miller and Phillip Gelb," *Education Theatre Journal*, 10.3 (October, 1958): 192.
26. Arthur Miller, *Death of a Salesman* (London: Penguin Books, 2000), 40–1.
27. Ibid., 38.
28. Martin Dworkin in "Arthur Miller's *Death of a Salesman*: A Symposium. Arthur Miller, Gore Vidal, Richard Watts, John Beauford, Martin Dworkin, David W. Thompson and Phillip Gelb," *The Tulane Drama Review*, 2.3 (May, 1958): 63–4.
29. Ibid., 64.
30. Miller, *Death of a Salesman*, 105.
31. Martin Heidegger, *The Fundamental Concepts of Metaphysics: World, Finitude, Solitude*, trans. William McNeill and Nicholas Walker (Indiana: Indiana University Press 1995), 365.
32. In *Being and Time*, Heidegger would describe Dasein's relation to facticity as follows: "In its factical Being, any Dasein is as it already was, and it is 'what it already was'. It *is* its past,

whether explicitly or not . . . whatever the way of being it may have at the time, and thus with whatever understanding of Being, it may possess, Dasein has grown up both into and in a traditional way of interpreting itself." *Being and Time*, trans. John Macquarrie and Edward Robinson, new edn. (New York: Harper Collins, 2008), 41.
33. Heidegger, *The Fundamental Concepts of Metaphysics*, 366.
34. Miller, *Death of a Salesman*, 106. Miller also adds that Loman is "seeking a kind of ecstasy in life which the machine civilization deprives people of": Miller and Gelb, "Morality and Modern Drama, Interview with Arthur Miller and Phillip Gelb," 192.
35. Miller, *Death of a Salesman*, 105.
36. Miller, "Tragedy and the Common Man," 5.
37. John Beauford, "*Death of a Salesman*: A Symposium," 65.
38. Miller, "Tragedy and the Common Man," 4–5.
39. Miller and Gelb, "Morality and Modern Drama, Interview with Arthur Miller and Phillip Gelb," 90.
40. Theodor W. Adorno, *History and Freedom, Lectures, 1964–1965*, trans. Rodney Livingstone (Cambridge: Polity Press, 2006), 86, 87.
41. Ibid., 87.
42. Ibid., 3, 4.
43. Ibid., 4.
44. Ibid., 7.
45. Ibid., 207.
46. Hannah Arendt, *The Life of the Mind* (San Diego: Harvest Books, 1978), 191.
47. Ibid., 191.
48. Ibid., 4.
49. Ibid., 4.
50. Adriana Cavarero, *Horrorism: Naming Contemporary Violence*, trans. William McCuiag (New York: Columbia University Press, 2011), 39.
51. Ibid., 39.
52. Ibid., 34.
53. Williams, *Modern Tragedy*, 53.
54. Ibid., 59.
55. Ibid., 59.
56. Ibid., 61.
57. Primo Levi, *If This is a Man*, trans. Stuart Woolf (London: Abacus Books, 1987), 96.
58. Giorgio Agamben, *Remnants of Auschwitz: The Witness and The Archive*, trans. Daniel Heller-Roazen (New York: Zone Books, 1999), 81.
59. Ibid., 55.
60. Ibid., 34.
61. Walter Benjamin, "The Storyteller," in *Illuminations*, trans. Harry Zorn (London: Pimlico, 1999), 83.
62. Benjamin, "The Storyteller," 84.
63. Giorgio Agamben, *Infancy and History: On the Destruction of Experience*, trans. Liz Heron (London: Verso, 2007), 15.
64. Ibid., 16.
65. Theodor W. Adorno, "Commitment," in *Notes to Literature, vol. two*, trans. Shierry Weber Nicholson (New York: Columbia University Press, 1992), 87.
66. Ibid., 88.
67. Ibid., 88.

68. Ibid., 88.
69. Ibid., 88.
70. Ibid., 88.
71. Ibid., 88.
72. Ibid., 88.
73. Ibid., 93.
74. Ibid, 94.
75. Theodor W. Adorno, *Aesthetic Theory*, trans. Robert Hullot-Kentor (London: Continuum, 2002), 243.
76. Ibid., 238.
77. Ibid., 238, 232.
78. Ibid., 82.
79. Ibid., 83.
80. Ibid., 253.
81. Ibid., 252.
82. Adorno, "Commitment," 90.
83. Heiner Müller, "Waterfront Wasteland," in *Theatremachine*, trans. Marc von Henning (London: Faber and Faber, 1995), 57.

Chapter Seven

1. The UK's hitched.co.uk surveyed thousands of newlywed couples, at http://hitched-wife.org/wedding-facts-economics/summary-stats/each-year-uk-weddings-are-worth-10-billion-pounds/ (accessed May 18, 2017). See also Andre Bourque, "Technology Profits and Pivots in the $300 Billion Wedding Space," *The Huffington Post*, January 5, 2015, updated May 1, 2016, at http://www.huffingtonpost.com/andre-bourque/technology-profit-and-piv_b_7193112.html (accessed May 18, 2017).
2. See e.g., Heather Widdows, "Border Disputes across Bodies: Exploitation in Trafficking for Prostitution and Egg Sale for Stem Cell Research," *International Journal of Feminist Approaches to Bioethics* 2.1 (2009): 5–24.
3. Donna Haraway discusses "naturecultures" in *The Companion Species Manifesto: Dogs, People, and Significant Otherness* (Chicago: Prickly Paradigm Press, 2003).
4. See e.g., Terry Eagleton, *Sweet Violence: The Idea of the Tragic* (Oxford: Blackwell, 2003): 95.
5. Eagleton, *Sweet Violence*, 55–6.
6. See esp. Gilles Deleuze and Félix Guattari, *Anti-Oedipus: Capitalism and Schizophrenia*, preface by Michel Foucault, trans. Robert Hurley, Mark Seem, and Helen R. Lane (Minneapolis: University of Minnesota Press, 1983).
7. Natalia Sarkisian and Naomi Gerstel, *Nuclear Family Values, Extended Family Lives: The Power of Race, Class and Gender* (New York and London: Routledge, 2012), 1.
8. The expression "leader of the free world" came increasingly into use with the Cold War. See John Fousek, *To Lead the Free World: American Nationalism and the Cultural Roots of the Cold War* (Chapel Hill and London: The University of North Carolina Press, 2000).
9. Aldous Huxley, *Brave New World* (London: Vintage Classics, 2007 [1932]).
10. Giorgio Agamben, *State of Exception*, trans. Kevin Attell (Chicago and London: The University of Chicago Press, 2005).
11. See Michel Foucault, "The Politics of Health in the Eighteenth Century," in Michel Foucault, *Power: The Essential Works of Foucault 1954–1984*, ed. James D. Faubion and trans. Robert Hurley and others, 3 vols., vol. 3 (London: Penguin Books, 2000), 90–105.

12. Julie A. Carlson, "Like Me: An Invitation to *Domestic/Tragedy*," *SAQ* 98.3 (1999): 332.
13. Hannah Arendt, *The Human Condition*, 2nd edn (Chicago: University of Chicago Press, 1998), 38.
14. Sara Ahmed, *Living a Feminist Life* (Durham and London: Duke University Press, 2017), 10–13ff.
15. "Affinities: Villa Gillet's Walls and Bridges Series | The New School for Public Engagement," available at https://www.youtube.com/watch?v=8k91WwJIhl8 (accessed 17 May, 2017).
16. "Affinities."
17. See http://blacklivesmatter.com/herstory/ and http://blacklivesmatter.com/guiding-principles/ (accessed October 3, 2016).
18. Mojisola Adebayo, "Everything You Know About Queerness You Learnt from Blackness: The Afri-Quia Theatre of Black Dykes, Crips and Kids," in *Queer Dramaturgies: International Perspectives on Where Performance Leads Queer*, ed. Alyson Campbell and Stephen Farrier (Houndmills, Basingstoke: Palgrave, 2016), 131.
19. Adebayo, "Everything You Know," 132.
20. See Jean-François Lyotard, *Enthusiasm: The Kantian Critique of History*, trans. Georges Van Den Abbeele (Stanford, CA: Stanford University Press, 2009), 29–41.
21. Joe Kelleher, *The Illuminated Theatre: Studies on the Suffering of Images* (London: Routledge, 2015).
22. Rachel Fensham, *To Watch Theatre: Essays on Genre and Corporeality* (Brussels: Peter Lang, 2009): 137ff.
23. Daniel Sack, "*L.#09-London Episode of the Tragedia Endogonidia*. By Socìetas Raffaello Sanzio. Directed by Romeo Castellucci. Alexander Kasser Theater, Montclair State University, New Jersey, 7 October 2005," *Theatre Journal* 58.3 (2006): 485.
24. David Román, "Introduction: Tragedy," *Theatre Journal* 54.1 (2002): 1–17, 1–3. See Raymond Williams, *Modern Tragedy* (Stanford, CA: Stanford University Press, 1966).
25. Román, 3.
26. See Julie Bindel, "The truth behind America's most famous gay-hate murder," *The Guardian*, October 26, 2014, https://www.theguardian.com/world/2014/oct/26/the-truth-behind-americas-most-famous-gay-hate-murder-matthew-shepard (accessed August 25, 2016). Though much maligned for bursting the bubble of Matt's martyrdom, investigative journalist Stephen Jimenez's thirteen-year inquiry into the case highlights the complex intertwinement of crystal meth dealing and prior sexual relations among the young men involved, in *The Book of Matt: Hidden Truths about the Murder of Matthew Shepard* (Hanover, NH: Steerforth Press, 2013).
27. Moisés Kaufman, "Introduction," in Moisés Kaufman and the members of Tectonic Theater Project, *The Laramie Project* (New York: Vintage Books, 2001), vi–vii.
28. See Amy L. Tigner, "The Laramie Project: Western Pastoral," *Modern Drama* 45.1 (2002): 141–42.
29. Jennifer Wallace, *The Cambridge Introduction to Tragedy* (Cambridge: Cambridge University Press, 2007): 85–7. See Tony Kushner, *Angels in America: A Gay Fantasia on National Themes*, complete and revised edn (New York: Theatre Communications Group, 2013).
30. Bonnie Honig, *Antigone, Interrupted* (Cambridge: Cambridge University Press, 2013).
31. This paradoxically individual yet pre-agential "tragic" situation is signaled by the drama of choicelessness which characters understood to suffer from *hamartia* (tragic flaw) typically embody.
32. Honig, 53. See Lee Edelman, *No Future: Queer Theory and the Death Drive* (Durham and London: Duke University Press, 2004). Edelman's argument is refuted, Honig notes, among

others by Christopher Castiglia and Christopher Reed, *If Memory Serves: Gay Men, AIDS, and the Promise of the Queer Past* (Minneapolis: University of Minnesota Press, 2011).
33. Honig, 151–3.
34. Honig, 154. See Mary Rawlinson, "Beyond Antigone: Ismene, Gender, and the Right to Life," in *The Returns of Antigone: Interdisciplinary Essays*, ed. Tina Chanter and Sean D. Kirkland (Albany: State University of New York Press, 2014): 101–21.
35. Honig, 156ff.
36. Honig, 161.
37. Honig, 162–4.
38. Honig, 168.
39. Honig, 168.
40. See n1 above.
41. Stefano Harney and Fred Moten describe the "undercommons" as a space of love and resistance beneath the radar of professionalized, polite politics, and beneath the radar of institutionalized expressions of dissent. In *The Undercommons: Fugitive Planning and Black Study* (Wivenhoe and New York: Minor Compositions, 2013).
42. Judith Butler, *Notes Toward a Performative Theory of Assembly* (Cambridge, MA: Harvard University Press, 2015): 160.
43. Nikolaus Antonakakis and Allan Collins, "The impact of fiscal austerity on suicide: On the empirics of a modern Greek tragedy," *Social Science and Medicine* 112 (July 2014): 39–50. See also Charles C. Branas et al., "The impact of economic austerity and prosperity events on suicide in Greece: a 30-year interrupted time-series analysis," *BMJ Open* 15.1 (2015), doi: 10.1136/bmjopen-2014-005619 (accessed October 3, 2016).
44. Eagleton, *Sweet Violence*, 2–3.
45. Butler argues that though Antigone appears to represent a "prepolitical opposition to politics," indeed to represent "*kinship as the sphere that conditions the possibility of politics without ever entering into it*," she does so paradoxically by imitating the linguistic mannerisms, the language gestures, performed by Creon. In *Antigone's Claim: Kinship between Life and Death* (New York: Columbia University Press, 2000): 2.
46. See Achille Mbembe, "Necropolitics," trans. Libby Meintjes, *Public Culture* 15.1 (2003): 11–40.
47. I borrow the notion of *form-of-life* from Giorgio Agamben, who writes that this is life not separable from its form. See e.g., *The Use of Bodies*, trans. Adam Kotsko (Stanford, CA: Stanford University Press, 2016 [2014]), esp. 195ff.
48. Giorgio Agamben, "What Is an Apparatus?" in *What Is An Apparatus? And Other Essays*, trans. David Kishik and Stefan Pedatella (Stanford, CA: Stanford University Press, 2009): 8–10.
49. Andrew Parker, *The Theorist's Mother* (Durham and London: Duke University Press, 2012), xii.
50. See Michel Foucault, "Governmentality," in *Power: The Essential Works of Foucault*, vol. 3, 206–7. See also esp. Foucault, *Security, Territory, Population: Lectures at the Collège de France 1977–1978*, ed. Arnold I. Davidson and trans. Graham Burchell (New York: Palgrave Macmillan, 2007).
51. Foucault, "The Politics of Health", 96.
52. Svetlana Boym, *Another Freedom: Alternative History of an Idea* (Chicago and London: University of Chicago Press, 2010): 11.
53. Félix Guattari and Antonio Negri, *New Lines of Alliance, New Spaces of Liberty* [*Les nouveaux espaces de liberté* (1985)], ed. Stevphen Shukaitis, trans. Michael Ryan, Jared

Becker, Arianna Bove, and Noe Le Blanc (London and New York: Minor Compositions/ Autonomedia and MayFlyBooks, 2010).

Chapter Eight

1. Hans-Thies Lehmann, *Theatre and Dramatic Tragedy* (London: Routledge, 2016), 6.
2. Hélène Cixous, "Enter the Theatre", in *Collaborative Theatre: The Theatre du Soleil Sourcebook*, ed. David Williams (London: Routledge, 1999), 26.
3. Ibid., 27.
4. See P.A. Skantze, *Stillness in Motion on the Seventeenth-Century Stage* (London: Routledge, 2003) and Pat Parker, *Literary Fat Ladies: Rhetoric, Gender and Property* (London: Routledge, 1988).
5. Hortense J. Spillers, "Mama's Baby, Papa's Maybe: An American Grammar Book," *Diacritics*, 17, No. 2, Culture and Countermemory: The "American" Connection (Summer, 1987): 64–81.
6. Because this chapter explores gender and sexuality and tragedy, race and indeed class cannot be separated from either as white gender and white sexuality inhabit a different space of power than women and homosexual/transsexual people of color. To leave out the word race in a chapter focussing on gender and sexuality implies the privileged position of false universal categories where "white" implies neutral.
7. In two rich paragraphs Catherine Clément directs our attention to how this works in the context of women and opera: Catherine Clément, *Opera, or the Undoing of Women* (London: Virago Press, 1989), 10–11.
8. Wynter's theories are rich with possibility for performance theorists. Wynter's use of Aimee Cesaire's (author of a tragic adaptation himself) and her own works of fiction and drama reiterate the aesthetic and the narrative as tools with which to navigate away from the tragic trap of patriarchy, heteronormativity, and imperialism.
9. Katherine McKittrick, ed. *Sylvia Wynter: on being human as praxis* (Durham, NC: Duke University Press, 2015), p. 18.
10. Sarah Trimble, "Trust Sylvia Wynter," *new formations: a journal of culture/theory/politics*, 89–90 (2017): 276.
11. Cixous, "Enter the Theatre," 30.
12. Ibid., 28. Emphasis in original.
13. I want to write "of whatever gender" here but in truth protagonists remain overwhelmingly white, heterosexual, and male.
14. Virginia Woolf, *Three Guineas* (1937; reprint Martino Books Fine Books, 2013).
15. In contemporary tragedy the tragic is often intensified by a woman's isolation; the woman at the center no longer even benefits from a chorus who watches and advises. No matter how annoying the platitudes of choruses in some tragedy, they still see the character and what she is suffering instead of the wholly internal maelstrom of pain that is, for example, Sarah Kane's Phaedra.
16. It must be said that the threat of a mobile woman in Creon's kingdom is so great that she must literally be contained until she dies, entombed alive.
17. Clément, *Opera, or the Undoing of Women*, 45.
18. Ibid., 45.
19. Marvin Carlson, *The Haunted Stage* (Ann Arbor: University of Michigan Press, 2001).
20. Lehmann, *Theatre and Dramatic Tragedy*, 125.
21. Ibid., 125.

22. Ibid., 6.
23. Ibid., 118.
24. Ibid., 118.
25. Ibid.
26. See P.A. Skantze, "Unaccommodated Woman: Mabou Mines' *Lear*, the Universal and the Particular in Performance," in *Shakespeare RE-Dressed: Cross-Gender Casting in Contemporary Performance*, ed. James Bulman (Cranbury, NJ: Fairleigh Dickinson University Press, 2008), 116–30.
27. While I suggest how fundamental the connection between the tragic and singing is in its more overt form in the musical, I do not have the space in this chapter to consider more thoroughly the power of the sonic in the form both of cadence and in speech and in the form of singing and lyric to raise the stakes of the tragic—indeed to change the time of the reception as all singing and music draws out time. In this production, the entire cast created a compelling polyphony in moments of sung stillness as well as when Bottom, cheerily in his own world, sang an AC/DC song in a voice most of us recognize as the belting of an unselfconscious singer in the shower. In an instant in both cases, whether beautiful chorus or solo silliness the vulnerability of the human body in the face of the forces around it resounded in the air.
28. This sensation was made more powerful by the extraordinarily funny Bottom and Company throughout. One hurt from laughing so hard and one hurt from an internal keening brought about by the staging and the players.
29. Caryl Churchill, *Escaped Alone* (London: Nick Hern Books, 2017).
30. Ibid., 5.
31. Ibid., 8.
32. Caryl Churchill, *Here We Go* (London: Nick Hern Books, 2015), 21. The instructions from Churchill in the play text (21) are: "One of these [speeches] is spoken by each of the characters directly to the audience. They should be inserted randomly into the previous dialogue in any order. The number of years later can be adjusted if necessary to make sense for the characters." The speeches quoted in this chapter are the "adjusted" ones used in the play's opening run at the National Theatre, London, November 2015, rather than the exact lines printed in the play text.
33. "Scientists confirm what women always knew: men are the weaker sex," *The Guardian*, January 17, 2018.
34. Katherine McKittrick uses the term "counter poetics" in the context of artistic creativity and Sylvia Wynter: "Rebellion/Invention/Groove," *Small Axe*, 20.1 (March 2016): 79–91. Jennifer Nash, returning us to the wisdom of June Jordan and Audre Lorde, invents with truly dazzling creativity and extraordinary generosity a vision of a future worth working for in "Practicing Love: Black Feminism, Love-Politics and Post Intersectionality," *Meridians: feminism, race, transnationalism*, 11.2 (2011): 18.

BIBLIOGRAPHY

Abel, Lionel. *Tragedy and Metatheatre*. Ed. Martin Puchner. New York: Holmes & Meier, 2003.
Ackerley, Duncan, Ben B.B. Booth, Sylvia H.E. Knight, Eleanor J. Highwood, David J. Frame, Myles R. Allen, and David P. Rowell. "Sensitivity of Twentieth-Century Sahel Rainfall to Sulfate Aerosol and CO_2 Forcing." *Journal of Climate*, 24.19 (2011): 4999–5014.
Ackerman, Robert. *The Myth and Ritual School: J. G. Frazer and the Cambridge Ritualists*. 1991. London: Routledge, 2002.
Adamson, Samuel and others. *Decade: Twenty New Plays about 9/11 and Its Legacy*. London: Nick Hern Books, 2011.
Adebayo, Mojisola. "Everything You Know About Queerness You Learnt from Blackness: The Afri-Quia Theatre of Black Dykes, Crips and Kids." In *Queer Dramaturgies: International Perspectives on Where Performance Leads Queer*, ed. Alyson Campbell and Stephen Farrier, 131–49. Basingstoke: Palgrave, 2016.
Adorno, Theodor W. *Aesthetic Theory*. Trans. Robert Hullot-Kentor. London: Continuum, 2002.
Adorno, Theodor W. *History and Freedom, Lectures, 1964-1965*. Trans. Rodney Livingstone. Cambridge: Polity Press, 2006.
Adorno, Theodor W. *Minima Moralia: Reflections from Damaged Life*. Trans. E.F.N. Jephcott. London: Verso, 1974.
Adorno, Theodor W. *Negative Dialectics*. Trans. E.B. Ashton. London: Routledge, 1973.
Adorno, Theodor W. *Notes to Literature*, vol. 2. Trans. Shierry Weber Nicholsen. New York: Columbia University Press, 1992.
Adorno, Theodor. *Prisms: Cultural Criticism and Society*. Trans. Samuel and Shierry Weber. London: Neville Spearman, 1967
Agamben, Giorgio, *Infancy and History: On the Destruction of Experience*. Trans. Liz Heron. London: Verso, 2007.
Agamben, Giorgio. *Remnants of Auschwitz: The Witness and The Archive*. Trans. Daniel Heller-Roazen. New York: Zone Books, 1999.
Agamben, Giorgio, *State of Exception*. Trans. Kevin Attell. Chicago: The University of Chicago Press, 2005.
Agamben, Giorgio. *The Use of Bodies*. Trans. Adam Kotsko. Stanford, CA: Stanford University Press, 2016.
Agamben, Giorgio. *What Is An Apparatus? And Other Essays*. Trans. David Kishik and Stefan Pedatella. Stanford, CA: Stanford University Press, 2009.
Ahmed, Sara. *Living a Feminist Life*. Durham, NC: Duke University Press, 2017.
Ai Weiwei. "Remembering" (2009), first exhibited Haus der Kunst, Munich, 2009.
Ai Weiwei. "Straight" (2008–12), first exhibited Hirschhorn Museum and Sculpture Garden, Washington D.C., 2012.
Akasha, Mohamed Osman. *Darfur: A Tragedy of Climate Change*. Hamburg: Anchor, 2013.
Albee, Edward. *Who's Afraid of Virginia Woolf*. London: Penguin, 1965.

Améry, Jean. *At the Mind's Limits: Contemplations by a Survivor on Auschwitz and its Realities*. Trans. Sidney and Stella P. Rosenfeld. Bloomington, IN: Indiana University Press, 2009.

Andrei Rublev. Directed by Andrei Tarkovsky. Moscow: Mosfilm, 1966. DVD.

Anouilh, Jean. *Antigone*. Trans. Barbara Bray. London: Methuen Drama, 2000.

Antonakakis, Nikolaus and Allan Collins. "The impact of fiscal austerity on suicide: On the empirics of a modern Greek tragedy." *Social Science and Medicine* 112 (July 2014): 39–50.

Arendt, Hannah. *Essays in Understanding, 1930-1954: Formation, Exile, and Totalitarianism*. New York: Schochen Books, 1994.

Arendt, Hannah. *The Human Condition*, 2nd edn. Chicago: University of Chicago Press, 1998.

Arendt, Hannah. *The Life of the Mind*. San Diego: Harvest Books, 1978.

Arendt, Hannah. *On Revolution*. New York: Penguin Books, 1990.

Arfara, Katia, Aneta Mancewicz, and Ralf Remshardt, eds. *Intermedial Performance and Politics in the Public Sphere*. Basingstoke: Palgrave Macmillan, 2018.

Arnold, Catharine. *Pandemic 1918: The Story of the Deadliest Influenza in History*. London: Michael O'Mara Books, 2018.

Artaud, Antonin. *Collected Works Vol. 4*. Trans. Victor Corti. London: Calder & Boyars, 1968.

Auslander, Philip. *Liveness: Performance in a Mediatized Culture*. London: Routledge, 2008.

Baldick, Chris. "Tragedy." In *The Online Oxford Dictionary of Literary Terms*. Oxford: Oxford University Press, 2015.

Balthasar, Hans Urs von. *The Glory of the Lord: A Theological Aesthetics*. Vol. 5. Edinburgh: T&T Clark, 1991.

Balthasar, Hans Urs von. *Theo-Drama: Theological Dramatic Theory*. 5 vols. San Francisco: Ignatius Press, 1988–98.

Barker, Howard. *Arguments for a Theatre*, 3rd edn. Manchester: Manchester University Press, 1993.

Barnett, David. "Resisting the Revolution: Heiner Müller's Hamlet/Machine at the Deutsches Theater, Berlin, March 1990." *Theatre Research International* 31, No. 2 (2006): 188–200.

Barth, Karl. *Church Dogmatics*, vol. 2. Edinburgh: T&T Clark, 1957.

Beard, Mary. *The Invention of Jane Harrison*. Cambridge, MA: Harvard University Press 2000.

Beauvoir, Simone de. *The Second Sex*. Trans. Constance Borde and Sheila Malovany-Chevallier. New York: Vintage Books, 2011.

Beauvoir, Simone de. *"The Useless Mouths" and Other Literary Writings*. Ed. Margaret A. Simons and Marybeth Timmermann. Champaign, IL: University of Illinois Press, 2011.

Beckett, Samuel. *Endgame*. London: Faber and Faber, *c*. 1957, 2009, 6.

Beckett, Samuel. *The Complete Dramatic Works*. London: Faber and Faber, 2006.

Beckett, Samuel. *Imagination Dead Imagine*. London: Caldar Publications Ltd, 1966.

Beckett, Samuel. *Molloy; Malone Dies; The Unnameable*. London: Caldar & Boyars, 1959.

Beistegui, Michel and Simon Sparks, eds. *Philosophy and Tragedy*. London: Routledge, 2000.

Benjamin, Walter. *Illuminations*. Trans. Harry Zohn, ed. and intro. Hannah Arendt. London: Fontana, 1992.

Benjamin, Walter. *The Origin of German Tragic Drama*. Trans. John Osborne. New York: Verso, 1998.

Benjamin, Walter. "The Work of Art in the Age of Mechanical Reproduction" (1936). In *Illuminations*, trans. H. Zorn, 211–44. London: Fontana, 1992.

Berg, Alban. *Lulu*. Libretto: Frank Wedekind. Premiere: Opera House, Zurich, 1937.

Berg, Alban. *Wozzeck*. Libretto: Alban Berg. Premiere: Berlin State Opera, 1925.

Bharucha, Rustom. "Between Truth and Reconciliation: Experiments in Theatre and Public Culture." *Economic and Political Weekly*, 36.39 (2001): 3763–73.

Billings, Joshua. *Genealogy of the Tragic: Greek Tragedy and German Philosophy*. Princeton, NJ: Princeton University Press, 2014.

Billings, Joshua, Felix Budelmann, and Fiona Macintosh, eds. *Choruses, Ancient & Modern*. Oxford: Oxford University Press, 2013.

Bindel, Julie. "The truth behind America's most famous gay-hate murder." *The Guardian*, October 26, 2014. https://www.theguardian.com/world/2014/oct/26/the-truth-behind-americas-most-famous-gay-hate-murder-matthew-shepard (accessed August 25, 2016).

Birch, Anne and Joanne Tompkins, eds. *Performing site-specific theatre: Politics, place, practice*. Basingstoke: Palgrave Macmillan, 2012.

Blade Runner. Directed by Ridley Scott. Los Angeles: Warner Home Video, 2008, DVD.

Blanchot, Maurice. *The Writing of the Disaster*. Trans. Ann Smock, 2nd edn. Lincoln, NE: University of Nebraska Press, 1995.

Blind Chance. Directed by Krzysztof Kieslowski. PP Film Polski, 1987. DVD.

Blue Planet II. Executive producers: James Honeyborne and Mark Brownlow. BBC Natural History Unit. October–December 2017.

Boal, Augusto. *Theatre of the Oppressed*. Trans. Charles A. and Maria-Odilia Leal McBride and Emily Fryer, 2nd edn. London: Pluto Press, 2000.

Bond, Edward. *Plays: One*, rev. edn. London: Bloomsbury Methuen Drama, 2008.

Bond, Edward. *Plays: Two*. London: Bloomsbury Methuen Drama, 1998.

Bonikowski, Wyatt. *Shell Shock and the Modernist Imagination: The Death Drive in Post World War I British Fiction*. Burlington: Ashgate, 2013.

The Book of Common Prayer. Oxford: Oxford University Press, 1964.

Bourque, Andre. "Technology Profits and Pivots in the $300 Billion Wedding Space." *The Huffington Post*, January 5, 2015, updated May 1, 2016, at http://www.huffingtonpost.com/andre-bourque/technology-profit-and-piv_b_7193112.html (accessed May 18, 2017).

Boym, Svetlana. *Another Freedom: Alternative History of an Idea*. Chicago: University of Chicago Press, 2010.

Branas, Charles C., et al. "The impact of economic austerity and prosperity events on suicide in Greece: a 30-year interrupted time-series analysis." *BMJ Open* 15.1 (2015), doi: 10.1136/bmjopen-2014-005619 (accessed October 3, 2016).

Breaking the Waves. Directed by Lars von Trier. New York: October Films, 1996. DVD.

Brecht, Bertolt. *Brecht on Theatre*. Trans. and ed. John Willett. London: Methuen, 1964.

Brecht, Bertolt. *Collected Plays: Five, Life of Galileo; Mother Courage and her Children*. Trans. John Willett. London: Methuen Drama, 1995.

Brecht, Bertolt. *Collected Plays: Six, The Good Person of Szechwan; The Resistible Rise of Arturo Ui; Mr Puntila and his Man Matti*. Trans. John Willett and Ralph Manheim. London: Methuen Drama, 1994.

Brecht, Bertolt. *Collected Plays: Seven, The Visions of Simone Machard; Schweyk in the Second World War; The Caucasian Chalk Circle; The Duchess of Malfi*. Trans. Hugh and Ellen Rank, William Rowlinson, James and Tania Stern with W.H. Auden. London: Methuen Drama, 1994.

Brecht, Bertolt. *Collected Plays: Eight, The Antigone of Sophocles; the Days of the Commune; Turondot or the Whitewashers' Congress*. Ed. and trans. David Constantine and Tom Kuhn. London: Methuen Drama, 2004.

Brecht, Bertolt. *Journals 1934–1955*. Trans. Stephan S. Brecht. London: Routledge Chapman & Hall, 1995.

Bridge over the River Kwai. Directed by David Lean. Los Angeles: Columbia Pictures, 1957. DVD.
Brief Encounter. Directed by David Lean. Los Angeles: Eagle-Lion, 1945. DVD.
Britten, Benjamin. *Peter Grimes*. Premiere: Sadler's Wells Theatre, London: 1945.
Brody, Richard. "The Inadequacy of Berlin's 'Memorial to the Murdered Jews of Europe.'" *The New Yorker*, July 12, 2012.
Brook, Peter. *The Empty Space*. London: Penguin, 1972.
Broswimmer, Franz J. *Ecocide: A Short History of the Mass Extinction of the Species*. London: Pluto, 2002.
Browne, E. Martin. *The Making of T. S. Eliot's Plays*. Cambridge: Cambridge University Press, 1969.
Bushnell, Rebecca, ed. *A Companion to Tragedy*. Oxford: Blackwell, 2005.
Bushnell, Rebecca. *Tragic Time in Drama, Film and Videogames: The Future in the Instant*. London: Palgrave Macmillan, 2016.
Butler, Judith. *Antigone's Claim: Kinship Between Life and Death*. New York: Columbia University Press, 2002.
Butler, Judith. *Frames of War: When is Life Grievable?* London: Verso, 2009.
Butler, Judith. *Notes Toward a Performative Theory of Assembly*. Cambridge, MA: Harvard University Press, 2015.
Butler, Judith. *Precarious Life: The Powers of Mourning and Violence*. London: Verso, 2004.
Butterworth, Jez. *Jerusalem*. London: Nick Hern Books, 2009.
Butterworth, Jez. *The Ferryman*. London: Nick Hern Books, 2017.
Caché. Directed by Michael Haneke. Los Angeles: Sony Pictures, 2006. DVD.
Camus, Albert. *The Myth of Sisyphus and Other Essays*. Trans. Justin O'Brien. New York: Vintage Books, 1991.
Camus, Albert. *The Outsider*. Trans. Joseph Laredo, repr. edn. London: Penguin, 2000.
Carey, John. *The Intellectuals and the Masses: Pride and Prejudice among the Literary Intelligentsia, 1880-1939*. London: Faber and Faber, 1992.
Carlson, Julie A. "Like Me: An Invitation to *Domestic/Tragedy*." *SAQ* 98.3 (1999): 331–47.
Carlson, Marvin. *The Haunted Stage*. Ann Arbor: University of Michigan Press, 2001.
Carney, Sean. *The Politics and Poetics of Contemporary English Tragedy*. Toronto: University of Toronto Press, 2013.
Carpenter, Elle, ed. *The Nuclear Culture Sourcebook*. London: Black Dog, 2016.
Carpentier, Martha. *Ritual, Myth and the Modernist Text: The Influence of Jane Ellen Harrison on Joyce, Eliot and Woolf*. London: Routledge, 1998.
Carson, Anne, *Antigonick (Sophokles)*. Illustrated by Bianca Stone. New York: New Directions Books, 2012.
Carson, Christie and Farah Karim-Cooper, eds. *Shakespeare's Globe: A Theatrical Experiment*. Cambridge: Cambridge University Press, 2008.
Castiglia, Christopher and Christopher Reed. *If Memory Serves: Gay Men, AIDS, and the Promise of the Queer Past*. Minneapolis: University of Minnesota Press, 2011.
Cavarero, Adriana. *Horrorism: Naming Contemporary Violence*. Trans. William McCuaig. New York: Columbia University Press, 2011.
Charry, Ellen T. *Psalms 1-50: Sighs and Songs of Israel*. Brazos Theological Commentary on the Bible. Grand Rapids, MI: Brazos, 2015.
Ch'ien Chung-Shu. "Tragedy in Old Chinese Drama." *T'ien Hsia Monthly*, 1 (Aug. 1935): 37–46; reprinted in *Renditions*, 9 (Spring 1978): 85–91.

Chou, Mark. "Postmodern Dramaturgy, Premodern Drama: The Global Resurgence of Greek Tragedy Today." *Journal for Cultural Research*, 15.2 (2011): 131–52.
Chu Kwang-Tsien. *The Psychology of Tragedy*. PhD diss., University of Alsace, 1933.
Churchill, Caryl. *Escaped Alone*. London: Nick Hern Books, 2017.
Churchill, Caryl. *Here We Go*. London: Nick Hern Books, 2015.
Cixous, Hélène. "Enter the Theatre." In *Collaborative Theatre: The Theatre du Soleil Sourcebook*, ed. David Williams. London: Routledge, 1999.
Clark, Christopher. *The Sleepwalkers: How Europe Went to War in 1914*. London: Penguin, 2013.
Climates. Directed by Nuri Bilge Ceylan. New York: Zeitgeist Films, 2007. DVD.
Climenhaga, Royd. *Pina Bausch*. London: Routledge, 2009.
Climenhaga, Royd, ed. *The Pina Bausch Sourcebook: The Making of Tanztheater*. London: Routledge, 2013.
Clément, Catherine. *Opera, or the Undoing of Women*. London: Virago Press, 1989.
Cless, Downing. *Ecology and Environment in European Drama*. New York: Routledge, 2010.
Cocteau, Jean. "Preface to *The Wedding on the Eiffel Tower*." 1922. In *Modern French Plays: An Anthology from Jarry to Ionesco*, 96–7. Trans. Michael Benedikt. London: Faber and Faber, 1964.
Cohn, Ruby. *From Desire to Godot: Pocket Theatre of Postwar Paris*. Berkeley, CA: University of California Press, 1987.
Cooke, Mervyn, ed. *The Cambridge Companion to Twentieth Century Opera*. Cambridge: Cambridge University Press, 2005.
Coward, Noel. *Private Lives*. New edn. London: Methuen Drama, 2000.
Craig, Edward Gordon. *The Mask*. 1908–24. Florence: The Arena Goldoni. Reprinted with index by Lorelei Guidry. New York: Benjamin Blom, 1967.
Craig, Edward Gordon. *The Theatre Advancing*. London: Heinemann, 1921.
Critchley, Simon. *Very Little . . . Almost Nothing: Death, Philosophy, Literature*. London: Routledge, 1997.
Cruz, Decio Torres. *Postmodern Meta-narratives: Literature in the Age of the Image. Scott's Blade Runner and Puig's novels*. PhD Diss. State University of New York Buffalo: Proquest Dissertations Publishing, 1998.
Cubitt, Sean. *Ecomedia*. Amsterdam: Rodopi, 2005.
Cubitt, Sean, Stephen Rust, and Salma Monani, eds. *The Ecocinema Reader: Theory and Practice*. London: Routledge, 2012.
Cudden, J.A. *The Penguin Dictionary of Literary Terms and Literary Theory*, 3rd edn. London: Penguin, 1991.
Dancer in the Dark (2000). Directed by Lars von Trier. Los Angeles: Warner Brothers, 2005. DVD.
Danaher, William J. Jr. "Lamentation in Art: On Art, Ritual and Religion in Detroit." Paper delivered at the conference of the Society for the Study of Theology, University of Durham, 2016.
Davis, Miles. *Kind of Blue*. New York City: Columbia Studio. Audio CD. 1959.
Davis, Walter A. *Death's Dream Kingdom: the American Psyche Since 9-11*. London and Ann Arbor: Michigan University Press, 2006
Davis, Walter A. *Deracination: Historicity, Hiroshima, and the Tragic Imperative*. Albany: State University of New York Press, 2001.
Debord, Guy. *Society of the Spectacle*. Detroit: Black & Red, 1977.

Debord, Guy. *Comments on the Society of the Spectacle*. Trans. Malcolm Imrie. London: Verso, 1990.

Deleuze, Gilles. *Nietzsche and Philosophy*. Trans. Hugh Tomlinson. New York: Continuum, 2005.

Deleuze, Gilles and Felix Guattari. *Anti-Oedipus: Capitalism and Schizophrenia*. Trans. Robert Hurley, Mark Stern, and Helen R. Lane. Minneapolis: University of Minnesota Press, 1983.

Derrida, Jacques. *Dissemination*. Trans. Barbara Johnson. New York: Continuum, 1981.

Derrida, Jacques. "The Law of Genre." Trans. Avital Ronell. *Critical Inquiry* 7 no. 1 (1980): 55–81.

Derrida, Jacques. *Spectres of Marx: The State of the Debt, the Work of Mourning, and the New International*. Trans. Peggy Kamuf. New York: Routledge, 1994.

Desser, David. "The New Eve: The Influence of Paradise Lost and Frankenstein on Blade Runner." In *Retrofitting* Blade Runner: *Issues in Ridley Scott's* Blade Runner *and Philip K. Dick's* Do Androids Dream of Electric Sheep, ed. Judith B. Kerman, 53–65. Bowling Green, OH: Bowling Green State University Popular Press, 1991.

Distant. Directed by Nuri Bilge Ceylan. Istanbul: NBC Ajans/ NBC Film. 2002. DVD.

Dr Zhivago. Directed by David Lean. Los Angeles: MGM, 1965. DVD.

Dogville. Directed by Lars Von Trier. Hvidovre, Denmark: Zentropa. 2003. DVD.

Dostoevsky, Fyodor. *Notes from Underground* and *The Double*. Trans. Ronald Wilks. London and New York: Penguin Classics, 2009.

The Double. Directed by Richard Ayoade. London: Alcove Entertainment/British Film Institute/Film4. 2014. DVD.

Dower, John W. *Ways of Forgetting, Ways of Remembering: Japan in the Modern World*. New York: The New Press, 2012.

Drive. Directed by Nicolas Winding Refn. Los Angeles: FilmDistrict, 2011. DVD.

Duncan, Isadora. *The Art of the Dance*. New York: Theatre Arts Books, 1928.

Duncan, Isadora. *My Life*. 1927. New York: Liveright, 1996.

Eagleton, Terry. *Sweet Violence: The Idea of the Tragic*. Oxford: Blackwell, 2003.

Edelman, Lee. *No Future: Queer Theory and the Death Drive*. Durham, NC: Duke University Press, 2004.

Eklund, Rebekah. *Jesus Wept: The Significance of Jesus' Laments in the New Testament*. London: Bloomsbury T&T Clark, 2015.

Electra. Directed by Michael Cacoyannis. Athens: Finos Film, 1962. DVD.

Eliot, T.S. *Complete Poems and Plays*. London: Faber & Faber, 2004.

Eliot, T.S. *The Complete Prose of T. S. Eliot, Vol. 2: 1919-1926*. Ed. Anthony Cuba and Ronald Schuchard. London: Faber and Faber, 2014.

Eliot, T.S. "Poetry and Drama" (1951). In *Selected Prose of T. S. Eliot*, ed. Frank Kermode, 132–47. New York: Farrar, Straus and Giroux, 1975.

Ellison, Ralph. *The Invisible Man* (1952). New edn. London: Penguin, 2001.

Eno, Will. *Tragedy: A Tragedy*. London: Oberon Books, 2001.

Exum, Cheryl J. *Tragedy and Biblical Narrative: Arrows of the Almighty*. Cambridge: Cambridge University Press, 1992.

Farber, Yael. *Molora*. London: Oberon Books, 2008.

Felman, Shoshana. *The Juridical Unconscious: Trials and Traumas in the Twentieth Century*. Cambridge, MA: Harvard University Press, 2002.

Felski, Rita, ed. *Rethinking Tragedy*. Baltimore: Johns Hopkins University Press.

Fensham, Rachel. *To Watch Theatre: Essays on Genre and Corporeality*. Brussels: Peter Lang, 2009.

Ferguson, Niall. *The War of the World: History's Age of Hatred*. London: Allen Lane, 2006.
Festen. Directed by Thomas Vinterberg. Copenhagen: Scanbox Danmark, 1998. DVD.
Finburgh, Clare. *Watching War on the Twenty-First Century Stage: Spectacles of Conflict*. London: Bloomsbury, 2017.
Fioupou, Christiane. "Variations on Wole Soyinka's *Death and the King's Horseman*." In *New Theatre in Francophone and Anglophone Africa*, ed. Anne Fuchs, 229–40. Amsterdam: Rodopi, 1999.
Fischer-Lichte, Erika. *Tragedy's Endurance: Performances of Greek Tragedies and Cultural Identity in Germany since 1800*. Oxford: Oxford University Press, 2017.
Fischer-Lichte, Erika and Matthias Dreyer. *Antike Tragödie Heute. Vorträge und Materialien zum Antikenprojekt des Deutschen Theaters*. Berlin: Henschelverlag, 2007.
Fisher, Tony. *Theatre and Governance in Britain 1500–1900: Theatre, Disorder and the State*. Cambridge: Cambridge University Press, 2017.
A Fistful of Dollars. Directed by Sergio Leone. Los Angeles: United Artists, 1964.
Fitzgerald, F. Scott. *The Great Gatsby* (1925). Ed. Tony Tanner. New edn. London: Penguin, 2000.
For a Few Dollars More. Directed by Sergio Leone. Los Angeles: United Artists, 1965
Foley, Helene P. "Modern Performance and Adaptation of Greek Tragedy." *Transactions of the American Philological Association*, 129 (1999): 1–12.
Foley, Helene P. and Jean E. Howard. "The Urgency of Tragedy Now." *PMLA*, 129.4 (2014): 617–33.
Ford, David. "Tragedy and Atonement." In *Christ, Ethics and Tragedy: Essays in Honour of Donald MacKinnon*, ed. Kenneth Surin, 117–30. Cambridge: Cambridge University Press, 1989.
Foucault, Michel. *Power: The Essential Works of Foucault 1954–1984, Vol 3*. Ed. James D. Faubion, trans. Robert Hurley and others. London: Penguin Books, 2000.
Foucault, Michel. *Security, Territory, Population: Lectures at the Collège de France 1977–1978*. Ed. Arnold I. Davidson, trans. Graham Burchell. New York: Palgrave Macmillan, 2007.
Fousek, John. *To Lead the Free World: American Nationalism and the Cultural Roots of the Cold War*. Chapel Hill, NC: The University of North Carolina Press, 2000.
Frank, Anne. *The Diary of Anne Frank*. Trans. Susan Massotty. London: Penguin, 2000.
Freud, Sigmund. *Civilization and Its Discontents*. Trans. James Strachey. New York: W.W. Norton and Co., 1961.
Frisch, Max. *Homo faber. A Report*. Trans. Michael Bullock. Orlando, FL: Harvest Books, 1959.
Frisch, Max. *Homo Faber. Ein Bericht*. 1957. Frankfurt/Main: Suhrkamp, 1977.
Fugard, Athol. *Sizwe Bansi is Dead & The Island*. London: Viking, 1976.
Fukuyama, Francis. *The End of History and the Last Man*. New York: The Free Press, 1992.
Funny Games. Directed by Michael Haneke. Vienna: Wega Films/Filmfonds Wien, 1997. DVD.
Garafola, Lynn. *Diaghilev's Ballets Russes*. Oxford: Oxford University Press, 1989.
Gardiner, Stephen. *A Perfect Moral Storm: The Ethical Tragedy of Climate Change*. Oxford: Oxford University Press, 2011.
Giacometti, Alberto. "Walking Man II." Otterlo, Netherlands: Kröller-Müller Museum, 1960.
Giannchi, Gabriella and Nigel Stewart, eds. *Performing Nature: Explorations in Ecology and the Arts*. Bern: Peter Lang, 2005.
Girard, René. *Violence and the Sacred*. Trans. Patrick Gregory. Baltimore: Johns Hopkins University Press, 1977.

Goldenberg, Oren. *A Requiem for Douglass*. Detroit, MI: Museum of Contemporary Art, 2015.

Goldhill, Simon. *How To Stage Greek Tragedy Today*. Chicago: Chicago University Press, 2007.

Goldhill, Simon. "Greek tragedy: setting the stage today," Cambridge University Website (February 1, 2008). http://www.cam.ac.uk/research/news/greek-tragedy-setting-the-stagetoday (accessed March 6, 2017).

Goldman, Emma. "Marriage and Love." In *Anarchism and Other Essays*, 227–39. 3rd edn. New York: Dover, 1969 (1917).

Goldmann, Lucien. *The Hidden God: A Study of Tragic Vision in the Pensées of Pascal and the Tragedies of Racine*. Trans. Philip Thody. London: Routledge & Kegan Paul, 1964.

The Good, the Bad and the Ugly. Directed by Sergio Leone. Los Angeles; United Artists, 1966. DVD.

Gordon, Paul. *Tragedy After Nietzsche: Rapturous Superabundance*. Champaign, IL: University of Illinois Press, 2001.

Gray, Richard. *After the Fall: American Literature since 9/11*. Oxford: Wiley-Blackwell, 2011.

Greer, Bonnie. *The Hotel Cerise*. Premiere: Theatre Royal, Stratford East, London. October 2016.

Guattari, Félix and Antonio Negri. *New Lines of Alliance, New Spaces of Liberty*. Ed. Stephen Shukaitis, trans. Michael Ryan, Jared Becker, Arianna Bove, and Noe Le Blanc. London and New York: Minor Compositions/Autonomedia and MayFlyBooks, 2010.

Hall, Edith, Fiona Macintosh, and Amanda Wrigley, eds. *Dionysus since 69: Greek Tragedy at the Dawn of the Third Millennium*. Oxford: Oxford University Press, 2004.

Halliwell, Stephen. *The Aesthetics of Mimesis: Ancient Texts and Modern Problems*. Princeton: Princeton University Press, 2002.

Hamilton, Christopher. *A Philosophy of Tragedy*. London: Reaktion books, 2016.

Hansberry, Lorraine. *A Raisin in the Sun*. London: Methuen Drama, 2001.

Haraway, Donna. *The Companion Species Manifesto: Dogs, People, and Significant Otherness*. Chicago: Prickly Paradigm Press, 2003.

Hardy, Thomas. *Jude the Obscure* (1895). Ed. Patricia Ingham. Oxford: Oxford University Press, 1985.

Harney, Stefano and Fred Moten. *The Undercommons: Fugitive Planning and Black Study*. Wivenhoe and New York: Minor Compositions, 2013.

Hart, David Bentley. *The Beauty of the Infinite: The Aesthetics of Christian Truth*. Grand Rapids: Eerdmans, 2003.

Heaney, Seamus. *The Cure at Troy*. London: Faber and Faber, 1990.

Hecht, Werner. *Brecht Chronik 1898–1956*. Frankfurt/Main: Suhrkamp, 1997.

Heidegger, Martin. *Being and Time*. Trans. John Macquarrie and Edward Robinson. New edn. New York: Harper Collins, 2008.

Heidegger, Martin. *The Fundamental Concepts of Metaphysics: World, Finitude, Solitude*. Trans. William McNeill and Nicholas Walker. Indiana: Indiana University Press, 1995.

Heidegger, Martin. *Introduction to Metaphysics*. Trans. Gregory Fried and Richard Polt. New Haven: Yale University Press, 2000.

Heidegger, Martin. *Nietzsche*, 2 vols. Trans. David Farrell Krell. San Francisco: Harper San Francisco, 1979–84.

Heidegger, Martin. "The Origin of the Work of Art." In *Basic Writings*, trans. David Farrell Krell, 139–212. San Francisco: Harper San Francisco, 1993.

Heise, Ursula K. *Sense of Place and Sense of Planet: The Environmental Imagination of the Global*. Oxford: Oxford University Press, 2008.

Hermand, Edward S. and Noam Chomsky. *Manufacturing Consent: The Political Economy of the Mass Media*. New York: Pantheon Books, 1988.
Hiroshima Mon Amour. Directed by Alain Resnais. Paris: Argos Films. 1959. DVD.
Hölderlin, Friedrich. *Essays and Letters on Theory*. Trans. Thomas Pfau. Albany: State University of New York Press, 1988.
Holiday, Billie. *The Complete Decca Recordings* (1944–50). 2 CD. Los Angeles: Verve, 1991.
The Holy Bible. New Revised Standard Version. Oxford: Oxford University Press, 1989.
Honig, Bonnie. *Antigone, Interrupted*. Cambridge: Cambridge University Press, 2013.
Horkheimer, Max and Theodor W. Adorno. *Dialectic of Enlightenment: Philosophical Fragments*. Ed. Gunzelin Schmid Noerr, trans. Edmund Jephcott. Stanford: Stanford University Press, 2002.
The Hunt. Directed by Thomas Vinterberg. Copenhagen: Nordisk Film, 2012. DVD.
Huxley, Aldous, *Brave New World* (1932). London: Vintage Classics, 2007.
Ibironke, Olabode. "The Fourth Stage: Wole Soyinka and the Social Character of Ibadan." *History Compass*, 13/11 (2015): 541-549.
Iden, Peter. *Die Schaubühne am Halleschen Ufer 1970-1979*. München: Carl Hanser Verlag, 1979.
In The Mood for Love. Directed by Wong Kar-wei. Hong Kong: Block 2 Pictures/Jet Tone Production/Paradis Films, 2000. DVD.
Ingram, David. *Green Screen: Environmentalism and Hollywood Cinema*. Exeter: Exeter University Press, 2000.
Iphigenia. Directed by Michael Cacoyannis. Athens: Greek Film Center, 1977. DVD
Irigaray, Luce. "Civil Rights and Responsibilities for the Two Sexes." In *Luce Irigaray: Key Writings*, ed. Luce Irigaray, 202–13. London and New York: Continuum, 2004.
Jaspers, Karl. *Tragedy Is Not Enough*. Trans. H. A. T. Reiche, H. T. Moore, and K.W. Deutsch. London: Victor Gollancz, 1953.
Jeyifo, Biodun. *Wole Soyinka: Politics, Poetics, and Postcolonialism*. Cambridge: Cambridge University Press, 2003.
Jimenez, Stephen. *The Book of Matt: Hidden Truths about the Murder of Matthew Shepard*. Hanover, NH: Steerforth Press, 2013.
Jenkins, Karl. *The Armed Man: A Mass for Peace*. Warner Classics. Audio CD. 2005.
Johnson, Lonnie. *Blues*. Audio CD. Obc: 1992.
Jones, David, E. *The Plays of T. S. Eliot*. London: Routledge & Kegan Paul, 1960.
Kafka, Franz. *The Trial*. Trans. Idris Parry. New edn. London: Penguin, 2000.
Kalb, Jonathan. *The Theater of Heiner Müller*. New York: Cambridge University Press, 1998.
Kane, Sarah. *Complete Plays*. London: Methuen Drama, 2001.
Katrak, Ketu H. *Wole Soyinka and Modern Tragedy: A Study of Dramatic Theory and Practice*. Westport, CT: Greenwood, 1986.
Kaufman, Moisés. *The Laramie Project*. New York: Vintage Books, 2001.
Kaye, Nick. *Site-Specific Art: Performance, Place and Documentation*. London: Routledge, 2000.
Keats, John. *The Letters of John Keats, 1814-1821*. Ed. Hyder Edward Rollins. Cambridge, MA: Harvard University Press, 1958.
Kehl, Medard and Werner Löser, eds. *The Von Balthasar Reader*. Edinburgh: T&T Clark, 1982.
Kelleher, Joe and Nicholas Ridout. *The Theatre of Societas Raffaello Sanzio*. London: Routledge, 2007.
Kelleher, Joe. *The Illuminated Theatre: Studies on the Suffering of Images*. London: Routledge, 2015.

Kershaw, Baz. *Theatre Ecology: Environments and Performance Events.* Cambridge: Cambridge University Press, 2007.

Keniston, Ann and Jeanne Follansbee Quinn, eds. *Literature after 9/11.* New York and London: Routledge, 2008.

Kennedy, Dennis, ed. *Foreign Shakespeare: Contemporary Performance.* Cambridge: Cambridge University Press, 1993.

Kennedy, Dennis. *Looking at Shakespeare: A Visual History of Twentieth Century Performance.* Cambridge: Cambridge University Press, 1993.

Kiefer, Anselm. "Lot's Wife." Cleveland, OH: Cleveland Museum of Art, 1989.

Kiefer, Anselm. "Margarete." London: Saatchi Collection, 1981.

Kierkegaard, Søren. *Fear and Trembling: Dialectical Lyric by Johannes De Silentio.* Trans. Alastair Hannay. Harmondsworth: Penguin Classics, 1985.

King, Jeanette. *Tragedy and the Victorian Novel. Theory and Practice in the Novels of George Eliot, Thomas Hardy, and Henry James.* Cambridge: Cambridge University Press, 1978.

Kliger, Ilya. "Dostoyevsky and the Novel-Tragedy: Genre and Modernity in Ivanov, Pumpyansky and Bakhtin." *PMLA*, 126, no. 1 (January 2011): 73–87.

Kolbert, Elizabeth. *The Sixth Extinction: An Unnatural History.* London: Bloomsbury, 2014.

Kornhaber, David. *The Birth of Theater from the Spirit of Philosophy: Nietzsche and the Modern Drama.* Evanston, IL: Northwestern University Press, 2016.

Kolocotroni, Vassiliki. "Still Life: Modernism's Turn to Greece." *Journal of Modern Literature* 35, no. 2 (2012):1–24.

Kott, Jan. *Shakespeare our Contemporary.* Trans. Boleslaw Taborski, rev. edn. New York and London: W.W. Norton, 1974.

Kushner, Tony. *Angels in America: A Gay Fantasia on National Themes*, complete and revised edn. New York: Theatre Communications Group, 2013.

Lacan, Jacques. *The Ethics of Psychoanalysis, 1959-1960*, vol. VII. Ed. Jacques-Alain Miller. Trans. Dennis Porter. London: Routledge, 1992.

Lacey, Vanessa. "The History of the Cambridge Greek Play" (2015). http://www.cambridgegreekplay.com/the-history-of-the-cambridge-greek-play (accessed August 5, 2018).

Lacoue-Labarthe, Philippe. "Hölderlin's Theatre." In *Tragedy and Philosophy*, ed. Miguel de Beistegui and Simon Sparks. London: Routledge, 2000.

Lanzmann, Claude. "Why Spielberg has distorted the truth." *The Guardian Weekly* (April 3, 1994): 14.

Lawrence of Arabia. Directed by David Lean. London: Horizon Pictures, 1962. DVD.

Leavis, F.R. *Mass Civilisation and Minority Culture.* Cambridge: The Minority Press, 1930.

Lee, Young Jean, ed. *New Downtown Now: An Anthology of New Theater from Downtown New York.* Minneapolis: University of Minnesota, 2006.

Lehmann, Hans-Thies. *Postdramatic Theatre.* Trans. Karen Jürs-Munby. London: Routledge, 2006.

Lehmann, Hans-Thies. *Tragedy and Dramatic Theatre.* Trans. Erik Butler. London and New York: Routledge, 2016.

Lenson, David. *Achilles' Choice. Examples of Modern Tragedy.* Princeton: Princeton University Press, 2015.

Leonard, Miriam, *Tragic Modernities.* Cambridge, MA: Harvard University Press, 2015.

Lessing, Gotthold Ephraim. *Laocoon, An Essay on the Limits of Painting and Poetry*, 2nd edn. Trans. Edward Allen McCormick. Baltimore: Johns Hopkins University Press, 1984.

Levi, Primo. *If This Is a Man* and *The Truce.* Trans. Stuart Woolf. 1958. London: Abacus, 1987.

Ley, Graham. "Modern Visions of Greek Tragic Dancing." *Theatre* Journal, 55.3 (2003): 467–80.

Lillo, George. *The London Merchant* (1731). Lincoln, NE: University of Nebraska Press, 1965.

Linfield, Susie. *The Cruel Radiance: Photography and Political Violence*. Chicago: University of Chicago Press, 2010.

Lorca, Frederico Garcia. *Four Major Plays*. Trans. John Edmunds. Oxford: Oxford University Press, 1997.

Lu Xun. *The Real Tale of Ah-Q , and Other Tales of China: The Complete Fiction of Lu Xun*. Trans. Julia Lovell. London: Penguin, 2010.

Lyotard, Jean-François. *Enthusiasm: The Kantian Critique of History*. Trans. Georges Van Den Abbeele. Stanford, CA: Stanford University Press, 2009.

McCarthy, Cormac. *The Road*. London: Picador, 2006.

McDonald, David. "The Trace of Absence: a Derridean Analysis of 'Oedipus Rex.'" *Theatre Journal* 31.2 (May 1979): 147–61.

Mackinnon, Donald. *The Borderlands of Theology and Other Essays*. Ed. G.W. Roberts and D.E. Smucker. London: Lutterworth Press, 1968.

MacKinnon, Donald. *Explorations in Theology 5*. London: SCM, 1979.

MacKinnon, Donald. *Themes in Theology: The Threefold Cord*. Edinburgh: T&T Clark, 1987.

Macintosh, Fiona. "From the Court to the National: The Theatrical Legacy of Gilbert Murray's *Bacchae*." In *Gilbert Murray Reassessed: Hellenism, Theatre, and International Politics*, ed. Christopher Stray, 145–65. Oxford: Oxford University Press, 2007.

Macintosh, Fiona. "Tragedy in performance: nineteenth- and twentieth-century productions." In *The Cambridge Companion to Greek Tragedy*, ed. P.E. Easterling, 284–323. Cambridge: Cambridge University Press, 1992.

Marker, Chris. *Sans Soleil* (1983). Translation of the spoken script: https://www.markertext.com/sans_soleil.htm (accessed August 5, 2018).

McKibben, Bill. *The End of Nature*. New York: Random, 1989.

McKitterick, Katherine. "Rebellion/Invention/Groove." *Small Axe*, 20.1 (2016): 79–91.

McKitterick, Katherine, ed. *Sylvia Wynter: on being human as praxis*. Durham, NC: Duke University Press, 2015.

McNeill, David and Lucy Birmingham. *Strong in the Rain: Surviving Japan's Earthquake, Tsunami, and Fukushima Nuclear Disaster*. Basingstoke: Palgrave Macmillan, 2012.

Mamet, David. "The Art of Theatre No. 11." Interviewed by John Lahr. *The Paris Review*, Issue 142 (1997).

Mamet, David. *Oleanna*. New York: Vintage Books, 1992.

Marder, Michael. *The Chernobyl Herbarium: Fragments of an Exploded Consciousness*. London: Open Humanities, 2016.

Margolles, Teresa. *Plancha* (2010). Gallerie Peter Kilchmann, Zurich.

Martin, Randall. *Shakespeare and Ecology*. Oxford: Oxford University Press, 2015.

Mason, David V. "The Classical American Tradition: Meta-Tragedy in Oleanna." *Journal of American Drama and Theatre*, 13.3 (2001): 55–72.

Mbembe, Achille. "Necropolitics." Trans. Libby Meintjes. *Public Culture* 15.1 (2003): 11–40.

McCurry, Justin. "Fukushima's radioactive wasteland turns into art gallery." *The Guardian*, November 16, 2015.

Mee, Charles. *the (re)making project*. Online resource. http://www.charlesmee.org/index.shtml

Mee, Erin B. and Helene P. Foley, eds. *Antigone on the Contemporary World Stage*. Oxford: Oxford University Press, 2011.

Melinda and Melinda. Directed by Woody Allen. Hollywood: Fox Searchlight, 2005. DVD.

Merchant, Carolyn. *The Death of Nature: Women, Ecology and the Scientific Revolution*. San Francisco: Harper & Row, 1980.

Metz, Johann Baptist. *Followers of Christ: The Religious Life and the Church*. Trans. Thomas Linton. New York, NY: Paulist, 1978.

Michaels, Anne. *Fugitive Pieces*. Toronto: McClelland & Stewart Inc., 1996.

Michelakis, Pantelis. "Theater Festivals, Total Works of Art, And the Revival of Greek Tragedy on the Modern Stage." *Cultural Critique*, 74 (Winter 2010): 149–63.

Miller, Arthur. *All My Sons*. London: Penguin Books, 2000.

Miller, Arthur. *Death of a Salesman*. London: Penguin Books, 2000.

Miller, Arthur. "*Death of a Salesman*: A Symposium. Arthur Miller, Gore Vidal, Richard Watts, John Beauford, Martin Dworkin, David W. Thompson and Phillip Gelb." *The Tulane Drama Review*, 2.3 (May, 1958): 63–4.

Miller, Arthur. "Tragedy and the Common Man." In *The Theater Essays of Arthur Miller*, ed. Robert A. Martin, 3–7. London and New York: Penguin, 1978.

Miller, Arthur. *A View from the Bridge*. London: Penguin Books, 2010.

Miller, Arthur and Phillip Gelb. "Morality and Modern Drama: Interview with Arthur Miller and Phillip Gelb." *Education Theatre Journal*, 10.3 (October, 1958): 190–202.

Mishra, Pankaj. "How to Think about Islamic State." *The Guardian*, July 24, 2015.

Mitman, Gregg. *Reel Nature: America's romance with wildlife on films*. Cambridge, MA: Harvard University Press, 1999.

Moltmann, Juergen. *The Crucified God: The Cross of Christ as the Foundation and Criticism of Christian Theology*. Trans. R.A. Wilson and John Bowden. London: SCM Press, 1974.

Moore, Jason M., ed. *Anthropocene or Capitalocene?: Nature, History, and the Crisis of Capitalism*. Oakland, CA: PM Press. 2016.

Moran, Cerness. *Jean-Paul Sartre: A Tragic Ontology of Freedom*. Washington DC: Catholic University of America, 1978.

Morrison, Toni. *Beloved*. New York: Random House, 1987.

Morton, Timothy. *Ecology without Nature: Rethinking Environmental Aesthetics*. Cambridge, MA: Harvard University Press, 2009.

Mosse, Richard. "Artist Statement." Artist's Website, http://richardmosse.com/projects/artist-statement#home (accessed July 30, 2017).

Mosse, Richard. *Heat Maps*. First exhibited at the Curve Gallery, Barbican Centre. London, 2017.

Mosse, Richard. *Incoming*. Video installation. First exhibited at the Curve Gallery, Barbican Centre. London, 2017.

Mnouchkine, Ariane. *Les Atrides*. Premiere: Halle Tony Garnier, Lyons, November 1990.

Mouchette. Directed by Robert Bresson. Paris: Argos Films/Parc Film, 1967. DVD.

Müller, Heiner. *Hamletmachine and Other Texts for the Stage*. Ed. and trans. Carl Weber. New York: PAJ Publications, 1984.

Müller, Heiner. *Theatremachine*. Trans. Marc von Henning. London: Faber and Faber, 1995.

Mulholland Drive. Directed by David Lynch. Hollywood: Universal Pictures, 2001. DVD.

Murdoch, Iris. "The Sublime and the Good." *Chicago Review* 13.3 (Autumn 1959): 42–55.

Nachtwey, James. *Inferno*. New York: Phaidon Press, 2003.

Nash, Jennifer. "Practicing Love: Black Feminism, Love-Politics and Post-Intersectionality." *Meridians: feminism, race, transnationalism*, 11.2 (2011): 1–24.

Natanson, Maurice. "Jean-Paul Sartre's Philosophy of Freedom." In *Sartre and Existentialism: Existentialist Ontology and Human Consciousness*, ed. William L. McBridge, 30–46. New York: Routledge, 1997.
Neal, Lucy, ed. *Playing for Time: Making Art as if the World Mattered.* London: Oberon, 2015.
Nelson, Richard. *Sorry.* Premiere: Public Theater, New York, October 2012.
Newman, L.M. *Edward Gordon Craig, Black Figures: 105 Reproductions with an Unpublished Essay.* Wellingborough: Christopher Skelton, 1989.
Newman, L.M. "Reinhardt and Craig?" In *Max Reinhardt: The Oxford Symposium*, ed. Margaret Jakobs and John Warren, 6–15. Oxford: Oxford Polytechnic, 1986.
Ngũgĩ wa Thiong'o. *Decolonising the Mind: The Politics of Language in African Theatre.* London: Heinemann, 1986.
Nietzsche, Friedrich. *The Birth of Tragedy and Other Writings.* Ed. Raymond Geuss and Ronald Speirs, trans. Ronald Speirs. Cambridge: Cambridge University Press, 1999.
Nietzsche, Friedrich. *Ecce Homo, The Genealogy of Morals and Ecce Homo.* Trans. Walter Kaufmann. New York: Vintage Books, 1989.
Nietzsche, Friedrich. *The Joyous Science ("La Gaya Scienza").* Trans. R. Kevin Hill. London: Penguin Books, 2018.
Ninagawa, Yukio. *Macbeth.* Premiere: Tokyo, 1980. International premiere: Edinburgh Festival, 1985.
Norrish, Peter. *New Tragedy and Comedy in France, 1945-1970.* Lanham, MD: Rowman and Littlefield, 1988.
Nozick, Robert. *The Examined Life: Philosophical Meditations.* New York: Simon & Schuster, 1989.
Nussbaum, Martha. "Compassion and Terror." *Daedalus*, 132 (2003): 10–26.
Nussbaum, Martha. *The Fragility of Goodness: Luck and Ethics in Greek Tragedy and Philosophy*, revised edn. Cambridge: Cambridge University Press, 2001.
Nuttall, A.D. *Why Does Tragedy Give Pleasure?* Oxford: Clarendon Press, 1996.
October: Ten Days that Shook the World. Directed by Sergei Eisenstein. Sovkino/Amkino Corporation. 1927. DVD.
Odin, Steve. *Tragic Beauty in Whitehead and Japanese Aesthetics.* New York and London: Lexington Books, 2016.
O'Hara, Frank. *What's with Modern Art: Selected Short Reviews & Other Art Writings.* Ed. Bill Berkson. Austin, TX: Mike and Dale's Press, 1999.
OJ: Made in America. Directed by Ezra Edelman. ESPN Films, 2016.
Once Upon a Time in Anatolia. Directed by Nuri Bilge Ceylan. Istanbul: Zeynofilm/Production 2006/1000 Volt, 2011. DVD.
O'Neill, Eugene. *The Iceman Cometh.* London: Nick Hern Books, 1993.
O'Neill, Eugene. *Long Day's Journey Into Night.* London: Nick Hern Books, 1991.
Orlemanski, Julie. "Genre." In *A Handbook of Middle English Studies*, ed. Marion Turner, 207–21. London: John Wiley & Sons, 2013.
Osborne, John, *Look Back in Anger.* New edn. London: Penguin, 1982.
Osofisan, Femi. *Tegonni: An African Antigone.* Ibadan: Opon Ifa, 1999.
Owen, Wilfred. *The Poems of Wilfred Owen.* Ed. Jon Stallworthy. London: Chatto and Windus, 1990.
Ozu, Yasujiro. *Tokio Story.* Tokyo: Shochiko, 1953. DVD.
Palmer, David, ed. *Visions of Tragedy in Modern American Drama: From O'Neill to the Twenty-First Century.* London: Bloomsbury, 2018.
Parker, Andrew. *The Theorist's Mother.* Durham, NC: Duke University Press, 2012.

Parker, Pat. *Literary Fat Ladies: Rhetoric, Gender and Property*. London: Routledge, 1988.
Parks, Suzan-Lori. *Father Comes Home From the Wars*. New York and London: TCG/Nick Hern Books, 2015.
Parks, Suzan-Lori. *Topdog/Underdog*. New York: TCG books, 2001.
Patterson, Ian. *Guernica and Total War*. Cambridge, MA: Harvard University Press, 2007.
Pearson, Mike. *Site-specific Performance*. Basingstoke: Palgrave Macmillan, 2010.
Peters, Julie Stone. "Jane Harrison and the Savage Dionysus: Archaeological Voyages, Ritual Origins, Anthropology, and the Modern Theatre." *Modern Drama* 51, no. 1 (2008): 1–41.
Picasso, Pablo. *Guernica*. First exhibited in the Spanish Pavilion, International Exposition, Paris. 1937.
Pinter, Harold. *The Birthday Party*. London: Faber & Faber, 1991.
Pinter, Harold. *The Caretaker*. London: Faber & Faber, 1991.
Pinter, Harold. *The Homecoming*. New York: Grove Press, 1965.
Plokhy, Serhii. *Chernobyl: The History of a Tragedy*. London: Allen Lane, 2018.
Poulenc, Francis. *Dialogues des Carmélites*. Libretto, Francis Poulenc. Premiere: La Scala, Milan, January 1957.
Pound, Ezra. *A Guide to Kulcher*. 1938. New York: New Directions, 1970.
Pound, Ezra. *Women of Trachis, A Version by Ezra Pound*. London: Faber and Faber, 1956.
Pound, Ezra, and Rudd Fleming. *Sophokles, Electra, A Version by Ezra Pound and Rudd Fleming*. Ed. Carey Perloff. New York: New Directions Books, 1990.
Prevot, Andrew, *Thinking Prayer: Theology and Modernity Amid the Crises of Modernity*. Notre Dame, IN: Notre Dame University Press, 2015.
Pritchard, Jane and Geoffrey Marsh, eds. *Diaghilev and the Golden Age of the Ballets Russes 1909-1929*. London: V. & A., 2010.
Quash, Ben. "Christianity as Hyper-Tragic." In *Facing Tragedies*, ed. Christopher Hamilton, Otto Neumaier, Gottfried Schweiger, and Clemens Sedmak, 77–88. Wien-Berlin-Münster: LIT Verlag, 2009.
Quash, Ben. "Four Biblical Characters: In Search of a Tragedy." In *Christian Theology and Tragedy: Theologians, Tragic Literature, and Tragic Theory*, ed. Kevin Taylor and Giles Waller, 15–34. Aldershot: Ashgate, 2011.
Quash, Ben. "Real Enactment: The Role of Drama in the Theology of Hans Urs von Balthasar." In *Faithful Performances: The Enactment of Christian Identity in Theology and the Arts*, ed. Trevor Hart and Steven Guthrie, 13–32. Aldershot: Ashgate, 2007.
Quayson, Ato, *Calibrations: Reading for the Social*. Minneapolis, MN: University of Minnesota Press, 2003.
Rainer, Yvonne. "Some retrospective notes on a dance for 10 people and 12 mattresses called 'Parts of Some Sextets.'" *The Tulane Drama Review*, 10, No. 2 (1965): 168–78.
Rancière, Jacques. *Aisthesis: Scenes from the Aesthetic Regime of Art*. Trans. Paul Zakir. London: Verso, 2013.
Rancière, Jacques, "The Archaeomodern Turn." In *Walter Benjamin and the Demands of History*, ed. Michael P. Steinberg, 24–40. Cornell: Cornell University Press, 1996.
Rancière, Jacques. *The Politics of Aesthetics: The Distribution of the Sensible*. Ed. Gabriel Rockhill. London and New York: Bloomsbury Academic, 2013.
Rattigan, Terence. *After the Dance* (1938). London: Nick Hern Books, 1995.
Rattigan, Terence. *The Deep Blue Sea* (1952). London: Nick Hern Books, 1999.
Mark Ravenhill. *Plays 1: Shopping and F**king; Faust; Handbag; Some Explicit Polaroids*. London: Methuen Drama, 2000.

Rawlinson, Mary. "Beyond Antigone: Ismene, Gender, and the Right to Life." In *The Returns of Antigone: Interdisciplinary Essays*, ed. Tina Chanter and Sean D. Kirkland, 101–21. Albany, NY: State University of New York Press, 2014.
Red Desert. Directed by Michelangelo Antonioni. Milan: Rizzoli, 1964. DVD.
Rev. BBC drama. London: Big Talk Productions/Ingenious Broadcasting. 2010–14.
Richter, Gerhard. *Birkenau*. Reichstag, Berlin, 2014.
Richter, Gerhard. *October 18 1977*. New York: MoMA, 1988.
Robinson, Marilynne. *Gilead*. New York: Farrar, Straus and Giroux, 2004.
Román, David. "Introduction: Tragedy." *Theatre Journal* 54.1 (2002): 1–17.
Rosen, Aaron. *Art + Religion in the 21st Century*. London: Thames and Hudson, 2015.
Rossiter, A.P. *Angels With Horns: Fifteen Lectures on Shakespeare*. London: Longmans Green, 1961.
Rotimi, Ola. *The Gods Are Not To Blame*. Oxford: Oxford University Press, 1971.
Royal Court. "Environmental Policy" (2012–18), website mission statement: https://royalcourttheatre.com/about/environmental-policy/ (accessed August 5, 2018).
Rupprecht, Philip. *Britten's Musical Language*. Cambridge: Cambridge University Press, 2001.
Sack, Daniel. "*L.#09-London Episode of the Tragedia Endogonidia*. By Socìetas Raffaello Sanzio. Directed by Romeo Castellucci. Alexander Kasser Theater, Montclair State University, New Jersey, 7 October 2005." *Theatre Journal* 58.3 (2006): 485–6.
The Sacrifice. Directed by Andrei Tarkovsky. Svenska Filminstitutet/Argos Films, 1986. DVD.
Said, Edward. "The Palestinian Experience." In *The Edward Said Reader*, ed. Moustafa Bayoumi and Andrew Rubin, 14–37. New York: Vintage Books, 2000.
Salcedo, Doris. *Atrabiliarios*. San Francisco: SFMOMA, 1992–2003.
Salcedo, Doris. *Plegaria Muda*. San Francisco: SFMOMA, 2008–10.
Salcedo, Doris. *Shibboleth*. London: Tate Modern, 2007.
Salcedo, Doris. *Unland: The Orphan's Tunic*. Barcelona: Fundacio La Caixa, 1997.
Samuels, Diane and Tracy-Ann Oberman. *Three Sisters on Hope Street*. London: Nick Hern Books, 2008.
Sans Soleil. Directed by Chris Marker. Paris: Argos Films, 1983. DVD.
Sarkisian, Natalia and Naomi Gerstel. *Nuclear Family Values, Extended Family Lives: The Power of Race, Class and Gender*. New York and London: Routledge, 2012.
Sartre, Jean-Paul. *Being and Nothingness: An Essay on Phenomenological Ontology*. Trans. Hazel E. Barnes. New York: Philosophical Library, 1956.
Sartre, Jean-Paul. *Existentialism is a Humanism*. Trans. Annie Cohen-Solal, ed. John Kulka. New Haven: Yale University Press, 2007.
Sartre, Jean-Paul. *Les Mouches*. Paris: Gallimard, 1943; translated in *Sartre on Theater*, ed. Michel Contat and Michel Rybalka. London: Quartet Books, 1976.
Sartre, Jean-Paul. *Un théâtre de situations*. Paris: Gaillmard, 1992; translated in Christina Howells, *Sartre: The Necessity of Freedom*. Cambridge: Cambridge University Press, 2009.
Sartre, Jean-Paul. *"What is Literature?" and Other Essays*. Trans. Bernard Frechtman Cambridge, MA: Harvard University Press, 1988.
Saunders, Graham. *"Love Me or Kill Me": Sarah Kane and the Theatre of Excess*. Manchester: Manchester University Press, 2002.
Schechner, Richard, ed. *Dionysus in 69*. New York: Farrar, Straus & Giroux, 1973.
Schechner, Richard. *Environmental Theatre*. 1973. New York: Applause, 1994.
Schechner, Richard. "9/11 as Avant-Garde Art?" *PMLA* 124, no. 5 (2009): 1820–9.
Schlegel, A.W. *A Course of Lectures on Dramatic Art and Literature*, 2 vols. Trans. John Black. London: Henry G. Bohn, 1846.

Scranton, Roy. "Learning to Die in the Anthropocene." *New York Times*, November 10, 2013.

Selby, Jan, Omar S. Dahi, Christiane Frölich, and Mike Hulme. "Climate change and the Syrian civil war revisited." *Political Geography*, 60 (September 2017): 232–44.

Seneca. *Thyestes*. Trans. Caryl Churchill. London: Nick Hern Books, 1993.

Senelick, Laurence. *Gordon Craig's Moscow Hamlet: A Reconstruction*. Westport, CT: Greenwood, Praeger, 1982.

A Separation. Directed by Asghar Farhadi. Paris: Asghar Farhadi Productions/Dreamlab Films, 2011. DVD.

The Seventh Seal. Directed by Ingmar Bergman. Stockholm: AB.Svensk Filmindustri, 1957. DVD.

Shakespeare, William. *Hamlet*. Ed. Ann Thompson and Neil Taylor. Rev. edn. London: Bloomsbury Arden Shakespeare, 2016.

Shakespeare, William. *King Lear*. Ed. R.A. Foakes. London: The Arden Shakespeare, 1997.

Shaw, George Bernard. *Saint Joan*. Ed. Jean Chothia. London: Methuen Drama, 2008.

Sierz, Aleks. *In-Yer-Face Theatre: British Drama Today*. London: Faber, 2001.

Simone, Nina. *The Nina Simone Collection*. New York: Union Square Music, 2006. 3 × CD.

Singleton, Brian. "Plague." In *Le Théâtre et son double*, 23–31. London: Grant & Cutler Ltd, 1998.

Skantze, P.A. *Stillness in Motion on the Seventeenth-Century Stage*. London: Routledge, 2003.

Skantze, P.A. "Unaccommodated Woman: Mabou Mines' *Lear*, the Universal and the Particular in Performance." In *Shakespeare RE-Dressed: Cross-Gender Casting in Contemporary Performance*, ed. James Bulman, 116–30. Cranbury, NJ: Fairleigh Dickinson University Press, 2008.

Smith, Bessie. *Bessie Smith Sings The Blues*. Brownsville, TN, 2007. CD.

Smith, Bradon. "Staging Climate Change: the last ten years" (2014), http://bradonsmith.com/wp-content/uploads/2014/04/Staging-climate-change-the-last-ten-years.pdf (accessed August 8, 2018).

Smith, Sylvia Rupani. "Japanese artists respond to Fukishima." *New York Times*, June 26, 2014.

Solzhenitsyn, Aleksandr. *One Day in the Life of Ivan Denisovich*. Trans. Ralph Parker. 1962: London, Penguin, 1963.

Sontag, Susan. "The Death of Tragedy." In *Against Interpretation and Other Essays*. New York: Dell, 1969: 138–45.

Sontag, Susan. *On Photography*. New York: Farrar, Straus and Giroux, 1977.

Sontag, Susan, *Regarding the Pain of Others*. London: Picador, 2004.

Soyinka, Wole. *The Bacchae of Euripides: A Communion Rite*, 2nd edn. New York: W.W. Norton & Co., 2004.

Soyinka, Wole. *Death and the King's Horsemen*. Ed. Simon Gikandi. New York: W.W.Norton & Co., 2003.

Soyinka, Wole. "The Fourth Stage." In *The Morality of Art: Essays Presented to G. Wilson Knight by his Colleagues and Friends*, ed. D.W. Jefferson, 119–34. London: Routledge, 1969.

Soyinka, Wole. *Myth, Literature and the African World*. Cambridge: Cambridge University Press, 1976.

Spillers, Hortense J. "Mama's Baby, Papa's Maybe: An American Grammar Book." *Diacritics*, 17, No. 2, Culture and Countermemory: The "American" Connection (Summer, 1987): 64–81.

Spotts, Frederic. *Bayreuth: A History of the Wagner Festival*. New Haven and London: Yale University Press, 1994.

Steiner, George, *The Death of Tragedy*. London: Faber and Faber, 1961.

Steiner, George. *Proofs and Three Parables*. London: Granta Books, 1992.
Stergiopoulou, Katerina. "'And a Good Job'? Elektrifying English at St. Elizabeth's." *Journal of Modern Literature* 39, no.1 (2015): 87–111.
Storm, William. *After Dionysus: A Theory of the Tragic*. Ithaca: Cornell University Press, 1998.
Styan, John L. *The dark comedy: The development of modern comic tragedy*. Cambridge: Cambridge University Press, 1962.
Styan, John L. *Max Reinhardt*. Cambridge: Cambridge University Press, 1982.
Suppliant Women. "Teaser Trailer." YouTube. Posted October 3, 2016, https://www.youtube.com/watch?v=2FdLq_vRKmE (accessed February 2, 2017).
Szondi, Peter. *An Essay on the Tragic*. Trans. Paul Fleming. Stanford, CA: Stanford University Press, 2002.
Taste of Cherry. Directed by Abbas Kiarostami. Abbas Kiarostami Productions/CiBy 2000. 1997. DVD.
Tate, Trudi. *History, Modernism and the First World War*. Manchester: Manchester University Press, 1998.
Tatlow, Anthony. *Brecht, Shakespeare and the Intercultural Sign*. Durham, NC: Duke University Press, 2001.
Taxi Driver. Directed by Martin Scorsese. Los Angeles: Columbia Pictures, 1976. DVD.
Three Colors. Directed by Krzysztof Kieslowski. Paris: MK2 Productions, 1993–4. DVD.
Tigner, Amy L. "The Laramie Project: Western Pastoral." *Modern Drama* 45.1 (2002): 138–56.
Torpey, John. *Making Whole What Has Been Smashed*. Cambridge, MA: Harvard University Press, 2006.
The Tree of Life. Directed by Terrence Malick. Cottonwood Pictures/River Road Entertainment/Brace Cove Entertainment/Plan B Entertainment. 2011. DVD.
Trimble, Sarah. "Trust Sylvia Wynter." *new formations: a journal of culture/theory/politics*, 89–90 (2017): 276.
Trojan Women. Directed by Michael Cacoyannis. London: Josef Shaftel Productions, 1971. DVD
Tuoi Sleng Image Database. Gallery of S-21 Prisoner Photographs. Cambodia Genocide Databases, Yale University. https://gsp.yale.edu/case-studies/cambodian-genocide-program/cambodian-genocide-databases-cgdb/tuol-sleng-image-database
Turpin, John. "Monumental Commemoration of the Fallen in Ireland, North and South, 1920–60." *New Hibernia Review / Iris Éireannach Nua*, 11.4 (2007): 107–19.
The Unforgiven. Directed by Clint Eastwood. Hollywood: Warner Bros. 1992. DVD.
Urban, Eva. *Community Politics and the Peace Process in Contemporary Northern Irish Drama*. Bern: Peter Lang, 2010.
Van der Dries, Luk. "Mount Olympus/24H." http://mountolympus.be/about
Vernant, Jean-Pierre and Pierre Vidal-Naquet. *Myth and Tragedy in Ancient Greece*. Trans. Janet Lloyd. New York: Zone Books, 1990.
Vicuña, Cecilia. *Spit Temple: the selected performance of*. Trans. Rosa Alcalá. Brooklyn, NY: Ugly Duckling Presse, 2012.
Vishniac, Roman. *Vishniac: Children of a Vanished World*. Ed. Mara Vishniac Kohn and Hartman Flacks. Berkeley and Los Angeles: University of California Press, 1999.
Wallace, Jennifer. *The Cambridge Introduction to Tragedy*. Cambridge: Cambridge University Press, 2007.
Wallace, Jennifer. "Tragedy in China." *Cambridge Quarterly*, 42.2 (2013): 99–111.
Wallace, Jennifer. "Tragedy, Photography and Osama bin Laden: Looking at the Enemy." *Critical Quarterly*, 57.2 (2015): 17–35.

Wallace, Jennifer. *Tragedy since 9/11: Reading a World Out of Joint*. London: Bloomsbury, 2019.

Wardle, Irving. "Comedy of Menace." *Encore*, 5 (September–October 1958): 28–33.

Waters, Steve. *The Contingency Plan*. London: Nick Hern Books, 2009.

Waters, Steve. "The truth behind the facts." *The Guardian*, February 11, 2004.

Wellbery, David. "Form und Funktion der Tragödie in Nietzsche." In *Tragödie. Trauerspiel. Spektakel*, ed. Christoph Menke and Bettine Menke. Berlin: Theater der Zeit, 2007.

West, Cornel. "On Prophetic Pragmatism." In *The Cornel West Reader*, 149–74. New York: Basic Books, 2000.

The White Ribbon. Directed by Michael Haneke. Berlin: X Filme Creative Pool/Vienna: Wega Film/Paris: Les Films de Losange/Los Angeles: Lucky Red, 2009. DVD.

Widdows, Heather. "Border Disputes across Bodies: Exploitation in Trafficking for Prostitution and Egg Sale for Stem Cell Research." *International Journal of Feminist Approaches to Bioethics* 2.1 (2009): 5–24.

Wiles, David. *Tragedy in Athens: Performance Space and Theatrical Meaning*. Cambridge: Cambridge University Press, 1997.

Wiles, David. *A Short History of Performance Space*. Cambridge: Cambridge University Press, 2003.

Wiles, David. "Sophoclean Diptychs: Modern Translations of Dramatic Poetry." *A Journal of Humanities and the Classics* 13, no. 1 (2005): 9–26.

Williams, Raymond. *Modern Tragedy*. London: Chatto & Windus, 1966.

Williams, Raymond. *Writing in Society*. London: Verso, 1983.

Williams, Rowan. *Grace and Necessity: Reflections on Art and Love*. London: Bloomsbury, 2005.

Williams, Rowan. *The Tragic Imagination*. Oxford: Oxford University Press, 2016.

Williams, Rowan. "Trinity and Ontology." In *Christ, Ethics and Tragedy: Essays in Honour of Donald MacKinnon*, ed. Kenneth Surin, 71–93. Cambridge: Cambridge University Press, 1989.

Williams, Rowan. *Writing in the Dust: Reflections on 11th September and its Aftermath*. London: Hodder and Stoughton, 2002.

Williams, Tennessee. *Cat on a Hot Tin Roof*. Ed. Philip Kolin. London: Methuen Drama, 2010.

Williams, Tennessee. *The Glass Menagerie*. Ed. Stephen Bottoms. London: Methuen Drama, 2008.

Williams, Tennessee. *A Streetcar Named Desire*. Ed. Michael Hooper and Patricia Hern. London: Methuen Drama, 2005.

Wilson, August. *Fences*. New York: Plume, 1986.

Winehouse, Amy. *Back to Black*. London: Island Records, 2006. CD.

Woolf, Virginia. *Three Guineas* (1937). Eastford, CT: Martino Fine Books, 2013.

The Wooster Group. "Hamlet." The Wooster Group Company Website: http://thewoostergroup.org/hamlet (accessed April 1, 2017).

Worthen, W.B. "Antigone's Bones." *TDR—Deb Margolin: I'm Just Sayin*, 52.3 (2008): 10–33.

Wynter, Sylvia. "The Pope Must Have Been Drunk, the King of Castile as a Madman: Culture as Actuality and the Caribbean Rethinking of Modernity." In *Reordering of Culture: Latin America, the Caribbean and Canada in the 'Hood*, 17–42. Ottawa: Carleton University Press, 1995

Yaari, Nurit. "Myth into Dance: Martha Graham's Interpretation of the Classical Tradition." *International Journal of the Classical Tradition*, 10.2 (2003): 221–42.

Yates, Richard. *Revolutionary Road*. Boston, MA: Little, Brown & Co., 1961.

Yeats, W.B. *The Collected Works of W. B. Yeats, Vol. II The Plays*. Ed. David R. Clark and Rosalind E. Clark. New York: Scribner, 2001.
Yeats, W.B. *Explorations*. London: Macmillan, 1962.
Yeats, W.B. "The Tragic Generation" (1914). In *Autobiographies*, 279–348. London: Macmillan, 1955.
Young, James E. *The Texture of Memory: Holocaust Memorials and Meaning*. New Haven: Yale University Press, 1993.
Young, Julian. *The Philosophy of Tragedy: From Plato to Žižek*. Cambridge: Cambridge University Press, 2013.
Zabriskie Point. Directed by Michelangelo Antonioni. Los Angeles: MGM. 1970. DVD.
Žižek, Slavoj. *Antigone*. London: Bloomsbury, 2016.
Žižek, Slavoj. "Femininity Between Goodness and Act." *Lacanian Ink* 14 (1999): 26–40.
Žižek, Slavoj. "Psychoanalysis in Post-Marxism: The Case of Alain Badiou." *The South Atlantic Quarterly* 97.2 (Spring 1998): 235–61.
Zola, Emile. "Naturalism on the Stage." In *Playwrights on Playwriting: From Ibsen to Ionesco*, ed. Toby Cole, 5–14. New York: Cooper Square Press, 2001.

INDEX

Abel, Lionel 26
  Metatheatre: A New View of Dramatic Form 25
abnormality 130
accident 112
Adams, John
  Death of Klinghoffer, The 52
  Doctor Atomic 52
adaptation 35–40
Adebayo, Mojisola 132
  Muhammad Ali and Me 132–3
Adorno, Theodore 15, 43, 50, 85, 89, 121–3
  Aesthetic Theory 122–3
  autonomous works 122–3
  freedom 118
Aeschylus 4
  Suppliant Women, The 30, 34, 82
aesthetics 57, 80, 123–4 (*see also* German Idealism)
Africa 103
African American history 8
Agamben, Giorgio 88, 119–20, 129, 141
Ahmed, Sarah 130
Ai Weiwei 18
AIDS epidemic 135, 136
Al Attar, Mohammad
  While I Was Waiting 50
Albee, Edward
  Who's Afraid of Virginia Woolf 6
alienation 6–7
Allen, Woody
  Melinda and Melinda 35–6
America 6, 7, 128–9
  race 13–14
anarchy 138–40
ancient Greece 4
Anouilh, Jean
  Antigone 7
Anti-Slavery Arch, Stroud 44
anti-theatricality 146
Antigone character 20, 31, 50, 75, 78, 80, 87–9, 131, 137, 139–40, 143, 149
  (*see also under* Anouilh; Brecht; Carson; Mendelssohn; Sophocles; van Hove)
Antonakakis, Nikolaos 139
Antonioni, Michelangelo 9
  Zabriskie Point 54
archeo-modern turn 61
Archive of Performances in Greek and Roman Drama 34
archives 34–5
Arendt, Hannah 15, 84, 130
  evil 118–19
  On Revolution 84
Aristotle 3
  Poetics, The 8, 64
art 4, 10
Artaud, Antonin 57, 73–4
  "End to Masterpieces, An" 60, 73
arts 108, 111, 121–2
  social truth content 123
assassinations 13
assemblies 138–40
Association of Teachers of the Revived Greek Dance 52
Athens and Epidaurus Festival 52
audience. *See* spectating
audio-visual recording devices 34–5
Auschwitz concentration camp 4, 15 (*see also* Holocaust, the)
austerity 138–9
autonomous works 122–3

Balthasar, Hans Urs von 98–9, 101, 102
  Theodrama 98
Barker, Howard 29
Barth, Karl 97–8, 101
Bartlett, Mike
  Earthquakes in London 49
Bate, Jonathan 7
Bausch, Pina
  Café Müller 52
Bayreuth Festival 26, 31, 52
Bean, Richard
  Heretic, The 49

bearing witness 120
Beauford, John 117
Beck, Julian 33
Beckett, Samuel 6, 10, 27, 123–5
　Breath 27
　Endgame 27, 42, 96, 123
　Happy Days 123, 124
　Unnameable, The 17
　Waiting for Godot 42, 54, 96, 110
Benjamin, Walter
　First World War 120
　Origin of German Tragic Drama, The 83–4
　Task of the Translator, The 58
　"Theses on the Philosophy of History" 28
　translatability 71–2
　Trauerspiel 83–4
　"Work of Art in the Age of Mechanical Reproduction, The" 26
Berg, Alban 9
　Lulu 52
Bergman, Ingmar 9
Berlau, Ruth
　Antigone-Model 71–2
Bible 105, 107
Black Lives Matter campaigns 132
Blue Planet II (BBC TV series) 54
Boal, Augusto 3
bodies 129–30
Bond, Edward 7
borders 130, 142–3
Bourke-White, Margaret 10, 12
Boym, Svetlana
　Another Freedom: The Alternative History of an Idea 142
Brecht, Bertolt 3, 6, 54, 57, 113, 123
　Antigone (of Sophocles) 7, 33, 61, 71, 74
　Antigone-Model 71–3
　Arturo Ui 123
　Coriolanus 60
　Greek tragedy 71–3
　Lehrstücke 34
　Life of Galileo, The 42
　Short Organum for the Theatre, A 71
Bresson, Robert 9
Breuer, Lee
　Gospel at Colonus, The 74
　King Lear 153
Britain 6–7, 28–9
　colonialism 55–6
Britten, Benjamin 9
Bronfen, Elizabeth 37
Brook, Peter 7, 52

Brown, John 34
Brown, Nicole 14
Buchenwald concentration camp 12
Buffini, Moira, Matt Charman, Penelope Skinner and Jack Thorne
　Greenland 49
Burrows, Larry 96
Burton, Richard
　Hamlet 35
Butler, Judith 88, 130, 138, 139
　kinship 131
　Notes Towards a Performative Theory of Assembly 132

Cacoyannis, Michael
　Electra 7
　Iphigenia 7
　Trojan Women 7
Cage, John 159
Cambridge Ritualists 60, 61, 66
Camus, Albert 4, 6, 77, 78
　"Myth of Sisyphus, The" 78–9
　Outsider, The 8
canons 6–12, 24–5, 36
　reviving 48
care 133–5, 136, 141, 143, 158–9
Carlson, Julie A. 130
Carney, Sean 48
Carson, Anne
　Antigonick 8
Carver, Raymond 8
Castellucci, Claudia 135
Castellucci, Romeo 135
　On the Concept of the Face, Regarding the Son of God 133–5
catastrophe 18–19, 42, 48–9, 55, 145 (see also war)
　AIDS epidemic 135, 136
　Benjamin, Walter 28
　Duse, Eleanora 64
　environment, the 19, 42, 48–55
　9/11 20–1, 42
　Steiner, George 110
　tragic experience 111–19
catharsis 3, 147
Cavarero, Adriana 119
Cenotaph, Whitehall, London 44
Cesaire, Aimé
　Tragedy of King Christophe 56
Ceylan, Nuri Bilge 9
Chekhov, Anton 7
　Cherry Orchard, The 49

Chernobyl 50–1
Cherry, Ellen 178 n.50
childbirth/childhood 127, 141–2
China 18
chorus 33–4, 59
   Eliot, T.S. 66–7
Christianity 93–4, 96 (*see also* religion)
   excess 102–3
   goodness 107
   lamentation 104–7
   oikonomia 141
   precariousness 107–8
   ritual 103–4
   suffering 98–104, 108
   theodicy 97–102
Christoulas, Dimitris 138–9
Churchill, Caryl 7
   Cloud Nine 156
   Escaped Alone 156–8, 159
   Here We Go 158–9
   Serious Money 156
   Thyestes 7
Churchill, Winston 161 n.2
cinema. *See* film
Ciulei, Liviu
   Midsummer Night's Dream, A 154
Civil Rights Movement 13, 25, 132
Cixous, Hélène 146, 147
   "Enter the Theatre" 145
classical discourse 112–14
classical tragedy 7, 127–8 (*see also* classical discourse; Greek tragedy)
Clément, Catherine
   Opera, or the Undoing of Women 150
climate change 19, 49–50 (*see also* environment, the)
Clough, Patricia Ticineto, Alan Frank, and Steven Seidman
   Intimacies: A new world of relational life 128
cohabitation 133
Cold War 13, 128–9
Collins, Alan 139
colonialism 55–6
comedy 89–90
common man 113–17, 118–19
communication 103
community 33, 133
   violence 33
concentration camps 4, 12, 15, 119–20
conflict. *See* war
conflict resolution 51

consciousness 4
Cook, Arthur Bernard 60
Coppola, Francis Ford
   Apocalypse Now 53
Cornford, Francis 60
courtroom dramas 46
Coward, Noël
   Private Lives 6
Craig, Edward Gordon 57, 60, 62, 63–5, 69
   "Actor and the Übermarionette, The" 59, 64
   Black Figures 64–5
   Hamlet and 64, 74
   Hecuba 65
   Übermarionette concept 62, 63–4
culture 1, 8
   rebelling against 25

dance 52, 58–9, 62–5
Danish Dogma group 9
Dasein 116
Davis, Anthony
   X, the Life and Times of Malcolm X 52
Davis, Miles
   Kind of Blue 9
de Beauvoir, Simone 77, 79, 80–1
   Second Sex, The 79
   Useless Mouths, The 82–3, 87
death 37, 102, 136, 158–9
   necropolitics 140
   of tragedy 109–10, 125
death drive 43, 76
Death of God 60
definitions 3–6, 17, 20, 23, 111
   Lehmann, Hans-Thies 32
   Online Oxford Dictionary of Literary Terms 25
Deflorian, Daria and Antonio Tagliarini
   We Decided to Go Because We Don't Want to Be a Burden to You 140
Deleuze, Gilles and Felix Guattari 128
   Anti-Oedipus 86, 87, 91
   Nietzsche and Philosophy 91
Derrida, Jacques
   Dissemination 87
   "Law of Genre, The" 25
   Monolingualism of the Other; or, The Prosthesis of Origin 142
   Spectres of Marx 90
Detroit 104–5

Dick, Philip K.
  Do Androids Dream of Electric Sheep? 37
digital media, as performance site 43
Dionysianism 32–3, 61, 68, 76, 127–8
domestic duties 141, 142
Doolittle, Hilda (H.D.) 60
Dostoevsky, Fyodor
  Double, The 94
  Notes from Underground 94
Doyle, John 150, 151, 152, 156
Dreyer, Carl Theodore
  Passion of Joan of Arc, The 53
Duncan, Isadora 52, 57, 58–9, 62–3, 64–5
Duras, Margaret and Alain Resnais
  Hiroshima Mon Amour 55
Duse, Eleanora 64
  Electra 64
Dworkin, Martin 115–16

Eagleton, Terry 109, 111, 112–13, 139
  Dionysianism 127–8
Eastwood, Clint 9
Edelman, Ezra
  OJ: Made in America 14
Edelman, Lee 137
Eichmann, Adolf 118
Eisenstein, Sergei
  October: Ten Days That Shook the World 55
Eklund, Rebekah
  Jesus Wept 105, 107
Eliot, George
  Middlemarch 8
Eliot, T.S. 57, 58, 74
  Cocktail Party, The 66, 67
  Confidential Clerk, The 66, 67
  Elder Statesman, The 66, 67
  Family Reunion, The 6, 66, 67, 68
  Greek tragedy 60, 65–8
  Murder in the Cathedral 6, 66–7
  Poetry and Drama 67
  Rock, The 66
  Sweeney Agonistes 66
Elizabethan Stage Society 52
Ellison, Ralph
  Invisible Man, The 8
endogonida 135
Enlightenment, the 87, 109
Eno, Will
  Tragedy: the Tragedy 41–2
environment, the 19, 42, 48–55

films 53–5
Greek tragedy 51–2
Epic Theatre 3, 48, 57, 71, 72
equality 145–9
Euripides 4
  Bacchae, The 32–3
  Children of Heracles 82
  Iphigenia at Tauris 82
  Trojan Women, The 82
Eurocentricity 85
Europe 6
evil 101, 102, 177 n.29
  Arendt, Hannah 118–19
  Williams, Raymond 119
Evreinov, Nikolai
  Storming of the Winter Palace, The 54–5
excess 102–3
existentialism 77, 79, 80–2, 114–15, 116
experience 118–25, 145
  tragic experience 111–19, 145, 147, 150–2, 159

Fabre, Jan 73, 74
  Mount Olympus: To Glorify the Cult of Tragedy 23, 24
family 127–8, 137, 142–3
  care 133–5, 136, 141–2, 143
  childbirth/childhood 127, 141–2
  chosen 140
  domestic duties 141, 142
  government of 141–2
  home, the 141–2
  kinship 131, 136, 140
  mutual dependence 133–5
  nuclear families 128–33
  oikologies 140–3
  private/public sphere 138
  proximity 132
  queer 136
  race 132
  Socìetas Raffaello Sanzio 133
  sorority/fraternity 136–7, 140
  state and 141–2
Farber, Yael
  Molora 7
Farhadi, Asghar 9
fascism 123
feelings 5
Felski, Rita 8, 9, 26, 36
feminism 130–2, 136–7
Fen Court, London 44
Festival of International Drama (F.I.N.D.) 40

fiction 51
film 7, 9, 53–4
   China 18
   environment, the 53–5
   Hamlet 35
   nature documentaries 54
   news 54–5
   as performance site 43
   technology 37–8
   western films 9, 53
film noir 37
First World War 1–2, 13, 43
   Benjamin, Walter 120
   escapism 2
Fitzgerald, F. Scott
   Great Gatsby, The 8
Foley, Helene 34
Ford, David 98, 99
Ford, John
   Grapes of Wrath, The 53
   Man Who Shot Liberty Valance, The 53
   Searchers, The 53
forum theater 48
Foucault, Michel 130, 141–2
France 6
Frank, Anne 15
   Diary of Anne Frank, The 8
fraternity 136–7
Frazer, James
   Golden Bough, The 60
freedom 78, 81–2, 118
Frend, Charles
   Scott of the Antarctic 53
Freud, Sigmund 4, 43, 128
   Civilization and Its Discontents 76, 88
   Interpretation of Dreams, The 75, 86
   Oedipus complex 86, 114
Frisch, Max
   Homo Faber 37
Fugard, Athol
   Island, The 7

gay writers 6
gender 131, 135, 145–9
   Escaped Alone 156–8, 159
   Here We Go 158–9
   Midsummer Night's Dream, A 153–6
   Pacific Overtures 150–3
Genet, Jean 6
genocide 51 (*see also* Holocaust, the)
genre 25, 145
   of human 147

German Idealism 24, 57, 58
Germany 1, 6
   fascism 123
   Müller, Heine 28
Gesamtkunstwerk 24, 26
Giacometti, Alberto 10
   "Walking Man II" 10
Girard, René
   Violence and the Sacred 33
global 43
   capital 130
   catastrophe 18–19, 42, 48–9, 55
   institutes 46
   migration 50
   tragedy 17–19
Goldenberg, Oren
   Requiem for Douglass, A 104, 178 n.47
Goldhill, Simon
   How to Stage Greek Tragedy Today 34
Goldman, Ron 14
goodness 107
Gordon, Paul 76
government 113, 129–30 (*see also* politics)
grace 102–3
Graham, Martha
   "Greek Cycle" 52
Granville Barker, Harley
   Waste 43
Gray, Ramin 34
Greece 138–40
   ancient Greece 4
Greek performance 52
Greek tragedy 31–2, 34, 131, 133, 139 (*see also* Hellenism)
   Antigone character 87–9, 131, 137 (*see also* Sophocles)
   Artaud, Antonin 73–4
   Brecht, Bertolt 71–3
   Camus, Albert 78–9
   chorus, the 33–4
   dance 62–5
   Eliot, T.S. 60, 65–8
   environment, the 51–2
   Heidegger, Martin 80
   Hölderlin, Friedrich 58, 71–2
   modernism 59, 60–1
   Oedipus character 77–9, 85–7, 89, 114, 131 (*see also* Sophocles)
   performance sites 51, 52
   perversion 130
   poetry 65–71
   Pound, Ezra 60, 65, 66, 69–70

Sartre, Jean-Paul 78, 81
translation 58, 60, 65–73
Yeats, W.B. 60, 65, 68–9
Greeks, the 59 (*see also* Hellenism)
Greer, Bonnie
   Hotel Cerise 7
Greig, David
   Suppliant Women, The 34
Guattari, Felix *see* Deleuze, Gilles
Guidi, Chiara 135
Guthrie, Tyrone 34

H.D. (Hilda Doolittle) 60
Hall, Edith 34
Hamilton, Christopher 4
Handke, Peter 124
Haneke, Michael 9
Hansberry, Lorraine 7
   Raisin in the Sun, A 7
Hardy, Thomas 8, 94
   Jude the Obscure 94
Harrison, Jane 60–1, 62–3
Hart, David Bentley 101–2
Hawks, Howard
   Red River 53
Heaney, Seamus
   Cure at Troy, The 7
Hegel, G.W.F. 75, 90, 107
   Lectures on Aesthetics 75
Heidegger, Martin 76–7, 79–80, 116–17
   Introduction to Metaphysics 77
   "Ode to Man" and 77
   Origin of the Work of Art, The 80
Hellenism 60–1, 70
heroism 94–7, 112 (*see also* common man)
Hick, John 99–101
Hill-Gibbins, Joe
   Midsummer Night's Dream, A 154–5
Hiroshima bombing 15, 17, 55
historical events 5, 10, 12–17
   Giacometti, Alberto 10
   Kiefer, Anselm 10
   Richter, Gerhard 10
history 27–8, 118, 139
Hölderlin, Friedrich 58, 71–2
Holiday, Billie 9
Hollow Crown, The (BBC TV series) 7
Holocaust, the 10, 15, 118–20
   Auschwitz concentration camp 4, 15
   Buchenwald concentration camp 12
   Kiefer, Anselm 10
   Levi, Primo 8–9, 119

memorials 16–17, 44, 46, 47
religion 15
Richter, Gerhard 10
Shoah 50
Holocaust Memorial 16–17
home, the 141–2
homosexuality 135–6
Honig, Bonnie 136, 137, 140
Horkheimer, Max 85
Huang, David Henry
   M. Butterfly 150
Hudlin, Reginald
   Marshall 46
human agency 49
human rights 13, 132
human tragedies 50, 97–8 (*see also*
   Holocaust, the; war)
   nuclear wars 15, 16, 17, 55, 128–31
humanness 147

Ibsen, Henrik
   Brand 49
   Doll's House, The 148
   Enemy of the People 49
   Hedda Gabler 148
identity politics 132–3
immersive theater 3
India Gate, New Delhi 44
individual, the 118
inequality 145–9
infidelity 148
Ionesco, Eugène 6
Iraq 161 n.2
Irenaeus of Lyons 99
Iribonke, Olabode 55
Irigaray, Luce 88
irreparable experience 118–25
irreparable tragedy 110, 118
Ito, Michio 68, 69

Jackson, Glenda 153
Japan 18, 151
Jarry, Alfred
   Ubu Roi 61
jazz 9
Jenkins, Karl
   Armed Man, The 9
Jewish Museum, Berlin 44
Johnson, Lonnie 9
Judas 98–9
Judenplatz Holocaust Memorial, Vienna
   46, 47

INDEX

Kafka, Franz
  Trial, The 8
Kamĩriithũ Community Education and
    Cultural Centre 56
Kane, Sarah 7, 102, 124
  Blasted 148
Kant, Immanuel 107
Kaufman, Moisés and the Tectonic Theater
    Project
  Laramie Project, The 135–6
Kenya 56
Khalidi, Ismail
  Truth Serum Blues 42
Khmer Rouge victims 10, 11
Kiarostami, Abbas 9
Kieslowski, Krzysztof 9
King, Jeanette 36
King, Martin Luther, Jr. 13, 14
kinship 131, 136, 140
Klee, Paul
  Angelus Novus 29
Kott, Jan 7
Kushner, Tony
  *Angels in America: A Gay Fantasia on
    National Themes* 136

LaBute, Neil
  Mercy Seat, The 42
Lacan, Jacques
  Ethics of Psychoanalysis, The 87–8
lamentation 104–7 (*see also* mourning)
Lang, Fritz
  Metropolis 53
Langsner, Meron
  Bystander 42
language 30–1
  Artaud, Antonin 73
  Eliot, T.S. 67–8
  family and society 131
  Pound, Ezra 69–70
  Yeats, W.B. 69
Lanzmann, Claude
  Shoah 50
Lash, Nicholas 98
"Last Post, The" 9
League of Nations 1
Lean, David 9
  Bridge Over the River Kwai 9
  Brief Encounter 9
  Dr Zhivago 9
Leavis, F.R.
  Mass Civilisation and Minority Culture 1

Lehmann, Hans-Thies 153
  Tragedy and Dramatic Theatre 32, 145–6
Lehrstücke 34
Leone, Sergio 9
Levi, Primo 119–20
  Drowned and the Saved, The 119
  If This is a Man 8–9
liberal tragedies 49–50
Libeskind, David 44
life as tragedy 76–9
lightheartedness 89–90
Lillo, George
  London Merchant, The 114
Lin, Maya 15–16
Littlewood, Joan
  Oh What a Lovely War! 43
Lorca, Federico Garcia
  Blood Wedding 6
  House of Bernarda Alba, The 6
  Yerma 6, 148, 149
Lu Xun 18
Lugné-Poë, Aurélien-Marie 61
Lumet, Sidney
  Twelve Angry Men 45
Luytens, Edwin 44
Lynch, David
  Mulholland Drive 9
Lyotard, Jean-François 133

Mac, Taylor
  Hir 148
McCarthy, Cormac 108
  Road, The 95, 108
McGuiness, Frank
  *Observe the Sons of Ulster Marching
    Towards the Somme* 43
MacKinnon, Donald 15, 98, 99, 100
McNally, Terrence
  Corpus Christi 135
Maleczech, Ruth 153
Malick, Terrence
  Badlands 100
  Thin Red Line, The 100
  Tree of Life, The 100
Malina, Judith 33
Mamet, David 30
  American Buffalo 3
  Cryptogram, The 30
  Oleanna 30–1
  Woods, The 30
Mann, Abby
  Judgment at Nuremberg 46

Margolles, Teresa 105
   Plancha 105, 106
Markaris, Petros
   Termination 139
Marker, Chris
   Sans Soleil 54
marriage 127
Marx, Karl
   Eighteenth Brumaire of Louis Napoleon, The 89
Marxism 90
masks 34
Mbembe, Achille 140
Mee, Charles 29–30
   Bacchae 2.1, The 30
   Big Love 30
   Iphigenia 2.0 30
   (re)making project 29–30
   Suppliant Women, The 30
memorials 15–16, 44, 46, 47
   Chernobyl 51
memory 9
Mendelssohn-Bartholdy, Felix
   Antigone 31
metatheatre 26, 27–31
Metz, Johann Baptist 178 n.51
Michaels, Anne
   Fugitive Pieces 8
migration 50, 140–1, 142
Milbank, John 101
Milestone, Lewis
   All Quiet on the Western Front 53
Miller, Arthur 114–15
   All My Sons 6
   Crucible, The 13
   Death of a Salesman 6, 36, 94, 114, 115–17
   "Tragedy and the Common Man" 114
   View from the Bridge, A 6, 153
Mishima Yukio
   Temple of the Golden Pavilion, The 18
Mishra, Pankaj 94
Mnouchkine, Ariane 73, 146
   Atrides, Les 7, 34
modern tragedy 36–7
modernism/modernity 1, 7, 57–61, 74
   Arendt, Hannah 84
   Artaud, Antonin 73–4
   Beckett, Samuel 123
   Benjamin, Walter 83–4
   Brecht, Bertolt 71–3, 123
   dance 62–5

   Eliot, T.S. 60, 65–8
   experience, impoverishment of 120–1
   Greek tragedy 59, 60–1
   poetry 65–71
   Pound, Ezra 60, 65, 66, 69–70
   war 120
   Yeats, W.B. 60, 65, 68–9
Moltmann, Juergen 15
morality 113, 114, 115
Morpurgo, Michael and Nick Stafford
   War Horse 43
Morrison, Toni
   Beloved 8
Mosse, Richard
   "Heat Maps" 39–40
   "Incoming" 39–40
   Moira in Snow, Lesbos Greece 38–9
mourning 136 (*see also* lamentation)
Müller, Heine 6, 27, 74, 124–5
   Hamletmachine 27–8
   Philoctetes 27
   Waterfront Wasteland Medea Material, Landscape with Argonauts 124
Mulligan, Robert
   To Kill a Mockingbird 46, 53
Murdoch, Iris
   "Sublime and the Good, The" 107
Murnau, F.W.
   Sunrise 53
Murray, Gilbert 60
   Trojan Women 7
music 9, 152
musicals 152
myth 103–4

Nagasaki bombing 15, 16, 17
Nash, Jennifer 159
Nash, Paul
   We Are Making a New World 2
National Holocaust Museum, Ottawa 44
nature documentaries 54
necropolitics 140
Nelson, Anne
   Guys, The 42
Nelson, Richard
   Sorry 7
Ngũgĩ wa Thiong'o
   Decolonising the Mind 56
Nichols, Mike
   Silkwood 53
Nietzsche, Friedrich 23–4, 61, 76

Birth of Tragedy, The 8, 24, 57, 59, 62–3, 75, 76
   Heidegger, Martin 76–7
   Joyous Science, The 4
Nigeria 7
Nijinsky, Vaslav
   L'après midi d'un faune 52
   Rite of Spring, The 52
Ninagawa, Yukio 7, 74
   Medea 74
9/11 20–1, 42
Noh drama 68, 69, 70
normality 130
novels 8, 25,
   film adaptations 53
   technology 36–7
nuclear families 128–33
nuclear wars 15, 16, 17, 55, 128–31
Nussbaum, Martha
   Fragility of Goodness, The 90

O'Casey, Sean
   Silver Tassie 43
O'Connor, Flannery 102
Oedipus character 77–9, 85–7, 89, 114, 131
   (*see also* Sophocles)
oikologies 140–3
oikonomia 141
O'Neill, Eugene
   Iceman Cometh, The 6
   Long Day's Journey Into Night 6
Online Oxford Dictionary of Literary Terms 25
opera 24, 52–3, 150, 152
   Bayreuth Festival 26, 31, 52
Orientalism 60
Orlemanski, Julie 25
Osborne, John
   Look Back in Anger 6
Osofisan, Femi 7
Ottoman Empire 1
Owen, Wilfred
   "Futility" 13
Ozu, Yasujiro 9
   Tokyo Story 53

Palmer, David
   Visions of Tragedy in Modern American Drama 48
Parker, Andrew
   Theorist's Mother, The 141
patriarchy 146, 147–9

performance 31–5, 145–50
   language 58, 60
   modernism 58–9
performance sites 41, 51–6
   courtroom dramas 46
   global institutions 46
   Greek tragedy 51, 52
   Guernica 46, 47
   intermedial 35, 43
   memorials 44
   Shakespeare, William 51, 52
   television news 43
   Tragedy: the Tragedy 41–2
   Women of Trachis, The 70
Performance Studies 33
performing body 58–9, 62–5
perversion 130
philosophy 4–5, 23–4, 57, 75–6 (*see also* German Idealism)
   Antigone character 87–9
   life as tragedy 76–9
   Oedipus character 77, 78–9, 86–7, 89
   pragmatism 90
   recovering tragedy 89–91
   rejection of tragedy 83–6
   tragedy as 79–83
photography 10–12, 34, 38–9
   Berlau, Ruth 71
   Mosse, Richard 39–40
   Nachtwey, James 163 n.37
   war 96
Picasso, Pablo
   Guernica 12, 46, 47
Pinter, Harold 6–7
   Birthday Party, The 6
   Caretaker, The 6
   Homecoming, The 6
Plato
   Republic 64
poetry 57, 58
   modernism 65–71
Polanski, Roman
   Chinatown 53
politics 84–5, 109–11, 129
   Adorno, Theodor 122–3
   autonomous works 122–3
   Brecht, Bertolt 123
   classical discourse 113
   common man, the 113–17, 118–19
   Death of a Salesman 115–17
   government agendas 113
   Greece 138–40

identity politics 132–3
Pollard, Clare
    Weather, The 49
Pontecorvo, Gillo
    Battle of Algiers, The 53
Potsdam *Antigone* 31
Poulenc, Francis 9
Pound, Ezra 74
    Electra 58, 69–70
    Greek tragedy 60, 65, 66, 69–70
    Women of Trachis, The 58, 69–70
pragmatism 90
precariousness 107–8
prejudice 145–7
Prevot, Andrew 107–8
Primitivism 60, 61
private sphere 129–30, 138
private tragedy 36, 111
proximity 132
psychoanalysis 4
public events 5
public sphere 129, 130, 138–40
public square 138–40
Puccini, Giacomo
    Madame Butterfly 150

Quảng Đức, Thích 139
queer theory 135–6

race 7, 13–14, 129, 132, 145–9
    African American history 8
    Civil Rights Movement 13, 25, 132
    Colour of Justice, The 46
    Here We Go 158–9
Rainer, Yvonne
    "No Manifesto" 52
Rancière, Jacques 70–1
Rattigan, Terence
    After the Dance 2, 6
    Deep Blue Sea, The 6
Ravenhill, Mark 7
    Shopping and Fucking 148
recognition 5
Refn, Nicolas Winding
    Drive 9
Reinhardt, Max 32
    Oedipus Rex 64
religion 4, 5, 93–4 (*see also* Christianity)
    absence of 60
    arts, the 108
    Benjamin, Walter 83–4

Eliot, T.S. 67, 68
heroism 94–7
Holocaust, the 15
modernism 60
9/11 20
ritual 93, 103–5, 108
theodicy 96–102
theology 97–108
Yeats, W.B. 68
reproduction 127, 130
Resnais, Alain and Margaret Duras
    Hiroshima Mon Amour 55
Rev (BBC TV series) 100–1
revolution 54–5
rights protests 132
ritual 93, 103–5, 108
Robinson, Marilynne 95, 108
    Gilead 95
Román, David 135
Ronell, Avital 131
Rotimi, Ola 7
Royal Court Theatre, London 48
Russia 1
Rwanda 11, 51

Sack, Daniel 135
Said, Edward 84–5
Salcedo, Doris 105
    Atrabiliarios 105
    Plegaria Muda 105
    Shibboleth 105, 106
    Unland: The Orphan's Tunic 105
Samuels, Diane
    Three Sisters on Hope Street 7
Sartre, Jean-Paul 4, 6, 77–8, 81, 122
    Being and Nothingness 78
    Flies, The 78, 81
    "For a Theater of Situations" 78
    No Exit 81–2
Sasaki, Sadako 15
Schechner, Richard 32–3, 42
    Dionysus in '69 32
Schelling, Friedrich 75
    Philosophical Letters on Dogmatism and Criticism 75
science fiction 37–8
Scorsese, Martin
    Taxi Driver 9
Scott, Ridley
    Blade Runner 37–8
Second World War 13, 43 (*see also* Holocaust, the)

self-consciousness 5
sexual difference 79
sexuality 145–9
   Escaped Alone 156–8, 159
   Here We Go 158–9
   homosexuality 135–6
   Midsummer Night's Dream, A 153–6
   Pacific Overtures 150–3
Shakespeare, William
   Coriolanus 60
   Cranach Hamlet, The 64
   Hamlet 35, 60, 64
   King Lear 7, 153
   Macbeth 147
   Midsummer Night's Dream, A 153–6
   modernism 60
   Othello 148
   performance sites 51, 52
   Titus Andronicus 7
Shaw, George Bernard
   Heartbreak House 49
   St Joan 5
Shepard, Matthew 135–6
Shepard, Sam
   God of Hell, The 42
Sherriff, R.C.
   Journey's End 43
Shostakovich, Dmitri
   Lady Macbeth of Mtensk 52
Simone, Nina 9
Simpson, O.J. 13–14
singing 152, 184 n.27 (*see also* opera)
"Slave Route" memorial, Ouidah, Benin 44, 45
slavery 44
Smith, Bessie 9
Smith, David 46
social class/rank 112–17, 158
   common man, the 113–17
social truth content 123
Socìetas Raffaello Sanzio 48, 132, 133
   Genesi: The Museum of Sleep 135
   Tragedia Endogonidia 48, 135
society 127–8, 130, 133
socius 128
Solzhenitsyn, Aleksandr 13
Sondheim, Stephen
   Pacific Overtures 150–3, 156
Sontag, Susan 10, 38
Sophocles 4
   Antigone 5, 33, 77, 137, 153 (*see also* Antigone character)

Oedipus at Colonus 84, 89
Oedipus Rex 5, 34, 60, 64, 89 (*see also* Oedipus character)
sorority 136–7, 140
Soyinka, Wole 7, 18, 103–4
   Bacchae of Euripides, The 7
   Death and the King's Horseman 18
   fourth stage concept 55
spectacle 42
spectating 145–50
   Escaped Alone 156–8, 159
   Here We Go 158–9
   Midsummer Night's Dream, A 153–6
   Pacific Overtures 151–3
Spielberg, Steven
   Schindler's List 53
Spiller, Hortense
   "Mama's Baby, Papa's Maybe" 146
Stanislavsky, Konstantin
   Hamlet 60, 64
state, the 141–2, 143 (*see also* politics)
Stein, Peter
   Antiquity Project I 33
Steiner, George 3, 60, 109, 110
   Death of Tragedy 25
Student Movement 25
subject, crisis of 118–25
sublime, the 107
suffering 98–104, 108, 112, 121, 135, 136
suicide 138–40
Syria 50
Szondi, Peter
   Essay on the Tragic, An 57, 75

Tagliarini, Antonio and Daria Deflorian
   We Decided to Go Because We Don't Want to Be a Burden to You 140
Taplin, Oliver 34
   Greek Tragedy in Action 34
Tarkovsky, Andrei 9
technology 1, 26, 34, 49
   Homo Faber 37
   Blade Runner 37–8
Tectonic Theater Project and Kaufman, Moisés
   Laramie Project, The 135–6
television 41–3
   nature documentaries 54
   news 41–3, 54–5
   as performance site 43
   TV series 7, 54, 100–1
terror 20

Terzopoulos, Theodoros 73, 74
The Living Theatre 33
The Performance Group 32–3
Theatre of Catastrophe 29
Theatre of Cruelty 57, 73
Theatre of the Absurd 6, 27
Theatre Workshop
   Oh What a Lovely War! 43
theodicy 96–102
theology 97–108 (*see also* religion)
Thiepval Monument to the Missing of the Somme, France 44, 45
Tieck, Ludwig 31
Tigner, Amy L. 135–6
Tolstoy, Leo
   Anna Karenina 8
Torpey, John 40
tragic chorus, the 33–4
tragic experience 111–19, 145, 147, 150–2, 159
tragic sites 50
translation 58, 60, 65–71
   Benjamin, Walter 71–2
   Eliot, T.S. 65–8
   Hölderlin, Friedrich 58, 71–2
   Pound, Ezra 65, 66, 69–70, 74
   Yeats, W.B. 65, 68–9
Trauerspiel 83–4
Tricycle Theatre
   Colour of Justice, The 46
Trimble, Sarah 147
twenty-first century 20–1

uncanny, the 77
United Nations 46

van Hove, Ivan
   Antigone 153
   Roman Tragedies 7
   View From the Bridge, A 153
Vernant, Jean-Pierre
   "Oedipus without the Complex" 87
vibrant affiliations 127
victims 119–21
Vicuña, Cecilia
   Spit Temple 56
video 34
Vietnam War Memorial 15–16
violence 28–9, 119, 132 (*see also* terror; war)
   Brecht, Bertolt 33
   community, the 33

Laramie, Wyoming 135–6
photography 38
Vishniac, Roman 10
von Trier, Lars 9, 102–3
   Breaking the Waves 103
   Dogville 103

Wagner, Richard 23, 24, 26, 31
Wallace, Jennifer 38, 136
war 1–2, 13, 20, 43, 122, 129 (*see also* revolution)
   Cold War 13, 128–9
   First World War 1–2, 13, 43, 120
   nuclear wars 15, 16, 17, 55, 128–31
   photography 96
   Second World War 13, 43
   social order 112–13
   Syria 50
   Williams, Raymond 26
war memorials 44
Warner, Deborah
   King Lear 153
Waters, Steve
   Contingency Plan, The 49
   World Music 51
Wedekind, Frank
   Lulu plays 148
West, Cornel 90–1
western films 9, 53
Whiteread, Rachel 46
   House 46
   Judenplatz Holocaust Memorial 46
Williams, Raymond 24–6, 36, 109, 119, 135
   Modern Tragedy 5–6, 25, 111–12
   tragic sites 50
Williams, Rowan 98, 103
   Grace and Necessity 102
   Tragic Imagination, The 102
Williams, Tennessee
   Cat on a Hot Tin Roof 6
   Glass Menagerie, The 6
   Streetcar Named Desire 6, 148
Wilson, August 7
   Fences 7, 17
   Pittsburgh Cycle, The 7
Wilson, John Dover
   Cranach Hamlet, The 64
Winehouse, Amy 12
   Back to Black 9
witnesses 120

women (*see also* gender)
    domestic duties 141, 142, 158–9
    enfranchisement 1
    infidelity 148
    as protagonist 153
    opera 150
    theatrical roles 148–9
    violence 14
Wong, B.D. 150
Wong Kar-wai
    In the Mood for Love 9
Woolf, Virginia
    Three Guineas 148
Wooster Group 35
World Trade Center
    attack 20–1, 42
    rebuilt 44
Worthen, William 35
Wynter, Sylvia 147, 153

Yates, Richard
    Revolutionary Road 8
Yeats, W.B. 57, 58, 61
    Explorations 69
    Four Plays for Dancers 68
    Greek tragedy 60, 65, 68–9
    Oedipus plays 68–9
    Purgatory 5
    Resurrection 68
    "Tragic Generation, The" 61
Yoruban drama 55, 103–4

Zhang Yimou 18
    Not One Less 18
    Red Sorghum 18
Žižek, Slavoj 88–9
    First as Tragedy, then as Farce 89
Zola, Emile 36
"zone rouge," France 50